Lost and Now Found

Previous volumes published from ASTENE Conferences:

Desert Travellers from Herodotus to T E Lawrence (2000), edited by Janet Starkey and Okasha El Daly. Durham, ASTENE.

Travellers in the Levant: Voyagers and Visionaries (2001), edited by Sarah Searight and Malcolm Wagstaff. Durham, ASTENE.

Egypt Through the Eyes of Travellers (2002), edited by Paul Starkey and Nadia El Kholy. Durham, ASTENE.

Travellers in the Near East (2004), edited by Charles Foster. London, Stacey International.

Women Travellers in the Near East (2005), edited by Sarah Searight. ASTENE and Oxbow Books.

Who Travels Sees More: Artists, Architects and Archaeologists Discover Egypt and the Near East (2007), edited by Diane Fortenberry. Oxford, ASTENE and Oxbow Books.

Saddling the Dogs: Journeys through Egypt and the Near East (2009), edited by Diane Fortenberry and Deborah Manley. Oxford, ASTENE and Oxbow Books.

Knowledge is Light: Travellers in the Near East (2011), edited by Katherine Salahi. Oxford, ASTENE and Oxbow Books.

Souvenirs and New Ideas: Travel and Collecting in Egypt and the Near East, edited by Diane Fortenberry. Oxford, ASTENE and Oxbow Books.

Every Traveller Needs a Compass, edited by Neil Cooke and Vanessa Daubney. Oxford, ASTENE and Oxbow Books.

Lost and Now Found

Explorers, Diplomats and Artists in Egypt and the Near East

Edited by

Neil Cooke and Vanessa Daubney

ASTENE
and
Archaeopress Publishing Ltd., Oxford

ARCHAEOPRESS PUBLISHING LTD

Gordon House
276 Banbury Road
Oxford OX2 7ED
www.archaeopress.com

ISBN 978 1 78491 627 5
ISBN 978 1 78491 628 2 (e-Pdf)

Cover image: Constantinople from the Swedish embassy at Pera with the Topkapi Palace (at centre) and imperial caiques on the Bosphorus. Oil painting (SK-A-2056) by Antoine van der Steen c1770-1780. © Rijksmuseum, Amsterdam.

Printed in England by Holywell Press, Oxford

This book is available direct from Archaeopress or from our website www.archaeopress.com

Contents

Introduction

Neil Cooke

Since its foundation in 1997, members of the Association for the Study of Travel in Egypt and the Near East (ASTENE) have researched and published, together with those in this present 14th volume, some 200 essays revealing the lives, journeys and achievements of men and women who have often been left out of history, including those who gave first-hand descriptions of long-forgotten events that they alone witnessed and which were often not recorded in the countries where they took place.

Over the centuries, while people of wealth living in Europe, the Americas and countries adjoining the Near East were able to afford the luxury of travel and returned home to write and publish about their journeys, it is now known that there were many people from more modest backgrounds who wrote about their own travels, a few finding a publisher but many languishing as forgotten manuscripts in archives and libraries. This trove of travellers' tales includes the writings of farmers who wanted to learn about potential new crops or other methods of animal husbandry; of those who were recruited by the army or press-ganged into the navy; of servants taken along on lengthy overseas journeys without having a choice in the matter; and of artisans with a skill who travelled because they needed employment but sometimes because they fancied the adventure of visiting foreign lands. Others, in less fortunate circumstances, filled scraps of paper writing about their imaginary travels. One such was the imprisoned Xavier de Maistre who penned A journey around my room to describe the many different routes he could take traversing his prison cell, following the format and typical content of any number of books about real journeys that he might once have read.

It is now also appreciated that the journeys made by people over the centuries were not just one way. In Cannon Hall Museum, Barnsley, is a painting from c. 1715–20 described as 'Philip Stanhope (1673–1726), 3rd Earl of Chesterfield, with his wife, Lady Elizabeth Savile, children and Nubian slave'. A century later, the Spencer-Stanhope family were supporters of the anti-slavery movement and William Wilberforce came to meetings at Cannon Hall. It is not known how the Nubian boy came to be living with the Earl of Chesterfield and his family and why he is described as a slave, unless the title for this painting is a modern interpretation. Sadly, nothing more is known about him.

In 1813, the Cacheef of Dehr, in return for the gift of a sword, presented Thomas Legh with a Nubian slave boy from Dongola. The ten-year-old boy was brought to England to live with Legh's travelling companion the Reverend Charles Smelt, at Gedling, in Nottinghamshire, a parish, by coincidence, then under the patronage of the Earls of Chesterfield. Again, nothing more is known about this Nubian boy other than that 'he has nearly forgotten his own language, retains only a few Arabic words, but he speaks English well'.

Another Nubian who arrived in Europe with travellers was Kalima, a 14- or 15-year-old slave girl. She reached Florence in 1827 with Champollion and Rossellini, having attached herself to their expedition party for the journey from Egypt to Europe. It is suggested her freedom was bought by Ippolito Rossellini's uncle, but it might simply be that he employed her as a servant in his household. Although the facts are unclear, Kalima might then have been employed in the Russian colony by the Kasincov family, who had moved to Florence for health reasons. With her new family, Kalima was baptized into the Russian Orthodox church with a new name, Nedezhda, meaning 'Hope'. She married, and died in 1851, and is buried at the English Cemetery in Florence with a memorial written in Cyrillic. Whether she spoke Arabic, Russian, Italian or English is not known.

There is also the case of Hassan el-Bakkeet, who was taken in by Alexander and Lucie Duff-Gordon when, after an evening with Charles Dickens, they found him on the doorstep of their home in London. Hassan was born in Nubia or northern Sudan in c.1832, and it is reported that as a baby he came under the protection of missionaries, who taught him English. How he reached London is not known, but in 1844 he was the servant to a man who lived in the same house as Signor Prandi, an Italian refugee who translated books and gave language lessons at Miss Shepherd's school on Bromley Common, where Lucie had been a pupil. Because it was suspected that Hassan was going blind and likely to become a burden, at the age of 12, he was abandoned to the streets and so, having hand delivered letters there before, he found his way to the Duff-Gordon's home in Queen's Square (now Queen Anne's Gate), Westminster, expecting a sympathetic welcome. As he hoped, Lucie took him in, had his eyes treated by an occulist, and from then onwards he was employed as a servant. Hassan, or Hatty, as he was called by children in the family who could not pronounce his name, became a happy and trusted member of the family. Late in 1848, while attending to Lucie at the Gordon's house in Weybridge, Hassan, like several other members of the family caught a bad cold. During November, Hassan's cold became bronchitis which then developed as tuberculosis. Lucie nursed Hassan for several weeks before he died on Christmas Day in the arms of her husband, Alexander.

In contrast, a good deal is known about the eight-year-old Selim Aga, from Taqali in the Nuba mountains, who had been brought by traders to Cairo as a slave. In 1834, Robert Thurburn, the British Consul in Alexandria, purchased Selim and brought him to Scotland, where he was sent to school. In 1846, with the help of Thurburn,

Selim published Incidents Connected with the Life of Selim Aga, perhaps the only autobiography to be written giving the experiences of a Muslim slave. Later in life, Selim lectured at the Egyptian Hall in London, describing the 'Grand Moving Panorama Picture of the Nile' painted in 1849 from the original drawings of Joseph Bonomi. In 1857, Selim acted as a steward for an expedition that went up the river Niger, and in 1861, he became factotum to Sir Richard Burton on his journeys in the Cameroon Mountains and to the Cataracts of the Congo river. During this journey, Selim sent communications to be published in the Journal of the Royal Geographic Society. Selim also put forward plans to the British foreign secretary for an east-west railway across Africa. In his last years, Selim settled in Liberia, the colony on the west coast of Africa set up for freed slaves, where he held on to the hope of being elected its first President. Sadly, Selim Aga was killed in a war between the first settlers and locals in 1875. His death was deemed important enough to have been reported in The Times.

It is also now known that Muhammad ʿAlī Pasha (1769–1849) sent students from Egypt to Europe to learn about such matters as science and industry with a view to establishing manufacturing as a key element of the Egyptian economy. In return, the students were to promote Islamic and Egyptian culture in the various western European countries to which they were sent. Four students, who were probably from the army, and might have been low-level officials in the pasha's household, came to England in 1826. Their names were ʿAlī Effendi, Muhammad Effendi, Omar Effendi and Selim Aga (not the former Nubian slave). Although little is known of their stay in England, in 1833 Selim Aga, probably after learning about gunpowder and artillery at Woolwich Arsenal, visited Birmingham as was reported in a letter between James Watt junior and Matthew Robinson Boulton.

> My dear Sir ... Yesterday I shewed your Mint to Selim Aga and Mr. Sanderson. The former is a young military officer, who has been compleating his education at Woolwich, and is quite unacquainted with the subject of Coinage. He is however a very intelligent, civil person... Selim is about to return to Egypt, and I have no doubt that... he should report personally to the Pacha what he had seen; which I have little doubt he will do favourably, as well as our progress with his Engines.

As the letter suggests, the firm of Boulton and Watt benefited by building a steam-boat named The Nile for the Pasha (either Muhammad ʿAlī Pasha or his son, Ibrahim Pasha). Clearly, a great deal more research is needed so that more can be learned about these anonymous Nubian slaves and other people from Egypt and the Near East who travelled to the west for whatever purpose.

This present volume of essays is a selection of papers from the 11th biennial ASTENE Conference held at the University of Exeter in July 2015. The title of the collection is Lost and Now Found: Explorers, Diplomats and Artists in Egypt and the Near East, which reflects the common theme to be found in the different chapters.

The first paper by Susanne Binder and Boyo Ockinga helpfully introduces the 'lost and now found' theme. It concerns the manuscript diary of Max Weidenbach who at the age of 19, together with his brother Ernst, then aged 24, were invited by Karl Richard Lepsius to be artist members of the Royal Prussian Expedition to Egypt between 1842 and 1845. Max Weidenbach had studied under Lepsius and trained to draw accurate hieroglyphics, therefore his role with the expedition was to prepare drawings of inscriptions, many of which were later used in lithographic plates for the multi-volume *Denkmäler aus Aegypten und Aethiopien* (Monuments from Egypt and Ethiopia), published in Berlin between 1849 and 1859. In 1849, Max Weidenbach took his diary to Australia where he joined several of his brothers who had already emigrated from Prussia and were living around the area of Adelaide. Following Max's death in 1890, his family gave the diary, and the ancient Egyptian artefacts he had collected, to the South Australia Museum. Several years later, the diary went missing – although in truth it was really hiding in plain sight. It transpired that to preserve the diary the Manuscript department had sent the handwritten pages for rebinding. On its return to the Museum, and because its new leather binding gave it the same appearance as other printed books returned the same day, the diary was shelved with the rare books collections rather than being returned to the Manuscript department where it really belonged. Now found decades later, the diary, which is currently being translated from German into English, and comprehensively annotated, is important for offering an unknown account of the Lepsius expedition, and providing details of encounters by expedition members with other scholars and travellers who were in Egypt during the early 1840s.

Over the centuries, travellers from Europe, America, Russia and other countries have published accounts of their visits to Egypt. However, it is less well known that a few of them were written by travellers who were born in Wales. Of particular interest in the paper from Tessa Baber is a handful of accounts written by authors wishing to bring their enthusiasm for *Y tir y Aifft* (the land of Egypt) to those people for whom Welsh was their native tongue, and their books were never published in any other language except Welsh. Two such unique works are *O'r Aifft* (From Egypt) by John Davies Bryan, and *Y Môr Canoldir a'r Aifft* (The Mediterranean Sea and Egypt') by Thomas Gwynn Jones. The first was published in the mid-19th century, the second in the early 20th century. The two authors not only convey their experience of travel relative to the time period when they visited Egypt but, interestingly, they also wrote in a way that offered a different perspective to reach the audience for whom they were each writing.

The paper by Malden Tomorov introduces Jakob Šašel who was born into a family of gunsmiths living in Croatia, which at the time was part of Austria. During 1853 and 1854, Šašel travelled to Egypt, Nubia and the Sudan, working as a carpenter for the Catholic Mission based at Khartoum under the guidance of Monseigneur Ignatio Knoblecher (1819–58). Having completed his studies in Rome, Knoblecher had been dispatched to Africa in 1847 to build mission stations and schools. Using boats on the river Nile and cross-country camel trains, Knoblecher reached the Bari and Dinka peoples in what is now South Sudan. In 1853, Knoblecher recruited Šašel for his return journey to Khartoum, having been in Europe to raise funds and recruit artisans to construct further mission buildings. Šašel described what he saw during his travels and the people he met in a journal written after he returned home. He illustrated it with the watercolours he had made during his journey. Šašel was fascinated with the remains of the ancient Egyptian temples and tombs he saw, and in the journal he refers to details from the published works of Belzoni and Wilkinson he had been able to obtain and study. However, what is perhaps most fascinating about his journal are descriptions of the everyday life of people indigenous to the Sudan who sadly, at the time, were still being exploited by slave traders.

While many Egyptian collections in the great museums of Europe were bought at auction during the first half of the 19th century from independent entrepreneurs such as Giovanni Battista Belzoni, Henry Salt, Bernardino Drovetti, Giuseppe Passalacqua, James Burton and others, the collections of American museums founded in the late 19th and early 20th centuries were acquired by sponsoring scientific excavations in Egypt from the 1890s to the 1930s. Thanks to the Egyptian Service des Antiquitiés developing 'division of finds' agreements with the museums or universities sponsoring the archaeological work, large, diverse and well-documented collections of artefacts – from humble pottery to great works of art – have over time been placed with museums such as the Metropolitan Museum of Art in New York, the Museum of Fine Arts, Boston, the Phoebe Apperson Hearst Museum of Archaeology in Berkeley and the Oriental Institute in Chicago. The paper by Susan Allen is a timely reminder that many of the museums, institutions and their publicly accessible collections – which today we so easily take for granted – were gifted to us through the philanthropy of men and women who were happy to share their wealth for the benefit of others. Among those included in this paper are: J. Pierpont Morgan, John D. Rockerfeller Sr, Phoebe Apperson Hearst, Charles Edwin Wilbour, Theodore Davis and Edward S. Harkness, the latter two both having funded the archaeological work in Egypt of George A. Reisner, Albert Lythgoe and Herbert Winlock and also paid for building the new galleries in which to exhibit their division of the finds.

Andrew Oliver brings to our attention another American, Henry Benjamin Humphrey, a dry goods merchant from Boston, who visited Egypt and countries in the Near East in 1839–41 and records meetings with Frederic Goupil and Pierre-Gustave Lotbinière, pioneering travelling photographers using the cameras and processes invented by Louis Daguerre. Humphrey's unpublished journal is now owned by the Massachusetts Historical Society, and it contains details of his meetings with British and American travellers, including George Robins Gliddon, the young British-born American Consul in Cairo who later toured the USA lecturing on Ancient Egypt, and Dr Henry Abbott, whose collection in Cairo was visited by many travellers, and was eventually purchased by the New York Historical Society –

the first collection of Egyptian antiquities owned by a public institution in the USA, and now in the Brooklyn Museum. Clearly, the region fascinated Humphreys and, in 1846, he was nominated as American Consul in Alexandria. However, he declined the appointment because the government would not revise the title to the more important role of Consul-General.

Two more Americans are the subjects of the paper by Susan Cohen. In 1838, and again in 1852, the biblical scholar Edward Robinson and a missionary, Eli Smith, travelled throughout the Middle East. The purpose of their journeys was to find and map the lost locations of events described in the Bible. With only compasses, a thermometer, measuring tapes and their Bibles for reference, Robinson and Smith wandered through Egypt and Palestine in search of historical sites and landscape features that could be fitted within the modern geographical reality and thereby illustrate the biblical landscape. To locate with greater certainty many less obvious locations, the two men made use of Smith's knowledge of Arabic and modern place names, combined with descriptions of battlefields, sites, landmarks and routes given within the biblical text. The result of this pioneering work by Robinson and Smith was to create an academic discipline – Biblical Historical Geography – and this provides modern scholars with the context to understand better events in the ancient world.

While we generally think that it is people who travel and occasionally become lost, the same fate can also happen to antiquities which were once found during archaeological excavations. In his paper, Lawrence Berman describes how a great masterpiece of ancient Egyptian sculpture from the 4th century BC disappeared for decades – between 1857, when it was excavated by Auguste Mariette, and 1904, when it was purchased by the Museum of Fine Arts, in Boston. What is better known today as the Boston Green Head is an exquisite portrait by a master sculptor of a priest's head in hard dark-green stone and is all that now remains of a life-sized statue. Mariette sent the head to Paris with other antiquities as a gift to Prince Napoleon Bonaparte, known to his friends as 'Plon Plon', as one among a group of souvenirs of a trip to Egypt that never happened. The head was then displayed in Plon Plon's faux Pompeian palace at 16–18 Avenue Montaigne, Paris (built 1856–80, and demolished 1891). After disappearing from Paris, the head turned up in the collection of Edward Perry Warren, a wealthy American expatriate and connoisseur of Greek and Roman art, who lived with like-minded aesthetes at Lewes House in East Sussex, England. It was Warren who, in 1904, sold the head to the Museum of Fine Arts. It is interesting to conjecture that the head might have been lost for several decades because it had been imagined as too refined to have been created by a lesser civilization. That is, until its qualities were noted by Edward Warren when he saw it and decided to purchase it. Today, the Boston Green Head is recognized as the creation of a skilled master sculptor and produced within what was a very sophisticated ancient cultural framework.

Finding routes through the Middle East to be used as safe trading links from Europe to India and beyond was a major objective of travel for many entrepreneurs during the second half of the 18th century, and especially for those doing business with, or in, the employ of the East India Company. But nothing was that simple, as others, particularly Warren Hastings and Lieutenant General Sir Eyre Coote, were more interested in the fastest routes by which military and political 'intelligence' could be transferred back and forth. The paper by Janet Starkey introduces Alexander Dalrymple, James Capper and Eyles Irwin and describes their adventures travelling over land, across desert and by sea, with the possibility of being captured by pirates as they tried to figure out the easiest and quickest land routes that would avoid having to sail the long way around the east and west coasts of Africa via the Cape of Good Hope. Each of the travellers published accounts of their peregrinations with details of the political, religious and cultural climate of the different areas they passed through, together with accounts of the people they met and maps showing routes that could be followed. Interestingly, the routes included sailing from India to Suez in Egypt, and transferring overland to Alexandria before sailing onwards to England.

The paper by Brian Taylor recovers from anonymity the artist Antoine van der Steen and identifies several of his paintings that have either been ascribed to 'an unknown artist' or credited to another. The quest for this artist began with a challenge to identify the anonymous travelling companion of George Baldwin, whom he referred to in the published account of his travels as variously 'Mr.—, a painter by profession', 'my friend the painter', or just plain 'Mr —'. Baldwin and his artist friend are believed to be the first Europeans to have visited the carved rock monuments in the Phrygian Highlands of Anatolia with the only illustration from their journey being an engraving of the Midas Monument – an illustration that could only have been created from a drawing made at the time by 'my friend the painter'. The identity of Antoine van der Steen and piecing together his life and travels have required linking tiny fragments of information about people, places and events found in letters in public and private archives around Europe. From these fragments, it has been possible to learn of van der Steen's employment as 'artist in residence' at the Swedish embassy in Constantinople, his wish to travel overland to India with a first failed attempt in the group led by George Baldwin, and his finally reaching India, having joined the East India Company under the name Anthony Vendersteen, and being employed as a Lieutenant Fireworker in the Bombay Artillery.

Although Edmond G. Reuter was employed as an artist by Édouard Naville, for his journey along the river Nile in 1868–69, the paper by Hélène Virenque explains that his greater interest was in drawing architectural ornament and floral patterns, possibly encouraged by his father who had been Director of the Botanical Garden of Geneva. Soon after his return from Egypt, Reuter moved to England, where he taught at the National Art Training School in Kensington, better known today as the Royal College of Art. While teaching there, he was encouraged by the French designer, Leon Arnaud, to work with him at the famous Minton Art Pottery Studio. After a major fire in 1875, the Minton studio was not rebuilt in Kensington and production moved to the firm's main factory in Stoke-on-Trent. Reuter decided to move there too, and letters to his family in Geneva contain watercolours of Stoke showing the smoking kiln chimneys, sketches of people he lived or worked with and pattern ideas for his ceramic works. Reuter became such a master of floral decoration that he came to the attention of William Morris, who invited him to create illuminated pages in the medieval style for several unique manuscript books. Having lived in England for more than two decades, Reuter returned home to Geneva where he continued to create decorative objects in the Arts and Crafts style, including painted tapestries and book illustrations.

Having compared the different contributions made by William John Bankes and Charles Barry towards recording the ruins of Gerasa (Jerash) in drawings, in the last volume of ASTENE papers *Every Traveller Needs a Compass*, Don Boyer's additional paper sheds new light on the subsequent Action for Libel in the Case of Buckingham versus Bankes, tried at the Court of King's Bench, London, in 1826, in which the drawings formed part of the evidence. The libel action had been triggered by Bankes' claim that Buckingham's 1821 publication of the description and plans of the Bankes' party's visit to Jerash, in 1816, had been based on material copied without Bankes' permission. It was subsequently argued in court that Buckingham was entitled to retain and publish his notes and plans taken during his visit to Jarash in Bankes' company, although Buckingham was insistent that his published plan of the ruins was entirely the result of his subsequent solo visit to the site a month later. Concluded in one day, the case attracted considerable attention, with newspapers and journals reporting it as being the result of a very effective prosecuting counsel and an ineffective defence. The jury found in Buckingham's favour and damages of £400 were awarded against Bankes, although Buckingham later claimed that the cost of the litigation to Bankes was closer to £6,000. Further information as to the attribution of guilt or innocence in the case is the result of a careful analysis of unpublished documents found within the Bankes archive at the Dorset History Centre.

Anyone visiting Lyme Park, Cheshire, will remember looking at the portrait of Thomas Legh by the artist William Bradley. The large painting shows Legh wearing Turkish dress, probably the outfit he described purchasing in Istanbul. He stands beside a black Arabian stallion. In one corner of the painting and sitting cross-legged on the ground is a young man also wearing oriental clothing. This is now believed to be James Curtin, an Irishman who had first travelled as a servant with Giovanni Battista Belzoni and who was later gifted to Thomas Legh by Sarah Belzoni, as Curtin had expressed a wish to return to London – although this was not to happen for several more years. Legh was among the first to visit the temples of

Nubia, largely avoided by earlier travellers, according to William Richard Hamilton by the difficulty of the roads and the inhospitable disposition of the inhabitants. Legh travelled into Nubia with Charles Smelt, as well as a Greek cook and a Swiss servant named Lavanchy. He also engaged as a dragoman the enigmatic American, Françoise Barthow, who previously had worked for Lord Valentia. The paper by Robert Morkot compares Legh's published account of Nubia and its temples with reports written by other near contemporary travellers.

The paper by Cathy McGlynn resurrects Augusta, Lady Gregory, famed for her involvement in Irish cultural nationalism at the turn of the 20th century and for her patronage of such literary luminaries as the poet W. B. Yeats and the playwright J. M. Synge. In the years 1881 and 1882, Lady Gregory accompanied her husband, the politician and writer Sir William Gregory, on his second visit to Egypt. During her time there, she became deeply involved in the turbulent cultural climate in Cairo, where Arabi Bey, a young and powerful Egyptian nationalist, was waging a political war against the Khedive's government and British and French influence. Lady Gregory aligned herself with the nationalist cause and, when Britain crushed the rebellion, she attempted to win British sympathy for Arabi Bey in a letter to *The Times* entitled 'Arabi and his Household', later published in pamphlet form. While Lady Gregory's involvement in the Arabi cause is well-documented in her diaries, autobiography and letters, her unpublished An Emigrant's Notebook, composed a year after her travels, fills gaps in the narrative of her published political writings. This part-memoir also includes details of Lady Gregory's trip on the Nile and her impressions of daily life in Egypt.

Sir William Wilde is now remembered primarily as being the father of the author and playwright Oscar Wilde. Yet he was also a respected eye and ear surgeon, as well as being an archaeologist, ethnologist, antiquarian, biographer, statistician, naturalist, topographer and historian. In 1837, Wilde agreed to travel as personal medical attendant to the wealthy traveller, Robert Meiklam, on a voyage aboard his yacht. During the journey around the Mediterranean and into countries of the Near East, that Meiklam hoped would restore his health, Wilde penned *The narrative of a voyage to Madeira, Teneriffe [sic], and along the shores of the Mediterranean.* This became a popular account and quickly sold out, and was reprinted in 1844. Though this travel narrative was widely read at the time, it has since been neglected. This paper by Emmet Jackson presents a summary and analysis of Wilde's neglected travels and his observations on Egypt, in particular.

The paper by Sheila McGuirk serves as an introduction to the travels of the Marquis Charles-Jean-Melchior de Vogüé, an episodic French diplomat and an important scholar of Palestine and Syria. He travelled widely in the Near East over a period of nearly 60 years between 1853 and 1911, and to assist with his work, he mastered the Greek, Latin, Phoenician, Syriac and Hebrew languages. A current list of de Vogüé's publications fills more than 14 pages but does not yet include everything he produced. Perhaps his most famous discoveries are the 'dead' Byzantine cities of northern Syria, which he recorded in great detail in the three-volume *Syrie Centrale*. In 2011, many of these 'ghost' cities were incorporated into a UNESCO World Heritage Site. Another of de Vogüé's memorable publications is *Churches of the Holy Land*. Like many of his books, it is lavishly illustrated with meticulously accurate drawings of the sites and inscriptions. The Marquis de Vogüé's publications are, in many instances, the best record of places in the region that have since been destroyed. In recognition of his work, de Vogüé became an honoured member of many French learned societies, including the Académie Française.

It is well known that over the centuries people have made tourist visits to the sites of battles. Visits were made to the Waterloo battlefield almost before it ended and the author Sir Walter Scott is known to have visited within weeks. Tourists, including the writer Mark Twain, also visited the battlefields of the Crimea, with some making every effort to watch from overlooking hills as the events unfolded. This war was also the first to be recorded in photographs, when in 1854 Roger Fenton arrived in the Crimea with his wagon of equipment and chemicals. This was seven years before Mathew Brady embarked on a similar recording exercise of the American Civil War. The paper by Peta Rée describes a visit to Constantinople made by Emilia and Edmund Hornby in September 1856, roughly 18 months after the Crimean War began. While her husband was busy managing a loan of £5 million to the Turkish government on behalf of the British foreign secretary, Emilia Hornby and her friend Mrs Brett went off to Balaklava to visit the vast camp at Sebastopol before it was disbanded. From there, the two women visited the 'Valley of the Shadow of Death' where they met a large party of Russian officers surveying the recent battlefield. The two women also visited English soldiers and observed their reminders of home provided by boards bearing names such as Albert Terrace, Prospect Cottage and Marine Village standing in well-tended flower gardens outside their wooden huts. Emila Hornby wrote about all she saw in very full letters sent home to her family and friends, which were later published. Many years later, Edmund wrote in his autobiography about his time in Constantinople. The two different accounts by husband and wife cast a light on that time and place quite different from those by military historians such as Alexander William Kinglake.

Many will be familiar with *Eothen*, a classic of Middle Eastern travel writing by Alexander William Kinglake that was produced many years before he wrote about the Crimean War. Eothen is the travelogue of a young Englishman's journey through Syria, Palestine and Egypt in the mid 1830s. Part of the book's fascination lies in the fact that one chapter is entirely devoted to his meeting with the eccentric adventurer Lady Hester Stanhope who, in 1831, had settled in the Lebanese mountain village of Joun, near Sidon, and become a magnet attracting every traveller who had read about her. The paper by Paul Starkey considers the circumstances that brought two of the most notable English adventurers of the period together for a few days, and describes the turbulent background conditions then prevailing in Syria and Lebanon following the Egyptian invasion of Syria in 1831–32 under Ibrahim Pasha.

Whereas Kinglake returned to England and began a successful legal career, dying in 1891, Lady Hester remained at Joun, dying in poverty in 1837. Interest in Lady Hester continues to this day and in 1988, with the Lebanese civil war in its final stages, the British Foreign Office received news that the 'earthly remains' of Lady Hester had been found in the hills around Sidon. The remains were then transferred to the British Ambassador's office and, on 2 February 1989, were interred in the garden of their summer residence in the hills overlooking Beirut. On 23 June 2004, Lady Hester's ashes were thought to have been scattered across the garden of her house at Joun – that is, until a biographer was shown a container holding her remains during a recent visit. It transpired that soon after being scattered all the pieces had been gathered up by the local priest to ensure their long-term preservation.

This present collection ends with a final paper by John Chapman about Patrick Leigh Fermor's modern classic of travel writing *Mani: Travels in the Southern Peloponnese*. First published in 1958, the book has never been out of print. Like all good travel books produced over the centuries, this work can still dominate everyone's perception of a place such as the Mani and its people, villages and landscapes. Like other good travel books, Mani has influenced many modern travel writers and will continue to do so long into the future.

The Diary of Max Weidenbach:
Encounters with Scholars and Travellers during the
Prussian Scientific Expedition to Egypt 1842–45

Susanne Binder and Boyo G. Ockinga

To the great delight of scholars who share an interest in 19th-century travel narratives, reception studies and Egyptology, an exciting discovery was made in the South Australian Museum in Adelaide in April 2013: a 440-page manuscript, a diary kept from 1842 to1845 by one of the members of the pioneering expedition to Egypt led by Karl Richard Lepsius, was found![1] It belonged to the youngest member of this Royal Prussian Expedition, Max Weidenbach (Fig.1.1), who at the age of 19 had joined Lepsius and his team on this scientific enterprise to record the ancient monuments of Egypt on the request, and with the support, of the King of Prussia Friedrich Wilhelm IV.[2]

The Royal Prussian Expedition in the context of other major expeditions to Egypt

Several decades earlier, the scientific aspect of Napoleon's expedition to Egypt 1798–1801 had laid the foundations for enhanced interest in ancient Egypt and its monuments as well as the natural world of Egypt and contemporary life and traditional crafts. Two decades later, by the 1820s, scholars had entered a highly competitive race, reaching the decisive breakthrough in 1822, to read hieroglyphs. When the two-year, Franco-Tuscan expedition, supported by the King of France Charles X and the Grand Duke of Tuscany Leopold II, set out in 1828 with Ippolito Rosellini and Jean-François Champollion, the members had philological skills and a fundamental knowledge of the historical framework for ancient Egypt guiding their choices on which monuments and inscriptions to describe and record. The untimely death of Champollion in 1832 (at the age of 41) meant that other scholars stepped up to take on the challenges of furthering the understanding of the complexities of the ancient script and its language.

The Prussians mounted the next large-scale expedition in 1842–45, expressly following in the footsteps of those who had recorded the monuments before them but with the aim of focusing on the ancient monuments only and

Fig 1.1 Members of the Prussian expedition on top of Khufu's pyramid on October 15, 1842. From left to right (standing): Carl Richard Lepsius, K.W. Isenberg, Carl Franke, Max Weidenbach (behind the pole), Ernst Weidenbach, Georg Erbkam, James Wild, Joseph Bonomi, Johann Frey. Drawing by J. Frey (1842). Z.2544 (detail) courtesy of the Berlin-Brandenburgische Akademie der Wissenschaften (BBAW), Archiv Altägyptisches Wörterbuch.

documenting the temples and tombs less selectively but more systematically by working with, checking and expanding on the records of the earlier expeditions and by producing facsimile drawings of complete walls and their decoration. New methods and tools were applied in the field, such as the production of so-called 'squeezes' (German: *Abklatsch*) that provide one-to-one copies of relief-cut inscriptions and decoration and the use of the *camera lucida* for the landscape panorama drawings, as well as conducting experiments with photographic equipment that Lepsius had acquired on the recommendation of Henry Fox Talbot in London on the way to Egypt in 1842. Also, the Prussian expedition was to venture as far south as Khartoum, into what they then called 'Ethiopia', to the furthest reaches of ancient Egyptian influence. By contrast, Napoleon's mission had only gone as far as the Island of Philae just south of the first cataract of the Nile, and the rock-cut temples Abu Simbel were the southernmost site recorded by the Franco-Tuscan team.

While these three expeditions differ in scale and scope, the length of time spent in Egypt and the number of specialists involved in completing the task (2000 scholars in the case of Napoleon's mission), they share the grand vision for the publication of the extensive documentation they compiled. All three expeditions published large folio volumes, which to the present day are among the treasures of many libraries. The first edition of Napoleon's *Description de l'Egypte* (1809–22) comprised nine volumes of text and 13 volumes with a total of 894 plates of engravings (1000 x 810 mm). The first edition of Rosellini's and Champollion's *I Monumenti dell'Egitto e della Nubia* (1832–44) was published in nine volumes of text and three large folio volumes with 395 plates of engravings (642 x 503 mm). The first and only edition of Lepsius's *Denkmäler aus Aegypten und Aethiopien* (1849–59) appeared in 12 folio volumes of plates with 900 plates of lithographs (760 x 615 mm) and five volumes of text.[3] It is interesting to note that the *Denkmäler aus Aegypten und Aethiopien* is the first of these works to reproduce the original drawings not as copper plate etchings but as lithographs. The publication history of all these works is, of course, a topic in its own right.

The members of the team

To realise the grand plan for the expedition, Karl Richard Lepsius, who had just become the first professor of Egyptology at the Friedrich-Wilhelm University in Berlin (now Humboldt Universität) in 1841, carefully selected a core team of five fellow-countrymen: the architect and surveyor Georg Erbkam, the artists and draughtsmen Johann Jakob Frey and the brothers Ernst and Max Weidenbach, as well as a master craftsman for plaster casting, Carl Franke. From December 1842 onward, the theologian and diplomat Heinrich Abeken was with the team in more of a freelance capacity. When, in August 1843, Frey became very ill, requiring him to return to Europe,[4] the artist Otto Georgi was invited to replace him on the team and by then he had to travel as far south as Gebel Barkal finally to meet up with the expedition in May 1844. On their way to Egypt from Berlin in August 1842, Lepsius and Max Weidenbach spent time in London to procure some final items of equipment. There they met two English artists, the sculptor Joseph Bonomi and the architect James William Wild, who quite spontaneously decided also to board the steamship from Southampton to Alexandria and take part in the expedition. They made a significant contribution to the team in the north of Egypt during the first year: Wild until May and Bonomi until July 1843. Bonomi's extensive knowledge of Egypt and his experience gained by travelling with earlier scholars and cartographers (1824–33) was invaluable to the Prussian team at the beginning of the expedition.[5]

Max Weidenbach's expedition diary (Figs.1.2, 1.3, 1.4)

Max Weidenbach's diary is in good condition. The pages have a format of 209 x 172 mm. Its modern cover has been removed to reveal that it consists of a series of quires, which may well be the original bindings. The entries are written in a very neat hand in German Kurrent script. The diary was donated to the South Australian Museum in 1944 by one of his descendents. On the last pages of this same expedition diary, Max Weidenbach himself added further biographical information in pencil, providing details of his departure from Berlin and the sea voyage to the colony of South Australia in 1849, only four years after the return from Egypt. The expedition diary must have been his to keep, which meant that he was able to bring it with him to the land where he found a new home. The diary is currently being transcribed and translated into English by the authors in preparation for publication.

Max Weidenbach's specific role in the team

In the years prior to the expedition, Karl Richard Lepsius had studied Egyptian texts on ancient monuments and papyri in Paris, Rome and Turin. For the publication of the *Todtenbuch der Aegypter* (1842),[6] the first facsimile reproduction of a papyrus scroll with the text of the so-called Book of the Dead, Lepsius required the assistance of an artist for the creation of the lithographs, someone with specialist knowledge and an eye for the reproduction of hieroglyphs. From his hometown Naumburg (about 200 km southwest of Berlin), Lepsius knew the Weidenbachs as a family of artists, and from 1840 onwards, when Max was only 16 years old, he began training him for this particular task of copying and writing hieroglyphs.

Max Weidenbach's diary: contents and writing style

During the three years of the expedition, Max Weidenbach made regular entries in his diary describing and commenting on the journey; the social and political circumstances in Egypt; the people they encountered and worked with; the work of the team in their endeavour to document the monuments and, of course, the stages of their journey that led them from Alexandria all the way to Khartoum and back to Cairo, travelling on the Nile and through the deserts. Max Weidenbach's diary differs from other published personal accounts of the Prussian expedition in several ways.[7] He was the only member of the core team to accompany Lepsius on the six-week expedition from Luxor through the Wadi Hammamat and the Eastern Desert to the Red Sea and the Sinai peninsula. More than the others do, he writes about the locals who were constantly with them and without whom they could not have fulfilled their task of recording the monuments or have travelled from site to site over thousands of kilometres: the dragoman (the interpreter and guide); the *kawass* (an official, police guard); the janissary (élite soldier); the cook; the workforce on site; the donkey-men and camel-drivers; the boat captains and sailors. Being the youngest in the team, Max would have felt closer to these participants in the expedition, not having to observe the hierarchies with the same rigour as the director. This group of people was crucial for the provisioning and well-being of the team and ultimately to the success of the entire expedition as well.

With regard to the work of the expedition, Max noted in more detail than others how the recording of the monuments was distributed, executed and shared, indicating to what extent so many of the original drawings are the product of a team effort. Max's diary entries are brief and to the point, taking note of what is new to him in the respective surroundings. There are regular records of facts: the weather; temperature; times; tasks and their distribution; the location for the tasks; how many workmen were hired for the excavations and their rate of pay; the sequence of the events of the day, and what was on the menu. The comings and goings of the people they encountered are mentioned in almost as brief and factual a manner. Only occasionally are there longer descriptions of the landscape or of the flora and fauna, revealing Max's keen interest in natural history. On very rare occasions, and then by using qualifying adjectives rather than full sentences let alone paragraphs, does Max add comments about the people and personalities around him. In other words, the diary neither contains what one might call gossip nor is it introspective or self-reflective. The diary must have been self-motivated and considered a personal document, as opposed to an official report expected to be handed over at the end of the expedition.

Fig 1.2 Pages of the manuscript diary kept by Max Weidenbach.

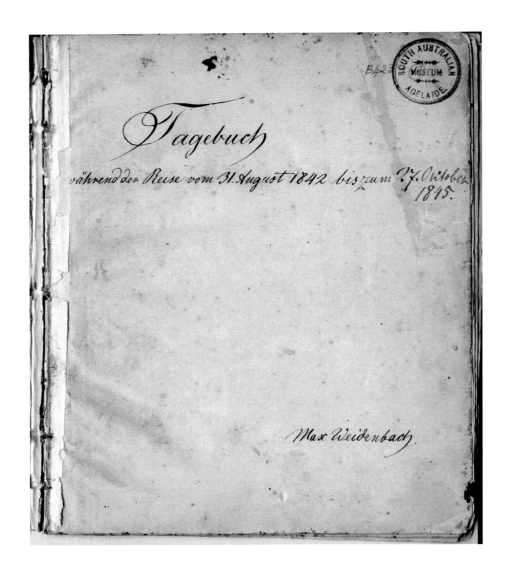

Fig 1.3 Title page of Max Weidenbach's expedition diary 1842-45.

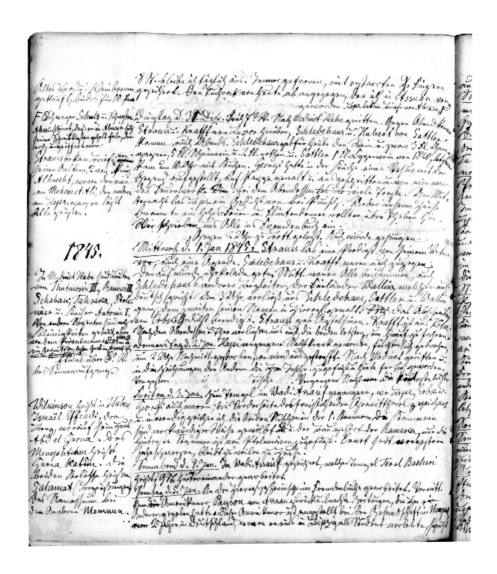

Fig 1.4 Weidenbach, *Tagebuch während der Reise*, page 304: 30 December 1844 to 5 January 1845.

Officials, consuls, antiquarians, scholars, painters, travellers

One interesting aspect of diaries such as Max Weidenbach's is the frequent reference to the people the team officially met, those they worked with and those who happened to pass by or specifically came to see them and spend time with them in the course of their three years in Egypt. Hundreds of people are mentioned by name, some by their official function, others in a more generic manner. There are encounters with the Ottoman officials, the village elders and local Egyptians, but also the Europeans, expatriates or travellers from Austria, Belgium, England, Finland, France, Germany, Greece, Russia and Sweden, as well as persons from America and one from India.

The focus in the second part of this paper is on the Europeans and Americans the team came in contact with. Some of the persons are unnamed and unknown, others indeed famous. They are presented here by location, from north to south, with a focus on the people they met in Alexandria, Cairo, Giza, the Fayum, Middle Egypt and Luxor. The following pages contain a selection and provide a first overview. An in-depth study of all the persons mentioned will follow at some later stage in the Weidenbach-Diary Project.

On arrival in Alexandria

When they first arrive in Alexandria on 18 September 1842, there are the diplomats who assist in arranging the decisive meeting with Viceroy Muhammad ʿAlī on 23 September 1842, which provides the permission to proceed with the expedition: the Swedish consul, antiquarian and merchant Giovanni Anastasi,[8] and in the absence of a Prussian consul in 1842[9] the Danish Consul-General Daniel Dumreicher[10] and the Austrian Consul-General von Laurin.[11] The team also has the opportunity of meeting these envoys socially:

> [9] (...) Today Wednesday 21 Sept 1842[12] (...) At 6 o'clock in the evening the whole expedition was invited for dinner to Herr Anastasi's, the Swedish Consul. It was very grand, we thought we weren't in Africa. Indeed, Alexandria is an almost semi-European city as very many Europeans live here. An English church is now being built here because the chapel used now [10] is too small. In this respect and in general, Cairo is very different to Alexandria. Apart from the seven of us, Herr Anastasi with his beautiful young foster daughter, a Greek lady, four other gentlemen were of the party, amongst whom was also Herr von Laurin, the Austrian Consul-General. After dinner, the company separated into two rooms. In one the tobacco smokers gathered, to whom I also belonged, and were provided with beautiful Turkish pipes 6 to 8 feet long, and also had coffee. At 10 o'clock we left and went home.

This extract from the entry for 21 September 1842 is also interesting because it notes Max's first impressions of Alexandria and his commentary on its international character. Here, 'going home' refers to the Hôtel d'Orient where the team stayed when they first arrived.[13]

In Cairo

In Cairo, where the team stayed for about four weeks until early November 1842, their introduction to the many facets of life in the metropolis continued with them meeting a wide range of persons: compatriots who assisted them in the setting up the practical aspects of the expedition, more officials and diplomats, and also a good number of travellers from Europe.

Some of these unnamed persons, individuals and the small groups that they usually move around in, are of interest as they illustrate that already in the 1840s it was not, as in the early decades of the 19th century, only the élite who were travelling. Max Weidenbach's diary bears witness to these very first beginnings of tourist traffic that Egypt was to become so famous for in the later 19th and 20th centuries. A selection of diary entries is presented here, concentrating on the English because they are in fact the nationality most frequently mentioned. In their first weeks in Cairo, on 23 October 1842, Max writes:

> |29| (...) On our way back [from Mohamed Ali's Palace in Shubra] we came across a big, chained elephant. (...) we went into a coffee house with an Englishman who had joined us in Shubra. There we saw a large part of the European Cairenes, amongst whom there were very attractive ladies.

On Friday 4 November 1842, on a visit to the German missionary Lieder (see below) on the last day of Ramadan, the Prussians meet up with English nationals whom they had already met on the steamship *Oriental* coming from Southampton:

> |34| (...) At Lieder's we encountered, apart from his wife, his English governess Louise, another pretty young English lady who had travelled with me on the English ship from Gibraltar to Malta and has now been in Cairo for 14 days with her father who is accompanying her, two Arab women and the brother of the governess. (...) The younger of the Arab women, who attracted most attention, was Madame Fresnel, the wife of a European scholar in Cairo.

These comments indicate on the one hand, that the Europeans were keen to get to know each other and that some entered into service with each other, and on the other that at this level of society, mixing with the local Arabs took place. Madame Fresnel mentioned by name in this entry would have to be the wife of the French orientalist and diplomat Fulgence Fresnel (1795–55). She appears to have befriended the young English lady and her father and was to pay a visit to the team on site in Giza:

> |40| (...) Thursday 17 Nov. 1842 Less diarrhoea. After morning coffee I went again with Frey and Ernst to draw in the old tomb. In the afternoon, Madame Fresnel with the English lady and her father whom we had seen at Lieder's came from Cairo to visit us and brought with them the tent that Wild had ordered. Madame Fresnel and her companion returned to Cairo, but the Englishman with his daughter stayed here, dined with us and spent the night over at the guesthouse of the pyramids. Went to bed at 11 o'clock.

When the Prussians organise their very first excursion to the pyramids on the Giza plateau, they select the day of their king's birthday, 15 October 1842. This was a momentous occasion and an opportunity for other dignitaries to join them, among them the Austrian Consul Franz Champion.

> |24| (...) <u>Saturday 15 Oct. 1842</u> Today is the birthday of our King, which we celebrated at the pyramids of Giza. We got up early while it was still dark, between 4 and 5 o'clock. At half past 5, Herr Lieder arrived, quarter of an hour later Herr Isenberg und Herr Mühleisen, missionaries. At 6 o'clock at sunrise, the procession of 14 persons, that is the 3 gentlemen Lieder, Mühleisen and Isenberg just mentioned, the 8 of us, the kawass and the 2 attendants, set out towards Old Cairo riding on donkeys, enjoying the beautiful Egyptian morning. We took the route that I had gone 3 days ago. In Fustat, the Austrian Consul Herr Champion, who had come to Old Cairo the night before, was waiting for us and joined us. (...) We were ferried across the river Nile on three barges (...) with our donkeys and all the bags and reached the other |25| shore and Giza at exactly half past 7 o'clock. It took us a quarter of an hour before we could continue our journey, and on account of the inundation we had to take a route more than twice as long as the direct road from Giza.

The German gentlemen John (Johann) Rudolph Theophilus Lieder (1798–1865), Mühleisen and Wilhelm Isenberg (1806–64) were missionaries all based in Cairo.[14] Particularly Lieder, an Anglican minister of German origin and founder of a school in Cairo, assisted the team in practical and organisational matters throughout the three years of the expedition and remained their main contact in the capital.[15] In a similar way, the medical doctor Franz Pruner (1808–83), who was in Cairo to assist the French surgeon Antoine Clot Bey (1793–68) in setting up the health system in Egypt and to research infections and tropical diseases on the request of Vice-Roy Mohamed ʿAlī, supported the team:[16]

> |32| (...) <u>Saturday 29 Oct 1842</u> Spent 2 hours at Lieder's with Lepsius. At noon, our two servants were dismissed and two others hired: the first, again called Mohamed, was organised through Dr Pruner, and is paid 6 dollars a month, the previous one got 20 dollars. The other, called Ali, was organised through Dr Lieder and is only paid 4 dollars. The one before him, Saïd, got 10 dollars, in other words, a very big difference. Around 2 o'clock we heard faint thunder. In the evening again much sheet lightning. Went for a walk with Ernst and Franke.

But there is also time for leisure, and another German doctor working for the Egyptian authorities, Dr Koch,[17] organises tickets for the theatre in Cairo, which is the opportunity to take part in a mixed social gathering:

> |34| <u>Thursday 3 Nov. 1842</u> (...) Dr Koch organised 5 tickets for us for today's theatre performance. Some of the actors are paid, some are amateurs, in other words, it is a theatre for enthusiasts. At half past 7 in the evening, we – Erbkam, Frey, Ernst, Franke and I – went to Dr Pruner's and found there Dr Koch who, along with another German,

joined us to the theatre at 8 o'clock. The place is quite spacious and well lit. The audience sit in a semi-circle, the men on the main floor, the women in the loggias of the gallery. There is now a performance every Thursday, Italian and French alternate. Today we heard an Italian comedy, 'The young lady in love' [*Die Liebhaberin von 16 Jahren*] in 5 acts. In the intermission music was being played: grand piano, 4 violins and 1 flute, very pleasant. The piece was very humorous and the acting was excellent. The characters were 2 very beautiful ladies and 6 gentlemen. It was a very pleasant evening. The Turkish ladies were not veiled and wore their original national costume with the splendid headdress. The European ladies also displayed their finery. The sets were average, the players wore no makeup. The play ended at half past 11 o'clock and all went home.

Cairo is also the place where encounters with collectors occur. On 18 October 1842, there is the opportunity to pay a visit to Dr Abbott (1807–59):[18]

> |28| (...) <u>Tuesday 18 Oct 1842</u> At midday I went with Lepsius and Bonomi to Dr Abbott's but did not find him at home. Made squeezes of some monuments in his Egyptian collection. Went from there to Clot Bey and found him at home. He is a Frenchman, Lieutenant General of the whole Egyptian army, looked at his Egyptian collection, smoked a pipe of tobacco and drank coffee. He has a small menagerie, amongst which are 6 giraffes. Around 6 o'clock we went home again.

Getting to meet Antoine Clot Bey and see his Egyptian collection instead would have been just as engaging. Ten days later, finally, they manage to see Dr Abbott:

> |32| (...) <u>Friday 28 Oct 1842</u> Spent 2 hours at Dr Abbott's with Lepsius. Looked at his Egyptian collection and copied several things. He is an Englishman.

Objects from both Dr Abbott's and Clot Bey's collections seen on this occasion were described and sketched and are even mentioned in the *Denkmäler*.[19]

Another interesting person they met, in a completely different profession, is the Scottish horticulturalist James Traill, who in 1828–48 worked on the island of Roda in the Nile at Cairo.[20] Here is Max's account of the meeting with this friend of Bonomi's:

> |33| (...) <u>Tuesday 1 Nov. 1842</u> (...) At 4 o'clock with Lepsius, Bonomi, Erbkam and Frey, I rode off and crossed over in ½ an hour to the island of Roda. First we visited the gardener of this island, which belongs to Ibrahim Pasha[21], an Englishman by name of Traill. Since we couldn't see the Nilometer on the island because it was still submerged, Traill, a friend of Bonomi's, guided us around the beautiful garden. There, one can probably see all types of palms, bamboo, many Indian plants, European trees, even an oak growing miserably, however, into a bush. The fences here are formed of myrtle and many coffee plants. Unfortunately the water level didn't allow us to see much. After taking coffee we left the friendly man and set out on our way home without having achieved our goal of seeing the old Nilometer. After 6 o'clock we reached home. After dinner Lepsius told entertaining stories about his student years.

Erbkam, the architect on the team, also mentions this visit to the gardens on Roda Island in his diary. This is how his entry reads:[22]

> [77] (...) <u>Tuesday 1 Nov. 1842</u> (...) At half past 4 o'clock Lepsius, Bonomi, Frey, Max and I ride off to Old Cairo where we asked to be ferried across to the island of Roda to see the Nilometer there. An Englishman is the gardener of the beautiful garden set-out like a park, a pleasant and polite gentleman, who we go to see and who shows us as much of the garden as was possible during this time of inundation. Unfortunately the most beautiful garden beds, grassy areas and park sections are flooded whereby everything suffers extremely, of course. Beautiful roses, oleander, rare species of palms, expansive lawns and exquisite deciduous trees, long hedges of myrrh looking like box shrubs, hedges of aloe. Rows of lemon trees line the beds and are pleasing to the eye. We are unable to see the Nilometer on account of the water level being too high and that part of the garden still being under water. – Giraffes in the garden. Many sakiyehs [water wheels] along the riverbank under leafy canopies. Strange vase-like flower-pots. After a walk in the garden we return to the house of the Englishman, drink some coffee there and then go back home through the now very crowded streets. In the evening we drink a delicious infusion made from orange leaves we brought back with us. – Late in the evening, Lepsius talks about his youth in Schulpforta,[23] which was amusing. – Before that we study Arabic.

While Erbkam's description contains much more informative detail about the plants, it is Max who provides the name of the gardener and allows us to identify him as James Traill, who with William McCulloch, spent two decades in Egypt designing and creating these special botanical and horticultural gardens for the recreation and pleasure of Ibrahim Pasha and as a place to entertain guests.[24]

Visitors to the sites in Giza

For three months from early November 1842 to early February 1843, the team was camped in Giza in and around rock-cut tombs south-west of the Sphinx. During this time, Max makes notes about the casual visitors. Only a few are mentioned by name. Some, like the group with Madame Fresnel mentioned above, help the team by bringing equipment out to Giza, and Max mentions an established place where visitors can stay overnight near the pyramids. Others chose to camp:

> [44] (...) <u>Thursday 1 Dec 1842</u> Two Englishmen, who have pitched their tent near us under the sycamores and palms and plan to stay several days here, dined with us.

These same two Englishmen joined them for dinner again the following day. The location 'under the sycamores and palms' appears to be the group of trees that features in Erbkam's plan of the Giza plateau, south-east of the Sphinx.[25] The shade of the trees would have made it a good place to set oneself up.

When Heinrich Abeken joined the expedition, on 10 December 1842, he arrives in the late morning with a large group comprising nine Englishmen and a man from India:

> [47] (...) <u>Saturday 10 Dec. 1842</u> We had hardly risen and the day was overcast. Lepsius and Erbkam rode to the pyramids of Saqqara immediately after coffee. Went to the tomb of Merhet with Frey, he drew the decoration and I inserted the hieroglyphs. Finished at noon, went to the tents, took breakfast and there met Herr Abeken who had come from Cairo with 10 gentlemen, all English apart from one Indian.

The Englishmen stay to visit the monuments for another day, four of them for another two days:

> [48] (...) <u>Sunday 11 Dec. 1842</u> (...) The Englishmen climbed the 1st pyramid. After their return, Abeken conducted divine service for them, they returned to Cairo, but 4 stayed back. (...) <u>Monday 12 Dec.</u> Overcast. Drank coffee with the Englishmen. Later, Abeken rode to Cairo with them.

Six weeks later, when Max was working in the tomb of Senedjemib, there is an encounter with two other Englishmen:

> [74] (...) <u>31 Jan. 1843</u> (...) Then went back home and after breakfast to the tomb of Senedjemib. In the afternoon I guided 2 young Englishmen around the tomb who had come from Upper Egypt. One spoke very good German.

Particularly at the beginning of the expedition, communication with other nationalities would have been difficult for Max. Meeting someone with 'very good German' is therefore special and gets a mention in the diary.

On various days in December 1842 and January 1843, Max refers to groups of persons who are interesting for their social backgrounds, and this, more generally, provides intriguing insight into who was beginning to travel to Egypt.

> [49] (...) <u>Wednesday 14 Dec. 1842</u> Went early to the tomb I had left yesterday, and by sunset I finished drawing there. Before dinner I went to the Sphinx, which Erbkam had measured the day before yesterday, and looked at the excavation. In the evening, 2 strangers, tourists [*Vergnügnungsreisende*], one a rich landowner from the vicinity of Bromberg, the other from Kurland, drank tea with us.

> [63] (...) <u>Thursday 12 Jan. 1843</u> (...) [64] (...) 2 Germans and a Belgian visited us and pitched their tents in the vicinity of ours. In the evening they drank tea with us.

> [66] (...) <u>Tuesday 17 Jan.</u> (...) After a short time there came to the entrance 3 craftsmen, Germans: the eldest half-blind, 54 years old from Braunschweig, a wheelwright; another, a Hanoverian, a clothier; the third a Silesian, a baker.

Max would have entered a conversation with them to have found out these details about their home towns and professions.

In the Fayum and Middle Egypt

While still in Giza, shortly before their move to Saqqara in February 1843, the expedition came into contact with a person who was to meet up with them on several occasions throughout that year, particularly in the Fayum and in Middle Egypt: George Robins Gliddon (1809–57), who had been appointed American consul in 1837.

> |75| (...) <u>Thursday 2 Feb. 1843</u> (...) After breakfast went into [the tomb of] Sekhemkare and inserted the hieroglyphs into the sheets of Frey and Ernst. A son of the American consul Gliddon was here at midday, took along 50 skulls for the collector from the tomb of Hetepheres.

This man is here referred to in relation to his father, John G. Gliddon, an English merchant who at the time was the American consul in Alexandria.[26] The collector mentioned here is presumably the physician and physical anthropologist Samuel George Morton (1799–51) who, in 1837, had requested Gliddon to provide him with ancient skulls from Egypt, and in 1840 had received 143 skulls from him.[27]

Later, in the Fayum, the 'younger Gliddon', as Weidenbach calls him, formed an attachment to the Prussian expedition. At first, Weidenbach speaks of him as 'imposing' himself.[28] But this perception changes in the course of the following weeks:

> |124| (...) <u>Wednesday 24 May 1843</u> (...) Towards evening the younger Gliddon, who is now staying at Medinet, rode over and imposed himself on us as a guest for the evening and the night. Lepsius (who was suffering from a sore throat) did not eat with us. At sunset the kawass and Ali returned with the soldier, who is residing in Hawara instead of a sheikh, and promised us excavators, as many as we want. Ate late without Lepsius. Ali brought along a poor, green kind of apple. 8 watchmen. <u>Thursday 25 May</u> After the morning breakfast Gliddon rode off again.

Four days later there is the next mention of Gliddon, which appears to demonstrate he is a good bargainer, that he is sojourning in the Fayoum and keeping contact with the expedition. After that, on Pentecost Sunday 4 June, Max writes a longer description of an outing to Gliddon's estate:

> |125| (...) <u>Monday 29 May 1843</u> Completed the earlier drawings. Read Setepenra on a big block, i.e. Ramesses, lying near Lepsius's tent. In the morning the mudir of Medinet sent 15 piasters worth of greens; in the afternoon Gliddon just as much for 5 piasters. (...) <u>Tuesday 30 May</u> (...) The younger Gliddon came in the morning, had lunch with us and then left again in the afternoon. (...) |126| (...) <u>Pentecost 4 June</u> (...) |127| (...) Divine service was at 8 o'clock. At half past 9 o'clock we rode off – of our attendants, only

Eugen, Mohamed, the Berber and Hauad and a guard were with us – and took the longer route of ½ an hour via Hawara, from there along the main road to Medinet or el Fayum, but after ½ an hour we turned left and in ½ an hour arrived at the Bahr Yussef. Opposite, right on the river, pleasantly surrounded by tamarisks and acacia trees there lies the estate of Gliddon. He himself met us on this side. The river is a little over the height of a man deep, so we crossed, two by two, standing on a disused mill wheel which was being pushed by 5 Arabs. The crossing was quite interesting and enjoyable. A young Syrian and a Cairene, both of whom spoke Italian, were still there as administrators. We went through the houses and immediately into a beautiful big garden full of banana trees, oleander, olives, figs, apricots, peaches, oranges, trees and palms. Carpets and cushions had been laid out along a colonnade deeply shaded by vines. We soon ate bread and dates and drank coffee. Then, apart from Frey and the two administrators, along with Gliddon we mounted donkeys. Lepsius mounted a young, wild, still unbroken horse, which immediately threw him off without injuring Lepsius. He then mounted another and we rode off to the south along the Bahr en Neshet over a half-collapsed bridge. ¼ of an hour further on, Gliddon was riding the horse now, we reached a monastery situated in the middle of the desert. (...) Back at the village we bathed, Lepsius, Abeken, Erbkam, Ernst, Gliddon and I, in the Bahr Yussef. Then we went into the garden. Soon a big sheep, two types of pudding, stuffed vine leaves, and baked apples were being served and eaten, but before that soup. We had brought 3 bottles of sparkling wine. Coffee completed the excellent dinner. We were all very merry. We also sang.

Gliddon also joins them on 6 and 7 June, and returns on 10 June to introduce to the Prussians a young German called Müller, a nephew of the Danish Consul Dumreicher:

|129| (...) In the morning Gliddon came with a German, Müller, the nephew of Dumreicher, who comes from the region around Ansbach, and the young Syrian. Müller has been in the Fayum for several days and returns to Cairo with Gliddon tomorrow. They dined with us. In the afternoon they returned to Medinet.

Later, in September 1843, once the expedition moved on to Middle Egypt and Beni Hassan, Gliddon, coming from Minia, is instrumental in providing them with the mail parcels they were waiting for which included important works for the expedition library:

|152| (...) <u>Wednesday 13 Sept 1843</u> We hurried in the afternoon and finished the tomb, having determined to sail in the evening. Everything was taken aboard the boat, we used to leave much up in the tombs overnight. Shortly before sunset a messenger arrived with a short letter for Lepsius, who was in the southern tombs. Meanwhile we went down and bathed. Lepsius soon followed and informed us that the letter was from the younger Gliddon, from Minia, to where he had come and who had brought with him a chest and a package for us. We were to collect it. So it was decided that Abeken, along with Joseph, should sail there in his boat and that we would wait here for him. We now ate. Between 8 and 9 o'clock Abeken departed.

In the entry for the following day we are told that the chest and package contained the complete publication of Vivant Denon, with plates and text, although Lepsius had only requested the text, along with the first two quires and plates of a work by von Bunsen, presumably part of his historical treatise *Aegyptens Stelle in der Weltgeschichte* [*Egypt's position in world history*]. On Friday 15 September, finally, 'Gliddon came over early from Minia.'

The last we hear of the Gliddons is in late 1844, when Weidenbach, in Luxor, makes note of the American consul John Gliddon's death:

> |300| (...) Saturday 16 Nov 1844 (...) Joseph returned from Cairo, on the ship were two Englishmen. (...) The elder Gliddon has died.

The close contact George Gliddon, the son, kept with the expedition can be understood in the light of his intense interest in the antiquities of Egypt. Already in 1841,[29] he had written a pamphlet entitled *An appeal to the antiquaries of Europe on the destruction of the monuments of Egypt*. When he returned to America, he went on to lecture and publish on ancient Egypt and Egyptian archaeology, earning him the designation 'American Egyptologist' in *Who was Who in Egyptology*.[30]

The Fayum is also the region where, through the expedition interpreter and guide Giuseppe Scerabie, Max and the others meet the French scientist Portier. Erbkam in his letters calls him a *Muschelsammler* (shell collector)[31], whereas Max appears to have more time for him and mentions him over several days:

> |134| Thursday 22 June 1843 (...) At Scerabie's we met a French naturalist who then ate with us, a huge number of dishes. Lemonade beforehand, coffee afterwards. Afterwards, Lepsius and I went out with Scerabie and the latter showed us a fragment of two seated statues, it was King Amenemhet I with his wife, only the legs preserved, I quickly drew this. (...) |138| (...) Sunday 9 July At ¼ to 5 I climbed up the pyramid and saw the sun rise at 5. The illumination of the evening sun is, however, much more dazzling than the morning sun. After tea went for a walk by myself, behind Hawara along the Bahr Yussef, from where, from today onwards, we will get our water, because the water in the canal near us has gone off. I asked for figs in the fig garden but none are ripe yet. I returned after 2 to 3 hours. No divine service today. Shortly after the midday breakfast the naturalist Portier came with Scerabie. The former has been in Medinet for the last 3 days having returned from the lake und came today in order to say farewell because tomorrow he wants to leave for Cairo and from there he goes to the Red Sea for the second time (he mainly collects conches). (...) Monday 10 July At midday the messenger Kandil returned from Cairo and brought along a sturdy kawass with guns for Portier, as well as a packet of letters.

So far, it has not been possible to identify further details about this French naturalist.

In Luxor and Upper Egypt

Luxor was another important place where the expedition made interesting contacts with other travellers, scholars and artists. Like others, the Prussians stayed there twice. The first stop was only brief to take advantage of the north wind to carry their boats south swiftly. When travelling with the current of the river on the return journey it was much easier to stop more frequently and still make steady progress.

It is in the context of the team's first arrival in Thebes on Friday 6 October 1843 that mention is made of the French Egyptologist Émile Prisse d'Avennes (1807–79).[32] The descriptive passage in Max's diary ends with a statement of great disappointment:[33]

> [165] (...) Around noon we sailed on towards Thebes. At sunset [166] one still couldn't see anything, but an hour and a ¼ later in the moonshine, the giant hall of columns, comprising 7 columns, could be seen, but not the second row behind. Soon the smaller court beside it on the right, not long after, the obelisk could also be discerned to the left of the great court, and finally the village of Luxor in and around the temple. Between 8 and 9 o'clock we moored and, apart from Franke, disembarked immediately, found the chief guard and now viewed these temple remains in the moonlight, when they make the greatest impression. The village makes a much greater impression in that it gives a point of comparison. We also climbed up the western pylon, a little dangerous at night. When we had returned, Abeken also arrived, and the Egyptian antiquarian Castellari visited us and brought us the sad news that Prisse had completely destroyed the kings' chamber in Karnak, having cut out the walls with the king list block by block and is taking them to Alexandria, whereby in the process most of them had been spoilt.

The Chamber of Kings is part of Thutmosis III's Festival Hall complex with depictions of this 18th-Dynasty king presenting offerings to four rows of predecessors. As such, these reliefs are significant historical documentation of the ancient Egyptians' sense of their past. Today, casts of the relief blocks are on the walls in Karnak, the originals being in the Louvre (E 13481) in a reconstruction of the 'Chambre des ancêtres' ever since Prisse d'Avennes took them there in 1843.[34]

The antiquarian in this passage is Andrea Castellari (d. 1848), a well-known antiquities dealer who had taken residence on the roof of Luxor temple.[35]

Another antiquarian who compiled a significant and diverse collection of antiquities on the West Bank at Thebes is the Greek Triantophyllos, also known as Wardi (d. 1852).[36] The expedition met him on their return visit to the Luxor region in late 1844:

> [298] (...) Monday 4 Nov. 1844 (...) We didn't start drawing today, were still sorting things and setting up. In the afternoon went with the others to the Ramesseum. We have 4 night watchmen and 1 gate keeper. The Greek Triantophyllos, a long-time resident here, brought 1 letter from Wild and 1 from Bonomi who wrote that our doorman

> Hauad would show us a tomb only discovered a year ago and still completely unknown with a king list similar to the known one in Qurna. This Greek has built up a significant collection here, which he wants to get out of Egypt through us since he is not able to do it because of the current strict prohibition. On the shelves was one with 2 new princesses, see page 156 of my notebook.

The Lepsius expedition purchased a of variety objects from him, which are now in the Berlin collection and published in the *Denkmäler*: among them a group of Hieratic papyri, a Middle Kingdom statue fragment and two mummies.[37] Triantophyllos is also known to and mentioned by other travellers.[38]

On the West Bank, one of the places where Max Weidenbach meets English visitors is the tomb of the ancient vizier Rekhmire (today: Theban Tomb 100):

> |307| (...) <u>Friday 24 Jan 1845</u> Drew with Georgi in a nearby tomb where the Jews making bricks and interesting crafts are depicted. The stooped Reverend Cantley came by. Pleasant days are back again. (...) |308| (...) <u>Tuesday 28 Jan</u> With Georgi, I finished the tomb with the Jews making bricks (the deceased is called Rekhmire and lived under Thutmosis III). In the afternoon I explained the scenes to 2 English ladies and 3 English gentlemen.

There are two clergymen with the surname Cantley who are possible candidates: either the Reverend Joshua Cantley, incumbent at Thorney from 1853,[39] or one Richard Cantley.[40] Even if it is not possible to identify the clergymen at this point in time, this diary entry illustrates one of the factors that influenced people at the time to take an interest in ancient Egypt: the information one hoped to gain on Biblical history. We know what role this later played in British Egyptology and the formation of the Egypt Exploration Fund by Amelia Edwards and Reginald Poole in 1882.[41] The Prussian expedition also benefited from this intense interest in the Bible, the Prussian king being a very devout man and his confidant Karl Josias von Bunsen, Prussian ambassador to the Court of St James, in the process of writing a history of Egypt with the express purpose of contextualising ancient Israel.[42] Furthermore, one of the members of the expedition, Heinrich Abeken, was a theologian and had been chaplain to the Prussian Embassy in both Rome, when von Bunsen was Ambassador there, and later in London.[43]

Then there is the group with another Englishman, Thomas Robinson Woolfield (1800–88):

> |306| (...) <u>Thursday 16 Jan. 1845</u> Lepsius showed me 2 tombs a few paces to the north above our house, which I finished by the evening. Meanwhile, Woolfield with his wife and a major had visited us. I had seen these people the day before yesterday at the pylon in the Ramesseum.

Rather than for interest in Egypt, Woolfield is known for his connections with the French Riviera.[44] Egypt only gets a mention in passing in his book *Thomas Robinson*

Woolfield's Life at Cannes and Lord Brougham's First Arrival (London, 1890) where he states on page two that 'after seven years' travelling in Spain, Egypt, Palestine, Syria, Asia Minor, Turkey and Greece, hoping to find some spot where I might pass my remaining days, I found nothing to tempt me in comparison with Cannes.'

Also in January 1845, Max speaks of the visit by a group of Frenchmen who to appear to have made contact through Clot Bey:

> |307| (...) <u>Wed. 22 Jan 1845</u> (...) At midday the famous man of letters Ampère finally came with d'Artignes, Rousset and Durand with newspapers, cigars, ink, books and plaster from Clot Bey. Ampère speaks German, studied in Bonn for a year. Lepsius dined with them on the boat.

From 1841, Jean-Jacques Ampère (1800–64), son of the physicist Ampère, was a professor at the Sorbonne in Paris, a philologist and *homme de lettres*.[45] For Lepsius, this would have been an interesting meeting with colleagues. Ampère gives an account of his journey in *Voyage en* Égypte *et en Nubie,* which was published posthumously in 1867.[46]

Furthermore, on two consecutive days when working in Karnak, Weidenbach sees an Englishman by the name of Twiselton:

> |312| (...) <u>Wednesday 26 Feb. 1845</u> Made drawings in the temple of Khons and of the high gate in front of it. The German-speaking Englishman Twiselton visited us. (...) <u>Thursday 27 Feb.</u> Dreadful storm swirls up dust. At the high gate. Made drawings in the Ipet temple and the Khons temple. Twiselton was there as well.

Could this be the Reverend Frederick Benjamin Twisleton (1799–1887) whose dates fit the timeframe and who after this tour to Egypt, in 1847, succeeded to the title of 10th Baron of Saye and Sele and in 1849 changed his name to Frederick Benjamin Twisleton-Wykeham-Fiennes?[47]

While working on the West Bank in Luxor, the expedition stayed in what was known as Wilkinson's House, built in and around what is now Theban Tomb 83. Particularly around New Year 1845, there are people who stay with them: Christian Schledehaus (1810–58), the German doctor and personal physician of Mehemed Ali, in the company of the Austrian artist Huber Sattler (1817–1904) and the Finnish orientalist Georg August Wallin (1811–52),[48] as well as the theologian Friedrich Adolph Strauss (1817–88) and his cousin Krafft.

> |303| (...) <u>Sunday 29 Dec. 1844</u> At sunrise 7°. Devotions. At midday Schledehaus and Sattler ate with us. In the afternoon Domkandidat [pastor in training] Strauss with his cousin Krafft arrived here. All the Germans, except for Sattler, ate with us in the evening. Strauss gave a long flattering speech to toast the expedition. After 9 o'clock they took their leave. Lepsius read the introduction to his guestbook out loud, Erbkam presented his poem and Georgi's painting and nativity scene were exhibited. (...) |304| (...) <u>Tuesday 31 Dec.</u> In the morning 7°. I rode to Medinet Habu. Toward evening

Strauss and Krafft come across from Luxor, Schledehaus and Hubert von Sattler also came in the evening. Schledehaus contributed the wine for today, namely 3 bottles of champagne, 5 bottles of sparkling wine and 2 bottles of red, and Sattler 1 bottle of 1820 Cypriot wine. The latter arrived at 10 o'clock with cake. In the kitchen Georgi had set up a Vesuvius with its surroundings, painted on cardboard and cut out, and my contribution was the fireworks. During the evening meal many toasts. At midnight Lepsius read out a poem while we were having punch. Above the house [on the slope of the mountain] a large bonfire was burning and gunshots thundered and rolled across Thebes. We all wrote our names into the guestbook. (...) Went to bed around 2 o'clock. We also sang. Wednesday 1 Jan. 1845 Strauss read out a sermon by his father, and also an order of service. Schledehaus and Krafft were also present. Then we drank chocolate. At midday we all sat together, including Schledehaus's other companion, the Finn Wallin, who also speaks German. At 3 o'clock Schledehaus, Sattler and Wallin left us for good. For the second one, I wrote his name in hieroglyphs. Finished copying Erbkam's poem. Strauss brought oranges. Krafft is from Cologne. After the evening meal and tea these last two also left to travel up the river.

This passage describes the team's New Year's festivities and entertainment in the company of guests in the succinct style that is typical of Weidenbach's diary entries. It is at this point that Lepsius inaugurates the guestbook known as the *Fremdenbuch,* which was to remain in use until the 1970s.[49] That they indeed all entered their names as mentioned by Weidenbach is attested on page 14 of the volume.[50] Strauss was the son of the chaplain at the Prussian court, Gerhard Friedrich Strauss (1786–1863), whose sermons the team often read for the Sunday services they held regularly.[51] In this entry, Georg August Wallin (1811–52) is spoken of as if it were something special for him to take part in the gathering. He appears to have been travelling as an Oriental and was always cautious not to compromise his role.[52]

In the early days of 1845, another American visiting Egypt is mentioned in the diary: the American consul John Larkin Payson. Weidenbach writes about him on two consecutive days:

|304| (...) Sunday 5 Jan 1845 Worked on the hieroglyphic inscription in the visitors' book. In the morning the American Payson returned from Aswan and brought newspapers (...) This American is on the staff of the embassy in Naples, he was in Germany for two years, one of which he spent in Leipzig as a student. He speaks |305| excellent German. He comes from Boston. He spent the evening with us. Monday 6 Jan Made drawings in the temple at the Assasif [Deir el Bahari]. In the evening Payson dined with us. Drank tea. Between 9 and 10 in the evening, a Frenchman also came who gave us raw gypsum which he had with him to make casts but couldn't find a plaster caster and so gave it away since he had heard from Clot Bey that we need some.

From what one can gather from information about him, Payson was not an American envoy to Egypt, but rather travelled to the land on the Nile out of personal interest.[53]

Luxor being on the route of the travellers of the day makes the time anyone spent there particularly rich in encounters. The Prussians staying in and around Wilkinson's House, prominently located high on the slope of the Sheikh Abd el Gurna hill, would have also attracted visitors to seek them out. The *Fremdenbuch* and its entries attests to this, and research on those for the first months of 1845 would be an important lead to follow and would certainly bring to light more names of people than Weidenbach chose to mention in his diary.

This presentation of extracts from Max Weidenbach's diary could be continued. It could also be supplemented with comments from Erbkam's expedition diary and letters, as well as with information from Lepsius's published material and unpublished notes. For the moment, this representative sample from a few select locations and periods offers a flavour. The envisaged publication of the diary will include indices to allow the reader to follow up and study more comprehensively this interesting aspect of Max Weidenbach's account of his three years in Egypt with Lepsius and the Royal Prussian Expedition.

Endnotes

1 Manuscript (South Australian Museum, Adelaide): Max Weidenbach, *Tagebuch während der Reise vom 31. August 1842 bis zum 27. Oktober 1845.* The existence of this diary had been known for some time (Merrillees, R. [1990] *Living with Egypt's Past in Australia.* Melbourne, p. 9) but its location could not be identified. On the re-discovery of the diary, see South Australian Museum, Adelaide: 'Mystery of Ancient Egypt Diary Uncovered' (Media Release, October 2013), <http://www.samuseum.sa.gov.au/media/unlocked/mystery-of-ancient-egypt-diary-uncovered> (accessed: August 2016). For a further introduction to the diary, its discovery, its contents, its transcription and details about the Weidenbach-Diary Project, see S. Binder, 'The Diary of Max Weidenbach in the South Australian Museum in Adelaide: A new source on the Prussian expedition to Egypt 1842–45' in *Bulletin of the Australian Centre for Egyptology* 25 (2014): pp. 9–29. The authors would like to thank Dr Barry Craig (Senior Curator, World Cultures) at the South Australian Museum in Adelaide for his enthusiasm and generous on-going support for the Weidenbach Diary Project.

2 Friedrich Wilhelm IV (1795–61) was King of Prussia from 1840.

3 The text volumes are based mainly on Lepsius's extensive notebooks and diaries, now in the Lepsius Archive in Berlin. Only Volume I was published by Lepsius himself (1849). The remaining work was taken on and completed by Édouard Naville, Kurt Sethe, Walter Wreszinski and Hermann Grapow (1900–13). All the volumes of the publication are available online: < http://edoc3.bibliothek.uni-halle.de/lepsius/> (accessed Sept. 2016).

4 Weidenbach, *Tagebuch während der Reise*, p. 144.

5 For an overview of dates and short biographies of the team members, see, for example, Elke Freier and Stefan Grunert (1996) *Die Reise durch Ägypten nach Zeichnungen der Lepsius-Expedtion 1842–45*: pp. 174–176: Karl Richard Lepsius (1819–84), Heinrich Hermann Abeken (1809–72), Joseph Bonomi (1796–1878), Georg Gustav Erbkam

(1811–76), Carl Franke (1816–?), Johann Jakob Frey (1813–65), Friedrich Otto Georgi (1819–74), Theodor Ernst Weidenbach (1818–82), Maximilian Ferdinand Weidenbach (1823–90), James William Wild (1814–92). See also the relevant pages of the website at the Berlin-Brandenburg Academy of Sciences and Humanities relating to the Lepsius Archive: <http://aaew.bbaw.de/archive/lepsius-archiv> (accessed Sept. 2016) and the entries for Abeken, Bonomi, Frey, Lepsius, the Weidenbachs and Wild in M. Bierbrier (2012), *Who was Who in Egyptology*, 4th ed., London.

6   For early drawings and lithographs by Max Weidenbach, see Lepsius (1842), *Das Todtenbuch der Ägypter nach dem hieroglyphischen Papyrus in Turin mit einem Vorwort zum ersten Mal* herausgegeben, Leipzig, with 79 plates.

7   Richard Lepsius (1853), *Letters from Egypt, Ethiopia, and the Peninsula of Sinai*, Engl. translation: Leonora and Joanna B. Horner, London; E. Freier (ed.) (2013), '*Wer hier hundert Augen hätte...*' *G.G. Erbkams Reisebriefe aus* Ägypten *und Nubien*, Berlin; Georg Gustav Erbkam (1842–45), *Tagebuch meiner egyptischen Reise*, 3 vols., transcribed and edited by E. Freier, in: Deutsches Textarchiv <http://www.deutschestextarchiv.de/book/show/erbkam_tagebuch01_1842> (accessed Sept. 2016).

8   Weidenbach, *Tagebuch während der Reise*: pp. 9–12 and 15.

9   The first Prussian consul-general in Egypt, Johann Emil von Wagner, was appointed in 1843 and mentioned in the diary for the first time on 30 January 1843 (Weidenbach, *Tagebuch während der Reise*: p. 73).

10   Weidenbach, *Tagebuch während der Reise*: p. 9. Later, on 30 July 1843, Max mentions a letter Lepsius sent the team from Cairo with the news that Dumreicher had gone bankrupt (Weidenbach, *Tagebuch während der Reise*: p. 142).

11   Weidenbach, *Tagebuch während der Reise*: p. 10; Anton Joseph Ritter von Laurin (1789–1869) is mentioned three times in the Weidenbach diary (pp. 10, 73 and 83). He was in Egypt 1834–44: see Gottfried Hamernik, '*Anton Ritter von Laurin - Diplomat, Sammler und Ausgräber. Betrachtungen zu einer nicht gewürdigten Karriere*' in Johanna Holaubek, Wolf B. Oerter and Hana Navrátilová *(eds.) (2007), Egypt and Austria III: The Danube Monarchy and the Orient*, Prague: Czech Institute of Egyptology: pp. 91–98; Elke Freier (ed.), '*Wer hier hundert Augen hätte...*': p. 251; Bierbrier, *Who was Who*: p. 311; Patrick Richard Carstens (2014), *The Encyclopedia of Egypt During the Reign of the Mehemet Ali Dynasty 1798-1952. The People, Places and Events that Shaped Nineteenth Century Egypt and its Sphere of Influence*, Victoria, BC: pp. 408–09.

12   The text extracts from the diary are presented in this article in an English translation by the authors. The numbers between bars in superscript refer to the page of the original German manuscript. The underlining of the date and the use of numerals follow the practice in the original German text.

13   The Hôtel d'Orient, also Hôtel de l'Orient, was 'one of the two inns here' (Weidenbach, *Tagebuch während der Reise*: p. 9). See also Andrew Humphreys (2011), *Grand Hotels of Egypt in the Golden Age of Travel*, Cairo: p. 24.

14   Mühleisen and Isenberg were associated with the Basler Mission: Freier (ed.), '*Wer hier hundert Augen hätte...*', 253, Hartmut Mehlitz (2011), *Richard Lepsius. Ägypten und die Ordnung der* Wissenschaft, Berlin: pp. 252 and 362.

15   Lieder is mentioned on many occasions during the early stages of the expedition (until May 1843) and then again in June/July 1845 when the team had returned to Cairo.

16 Franz Ignaz Pruner (Bey): Bierbrier, *Who was Who*, p. 446; Antoine Barthélemy Clot Bey: Bierbrier, *Who was Who*: pp. 126–27.

17 Freier (ed.), '*Wer hier hundert Augen hätte...*': p. 251.

18 Henry William Charles Abbott: Bierbrier, *Who was Who*: pp. 1–2.

19 Lepsius (1849), *Denkmäler. Text*, Vol. I, Berlin: pp. 6–14. Today, Clot Bey's Egyptian collection is in the Musée d'Archéologie Méditerranéenne in Marseilles: Lucy Gordan-Rastelli (2015), 'Egypt in Marseille', *KMT* 26/4: pp. 52–63. On Abbott's collection of antiquities, see Andrew Oliver (2014), *American Travelers on the Nile. Early U.S. Visitors to Egypt, 1774-39*, Cairo: pp. 312–14.

20 Alix Wilkinson (2011), 'James Traill and William McCulloch: Two Nineteenth-Century Horticultural Society Gardeners in Egypt' in *Garden History* 39/1: pp. 83–98.

21 Ibrahim Pasha (1789–48): Viceroy Mohamed Ali's eldest son and general in the Egyptian army.

22 Georg Gustav Erbkam (1842–43), *Tagebuch meiner egyptischen Reise*, Vol. 1: pp. 77–78 (transcribed and edited by E. Freier) in Deutsches Textarchiv <http://www.deutschestextarchiv.de/book/view/erbkam_tagebuch01_1842?p=77> (accessed Sept. 2016).

23 Schulpforta is a public boarding school in an ancient monastery in Saxony with a long tradition of educating gifted students.

24 Traill's hospitality is also positively mentioned by other travellers: Oliver, *American Travelers on the Nile*: pp. 157, 174 and 243.

25 See, for example, Lepsius, *Denkmäler* I, pp. 14 and 18: trees drawn in the vicinity of the well.

26 Bierbrier, *Who was Who*: p. 215. For detailed information about both John Gliddon, the father, and George Gliddon, the son, see Oliver, *American Travelers on the Nile*: pp. 249–58, 312 and more.

27 Oliver, *American Travelers on the Nile*, pp. 251 and 264. Bierbrier, *Who was Who*: p. 388.

28 In the original: '*... und drang sich uns für den Abend und die Nacht als Gast auf*".

29 Not in 1849, as stated in Bierbrier, *Who was Who*: p. 215.

30 The year dates of 1842–43 for George Gliddon's lecturing in Boston might have to be revised in the light of the fact that he is attested in the Weidenbach diary to have been in Egypt for at least February to September 1843.

31 Erbkam, Letter 13: pp. 9, 13 and 17: Freier (ed.) '*Wer hier hundert Augen hätte...*': pp. 120–26.

32 Bierbrier, *Who was Who*: pp. 445–46.

33 See also: Leslie Greener |(1966), *The Discovery of Egypt*, New York: p. 166.

34 B. Porter and R. Moss (assisted by E. Burney) (1972), *Topographical Bibliography* of Ancient Egyptian Hieroglyphic Texts, Reliefs and Painting, vol. II, 2nd ed. Oxford: pp. 111–12, fig. XIII [2]; É. Delange (2015), *Monuments égyptiens du Nouvel Empire - Chambre des ancêtres, annales de Thoutmosis III, décor de palais de Séthi Ier*, Paris.

35 Bierbrier, *Who was Who*: p. 107. Carstens, *Encyclopedia of Egypt*: p. 148.

36 Bierbrier, *Who was Who*: p. 544. Lepsius, *Denkmäler. Text* III: pp. 288 and 306.

37 These are listed and described in Lepsius, *Denkmäler. Text* III: pp. 306–07 and published in Lepsius, *Denkmäler* VI: pp. 115–122, and II: pp. 120f, 120g and 140m.

38 For example: Jason Thompson (1992), *Sir Gardner Wilkinson and his circle*, Austin: pp. 105, 253 and n.23.

39   A Reverend Joshua Cantley is mentioned in *Journals of the House of Lords*, Vol. 88 (1855): p. 518.

40   The portrait of a Reverend Richard Cantley (1841) was an auction sales item: <http://www.artnet.com/artists/kingsman-cautley/portrait-of-reverend-richard-cantley-together-3oNnHZzi7oUXlYvOcPI5Gg2> (accessed Sept. 2016).

41   Margaret S. Drower, 'The Early Years' in T. G. H. James (1982), *Excavating in Egypt. The Egypt Exploration Society 1882–1982*, Chicago, London: pp. 9–10.

42   The work in question is already mentioned above, and at the time of the expedition was still in draft format: K. J. von Bunsen (1845–57), *Aegyptens Stelle in der Weltgeschichte* [*Egypt's position in world history*].

43   On Abeken, see Wolfgang Frischbier (2008), *Heinrich Abeken 1809–72. Eine Biographie*, Paderborn.

44   He is mentioned in Peter Thorold (2008), *The British in* France, London: p. 118.

45   Bierbrier, *Who was Who*: p. 19.

46   Mention of the encounter with Lepsius and his team: *Voyage en Egypte et en* Nubie, Paris, 1867: pp. 391–416.

47   Frederick Benjamin Twisleton: <https://en.wikipedia.org/wiki/Frederick_Fiennes,_16th_Baron_Saye_and_Sele> (accessed Sept. 2016).

48   Weidenbach, *Tagebuch während der Reise*: p. 300 (17 Nov 1844) mentions a first encounter before the group's departure for Wadi Halfa. For Schledehaus, see the Kulturgeschichtliche Museum Osnabrück, < http://www.osnabrueck.de/kgm/sammlungen/muenzkabinett.html> (accessed Sept. 2016). For Wallin, see Patricia Berg, Sofia Häggman, Kaj Öhrnberg, Jaakko Hämeen-Anttila and Heikki Palva (2014), *Dolce far niente in Arabia. Georg August Wallin and his travels in the 1840s*, Helsinki, and Patricia Berg, 'The Travels of G. A. Wallin and His View on Western Influence in the Middle East' in: Neil Cooke and Vanessa Daubney (eds.) (2015) *Every Traveller Needs a Compass. Travel and Collecting in Egypt and the Near East*, Oxford: pp. 23–31 (esp. pp. 25–26 for Wallin's comments on meeting Lepsius).

49   The history of this volume is a research project in itself. Today, it is part of the collection of the Neues Museum in Berlin, inventory no. 36103.

50   Many thanks to Caris-Beatrice Arnst (Neues Museum, Berlin) for the information and access to the documentation.

51   Freier (ed.), '*Wer hier hundert Augen hätte...*': p. 257.

52   Georg August Wallin: Bierbrier, *Who was Who*: p. 564; Sofia Häggmann, 'Wallin's Egypt – Quite like home' in *Dolce far niente in Arabia*: p. 58.

53   John Larkin Payson: see Debra J. Allen (2012), *Historical Dictionary of U.S. Diplomacy from the Revolution to Secession*, Plymouth: p. 320 (Appendix D).

O Cymru i Wlad y Nîl: Teithwyr Cymreig yn yr Aifft

From Wales to the Land of the Nile:
Welsh Travellers in Egypt

Tessa T. Baber

Y tir y Aifft, the land of Egypt, has long since captivated travellers from every corner of the globe, and numerous accounts have been published over the centuries by travellers from America, Europe and beyond. These include hundreds of British accounts, many of which have been the subject of extensive research in recent years. Among these accounts is a small number written by Welsh travellers, which have yet to be the focus of detailed study. As both Irish and Scottish travellers have been the subject of recent research (for example, the unpublished account of Lady Harriet Kavanagh [1799–1885]: see Jackson, 2011; 2013),[1] the author takes the opportunity to consider the Welsh contribution to our developing understanding of Western encounters with the East in the age of early travel,[2] through examination of the accounts left to us.

Of particular interest are the small number of travelogues published exclusively in the native Welsh tongue. These include: *I'r Aifft ac yn Ôl* (To Egypt and Back) by D. Rhagfr Jones,[3] *O'r Aifft* (From Egypt) by John Davies Bryan (1857–88) and *Y Môr Canoldir a'r Aifft* (The Mediterranean Sea and Egypt) by Thomas Gwynn Jones (1871–1949); the latter two sources will form the focus of this paper.[4]

These accounts are extraordinary in that they appear to be the only known British travelogues published in a native Gaelic language; so far it has been impossible to trace similar sources published in either Scottish or Irish Gaelic. These unique and interesting accounts offer an opportunity to experience the land of the Nile from a new perspective but also emphasize the need for consideration of the intended audience for whom these early travellers wrote. They also raise the question over the significance of language used in early travel accounts and how this may be a medium for the expression of the cultural identity of travellers.

The majority of Welsh travellers published their accounts in English, such as the accounts of John Petherick (1813–82) (Petherick, 1861; 1869), Hugh Price Hughes

(1847–1902) (Hughes, 1901) and John Foulkes Jones (1826–80) (Jones, 1860). Those with an interest in early travel literature may already be familiar with these accounts without necessarily knowing that the authors were Welsh and indeed, these accounts are often no different from those published by other British travellers. Nevertheless, they include a number written by some very interesting characters who appear to have made important contributions to the development of our knowledge and understanding of ancient Egyptian history and its dissemination among the general public.

Art & Architecture: Owen Jones' Travels in Egypt (1833–34)

Owen Jones (1809–1874),[5] an architect, artist and ornamental designer, was one of the earliest Welsh travellers to venture to Egypt. Born in London into a Welsh-speaking family, Owen's interest in ancient monumental architecture was likely influenced by his father (also named Owen Jones or 'Owain Myfyr' (1741–1815) who was an amateur Welsh antiquarian (Moser, 2012: p. 26).

In 1831, Jones embarked on a 'grand tour' of the continent where he studied the historical architecture of Italy, Greece, Turkey and Spain. He arrived in Egypt in 1833 in the company of French architect Jules Goury (1803–34),[6] whom he had met during his travels in Greece (Searight, 2006: 129). Together they measured and sketched the monuments of Egypt which were later published as *Views on the Nile* in 1843[7] (where some 31 plates were accompanied by descriptions by Samuel Birch (1813–85) of the British Museum (Moser, 2012: p. 28).

Jones' experiences in Egypt appear to have recommended him for several important and interesting design projects. In 1851, he was made Superintendents of Works for the Great Exhibition, where he was charged with the interior decoration of Joseph Paxton's Crystal Palace (Jespersen, 2008: p. 144). He used a bold, primary-colour, decorative scheme inspired by the polychromy he had encountered in the ancient architecture of Egypt[8] (Moser, 2012: p. 45). Although the exhibition's bold colour scheme drew some initial criticism[9] (from apparent 'chromophobists')[10] it was later lauded as a great success (Moser, 2012: pp. 7, 46–51 and 185–209) with some attendees claiming that Jones' use of colour produced similar effects to the work of J. M. W. Turner (1775–1851) (*Illustrated London News* Exhibition Supplement, 26 April 1851).

In 1854, Jones was appointed Director of Decorations for the new Crystal Palace at Sydenham[11] where he aided Matthew Digby Wyatt (1820–77) in the creation and installation of a number of Fine Arts Courts (Moser, 2012: p. 62). These were designed to represent a grand narrative of the history of design and ornament. Personally designing the 'Greek', 'Roman' and 'Alhambra' Courts,[12] Jones also aided Joseph Bonomi (1796–1878) in the creation of the 'Egyptian Court'[13] (Osslan, 2007: p. 67) where he was able to draw upon his own accurate sketches made of the monuments while he was in Egypt: 'The authorities which have served for the reproduction of portions of various Egyptian monuments forming the 'Egyptian Court' are a series of original drawings and measurements which I made on the spot in 1833, in company with the late Jules Goury [...]' (Sharpe, 1854: p. 3).

Jones' time spent in Egypt not only informed his decorative and architectural designs (Ferry, 2007) but also inspired him to develop new approaches to the use of pattern and colour (see Jones, 1856) which earned him the reputation as one of the most influential design theorists of his age (www4).

Exploration: John Petherick & Katherine Harriet Petherick's Travels in Egypt (1848-64)

John Petherick (1813–82),[14] another interesting character, ventured to Egypt a little after Owen Jones. A former mining engineer from Merthyr Tydfil, Petherick travelled to Egypt in 1845 to join the service of Mohammed Ali (1769–1849) where he was employed to use his expertise in what would prove to be an unsuccessful search for coal deposits in Upper Egypt (Petherick & Petherick, 1869a: p. 1).

In 1848, Petherick left government service to establish himself as an Arabic gum trader at Kordofan in the Sudan. He later became a successful ivory trader in Khartoum, personally hunting elephants on the White Nile (Humphries, 2013: pp. 39–41). In 1858, he was appointed British Vice-Consul in Khartoum and is known to have kept wild animals (including ostriches, leopards and hyenas) in the consulate garden (Verdcourt, 1995: p. 453), a testament to his somewhat eccentric character.

Returning home the following year, Petherick met and married Katherine Harriet Edelmann (1827–77) and made preparations for his return to the Sudan. The couple left England in 1861 in order for Petherick to take up a position offered to him by the Royal Geographical Society to provide relief stores for Captains John Hanning Speke (1813–82) and James Augustus Grant (1827–92) who would soon return from their expedition to discover the source of the Nile (Petherick & Petherick, 1869b: pp. 92–95).

However, the explorers were delayed by over a year, arriving in Gondokoro on 13 February 1863 rather than in November 1861 (Humphries, 2013: p. 73). In the meantime, the Pethericks decided to explore Bahr-el-Ghazal, where together they would make important collections of local flora and fauna (such as those detailed by J. E. Gray & Dr Albert Günther in the appendices in the second volume of the Petherick's 1869 travel account: pp. 189–272).

Speke and Grant eventually return in February 1863, arriving five days before John and Katherine's return from their explorations in the North, which would prove to be catastrophic for the Pethericks (Carnochan, 2006: p. 83). Although Petherick had left supplies for the men in the care of the British explorer Samuel White Baker (1821–93) (Humphries, 2013: p. 107), Speke saw Petherick's absence as a dereliction of duty and subsequently pursued an unrelenting campaign against his character, accusing him of being embroiled in the slave trade, and petitioning for him to be removed from office[15] (Jeal, 2011: p. 184). By 1864, Earl Russell (1792–1878),

British Secretary for Foreign Affairs, appears to have been persuaded to dissolve the post of British consul at Khartoum (Hall, 1980: p. 128), and despite travellers such as the Tinnés[16] (hailed as Central Africa's first (female) explorers (Willink, 2011: p. 19) showing support for Petherick and spurning Speke's boycott of his business,[17] his reputation was irrevocably damaged, a realization Katherine came to during the meal she had invited Speke and Grant to on 22 February 1863 to smooth matters over. Upon pleading with Speke to accept her husband's aid, he vehemently replied: 'I do not wish to recognise the succour dodge' (Petherick & Petherick, 1869b: p. 20).[18] In 1864, John and Katherine left the Sudan never to return (Humphries, 2013: pp.135–40).

In 1869, the Pethericks published a joint-account of their time spent in the East (Petherick & Petherick, 1869: 2 vols.) and despite being forced by Speke to fiercely defend their reputation in the public sphere,[19] the infamy of the 'Speke controversy' has unfortunately to this day served to overshadow the important contributions they made to our geographical, zoological and even ethnological knowledge of several important regions of Africa.[20]

In or around 1860, General Pitt-Rivers (1827–1900) (who himself took a short Cook's tour to Egypt in 1881 (Pitt-Rivers, 1882: p. 382), managed to acquire about 100 objects from John Petherick's personal collection which he had amassed during his explorations (Chapman, 1981: pp. 94–95). Many of these artefacts are now on display in the Pitt–River's Museum[21] and demonstrate both the importance and scope of his explorations in Africa.

Combat & Collecting: Field–Marshal Grenfell's Travels in Egypt (1882–98)

Field-Marshal Lord Francis Wallace Grenfell (1841–1925),[22] also formed important collections of artefacts whilst travelling throughout Egypt.[23]

Born in Swansea in 1841, Grenfell chose to join the army rather than enter into the family copper business, and was posted to Egypt in 1882 (Heathcote, 1999: p. 152). In 1885, he was appointed Commander-in-Chief of the British army in Egypt, and during his time spent in the country, he pursued his interest in archaeology and Egyptian history, enlisting the help of E. A. Wallis Budge (1857–1934)[24] in the procurement of Egyptian antiquities to form his own personal collection[25] (Budge, 1912: p. 74–75).

On 2 November 1888, Grenfell presented the mummy of 'Hor', a 22nd-Dynasty priest and scribe of the god Amun to the Swansea Museum (*Amgueddfa Abertawe*) (*The Cambrian*, 1888: p. 8). The mummy (www7), which is believed to be the first mummy to reach Wales, was donated in one of its original outer-coffins, together with a small collection of antiquities, including a wooden 18th-Dynasty shabti uncovered during Grenfell's excavations of the newly-discovered private tombs at Aswan in 1887, for which Grenfell provides an account in the aforementioned newspaper article: 'This Mummy was obtained at Echmim, an Arab town about 400 miles up the Nile, in 1887 [...] About three miles from the town are grottoes of great antiquity, and above the town are remains of a very ancient cemetery, which contains an immense number of mummy pits,[26] and from these pits this Mummy came.' (*The Cambrian*, 1888: p. 8)

Grenfell's collection in the Swansea Museum remained the most important collection of Egyptian artefacts in Wales for more than a hundred years, until 1971, when Egyptologist John Gwyn Griffiths (1911-2004) arranged for a selection of artefacts from the extensive collections of Sir Henry Wellcome (1853-1936) to come to Swansea University. John Gwyn Griffiths' wife, Kate Bosse-Griffiths (1910-98) (née Bosse), also an Egyptologist, spent most of her career studying the collection, which numbers some 5000 pieces (Lloyd, 1998: p. 192).

Displayed in part in various departments of the university over the years, the collection did not go on full display until 1998, when a new building built to house it was erected on the university campus. Known as the Egypt Centre this small museum contains the largest collection of ancient Egyptian artefacts in Wales (www8).

These are just a few brief examples of some of the interesting Welsh characters who ventured to Egypt during this early period of travel. I could go on to discuss many more at great length, however, I would now like to focus on some very unique and rare accounts.

Writing Home in Welsh

Until the recent discovery of a small number of accounts published in Welsh, the author was personally unaware that Welsh travel accounts were in any way different to those written by other travellers.

It is perhaps not remarkable to find that the majority of Welsh travellers published their accounts in English as this would ensure their experiences would reach a much wider audience. Therefore, it is interesting to discover that a few Welsh travellers chose to publish their accounts *exclusively* in Welsh.

The two accounts in question were written by working-class, North-Walian men who, although stemming from humble beginnings, both went on to become tremendously successful in their chosen professions. Travelling to Egypt in the late 19th and early 20th centuries, both men were greatly influenced by the land of the Nile, and their experiences changed their outlook on the world and their perceptions of their homeland. Our first traveller was so enamoured of Egypt, that after one visit, he felt no trepidation in moving his family business from wet North Wales to the exotic shores of north-east Africa.

John Davies Bryan: Entrepreneur in Egypt (1886–88)

John Davies Bryan (1857–1888)[27] (Fig.2. 1) was the first of these two men to venture to Egypt. Born in 1857 in the village of Llanarmon in North Wales to Edward Bryan (1823–86), a lead miner, and his wife Elinor (1827–78) ('John Davies Bryan', 1861), he was the eldest of four sons, and remained close to his brothers Robert (1859-1920),

Fig 2.1 John Davies Bryan (1857-1888) (from Bryan 1908).

Edward (1860–1929) and Joseph (1864–1935) throughout his life.[28] When Bryan was about three, the family moved to the Maelor Valley in Wrexham, where the children spent the rest of their childhood. It was here where, tutored at home by his mother in the company of his siblings, he learnt the Welsh language, (Bryan, 1908: p. vi).

As a young man Bryan sought work in Mostyn in nearby Flintshire, becoming an apprentice to the shopkeeper Enoch Lewis (1812–85) (Bryan, 1908: p. vi), who was an influential non-conformist Liberal and the father of John Herbert Lewis (1858–1933), a prominent Welsh Liberal politician, whose persistent campaigning led to the establishment of some of the most important cultural institutions in Wales, including the National Museum (*Amgueddfa Cymru*) and the National Library of Wales (*Llyfrgell Genedlaethol Cymru*) (www9). Both men instilled in John an appreciation for his own language and culture.

Bryan left Mostyn for Liverpool to work in a busy store on Bold Street. City life does not appear to have agreed with him and it was during this time that his health began to deteriorate, prompting him to return to his native Wales (Bryan, 1908: p. vi).

Settling in Caernarfon, where he worked for a time as an assistant to the drapers Pierce & Williams, Bryan later opened his own shop, Bryan Brother's Drapers at 12 Bridge Street (Jones, 2004: 68). The business thrived, and Bryan spent many years in the store working alongside his brother Edward, before his health took a turn for the worse.

In 1886, when in particularly frail health, Bryan was encouraged by his cousin Samuel Evans (1859–1935) (private secretary to Sir Edgar Vincent (1857–1941)[29] (Williams, 1995: p. 41) to join him that winter on a trip to Egypt. In October of that year, they set sail for the land of the Nile (Bryan, 1908: p. vii).

During his time in Egypt, Bryan wrote letters home to his family in Caernarfon, which were later published in 1887 in the local Welsh-language newspaper *Y Genedl Gymreig* (*The Welsh Nation*) (Jones, 2004: p. 97). In 1908, they were republished as a small pocket book entitled *O'r Aifft* (*From Egypt*). These letters were in large part humorous tales of his experiences of the country and of his impressions of its inhabitants.

Although motivated to travel to Egypt for the sake of his health, Bryan was evidently elated to be sojourning in a country which he describes as unrivalled in terms of its antiquity and wonder: 'Egypt! The Worldly things that are of interest to us are suggested to us in this word. Egypt; is on various considerations, the strangest country, in the afterglow of the sun. Where is there a river like the River of Egypt? – Buildings like the buildings of Egypt? – Where is the antiquity they hold compared for a moment with the antiquity of Egypt?'[30] (Bryan, 1908: p. 63)

Due to his ill-health, Bryan spent the entirety of his trip in northern Egypt and although enamoured of its antiquity, he appears to have been more interested in its modern culture, principally enjoying people-watching and especially intrigued by the various modes of dress he saw about him and he is unsparing in his criticism of the simple nature of some of the local attire, which he observed to consist of nothing more than old sugar-sacks and hats resembling halved coconuts:

> It appears that many of them [the Arabs] have decide that there was folly in dressing in any form of uniform of Cairo, there was no need for it, and for beauty – they did not care a bean, – so they took an old sack of sugar (the sugar manufacturer's name Joseph Tate & Sons, written clearly on the back), turned it upside down, cut a hole in the bottom big enough for their heads, and two holes in the sides for their arms [. . .] the whole suit for a shilling and tuppence! What more did they need? (However, I hope that my compatriots will not attempt to follow this fashion; otherwise, it will be very bad for the outfitters, – only gaining profit from a few old sacks). (Bryan, 1908: pp. 67–68)

Bryan's letters are laden with comedic renderings of his encounters with the new sights and scenes Egypt had to offer. He describes one local man as looking 'a bit like a man who had to pick out what to wear when his house was on fire, and having being chucked some of his wife's clothes – he put on the first things he could find before he escaped' (Bryan, 1908: 68).

From the very beginning of his account, Bryan relays amusing tales of the cunning and persuasion of the dragomen and donkey-handlers who swarmed around the new arrivals at Alexandria:

> They [the donkey drivers] have taken possession of both arms and both legs, each pulling in a different direction, one to his mule the other to his own vehicle. 'This way, sar – this good donkey, sar – Flying Dutchman, – sar – no, sar, that donkey no good, no go – this good donkey, sar, Lourd Shalusbury, sar, him go like steam engine,' &c. (the idea, Lord Salisbury goes like a steam engine)! (Bryan, 1908: pp. 69–70)

His account is very much tongue-in-cheek, and often appears suspiciously embellished and is evidently written by a man in high spirits despite his ill-health. John's tales of talking donkeys and his light-hearted descriptions of Egypt's modern inhabitants, no doubt would have kept the readers of The Welsh Nation eagerly anticipating the next instalment of his Egyptian escapades.

The Davies Bryan Company

Although filled with amusing and at times fantastical tales, what is however perhaps most interesting about John Davies Bryan's account is the biographical note written by his brother Robert which explains that John's first trip to Egypt would inspire him in a new business venture (Bryan, 1908: p. vii). He left Egypt with plans to return to open a store in Cairo, one which would provide travellers with everything they could possibly need.

Returning to Egypt in 1887, Bryan opened a shop in the Continental Hotel in Cairo, trading under the name Davies Bryan (Jones, 2004: p. 126). This small haberdashery sold an array of much-needed imported goods, including men's and ladies' hats, travel gear, draperies, hosiery and shoes; all under a 'fixed price' policy, ensuring a fair price for all (Jones, 2004: p. 95).

With the help of his brother Edward, Davies Bryan & Co soon earned itself a sterling reputation and proved to be such a success that John also enlisted the help of his youngest brother Joseph, to help run the busy Cairo store (Bryan, 1908: p. vi).

Two years later, John sold the Caernarfon store and made preparations to open a new branch of the Davies Bryan Company. in Alexandria. Located at 9 Sherif Pasha Street (Jones, 2004: p. 129), the Alexandrian store opened for business in 1888 and was christened 'Dewi Sant' ('St David'), after the patron saint of Wales (www10).

Following the success of the new store in Alexandria, the Davies Bryan brothers enlisted the help of Robert Williams (1848–1918), a Welsh architect from Merthyr Tydfil who had been working in Egypt as a consultant to the Egyptian government (Brodie, 2001: p. 1004) to design a new store. This was to be built in Cairo, in the Sharia Emad Al Din district (www10).

The new St David's of Cairo opened for business in 1910. Situated in a prime location fronting three of the busiest streets in the district (al-Maghrabi, Mohammed Farid and al-Manakh) and measuring some 1,900 sq m, it would prove to be the largest store of its kind in Egypt (www10).

Built from polished red granite from Aberdeen, and Doulting freestone from Somerset, the building's façades were embellished with ornate stucco motifs and with shields engraved with the initials 'D' and 'B' to immortalize the family name (www11). The building's decorations also included important Welsh cultural emblems such as those symbolizing the Welsh National Gorsedd of Bards, or 'Eisteddfod', an important cultural festival in Wales. A larger shield located above the street of Mohammed Farid, is engraved with the inscription: 'Y Gwir yn Erbyn y Byd' ('Truth against the World'), the principle tenet of this ancient Bardic gathering (Davies, 2012: pp. 30 and 35).

The brothers appear to have taken the opportunity to ensure that the new store would serve both to celebrate and memorialize the Welsh nation in Egypt, and onded, the Davies Bryan store in Cairo became a monument for the Welsh presence in Egypt and an important place of pilgrimage for all Welsh travellers who ventured to the land of the Nile.

J. D. Bryan did not unfortunately live to see the expansion of the family business, with further branches opening in both Port Saïd and Khartoum (Lewis, 1935: p. 176). In 1888, he succumbed to typhoid fever, passing away on 13 November that year. He was buried the next day in the British Cemetery in Cairo (Bryan, 1908: p. vii). John's brothers continued to run the family business until the time of their own passing (Lewis, 1935: p. 176). John's youngest brother Robert died in Cairo in 1920, and Edward, who had helped to set up and build the business, passed away in Alexandria in 1929, leaving a substantial sum to help establish the Cairo branch of the YMCA, which chose to locate its premises in the upper floors of the Davies Bryan building (www10) (Fig. 2.2).

Following Edward's death, Fred Purslow (1894–1972) (Fig. 2.3), who had worked as chief-accountant for the brothers, bought a share in the company, ensuring that the Davies Bryan family name survived well into the 1950s (Jones, 2004: p. 14). Fred continued to run the store, going above and beyond to welcome his Welsh compatriots, even inviting them to visit his family home in Coedpoeth when they returned to Wales (Jones, 2004: p. 180).

Circa 1957, the building was sold to two prosperous Syrian brothers, the Chourbaguis, whose name can now be seen painted over the original inscriptions above the store's entrance. In 1961, the building was taken over by a state-owned insurance company and in 2008 it was purchased by the real-estate investment firm Al-Ismailia; the building still awaits restoration (www11).

What was once the largest and one of the most successful stores in Cairo is now divided into a series of smaller shops and businesses, including Stephenson's Pharmacy (www9) which has preserved some of the original décor and serves as an historic emblem of the store's past. It stands as a monument to what was once the stronghold of a Welsh presence in Egypt but without the publication of Bryan's letters, we would know little about the history of this remarkable building or of the men who made the Davies Bryan Company a success.

During the late 19th and early 20th centuries, the Davies Bryan store in Cairo remained a site of pilgrimage for Welsh travellers, a place where they could speak the old language and where they were guaranteed a warm welcome from fellow countrymen.

One such traveller to seek the sanctuary of the Davies Bryan stores upon his arrival in Egypt is the author of our next account, the Welsh-language poet Thomas Gwynn Jones (1871–1949) (Fig. 2.4).

Thomas Gwynn Jones: Captivated 'Captive' in Egypt

> 'Every Welshman that passes through Egypt calls to look for the Bryan family, and none of them are disappointed with the really Welsh welcome. Into the store. Here we speak the old language, and are happy [...].' (Jones, 1912: p. 41)

Although John Davies Bryan and his brothers were well-known and respected traders in Egypt, they are perhaps unknown to most Welsh people. Thomas Gwynn

Jones (1871–1949) however, remains one of the most beloved of Welsh figures. A well-respected and influential poet in his time, he is affectionately known as 'T. Gwynn Jones' in Wales today.

Born in 1871 on the family farm (Gwyndy Uchaf) in Abergele, North Wales, T. Gwynn Jones[31] was the eldest son of Isaac Jones (1842–1929) and his wife Jane Roberts (1845–96). He had two brothers, Dafydd Morgan Jones (1874–1960) and Robert Isaac Jones (1878–1905) and a sister, Sarah Ellen Jones (1887–1973) ('Thomas Gwynn Jones', 1891). During his youth, the family moved to various farms in the area and Thomas worked alongside his father as a farm-hand (Beynon, 1970: p. 3).

Perhaps surprisingly, considering his status as one of the most influential poets of his time, Jones only received an elementary education and much of what he learnt was self-taught.

In order to seek admittance to the University of Oxford he sought instruction in Latin, Greek and mathematics from a neighbouring retired clergyman, but his consistent poor health caused him to abandon his academic career (www12).

Fig 2.2 Postcard depicting the Davies Bryan Store in Cairo (opened in 1910), once known as the 'pride of Sharia Emad Al Din' and which in the 1930s became the Cairo branch of the YMCA. © Darabanth Aukcióscház - Darabanth Auction House

Fig 2.3 Frederick Volance Purslow (1894-1972) outside his shop in Coedpoeth, Wrexham (once situated at 55 High Street, Coedpoeth, on the south side of Church Road). © Coedpoerth Historical Society Collection

A gifted writer, he began composing his own poetry in his early twenties. He would be declared author of the best 'ode' at the Bangor National Eisteddfod of 1902, for his poem 'Ymadawiad Arthur' ('The Passing of Arthur') (Koch, 2006: p. 1040). His second triumph came at the 1907 Eisteddfod in Swansea, which saw him named as the leading poet of his generation (Beynon, 1970: p. 14).

Jones spent his formative years working as a journalist for a number of Welsh and English newspapers. His first job at the age of 19 was as sub-editor for the 'Y Faner' ('The Flag'),[32] where he worked under Thomas Gee (1815–98), a Liberal advocate of the Welsh language who was an inspiration for much of Jones' life (Beynon, 1970: p. 24).

Jones remained in journalism until 1909, when he was offered the post of cataloguer in the newly-formed National Library of Wales (Llyfrgell Genedlaethol Cymru) in Aberystwyth, a role which

Fig 2.4 Thomas Gwynn Jones (1871-1949) (from Jones 1910)

later led him to his appointment as lecturer in Welsh at the University College of Wales (Aberystwyth) in 1913. He was made a professor of Welsh literature in 1919, a position that he held until his retirement in 1937 (Koch, 2006: p. 1041).

However, before he began his successful academic career in Aberystwyth, Jones once again had to contend with a bout of ill-health. In 1905, Jones contracted a stubborn cold and a doctor advised him to spend the winter in warmer climes and he duly left for the land of the Nile (Beynon, 1970: 19).

During his stay in Egypt, Jones wrote weekly letters to his wife Margaret (née Davies), which were published in 1912 under the title: Y Mor Canoldir a'r Aifft (The Mediterranean Sea and Egypt). Through these letters, he shared his experiences of being in a land of exotic wonders and antiquity:

> [...] [A]nd away in the distance the desert stretches, with its amber hues [. . .] I shall never forget that sight, for me a first glance at the wilderness. The palm trees like towers [...] the Bedouin and their tents in the distance [...] Arab children singing. There is nothing in the world like singing. Indeed, you would hardly have called it singing at all, as it is raucous, but that suited the space and time, somehow. The red light and then the mildewed yellow of the sun, nesting and sheltering in the black tops of the palms. The sea becomes darker and the children's song sounds stranger than before. Everything is strange and new to me. We are in the East [...].' (Jones, 1912: pp. 43–44)

Upon arriving in Egypt, Jones sought out the Davies Bryan store in Alexandria. Here, in a building which he described as ornately decorated with carved emblems of his homeland, he was greeted by its architect, the aforementioned Robert Williams and happily spent time speaking the 'old language' with the Welshman (Jones, 1912: p. 41).

Spending a little under two weeks in Alexandria, Jones wrote many observations of his fellow travellers and of the local life: the dress of Egyptian women, the antics of their wild-like children and the mysterious nature of the roaming Bedouin (Jones, 1912: 43). He was particularly fascinated by the local way of life, and sought out sights which tourists rarely ventured to see.

On one occasion, he visited the el-Azzar mosque in Cairo. After donning the 'slippers of the unfaithful' to permit him entry, he stopped to observe a group of students who were reading and studying the *Qur'an*: 'They sit on the floor like tailors, in a circle around the teacher, with books in their hands. In the blazing sun, without a shade in the world between them and him, and the leisure and the quiet serenity of the East rests on all of them' (Jones, 1912: p. 151).

Jones describes their teacher as a strong and handsome man and an excellent tutor, evident in the complete captivation of his students (Jones, 1912: p. 151). Jones was so entranced by the scene that he pulled out a pencil and paper from his pocket to sketch the students at work but advised himself against it, for fear of causing offence (Jones, 1912: p. 152).

Jones' poor health saw him sojourn Egypt for an extended period and allowed him to develop an appreciation and understanding of the local way of life. He spent a large part of his time in the health resort of Helwan, where, in constant contact with other travellers in poor health he felt an ever-growing sense of his own mortality, as he watched as others around him succumb to their illnesses: 'The Frenchman I mentioned [...] We were talking about Helwân immediately after we arrived. "Helwân?" says he, "Yes. When we can no longer live at home, we come here to die!"' (Jones, 1912: p. 85).

Jones developed an appreciation for the uniqueness of the land in which he had taken up temporary exile. With seemingly endless leisure time at his disposal, he read widely and learnt Arabic, in preparation for his later explorations of Egypt (Jones, 1912: p. 135). He appears to have been most captivated by Egypt's ancient past, especially the historical elements often overlooked by travellers and which required an imagination to bring them to life. He was particularly interested in the ancient quarries of el–Mokattam, which he persuaded his 'lazy' and 'unadventurous' English friend to explore one morning in January: 'We wandered there for an hour and a half or two hours, and when we came out into the light of day at last, the Englishman and I were willing to recognize each other, as two sons of the nations in partnership who made the empire "upon which the sun never sets" [...].' (Jones, 1912: p. 138)

He enjoyed the solitude of the place and its removal from the busy streets of Cairo and the tourist-ridden sites of the nearby Pyramids and the Egyptian Museum. Most of all, he was fascinated by the evidence of ancient activity in the quarries, remarking that the chisel marks felt freshly made and that at any moment the workers might return to continue their work (Jones, 1912: p. 139). Both men emerged with a renewed sense of wonder at the world and saw each other as equally insignificant in the presence of what Jones described to as 'the remains of greatness' (Jones, 1912: p. 138).

Jones was evidently captivated by the hidden history of Egypt and could sense the presence of the ancient past within its landscape. The historic events which the monuments, the desert and the river had witnessed stirred his imagination and left him with a lasting impression which would manifest itself in the poetry he composed about his own homeland: 'Smooth sand sank silently into the wilderness under my foot and I feel the beat of mild air on my face, as if it had come in waves of a certain distance. Where else is there a desert like this, where else does the spirit of times gone before remain even though they dwell quietly and without speech?' (Jones, 1912: p. 175)

Even the most famous of all Egypt's monuments, the pyramids, would prove an unexpected inspiration to the poet. Jones states that he had studied, mused over, imagined and reconstructed these magnificent structures time and time again in his mind to the point that he was certain that he would be disappointed when he finally laid eyes upon them (Jones, 1912: 170). He discovered, however, that such a thing was impossible, and he declared that his first sighting of the Great Pyramid of Giza was an experience he prized more than anything before or since:

> The golden light one finds in the East when the sun is about to set was like a flood over [the great pyramid], an amber haze, as if the sky had 'set' into a long lake of honey and it is as if we see and experience everything through it. To the east the sky is rose-coloured. Westward it is the colour of honey, the earth looks as though it were a denser layer of the same substance [...] It was like a scene from a dream, or like the view from parts of Snowdonia over the Menai Strait and across Anglesey, when the sun on a summer evening sinks within the middle of the clouds which look like mountains and valleys, forest and castles. (Jones, 1912: pp. 171–72).

Early one summer evening, soon after his arrival in Cairo, when the sight and scenes were still new to him, Jones awoke from an afternoon slumber to find the failing light of the evening sun pouring through the open window, drawing him towards it. Framed in the window was the Great Pyramid, illuminated by the rays of the setting sun (Jones, 1912: p. 171).

The aura of that summer evening is thought to have influenced his poems based on Celtic tales and characters, such as the opening passage of 'Broseliawnd' (1922) set in the forest of Broceliande and the scene of 'incomparable land' in the last part of 'Madog' (1917), a poem about Prince Madog, the legendary discoverer of marvellous lands (Davies, 1970: 20). Jones stated that he never described any scenery in his prose that he himself had not witnessed and the experience left a lasting impression on him which would inform his later imaginings of mythical Welsh landscapes.

It is clear that he was profoundly affected by the mysticism and exoticism of the Nile and the wonders Egypt had to offer him at a perilous time in his life: 'We feel nostalgia for times past and things that we do not know about them but they have to depart somewhere and the secret and wonders with them.' (Jones, 1912: p. 175).

These accounts, written by men who interpreted their surroundings with a child-like wonder are rare gems, inspiring interest in all that Egypt had to offer. It is mystifying therefore, that they have never been translated or shared with a wider audience. In attempting to understand why they have not previously been published in English there are several important factors to consider.

Both men hailed from North Wales, a predominantly Welsh-speaking part of the country and which during this period contained the highest percentage of Welsh speakers in Wales ('Language spoken in Wales. 1911: Report,' 1913: p. iv).[33] High literacy rates in the Welsh language during this period[34] also ensured that there was an audience for these accounts, something which is testified to by John's publication of his travels in his local Welsh-language newspaper (*Y Genedl Gymreig*).

It is evident that both men were proud of their heritage and language,[35] something which may have been instilled in them by the influential characters they had met during their lives. It is evident from these accounts that both men felt a marked separation from other British travellers and that their 'cultural identity' was at the forefront of their minds:

> I was in the company of the best class of Arabs once, never missing each time one of them called me an Englishman. I said that I am not an Englishman, but that I am a Welshman. The Arab thought for a moment, and then asked:
> "The same nation as Davies Bryan?"
> "Same place," I said.
> "Oh, well," was the reply, "welcome to you, that's a nation of gentlemen." (Jones, 1912: p. 63)

It is likely that neither felt the need to publish an English version of their accounts, not only because innumerable accounts had been published in English by this time[36] but also because of the nature of the Welsh language itself, which has been described as possessing an inherent beauty which is simply untranslatable.

In a paper entitled: 'English & Welsh' presented as an inaugural memorial lecture in Oxford on the 25 November 1955, the famous author and polymath, J. R. R. Tolkien (1892–1973) declared Welsh to be one of the most beautiful languages known to man and unrivalled in its lyricism: 'Most English-speaking people [...] will admit that cellar door is 'beautiful,' especially if dissociated from its sense (and from its spelling). More beautiful than beautiful. Well then, in Welsh for me cellar doors are extraordinarily frequent, and moving to the higher dimension, the words in which there is pleasure in the contemplation of the association of form and sense are abundant.' (Tolkien, 1963: p. 36)

It is perhaps more surprising, therefore, that there aren't a larger number of travel accounts published in the language.

Ultimately, however, John Davies Bryan and T. Gwynn Jones' use of language was governed by their primary audiences, which were their families and it has to be remembered that their accounts represent the unaltered, original correspondence written by them during their travels in Egypt.

Conclusions

There is still a great deal of research to be done on the Welsh presence in Egypt and it is not currently known how many unpublished accounts lie in archives and museum collections awaiting study, nor whether any of these were written in the Welsh language.

Potentially, Welsh travellers have a lot more to contribute to our understanding of the Egypt experience in this early period and the author hopes that, by sharing the translated accounts of John D. Bryan and T. Gwynn Jones, their experiences will reach a wider audience, thus allowing them to gain the appreciation they deserve.

Acknowledgements

The author would like to extend her gratitude to Prof. Katie Gramich and Prof. Paul T. Nicholson (both of Cardiff University) for the initial introduction to the accounts of T. Gwynn Jones, D. Rhagfyr Jones and John Davies Bryan; Gini Baber for her critical attention and advice on the original manuscript; Andrew Davies and Prof. Lloyd Llewellyn Jones (Cardiff University), for their help with the translation of the Welsh text and for further helpful suggestions on the Welsh language elements of this paper; ASTENE members Charles Newton and Sheila and Russell McGuirk for the information they provided on several of the Welsh travellers who appear in this paper (Owen Jones and Sam Evans respectively); Kathryn Ferry, for information on the Welsh-language biographical work on Owen Jones (Davies, 2004), and also to the Darabanth Auction House, Siân Jones (who sourced the image of the Davies Bryan brothers, owned by Jane Owen) and the Coedpoeth Historical Society for permission to use the photographs published in this chapter (with special thanks to Peter S. Fisher, Dewi Davies, David Kelly and Robert Edwards of the society, for their help and the information they provided on the photograph of Fred Purslow of Coedpoeth).

Endnotes

1   Information on Scottish (www1) and Irish travellers (www2) has also been made available to the general public on interesting and informative websites which contain new and important information of these early travellers.

2   Knowledge of which has been greatly expanded by research conducted by members of The Association for the Study of Travel in Egypt and the Near East (ASTENE).

3 Dates unfortunately unknown, however he is known to have been a clergyman and appears to have hailed from North Wales.

4 D. Rhagfr Jones' account was not considered for this paper as he was much less enamoured with Egypt and its native inhabitants, as Davies (2012) remarks: 'The Rev D. Rhagfyr Jones, in a 1904 travel memoir *I'r Aifft ac yn Ol* (*To Egypt and Back*), expresses a racism so virulent […] it should forever give the lie to the comforting myth that the Welsh have somehow been particularly enlightened in their intercultural dealings' (Davies, 2012: p. 32). It was thus considered best that Davies' Rhagfr Jones' account should be left for future study, perhaps in consideration of how early travellers perceived, interacted with and interpreted the East, and how this was not always with an open-mind (and in this case, there is the opportunity for discussion from a Welsh perspective).

5 For further information on Jones, a recommended read (published in Welsh) is Gareth Alban Davies': *Y llaw brofwwydol: Owen Jones, Pensaer (1809-74)* (2004) (I would like to thank Charles Newton & Kathryn Ferry for this reference) and in the context of Egypt: Stephanie Moser's *Designing Antiquity: Owen Jones, Ancient Egypt and the Crystal Palace* (2012).

6 Goury was assisting the German architect Gottfried Semper (1803–79) with his studies of the polychromy of Ancient Greek architecture when he met Owen Jones in Athens in 1831 (Flores, 1996: p. 19). Jones and Goury continued their travels together, where they made studies of the Islamic architecture of Cairo and those of the ancient Egyptian monuments at sites across Egypt, before moving onto Spain, where they studied the Islamic decoration of the Alhambra in Granada in 1834 (Jespersen, 2008: p. 143).

7 Several of his original sketches and illustrations are now housed in the Victoria & Albert Museum (Searight Collection) (such as his watercolours of a 'Tomb near Cairo' (1833) (SD.532 & SD.533); for example), as Jones was himself, a key figure in the foundation of the Victoria & Albert Museum (www3). Many of Jones' and Goury's sketches of Egypt, are wonderfully reproduced in Moser's *Designing Antiquity* (2012), as are many photographs and illustrations of the Egyptian Court at Sydenham.

8 For further information on the relationship between Jones' travels and his career as an architect and designer, consult Ferry's *Awakening a Higher Ambition* (2004).

9 Moser (2012) dedicates an entire chapter to the various critical reviews of the exhibition, where even early travellers such as Harriet Martineau (1802–76) expressed their disappointment in the vulgarity of the expression of the ancient architecture (Moser, 2012: pp. 158–83).

10 Batchelor (2000) has dedicated an entire book to this concept (see bibliography).

11 Following the success of the Great Exhibition of 1851 (which took place in the original Crystal Palace situated in Hyde Park), the palace was re-built in Sydenham in 1854, and remained standing until its destruction by fire in 1936 (Osslan, 2007: p. 73).

12 For more information on the 'Greek' and 'Roman' courts, see Nichols' *Greece and Rome at the Crystal Palace* (2015). For the 'Alhambra Court,' see: Ferry's *Printing the Alhambra* (2003).

13 The 'Egyptian Court' contained eight copies of Amenhotep III's granite lions ('The Prudhoe Lions') from the Temple of Soheb (now in the British Museum: EA1 & EA2) which flanked the entrance into the court. Osirian colossi, modelled after those in the Ramesseum filled the 'Outer Court' which preceded a room filled with a forest of

large, brightly-coloured columns modelled after the Hypostyle Hall at Karnak. The greatest attraction was however situated in the 'Inner Egyptian Court', where visitors could find colossal copies of the statues of the Great Temple of Ramesses II at Abu Simbel, cast in plaster and decorated in bold, polychromic colours (Osslan, 2007: pp. 69–70). For more information, see Moser's chapter on the court in *Designing Antiquity* (2012: pp. 81–119) and Jan Piggott's section on the Egyptian courts in her chapter: 'The Fine Arts Courts' in her *Palace of the People* (2004: pp. 84–87).

14   The travel journals and papers of John Petherick and his wife Katherine Harriet Petherick, are now housed in the Wellcome Library (London) (MSS.5787–5791).

15   That is putting it lightly, as Hall (1980) states, Speke was 'pathologically vengeful' (Hall, 1980: p. 91) in his pursuit of the ruination of John Petherick's reputation.

16   Dutch explorer Alexandrine (Alexine) P. F. Tinné (1835–69), her mother, Henriëtte Tinné-van Capellen (1799–1863) and her aunt, Adriana van Capellen (1814–63) travelled together through North Eastern in 1855–57, 1858, and Central Africa in 1861–63 (though Alexine remained in Egypt until her death in 1869) where, much like Petherick, they made important observations on the flora and fauna of the area. Their expedition resulted in one of the largest, most sumptuously illustrated botanical books ever published (Kotschy & Peyritsch, 1867) and although Henriëtte and Adriana sadly died during the third and final journey, an account of the women's travels was published both by Alexine (Tinné, 1869) and her half-brother, John A. Tinné (Tinné, 1864) (an earlier, shorter version of which was published by Alexine in *Trans. Hist. Soc. Lancs. & Chesh.* in 1860 (Tinné, 1860), and by their travel companion, Martin Theodor von Heuglin (1824–76) in 1869 (Heuglin, 1869).

17   The sentiment of the Tinné women, was expressed publicly in the aftermath of the controversy in John Tinné's aforementioned volume on the ladies' travels: '[T]hey never saw a more disappointed and dejected man than Mr. Petherick. He and his wife have had dreadful ill luck. He had made the best arrangements to meet Captain Speke [...], We hope Mrs. Petherick will publish her journal; it will make people at home start to see what they have suffered, and there can be no doubt of its accuracy.' (Tinné, 1864: p. 26).

18   The second volume of the Petherick's account (Appendix A), contains a detailed account of the Speke affair (Petherick & Petherick, 1869b: pp. 77–186).

19   The Speke–Petherick controversy made its way into several national newspapers, such as an extract of Speke's speech given at the Royal Geographical Society in Taunton in 1861, which was published in the *Overland Mail*, where Speke's (erroneous) accusation of Petherick being embroiled in the Slave trade was referenced:

> After a succession of fevers and a variety of illnesses that fastened upon my wife and myself [Petherick] during our return voyage and residence in Khartoum, as a substitute for the excitement of travel, I was laid up with a series of guinea-worms revelling in the fleshy part of my right leg and foot. Whilst in this state, a paragraph from the "Overland Mail" was placed in my hands, descriptive of a banquet in honour of Captain Speke on his return to Taunton. In that portion of this address touching upon the slave trade, he [...] obviously referred to me when saying, "men with authority emanating from our Government, who are engaged with the native kings in the diabolical slave trade."[...] (Petherick & Petherick, 1869b: p. 139).

The contention between the men involved several important figures of the era (such as Dr Joseph Natterer (1819–62), an Austrian physician and explorer who at the time was administrator of the Imperial Royal Austrian Consulate, the aforementioned German Zoologist and explorer Theodore von Heuglin (1824–76) and the French zoologist George Thibaut (1848–1914), who was administrator of the Imperial Vice-Consulate of France (Petherick & Petherick, 1869b: pp. 141–43), some of whom wrote letters of support to Petherick as he faced a very public humiliation following Speke's attempts to ruin his reputation (many of these letters were published by Petherick in 1869: Petherick & Petherick, 1869b: Appendix A).

20 Although John Humphries attempts to rectify this by petitioning the case from Petherick's perspective in his book: *Search for the Nile's Source: The Ruined Reputation of John Petherick, Nineteenth-Century Welsh Explorer* (2013).

21 For example, the Elephant Hide 'Fan Shield' (1884.30.34), from Gaboon & the Zande Shield (1884.30.33), from the southern Sudan, obtained by the museum in 1868 (www5).

22 More information can be found on the great man in his autobiography published in 1925 (see Bibliography).

23 Grenfell's archive material is housed in the Middle East Centre, St Antony's College, Oxford (e.g. MS diaries 1874–79, 1882, 1884–1925: Reference: GB165–0319).

24 Budge is quoted with describing Grenfell as: 'a true and powerful friend of myself and of every archaeologist' (Budge, 1912: p. 74).

25 Although Grenfell appears to have donated a mummy to Swansea Museum and one apparently to Malta (where he was Governor between 1889 and 1903 and to whom he apparently bequeathed a collection in 1912) (www6), the bulk of his collection of Egyptian antiquities seems to have been sold at auction (a three-day sale at Sotheby's) in 1917 (Thompson, 2015: p. 63).

26 The 'mummy pits' are the subject of ongoing research by the author more information on which can be sourced from www.mummpits.com and: Baber (2012) & (2016).

27 The Davies Bryan family papers and archive material are housed in the Gwynedd Archives (Caernarfon Record Office) (Reference: GB 0219 XM/8322; XS/3534).

28 Much information on the Davies Bryan brothers, their lives and their businesses in both Wales and Egypt is provided by Siân Jones in her: *O Gamddwr I Gairo: Hanes y Brodyr Davies Bryan (1851--1935)* (2004), which, as she words it, aims to: '[...] [F]ully introduce the history of the Bryan Davies brothers: John Davies, Robert Edward and Joseph, from the cradle to the grave.' She also promotes their cousin Samuel Evans (1859–1935) who has received very little attention despite his own remarkable travels and achievements and to whom she rightfully dedicates his own volume, and (Jones, 2004: p. 13).

29 See note above. Information on Evans can also be found in Llywelyn Williams' *Sam Nesa Wedyn* (1995) & John Griffiths' *Y Bererindod gyda Mr Samuel Evans, De Affrica* (1934). I would like to thank Russell and Sheila McGuirk for these references and additional information provided on Evans.

30 The quotes presented in this paper for both the accounts published by J. D. Bryan and T. G. Jones, have been translated from the original Welsh into English by the author. Due to the scope of this paper, the original Welsh text has been omitted here, but can be consulted in the original works cited.

31 T. Gwynn Jones' papers are currently housed in Aberystwyth University (Reference: GB 0982 TGJ).

32 He also spent time working for *Y Cymro* (based in Liverpool and edited by Isaac Foulkes), the *Liverpol Mercury*, the *Liverpool Post* and the *Manchester Guardian,* and later worked as sub-editor of *Yr Herald Gymraeg* and editor in another *Y Cymro* (based in Mold) and the weekly *Papur Pawr* in Caernarfon, before taking up his post in the National Library of Wales in 1909 (Beynon, 1970: pp. 3–4).

33 According to the 1911 Welsh census, although the use of the language had begun to decline (due to the influx of English workers during the Industrial Revolution, leading to a bilingual culture which prevails to this day), the counties with the highest percentage of Welsh-speakers were situated predominantly in North Wales (1911: p. iv).

34 In 1731, Welsh minister Griffith Jones (1864–1961), instigated a national education method which ensured that children were taught the Welsh language in school (known as the 'circulating school system', these educational bodies toured the country, teaching in each location for a period of around three months (Suggett, 2002: p. 69). This method is thought to have been responsible for teaching half of the population of Wales to read and significantly improved Welsh literacy rates from the mid 18th century onwards. By the time of Jones' death, it is estimated that up to 250,000 people had learned to read in schools throughout Wales (Jenkins, 1987: pp. 370–77).

35 T. Gwynn Jones was later quoted in 1928 as saying: 'we'll all be English when we stop writing in Welsh' (Elfyn, 2009: p. 7); a clear statement on the importance of the language to notion of a Welsh identity.

36 Enough for early traveller, Edward Hogg (1783–1848) to lament: 'Of late years we have had a literary inundation of the Nile, and so much has been published on that subject by learned and unlearned travellers, that the mere mention of the river, or the pyramids, the tombs, the mummy pits, crocodile, or temple at Dendera, gives us an unconquerable fit of yawning.' (Hogg, 1835: p. 375).

Bibliography

Baber, T. T. (2011) *The 'Mummy Pits' of Ancient Egypt: The Long-Kept Secret of Early Travellers.* MA Thesis, Cardiff University.

Baber, T. T. (2016) 'Ancient Corpses as Curiosities: Mummymania in the Age of Early Travel' *JAEI* 8: pp. 60–93.

Batchelor, D. (2000) *Chromophobia.* London, Reaktion Books.

Brodie, A. (ed.) (2001) *Directory of British Architects, 1834–1914.* Vol. 2 (L–Z). London and New York, Continuum.

Bryan, J. D. (1908) *O'r Aifft.* Gwrecsam: Swyddfa 'Cymru'r Plant'.

Budge, E. A. W. (1912) *By Nile and Tigris: a narrative of Journeys in Egypt and Mesopotamia on behalf of the British Museum between the years 1886 and 1913.* Vol. 1. London, John Murray.

Carnochan, W. B. (2006) *The Sad Story of Burton, Speke, and the Nile, Or, Was John Hanning Speke a Cad?:* Looking at the Evidence. Stanford, CA, Stanford University Press.

Chapman, W. R. (1981) *Ethnology in the Museum.* D.Phil. Thesis, Pitt Rivers Museum, University of Oxford.

Davies, G. A. (2004) *Y llaw broffwydol: Owen Jones, Pensaer (1809-74).* Talybont, Ceredigion: Y Lolfa.

Davies, G. (2012) 'On Mohammed Farid Street, A Response to David M Beddoe's the Lost Mameluke: A Tale of Egypt', *New Welsh Review* 96 (Summer): pp. 26–35.

Davies, W. B. (1970) *Writers of Wales: Thomas Gwynn Jones*. Cardiff, University of Wales Press.

Elfyn, M. (2009) 'Under the Influence' *Poetry Review* 99 (2) (Summer): 1-8.

Ferry, K. R. (2003) 'Printing the Alhambra: Owen Jones and Chromolithography', *Architectural History* 46 (January): pp. 175–88.

Ferry, K. R. (2007) 'Inspired by Egypt: Owen Jones and Architectural Theory' in D. Fortenberry (ed.) *Who Travels Sees More: Artists, Architects and Archaeologists Discover Egypt and the Near East*: pp. 101–17.

Fortenberry, D. (ed.) (2007) *Who Travels Sees More: Artists, Architects and Archaeologists Discover Egypt and the Near East*. Oxford, Oxbow Books & The Association for the Study of Travel in Egypt and the Near East (ASTENE).

Ferry, K. R. (2004) *Awakening a Higher Ambition: The Influence of Travel upon the Early Career of Owen Jones*. PhD. Thesis, University of Cambridge.

Flores, C. A. H. (1996) *Owen Jones: Architect*. PhD Thesis. Georgia Institute of Technology.

Fox, A. & D. R. Woolf (eds.) (2002) *The Spoken Word: Oral Culture in Britain, 1500-1850*. Manchester, Manchester University Press.

Grenfell, F. W. (1925) *Memoirs of Lord Grenfell*. London, Hodder & Stoughton.

Griffiths, J. (1934) *Y Bererindod gyda Mr Samuel Evans, De Affrica*. Publisher unidentified

Hall, R. S. (1980) *Lovers on the Nile: The Incredible African Journeys of Sam and Florence Baker*. London, Random House.

Heathcote, T. (1999) *The British Field Marshals 1736-1997*. Barnsley (UK), Pen & Sword.

Heuglin, M. T. von (1869) *Reise in das Gebiet des Weissen Nil und seiner westlichen Zuflüsse, 1862-64*. Leipzig, C. F. Winter'sche Verlagshandlung.

Hughes, H. P. (1901) *The Morning Lands of History: A Visit to Greece, Palestine and Egypt*. London, H. Marshall & Son.

Humphries, J. (2013) *Search for the Nile's Source: The Ruined Reputation of John Petherick, Nineteenth-Century Welsh Explorer*. Cardiff, University of Wales Press.

Jackson, E. (2011) *The Egyptian Travels of Lady Harriet Kavanagh With Specific Reference to Her Diaries and Antiquity Collection*. Certificate Thesis, Manchester University.

Jackson, E. (2013) 'An Irish Woman in Egypt: The Travels of Lady Harriet Kavanagh' in D. Fortenbury (ed.) *Souvenirs and New Ideas: Travel and Collecting in Egypt and the Near East*. Oxford, Oxbow Publications & The Association for the Study of Travel in Egypt and the Near East (ASTENE).

Jeal, T. (2011) *Explorers of the Nile: The Triumph and Tragedy of a Great Victorian Adventure*. New Haven and London, Yale University Press.

Jenkins, G. H. (1987) *The Foundations of Modern Wales: 1642-1780*. Oxford, Oxford University Press.

Jespersen, J. K. (2008) 'Originality and Jones' "The Grammar of Ornament" of 1856', *Journal of Design History* 21 (2) (Summer): pp. 143–53.

Jones, D. R. (1904) *I'r Aifft ac yn Ôl*. Gwrecsam: Hughes a'i Fab.

Jones, J. F. (1860) *Egypt in Its Biblical Relations and Moral Aspect*. London, Smith, Elder & Co.

Jones, O. (1856) *The Grammar of Ornament*. London, Day & Son.

Jones, O., Goury, J., Birch, S. & G. Moore (1843) *Views on the Nile: From Cairo to the Second Cataract: From Sketches Taken in 1832 and 1833, by Owen Jones and the late Jules Goury.* London, Graves & Warmsley.

Jones, S. W. (2004) *Delwedd: O Gamddwr i Gairo: Hanes y Brodyr Davies Bryan (1851–1935).* Wrecsam, Llyfrau'r Bont.

Jones, T. G. (1910) *Ymadawiad Arthur: A Chaniadau Ereill.* Caernarfon, Cwmni'r Cyhoeddwyr Cymreig.

Jones, T. G. (1912) *Y Môr Canoldir a'r Aifft.* Caernarfon, Cwmni'r Cyhoeddwyr Cymreig.

Koch, J. T. (ed.) (2006) *Celtic Culture: A Historical Encyclopedia.* Vol 1. Santa Barbara, CA; Denver, Colorado and Oxford, ABC-Clio.

Kotschy, C. G. T. & J. Peyritsch (1867) Plantae Tinneanae: Sive descriptio plantarum in expeditione tinneana ad flumen Bahr-el-Ghasal eiusque affluentias in septentrionali interioris Africae parte collectarum. /opus xxvii tabulis exornatum Theodori Kotschy et Ioannis Peyritsch. Consociatis stud. Vienna: C. Gerold fils.

Lewis, W. A. (1935) 'Anrhydedd y brodyr Davies Bryan yng Nghymru ac yng Ngwlad yr Aifft' *Y Ford Gron* (June): pp. 176–77.

Lloyd, A. B. (1998) 'Kate Bosse-Griffiths' [Obituary] *JEA* 84: pp. 191–93.

Moser, S. (2012) *Designing Antiquity: Owen Jones, Ancient Egypt and the Crystal Palace (The Paul Mellon Centre for Studies in British).* New Haven, Yale University Press.

Nichols, K. (2015) *Greece and Rome at the Crystal Palace: Classical Sculpture and Modern Britain, 1854–1936 (Classical Presences).* Oxford, Oxford University Press.

Osslan, C. (2007) 'The Egyptian Court of London's Crystal Palace' *KMT* 18 (3) (Fall): 64–73.

Petherick, J. (1861) *Egypt, the Soudan and Central Africa: with explorations from Khartoum on the White Nile to the Regions of the Equator: Being Sketches from Sixteen Years' Travel.* Edinburgh & London, William Blackwood & Sons.

Petherick, J. & K. Petherick (1869a) *Travels in Central Africa, and Explorations of the Western Nile Tributaries, by Mr and Mrs Petherick.* Vol. 1. London, Tinsley Brothers.

Petherick, J. & K. Petherick (1869b) *Travels in Central Africa, and Explorations of the Western Nile Tributaries, by Mr and Mrs Petherick.* Vol. 2. London, Tinsley Brothers.

Piggott, J. R. (2004) *Palace of the People: The Crystal Palace at Sydenham 1854-1936.* London, C. Hurst & Co.

Pitt-Rivers, A. H. L. F (1882) 'On the discovery of chert implements in stratified gravel in the Nile Valley Near Thebes', *The Journal of the Anthropological Institute of Great Britain and Ireland* 11, pp. 382–400.

Searight, S. (2006) 'Owen Jones: Travel and Vision of the Orient', *Alif: Journal of Comparative Poetics* 26: 128–146.

Sharpe, S. (1854) *The Fine Art's Courts in the Crystal Palace (First Series: North-West Side).* London, Bradbury & Evans Jones.

Suggett, R. & E. White (2002) 'Language, literacy and aspects of identity in early modern Wales' in A. Fox & D. R. Woolf (eds.) (2002) *The Spoken Word: Oral Culture in Britain, 1500-50.* Manchester, Manchester University Press, pp. 52–84.

Tinné, A. P. F. (1860) 'Geographical notes of expeditions in Central Africa by three Dutch ladies', *Trans. Hist. Soc. Lancs. & Chesh.* [new ser]. (4), pp. 107–48.

Tinné, J. A. (1864) *Geographical Notes of an Expedition in Central Africa by three Dutch Ladies.* Liverpool, T. Brakell.

Thompson, J. (2015) *Wonderful Things [Volume 2]: A History of Egyptology: 2: The Golden Age: 1881-1914.* Cairo, The American University in Cairo Press.

Tolkien, J. R. R. (1963) *Angles and Britons*: O'Donnell lectures. Cardiff, University of Wales Press.

Verdcourt, B. (1995) 'Collectors in East Africa No. 22: J. Petherick (1813–82)', *The Conchologists' Newsletter* 132 (March): 453–58.

Williams, L. (1995) 'Sam Nesa Wedyn' *Country Quest* (October): 41.

Willink, R. J. (2011) *The Fateful Journey: The Expedition of Alexine Tinné And Theodor von Heuglin in Sudan (1863–1864): A Study of their Travel Accounts and Ethnographic Collections.* Amsterdam: Amsterdam University Press.

Newspaper Articles

'A Remarkable Egyptian Mummy given to Swansea' *The Cambrian*, 2 November 1888: 8.

Census Records

'John Davies Bryan' (1861) *Census return for Ty Isaf, Parish of Hope, County of* Flintshire, North Wales. Class: RG9; Piece: 4278; Folio: 2; Page: 10; GSU roll: 543260. Available at: http://www.ancestry.co.uk [Accessed 21 September 2016].

'Thomas Gwynn Jones' (1891) *Census return for Tyddfyn Morgan, Parish of Abergele, St Asaph District, County of Denbighshire, North Wales.* Piece: 4628; Folio: 103; Page: 1. Available at: http://www.ancestry.co.uk [Accessed 21 September 2016].

'Language spoken in Wales. 1911: Report' (1913) *Census of 1911.* Pages: iii-xi. Available at: http://www.histpop.org/ohpr/servlet/PageBrowser2?ResourceT ype=Census&ResourceType=Legislation&SearchTerms=welsh%20speakers%20 1911&simple=yes&path=Results/Census/1911&active=yes&treestate=expand new&titlepos=0&mno=156&tocstate=expandnew&tocseq=200&display=sectio ns&display=tables&display=pagetitles&pageseq=first-nonblank [Accessed 21 September 2016].

Web Sources

www1: 'Scots and Egyptology', http://egyptology-scotland.squarespace.com/scots [Accessed 21 September 2016].

www2: Jackson, E. et. al. 'Irish Egyptology', http://www.irishegyptology.com/ [Accessed 21 September 2016].

www3: 'A higher ambition: Owen Jones (1809–74)', http://www.vam.ac.uk/content/articles/a/a-higher-ambition-owen-jones/ [Accessed 21 September 2016].

www4: Frankel, N. (2003) 'The Ecstasy of Decoration: The Grammar of Ornament as Embodied Experience', *Nineteenth Century Art Worldwide* [online] 2 (1) (Winter), pp. 1–32. http://www.19thc-artworldwide.org/winter03/79-winter03/winter03article/246-the-ecstasy-of-decoration-the-grammar-of-ornament-as-embodied-experience [Accessed 21 September 2016].

www5: Petch, A. 'Pitt Rivers and Shields: Shielding the Pitt Rivers Collection' http://web.prm.ox.ac.uk/england/englishness-Pitt-Rivers-and-shields.html [Accessed 21 September 2016].

www6: Cini, G. (2008) 'The Mummy with a Story to Tell', http://www.timesofmalta.com/articles/view/20080428/local/the-mummy-with-a-story-to-tell.205931 [Accessed 21 September 2016].

www7: 'Meet the Mummy', http://www.swanseamuseum.co.uk/our-collection/egyptian-artefacts/meet-the-mummy [Accessed 21 September 2016].

www8: 'How the Egypt Centre was Born' http://www.egypt.swan.ac.uk/index.php/history-of-the-egypt-centre. [Accessed 21 September 2016].

www9: 'Lewis, Sir John Herbert (1858–1933)', *Dictionary of Welsh Biography* http://yba.llgc.org.uk/en/s-LEWI-HER-1858.html [Accessed 21 September 2016].

www10: Raafat, S. 'Davies Bryan & Co. of Emad el Din Street: Four Welshmen who made Good in Egypt', *Egyptian Mail*, 27 May 1995: [n.p.], http://www.egy.com/landmarks/95-05-27.php [Accessed 21 September 2016].

www11: 'Buildings we Own: Davies Bryan Buildings', http://al-ismaelia.com/buildings/davies-bryan-buildings/ [Accessed 21 September 2016].

www12: Arthur ap Gwynn, (2001) 'Jones, Thomas Gwynn (1871–1949), poet, writer, translator and scholar', *Dictionary of Welsh Biography* [online], http://yba.llgc.org.uk/en/s2-JONE-GWY-1871.html [Accessed 21 September 2016].

Jakov Šašel (*Jacob Schaschel*) and his travels to Egypt, Nubia and Africa 1853–54

Mladen Tomorad

Croatian travellers to Egypt from the 16th century onwards

During the 16th–18th centuries, many travellers from the Austrian monarchy, which from 1527 included the Kingdoms of Croatia, Slavonia and Dalmatia, visited Egypt and the Sudan. Today, few of these travellers are known by the general public while even fewer of them wrote journals or published books describing their journeys, or donated ancient Egyptian collections to museums.

In Croatia, there are a number of travellers whose names have been remembered since the mid 16th century. Among the earliest is Juraj Hus Rasinjanin (Georges *Rasciniensis*) (end of 15th century–1566) who visited Egypt between 1540 and 1542. After returning to his homeland, he wrote a journal of his travels from Croatia to India and copies are to be found in libraries at the Vatican and in Budapest.[1]

Over the next three centuries, none of the names have survived, although travellers certainly existed, and in the collections of the archives in Dubrovnik there are manuscripts relating to merchants from the Dubrovnik (*Ragusa*) Republic and from cities around the Adriatic coast who, for commercial purposes, probably travelled to Egypt and the Sudan.

In the second half of the 19th century, two merchants from Dubrovnik who lived in Alexandria and Cairo, were the Amerling brothers, Nikola, or Niko (1823–92), and Frano (1821–?72). They lived in Egypt between 1842 and 1882, and collected more than 200 ancient Egyptian artefacts that now form a collection in the Archaeological Museum in Dubrovnik.[2]

In 1848–49, another Croatian, Mihael Barić (*c.*1791–1859), a clerk from Vienna, visited Egypt where he purchased a small collection of ancient Egyptian antiquities that are now kept in the Archaeological museum in Zagreb.[3]

A few years later, Jakov Šašel (German: Jakob Schaschel) (Fig.3.1) travelled in Egypt, Nubia and the Sudan, having been recruited as an artisan to work at the Catholic mission in Khartoum run by Ignatio Knoblecher. Several years after returning home, he wrote a memoire of his journey with the title *Bilder aus dem Oriente aufgenommen während einer Reise nach Aegypten, Nubien, Sudan in Jahren 1853 und 1854 (Pictures from the Orient taken during a journey to Egypt, Nubia and Sudan in 1853 and 1854).*[4] His manuscript is one of the first descriptions of Egypt and the Sudan to be written in Croatia since the middle of the 16th century.

Almost four decades after Šašel completed his manuscript, Fran Gundrum Oriovčanin (1856–1919), a medical doctor, amateur archaeologist, historian, anthropologist, ethnologist and collector of antiquities, visited Egypt to attend the First Egyptian Medical Congress (19–24 December 1902).[5] Returning to his home in Križevci, he wrote and published a series of journal articles about his travels.[6] In 1905, he published his travel journal as a book entitled *U Egiptu! (In Egypt),*[7] and this was reprinted in English and Arabic in 2003.[8]

Fig 3.1 Self portrait of Jakov Šašel (Jacob Schaschel). (All illustrations are © City Museum of Karlovac)

During the 1930s, Grga Novak (1888–1978), the Croatian scholar and university professor of ancient history, went to Egypt on two occasions, in 1932-33, and 1935. He described his visits in a series of newspaper articles and travellers' journals published between 1933 and 1945.[9] In 1935, Vladimir Nazor (1876–1949), a famous Croatian writer, also travelled to Egypt as a tourist, and recorded his impressions of the journey in *Iz Splita do piramida (From Split to the pyramids).*[10]

Jakov Šašel (1832-1903) – his life and work

Jakov Šašel was born on 25 July 1832 near Ferlach/Borovlje in Carinthia, a southern region of Austria, not far from the border with Slovenia.[11] His father, Janez, was a Slovenian gunsmith who travelled a lot because of his business. During Jakov's childhood, the family moved twice: the first time, when he was five years old, to Kranj in Slovenia, where between 1838 and 1842 Jakov completed four years of primary school. After a few years, the family moved to Ljubljana, where Jakov lived until 1857.[12] In Ljubljana, his father opened a workshop where he taught the trade of gunsmithing to three of his six sons – Jakov, Janez and Valentin.

In the summer of 1853, at the age of 21, Jakov went on his first journey to visit several gunsmiths working elsewhere in Austria.[13] During his travels, he learned that Monseigneur Ignatio Knoblecher (1819–1858),[14] from the Catholic mission in Khartoum, was looking for various craftsmen to work at his mission in Sudan.[15] Jakov decided to join the large group of missionaries and artisans, and in August 1853, he left his home on a journey to Egypt, Nubia and Sudan that lasted almost a year.

Returning from the Sudan in the summer of 1854, Jakov moved again to Novo Mesto, where he settled for the next three years. In Novo Mesto, he opened a gunsmith workshop, and also worked as a drawing teacher at the local Franciscan Gymnasium (school). Soon after, in 1856, he married Ana Kalčić, and in 1857, they moved to Karlovac in Croatia.[16] In Karlovac, Jakov opened his gunsmith workshop and there, until his death in 1903, he became a multi-talented craftsman and artist as a gunsmith and engraver,[17] illustrator, painter,[18] designer and constructor of church furnishings.[19] He also became a writer.[20] As a well-respected artist, his works were shown at the various exhibitions in Zagreb and Budapest from 1864 until his death in 1903.[21] During his lifetime, Jakov Šašel received several medals in Croatia, Hungary and Austria for his achievements in fine craftsmanship.[22] Sadly, many of his works only partially survive in the Karlovac Town Museum, and the Croatian History Museum in Zagreb. Jakov Šašel died in Karlovac on 28th March 1903 and is buried at the local cemetery.[23]

Jakov Šašel's journey to Egypt, Nubia and the Sudan during 1853 and 1854

Jakov Šašel's described his journey to Egypt, Nubia and Africa in a journal, which he completed in 1863. His manuscript, bound in leather with the title in gold letters, is today in the collections of Karlovac Town Museum, where it has the inventory number KP-493.[24] The manuscript consists of a foreword and 143 pages of text that are divided into four main chapters. The chapters are illustrated with 33 colourful drawings that Šašel made during his journey.[25] During 1884, the manuscript journal was published in sections in the journal *Svjetlo*.[26] In 2003, to mark the 140th anniversary of Jakov Šašel's journey to Africa, the Karlovac Town Museum published the manuscript of his travel diary in a bilingual German and Croatian edition.

Jakov Šašel's journey began in Ljubljana on 22 August 1853, when a party of five priests from Slovenia and Austria – Jeran, Jožef Lap, Joseph Gostner (or Gestner), Alojz Haller and Ignatz Kohl), together with Martin Ludvik Hansal, a teacher from Vienna, and seven craftsmen from Slovenia – Franc Bališ (carpenter), Janez Klančnik (cooper), Jakob Kobilica (waggon-builder, leather-worker, shoe-maker and fur-dresser), Jožef Kramar (shoe-maker), Martin Mikuž (waggon-builder), Lovrenc Pavlin (carpenter) and Jakov Šašel (gunsmith, illustrator, engraver and locksmith) – gathered together for their journey to the Sudan, where they were to join the Catholic mission in Khartoum lead by Ignatius Knoblecher.[27]

They set off from Ljubljana in several small groups and after walking for a couple of days,[28] on 25 August they reached Trieste. There, they were reunited and met with another group of missionaries from the Tyrol.[29] The party stayed in Trieste for two days, and on 27 August sailed from the harbour aboard the steamship *Calcutta*.[30]

In his description of the four day
voyage to the port of Alexandria in
Egypt, Šašel records the names of
various cities he saw from the ship
but did not stop to visit – Kopar,
Piran, Poreč in Istria, Methoni in
Greece – and several islands: Svetac,
Vis and Sušac in the Adriatic sea,
and Kérkyra and Pylos in Greece.[31]

Fig 3.2 Moga

The *Calcutta* arrived to
Alexandria harbour around 8
o'clock in the morning of Thursday
1 September.[32] As the party were
leaving the ship, a large group of
local Egyptians gathered around
the newly arrived passengers to try
and help them carry their luggage.
Not being used to this, Šašel noted
that he was rather annoyed.[33]
However, Ignatio Knoblecher was
there at the quayside to meet them,
and arranged their transport to
the Hôtel du Nord where they were
greeted by Moga, the chief of the Bari tribe from along the White Nile river, who
was dressed in a long red coat and small white trousers. Moga's head was adorned
by a hat with ostrich feathers.[34] Šašel was so fascinated with the chief that he
immediately began a painting of him.[35] (Fig.3.2) The party stayed in Alexandria from
1 to 17 September. Šašel's journal contains a short description of Alexandria, which
to him had 'started to lose its Oriental look'.[36] During his stay in Alexandria, Šašel
walked around the harbour and visited St Catherine's, which he described as the
most beautiful of the all churches in Alexandria.[37] The rest of his short entry mostly
contains lively descriptions of the way local men and women dressed.[38] (Fig.3.3)

For their journey through the Nile delta, the party hired small boats and left
Alexandria on 17 September. Their progress was slow, and was delayed by a storm
on 22 September. They arrived at Cairo on the evening of 25 September.[39] In 1853,
Cairo had two main harbours, one in the north for boats coming from Alexandria,
and the other at Bulaq that was used for boats from the south. In his description
of the journey to Cairo, Šašel was fascinated by the reforms of Muhammad Ali that
he could see along the banks of the Nile. Having described the small hovels of the
fellaheen[40] (Fig.3.4), he also noted the new stone buildings they passed by, including
schools, various manufacturing premises, stables for horses and granaries, all of
which were partly the result of the Pasha's reforms.[41]

Soon after arriving in Cairo, the party went to the Franciscan monastery where they stayed for the next eight days.[42] Šašel did his best to describe Cairo in his journal, referring to it as the 'Paris of the East',[43] with the beautiful Ezbekieh Square, the island where Moses was supposed to have been found by pharaoh's wife, and the pyramids of Giza.[44] (Fig.3.5) Šašel was fascinated with everything he saw in Cairo, from the different mosques, the promenades lined with acacia and palm trees, Old Cairo, the Coptic church built over the so-called 'Virgin Mary's cave', the old sycamore fig tree[45] (Fig.3.6) and the Citadel. He also described the modern Egyptian customs, houses and the harems he saw.[46] On the 29 September, Šašel was a witness to the slave trade being conducted in

Fig 3.3 Trachten in Alexsandrien (Costume in Alexandria)

Fig 3.4 Ein Fahlahs Wohnung (Houses of the fellaheen)

Fig 3.5 Kairo (Cairo - with Giza and the pyramids)

Fig 3.6 Sikomore oder wild. Feigenbaum
(A Sycamore Fig tree)

the Cairo streets, which happened every Friday, and he was 'touched to tears' by what he saw.[47] One day, he visited all three of the great pyramids in Giza, where he climbed to the top of one and went inside that built for Khufu. In his journal, he cites the ancient writer Herodotus and his description of how the greatest pyramid was built in 20 years.[48]

The party left Cairo by boat for Thebes on 3 October 1853. Along the banks of the Nile, Šašel saw fields where the Egyptians 'grow millet, beans and watermelons' in abundance, and he described the life in Upper Egypt. He also noted that such fields were seen 'all the way to Dendera, where the stone banks of the Nile begin'.[49]

During their voyage to Thebes, the party were threatened with attack from a 'pirate ship' just to the north of Asyut and had to stay awake and guard their boat the entire night. The next morning, happy that the pirates had left them unharmed, the party continued their journey to Asyut, which they sailed by the next day.[50] On the ninth day, the party passed Akhmim, and at around midnight they reached the small village of Girga (Fig.3.7) where they stayed for three days.[51] While waiting at Girga for a quantity of flat-bread to be baked, they watched two boats full of Egyptian soldiers and chained pirates sail by on their way to Cairo.[52]

The party continued their voyage on the Nile and passed Qena and Naqada (Fig.3.8) on their way to Thebes, where they arrived around 20 October.[53] They stayed among the ruins of ancient Thebes for several days, although Šašel does not mention how many. While there, the party visited almost all the ancient Egyptian monuments: the Ramesseum, the colossi of Memnon, the western Theban necropolis, the temple of Medinet Habu, the royal tombs in the Valley of the Kings,[54] and the temples at Karnak and Luxor.[55] (Figs.3.9, 10, 11, 12) Šašel's descriptions commonly refer to the publications of Giovanni Battista Belzoni and Sir John Gardner Wilkinson. For example he mentions Wilkinson's calculation of the number of stones used to build the Ramesseum,[56] the excavation of the tomb of Ramesses I (KV16), and Belzoni's work in the tomb of Seti I (KV17),[57] plus other details relating to the history of Egyptology.

The party left Thebes at the end of October. After two days, they reached Aswan and visited the temple at Philae.[58] During his stay there, Šašel's produced paintings, of the ruins of Aswan (Fig.3.13),[59] and the island of Philae. At Aswan, Luka Jeran, the

STADT GÖRGEH.

Bild / Slika 9

Fig 3.7 Stadt Görgeh (The town of Girga)

Fig 3.8 Kath Kirche in Negadez (Catholic church at Naqada)

Fig 3.9 Ruinen von Thebn (Ruins of Thebes)

priest from Ljubljana, became seriously ill with amoebic dysentery and returned to Cairo in the care of Jakob Kobilica the waggon-builder and shoe-maker.[60] It is not clear for how long the party stayed in the area of Aswan, but it was probably at least a week.

Fig 3.10 Memonsualen (Colossi of Memnon)

In Aswan, their luggage was taken from the boat and loaded onto camels, before being transported through the desert to Shellal, a small village on the banks of Nile. Šašel and his companions went ahead of the luggage on donkeys. In Shellal the party hired five smaller boats to continue their journey into Nubia. They sailed on 21 November, reaching the quayside at Kuruskū on 26 November.[61] Šašel's description of their arrival is illustrated with a painting showing the transportation of conscripted Egyptian recruits for the army that he had witnessed.[62]

In Kuruskū, the group met two priests originally from Verona: Giovanni Beltrame and Anton Lastenaro.[63] For the journey through the desert, the luggage was transferred from the boats and

Fig 3.11 Templeruin in Luxor (Temple ruins in Thebes)

Fig 3.12 Die Königsgräber (The king's tomb)
[Šašel appears to have confused the Valley of the Kings with the Temple of Ramses II at Abu Simbel]

Fig 3.13 Die katarcten und ruinen von Asuan (The cataracts and ruins of Aswan)

loaded onto a caravan of 500 camels. However, before they could begin the next part of their long journey, everybody in the party had to learn to ride his own camel.

DORF ABUHAMED.   Bild / Slika 23

Fig 3.14 Dorf Abuhamed (Village of Abu Hamed, Sudan)

Starting at the end of November, the huge caravan began walking slowly southward through the Nubian Desert to Abū Hamad. It is in this part of his journal that Šašel provides a good description of the desert phenomenon known as 'phatamorgana',[64] a type of mirage appearing on the horizon consisting of multiple images, such as of cliffs and buildings, which are distorted and magnified to resemble elaborate castles.

When Šašel arrived in Abū Hamad he made a painting (Fig.3.14) of the village and also of the wildlife he saw on the Nile.[65] In his journal, he describes the appearance of Nubians and how they hunted for crocodiles.[66] (Fig.3.15) On Monday 12 December, and for a further four days, the party continued their journey south, with their caravan following the river all the way to Barbar, a large Sudanese town that, in 1853, had a population of 8,000.[67]

After two weeks in Barbar, Šašel recorded in his journal that the fear of death then prevailed among his fellow travellers, following the death of the missionary priest Milharčič, who had greeted them on their arrival, on 18 December, just two days after they had arrived. A few days later, they learned about the death from dysentery of another priest, Kocijančič, at the mission in Khartoum.[68]

For the continuation of their journey, their luggage was transferred to a faster boat, the *Stella Matutina (Morning Star)*. From the boat, Šašel observed several hippopotamuses, which he first describes before explaining their value to the local population.[69] He also gave a detailed description of how the local people hunted the hippopotamus with spears.[70] During this part of the journey Šašel made further

Fig 3.15 *Eine krokodillsjargd (A crocodile hunt)*

Fig 3.16 *Stella Matutina (The Morning Star on the river Nile)*

paintings, showing the *Stella Matutina* and hippopotamuses in the shallows of the river Nile.[71] (Figs.3.16, 17)

Fig 3.17 Das Nilpferd (A Hippopotamus)

On 21 December, the party passed by the ruins of the ancient city of Meroe, and Šašel described in his journal the pyramids he saw in the distance.[72] The party stopped and moored their boats on 24 December in order to prepare for Christmas and, after two days of celebration, they continued with the last part of their journey[73] arriving at Khartoum on 28 December. It was now more than four months since Šašel had left Ljubljana.[74]

In Khartoum, the party were welcomed by Théodore von Heuglein, the naturalist and Austrian consul, and by Jenschek, a German doctor.[75] Khartoum was then the main city of Sudan with a population of 25,000 people who mostly lived in mud-brick houses. The party's quarters in the Catholic mission, together with the chapel and workshops, were also built of mud.[76] The climate was tropical with temperatures sometimes rising to 60°C. Šašel noted that the city was surrounded by fertile land cultivated with different vegetables and tropical fruits such as dates, oranges, lemons, bananas, grapes and figs.[77]

The last two chapters of Šašel's journal describe the everyday life of the local Sudanese population (Figs.3.18, 19, 21),[78] the city of Khartoum,[79] and details of their life in the Catholic mission.[80] Šašel did not like what he saw in Sudan, especially the moral corruption, slavery and the number of prostitutes.[81] This part of his travel journal is very valuable for future ethnographic and anthropological research of life in Central Africa in the middle of the 19th century.

For Šašel life in the mission was also far from ideal, especially for the craftsmen. Knoblecher did not treat everyone the same way, and did not pay any attention

Fig 3.18 Ein Negerdorf (A village in Sudan)

Fig 3.19 Schaukeln der Neger (A Sudanese 'see-saw')

to the craftsmen at all. Šašel had already noted that Knoblecher did not offer his hand to shake when greeting the party on their arrival in Alexandria. He wrote that he found this strange because the two men had been colleagues while studying

Fig 3.20 Missionsknabe am grabe seines wohltäters
(Mission boy by the grave of his benefactors
[the Catholic Mission])

theology. Knoblecher's greeting for all the Slavic priests and craftsmen was also very cold and he did not appear to like them. He even treated some of the priests from Slovenia in the same way, especially Jožef Lap. Knoblecher, noted Šašel, only ever appeared to greet warmly the Germans and Austrians.[82]

Over the next few weeks, death was a constant follower of every member of the Catholic mission. Priests and craftsmen began to die soon after they arrived in Khartoum. First they lost Jožef Lap, and then, in the next few weeks, Alojzij Haller, Ignatz Kohl, Gerstner (or Gostner),[83] Anton Lastenaro and the two masons, who died from sunstroke or fever.[84] After their deaths, the men were given a decent burial in graves marked with a cross. (Fig.3.20) Those who were not priests did not

Fig 3.21 Der Schlangenbandiger (A snake charmer)

get enough food to eat, so they either had to starve or buy very cheap bread from the local people. Yet, at the same time Knoblecher and some other German priests lived very well.[85] It is unclear how long Šašel stayed with the Catholic mission at Khartoum, where he worked daily as a metal craftsman. Soon, he too became sick and was also injured, so that he had to move around with the help of a wooden crutch, which he probably made himself.[86]

One day, a group of French merchants from Alexandria passed by, and they kindly offered to take Šašel and Andrej Hruška, the gardener, onto their boat. Their trip to the north went first to Barbar, then through the desert to Abū Hamad and Kuruskū.[87] While in the desert, a huge storm passed over. Many camels and other animals in the caravan died,[88] and Šašel made a painting of vultures eating the corpses of the dead animals. In Kuruskū, the party hired a boat in which they sailed to Aswan, where they changed to another that took them back to Cairo.

The party finally reached Cairo, exhausted, sick and hungry. Šašel again stayed for a time at the Franciscan monastery. When he had recovered, he left Cairo for Alexandria, where he embarked on a ship sailing to Trieste.[89] It is not clear how long his journey back to Slovenia took because Šašel did not record any dates in his diary, but it probably took place in the spring of 1854. This short final chapter describing the journey home brings the manuscript to a conclusion.

Šašel's travel journal is one of the most detailed and interesting dairies describing Egypt, Nubia and the Sudan that has survived from the middle of the 19th century. Today, Šašel's travel journal is a valuable source for multi-disciplinary research. It contains geographical, ethnological, anthropological and historical details of the route he travelled between the end of August 1853 and the late spring of 1854. His notes and impressions also provide valuable information for the field of Egyptology and about other explorers and travellers to Egypt and the Sudan. Šašel was obviously a well-read man with a very broad knowledge of ancient history and its sources. In various descriptions in his journal, he not only refers to the ancient sources such as Herodotus and Strabo, but also to the then newly available publications on Egyptology by Belzoni and Wilkinson.[90]

Sadly, until recently, the journal was not very well known to the wider public, although within the region of Karlovac, Jakov Šašel has always been recognized and known as a traveller, and his manuscript journal, together with the folk tales and articles about Khartoum that he published in 1884 in the journal *Svjetlo*, would have undoubtedly influenced other Croatian travellers to explore Africa.[91]

Endnotes

1   Tomorad. In the press.
2   Tomorad, 2001: p. 224; Menalo, 2003: pp. 6–7; Tomorad, 2003a: p. 56; Tomorad, 2015: p. 47; Tomorad & Stimac, 2016: p. 229.
3   Ljubic, 1892: p. 60; Tomorad, 2003a: p. 28; Tomorad, 2003b: p. 54; Tomorad, 2016: p. 329.
4   Schaschel, 1863; Šašel, 1884; Šašel, 2003; Kočever, 2008: pp. 6–9; Frelih, 2009: pp. 25–34.

5 Gundrum, 1903a.

6 Gundrum, 1903b.

7 Gundrum, 1904c.

8 Gundrum, 2003.

9 Novak, 1933a–m; Novak, 1935; Novak, 1945; Tomorad, 2003: pp. 117–19; Tomorad & Stimac, 2016: pp. 235–40.

10 Nazor, 1942.

11 Henkel, 2003; Kočever, 2003: p. 163; Kočever, 2008: pp. 6–7: Kočever, 2012: p. 95.

12 Kočever, 2008: pp. 6-7; Kočever, 2012: p. 95.

13 Kočever, 2003: p. 163; Kočever, 2008: pp. 6–7; Kočever, 2012: p. 95, fn. 11.

14 Ignatius Knoblecher (6 July 1819–13 April 1858) was a Slovenian Roman Catholic missionary in the Sudan. He was also one of the first explorers of the White Nile. Details of life and work can be found in Šašel, 2003: p. 173; Henkel, 2003: pp. 158–59; Frelih, 2005: pp. 41–64; Kočever, 2012: p. 95.

15 During the period 1852–58, 33 volunteer craftsmen joined the Knoblecher mission. Henkel, 2003: p. 158.

16 Kočever, 2003: p. 163; Kočever, 2008: pp. 6–7.

17 In his workshop at the centre of Haulikova 5 and Radićeva Street in Karlovac, Šašel hand crafted various types of guns, signet rings and gravestones. Kočever, 2008: pp. 6–7. One of his guns was made as a gift for the Austrian Emperor Franz Joseph I, and he was rewarded by a gift of 500 forints. Jeličić, 2008: pp. 14–15. More about his work as gunsmith and armourer can be found in: Jeličić, 2008: pp. 14–17.

18 During his lifetime, he made many drawing and painted many pictures. The first were made during his journey to Egypt, Nubia and Sudan in 1853–54. In later years, he made paintings of many subjects: landscape, genre, veduta, historical, sacral and portraits. More about his work as an illustrator, engraver and artist can be found in Škrtić, 2008: pp. 18–29; Škritić, 2012.

19 Šašel was a very successful Neo-Stylist designer whose work contributed to Historicism in Croatian art. More about his work as a designer and constructor of the church furnishings can be found in Čulig, 2008: pp. 30–50.

20 Šašel wrote the manuscript diary about his travels to Egypt, Nubia and the Sudan in 1863. He also wrote various texts in the local newspaper *Karlovački viestnik*, the journal *Svjetlo* and *Glasonoša*. Kočever, 2008: pp. 7–13.

21 His work was exhibited and rewarded at the First Economic Exhibition in Zagreb in 1864, and in Budapest in 1896. *Karlovački viestnik* 22 (1866): p. 173; *Svjetlo* 27 (1895): p. 3. His work was exhibited at the Economic Exhibition in Vienna in 1873, the local Karlovac Economic and Trade Exhibition in 1884 and in Zagreb in 1891. Kočever 2008: pp. 10–11.

22 Kočever 2008: pp. 10–11.

23 Kočever, 2003: p. 163; Kočever, 2008: pp. 6–7.

24 Kočever, 2008: p. 59, cat. No. 3.

25 Družak, 2003: pp. 168–70; Kočever, 2003: p. 164; Kočever, 2008: pp. 8–9; Škrtić, 2012.

26 It was named Chatum and published 6–24 April 1884 in numbers 29–34.

27 The Catholic mission in Khartoum was established in 1847 by Maximilian Ryllo from Poland. In 1848, Ignatio Knoblecher became the new 'general vicarious' (vicar) of the mission and soon found he was asking for new priests to come from Europe, and they gathered together at Ljubljana during the summer of 1853. Šašel, 2003: p. 173.

28 Part 1: Chapter 1, 'Ljubljana'. Šašel, 2003: p. 178
29 Part 1: Chapter 2, 'To Trieste and the Mediterranean Sea'. Šašel, 2003: p. 179.
30 Part 1: Chapter 2, 'To Trieste and the Mediterranean Sea'. Šašel, 2003: p. 179.
31 Part 1: Chapter 2, 'To Trieste and the Mediterranean Sea'. Šašel, 2003: pp. 179–80.
32 Part 1: Chapter 2, 'To Trieste and the Mediterranean Sea'. Šašel, 2003: p. 180.
33 Part 1: Chapter 3, 'Alexandria'. Šašel, 2003: p. 181.
34 Part 1: Chapter 3, 'Alexandria'. Šašel, 2003: p. 181.
35 Illustration 2 in Šašel's manuscript.
36 Part 1: Chapter 3, 'Alexandria'. Šašel, 2003: p. 183.
37 Part 1: Chapter 3, 'Alexandria'. Šašel, 2003: p. 182.
38 Part 1: Chapter 3, 'Alexandria'. Šašel, 2003: pp. 182–83, with illustrations 3 and 4 showing local costume.
39 Part 1: Chapter 4, 'From Alexandria to Cairo'. Šašel, 2003: pp. 184–85.
40 Illustration 5 in Šašel's manuscript, showing houses of the fellaheen.
41 Part 1: Chapter 4, 'From Alexandria to Cairo'. Šašel, 2003: p. 185.
42 Part 1: Chapter 5, 'Cairo'. Šašel, 2003: p. 188.
43 Part 1: Chapter 5, 'Cairo'. Šašel, 2003: p. 190.
44 Part 1: Chapter 5, 'Cairo'. Šašel, 2003: p. 187, with illustration 6 showing Cairo and the pyramids.
45 Part 1: Chapter 5 and 7, 'Cairo'. Šašel, 2003: pp. 188–90, with illustration 7 showing the sycamore fig tree.
46 Part 1: Chapter 9, 'Eunuchs and Muslim houses'. Šašel, 2003: pp. 200–01.
47 Part 1: Chapter 6, 'Slave trade in Cairo'. Šašel, 2003: pp. 191–93.
48 Part 1: Chapter 8, 'Pyramides'. Šašel, 2003: pp. 196–99.
49 Part 2: Chapter 1, 'From Cairo to Thebes'. Šašel, 2003: p. 204.
50 Part 2: Chapter 1, 'From Cairo to Thebes'. Šašel, 2003: p. 204.
51 Part 2: Chapter 1, 'From Cairo to Thebes'. Šašel, 2003: p. 205, with illustration 9 showing Girga.
52 Part 2: Chapter 1, 'From Cairo to Thebes'. Šašel, 2003: p. 205.
53 Part 2: Chapter 1, 'From Cairo to Thebes'. Šašel, 2003: p. 205, with illustration 10 showing the Catholic church at Naqada. The date for the party arriving at Thebes is not exactly clear. In his journal, Šašel writes of arriving at Esna (Isnā) on 20 October after a delay because there was not enough wind to continue sailing. Šašel further writes that after taking a break at Esna (Isnā) they arrived at the ruins of Thebes. Geographically, Esna is to the south of Thebes, therefore Šašel may have confused some dates and places when writing the final version of his journal during the early 1860s.
54 Part 2: Chapter 2, 'The Ruins of Thebes'. Šašel, 2003: p. 209. Šašel mentions that Strabo wrote of there being 40 tombs, and that only 17 had been discovered by 1853.
55 Part 2: Chapter 2, 'The Ruins of Thebes'. Šašel, 2003: pp. 206–12, with illustration 12 showing the ruins of Thebes, illustration 13 showing the Colossi of Memnon, illustration 14 showing the temple of Luxor, and illustration 15 titled the King's Tomb. (Illustration 15 clearly shows the Temple of Ramesses II at Abu Simbel, therefore Šašel may have again confused the places he visited when writing the final version of his journal during the early 1860s.)
56 Part 2: Chapter 2, 'The Ruins of Thebes'. Šašel, 2003: p. 207.
57 Part 2: Chapter 2, 'The Ruins of Thebes'. Šašel, 2003: p. 210.

58 Part 2: Chapter 3, 'Aswan and Kuruskū'. Šašel, 2003: p. 213.
59 Figures 16 and 17, in Šašel's manuscript, showing the cataracts at Aswan, and the granite cliffs at Philae.
60 Part 2: Chapter 3, 'Aswan and Kuruskū'. Šašel, 2003: p. 214.
61 Part 2: Chapter 3, 'Aswan and Kuruskū'. Šašel, 2003: p. 214.
62 Illustration 11, in Šašel's manuscript, showing the transportation of conscripted Egyptian recruits.
63 Part 2: Chapter 4, 'Desert'. Šašel, 2003: p. 216.
64 Part 2: Chapter 4, 'Desert'. Šašel, 2003: pp. 221–22.
65 Illustration 23 in Šašel's manuscript shows the village of Abū Hamad, and illustration 24 shows the crocodile hunt.
66 Part 2: Chapter 5, 'Nile, Nubians and Crocodiles'. Šašel, 2003: pp. 225–26.
67 Part 2: Chapter 6, 'Barbar, Stella Matutina and the Hypos'. Šašel, 2003: p. 227.
68 Part 2: Chapter 6, 'Barbar, Stella Matutina and the Hypos'. Šašel, 2003: p. 228.
69 Part 2: Chapter 6, 'Barbar, Stella Matutina and the Hypos'. Šašel, 2003: p. 229. Šašel mentions that hippopotamus meat is very good and tasty.
70 Part 2: Chapter 6, 'Barbar, Stella Matutina and the Hypos'. Šašel, 2003:p p. 229–31.
71 Illustrations 25 in Šašel's manuscript, showing the Stella Matutina, and illustration 26 showing a hippopotamus.
72 Part 2: Chapter 7, 'In Khartoum'. Šašel, 2003: p. 232.
73 Part 2: Chapter 7, 'In Khartoum'. Šašel, 2003: p. 232.
74 Part 2: Chapter 7, 'In Khartoum'. Šašel, 2003: p. 232.
75 Part 2: Chapter 7, 'In Khartoum'. Šašel, 2003: p. 232.
76 Part 2: Chapter 7, 'In Khartoum'. Šašel, 2003: p. 233.
77 Part 2: Chapter 7, 'In Khartoum'. Šašel 2003: p. 233.
78 Part 3: Chapter 1, 'Religion, Priests, Doctors and the Marriage of the Negroes'. Šašel, 2003: pp. 236–37. Chapter 2, 'War Celebrations and the Customs of the Negroes'. Šašel, 2003: pp. 236–37. Chapter 3 'Professions of the Negroes and Forging of the Iron'. Šašel, 2003: pp. 241–42. Chapter 4 'Slave Hunt and the Moral Corruption in Sudan'. Šašel, 2003: p. 245, with Illustration 29 showing a village in Sudan, illustration 30 showing a Sudanese 'see-saw' and illustration 34 showing a snake charmer.
79 Part 4: Chapter 1 'In Khartoum'. Šašel, 2003: pp. 248–49.
80 Part 4: Chapter 2 'Mission'. Šašel, 2003: pp. 250–52.
81 Part 3: Chapter 4 'Slave Hunt and the Moral Corruption in Sudan'. Šašel, 2003: p. 245.
82 Part 4: Chapter 2 'Mission'. Šašel, 2003: p. 251. While they were in Khartoum, Knoblecher never ate with them at the same table, and while walking he always passed by them as though they did not exist.
83 In his journal, Šašel used both names for the same person, therefore it is unclear which is the correct name.
84 Part 4: Chapter 2 'Mission'. Šašel, 2003: p. 251, with illustration 32 showing a missionary graves.
85 Part 4: Chapter 2 'Mission'. Šašel, 2003: pp. 251–52.
86 Part 4: Chapter 3 'In the Homeland'. Šašel, 2003: p. 253. Šašel did not mention what health problems he had. He just mentioned that he had to move with the help of a crutch.
87 Part 4: Chapter 3 'In the Homeland'. Šašel, 2003: p. 253.

88 Part 4: Chapter 3 'In the Homeland'. Šašel, 2003: p. 254, with illustration 33 showing vultures eating one of the dead animals from the caravan.
89 Part 4: Chapter 3 'In the Homeland'. Šašel, 2003: pp. 254–55.
90 Schaschel 1863; Šašel 1884; Šašel, 2003.
91 Dragutin Lerman (1863–1918), from Požega, and Napoleon Lukšić (1863–83) were members of Sir Henry Morton Stanley's expedition to the Congo. In 1882–96, Lerman travelled and explored the Congo where he discovered waterfalls at the river Kwil in 1893, and named it the Zrinski Chutes. In his youth, he worked in Karlovac as a sales assistant, so it is very likely that he heard stories about Jakov Šašel and his journey to Africa. More detail about his life can be found in: *Hrvatska enciklopedija*, Vol. 6 (2004) s.v. 'Lerman, Dragutin': 590. Kočever, 2012: pp. 96–98. Other famous Croatian explorers of Africa were the brothers Mirko (1871–1913) and Stevo (1876–1936) Seljan, from Karlovac, who explored Ethiopia between 1899 and 1902. Further details about their life can be found in *Hrvatska enciklopedija*, vol. 9 (2009) s.v. '*Seljan, Mirko i Stevo*': p. 679; Kočever , 2012: pp. 98–103.

Bibliography

Čulig, Igor (2008) *'Jakov Šašel kao projektant i graditelj crkvenog namještaja* ('Jakov Šašel as a designer and constructor of church furnishings') in: Kočevar, Sanda (ed.), *Jakov Šašel (1832-1903)*, Karlovac: pp. 30–55.

Družak, Antonija (2003) '*Zapažanja uz ilustracije*' in: (2003) *Slike s Orijenta nastale tijekom jednog putovanja u Egipat, Nubiju i Sudan godine 1853. i 1854*, Karlovac: pp. 168–70.

Frelih, Marko (2005) '*Afrika, ki odhaja in se vrača: dr. Ignacij Knoblehar - katoliški misijonar v južnem Sudanu in raziskovalec reke Nil*'. *Azijske in afriške studije* IX.3: pp. 41–64.

Frelih, Marko (2009) 'Thirty-three famous views of the Orient: Jakob Šašel and his impressions from his journey to Khartum in 1853' in: Lazar, Irene & Holaubek, Johanna (eds.) *Egypt and Austria V Proceedings*. Koper: pp. 25–34

Gundrum, Fran (1903a) '*Prvi egipatski medicinski kongres*'. Liečnički viestnik 3: pp. 94–101.

Gundrum, Fran (1903b) '*U Egiptu*', *Hrvatski planinar* nos. 7–12.

Gundrum, Fran (1905) *U Egiptu!*. Zagreb, Tisak Antuna Scholza.

Gundrum, Fran (2003) *In Egypt*. Križevci.

Henkel, Reinhard (2003) '*Predgovor*' in: Šašel, Jakov, *Slike s Orijenta nastale tijekom jednog putovanja u Egipat, Nubiju i Sudan godine 1853. i 1854*. Karlovac: pp. 158–62.

Jeličić, Janko (2008) '*Oružar Jakov Šašel* – Jakov Šašel the armourer'. In: Kočevar, Sanda (ed.), *Jakov Šašel (1832-1903)*. Karlovac: pp. 14–17.

Kočevar, Sanda (2003) '*Jakov Šašel i Slike Orijenta*' in: Šašel, Jakov, *Slike s Orijenta nastale tijekom jednog putovanja u Egipat, Nubiju i Sudan godine 1853. i 1854*. Karlovac: pp. 163–67.

Kočevar, Sanda (2008) '*Prilog za bibliografiju Jakova* Šašela *(1832-1903)* – A contribution ot the bibliography of Jakov Šašel (1832-1903)' in: Kočevar, Sanda (ed.), *Jakov Šašel (1832-1903)*. Karlovac: pp. 6–13.

Kočevar, Sanda (2012) '*Svoj o svome - ondašnji karlovački tisak o karlovačkim putnicima - istraživačima Afrike i Južne Amerike druge polovine XIX. i prve polovine XX. Stoljeća*'. *Časopis za suvremenu povijest* 44.1: pp. 93–109.

Kočevar, Sanda (ed.) (2008) *Jakov Šašel (1832-1903)*. Karlovac.

Ljubić, Šime (1892) 'Napisani povoji jedne mumije u narodnom muzeju u Zagrebu', Viestnik narodnoga zemaljskoga muzeja u Zagrebu XIV–2: pp. 59–60.

Menalo, Romana. (2003) Egipatska zbirka Dubrovačkog muzeja. Dubrovnik.

Novak, Grga. (1933a) 'Iz Trsta u Egipat. Na parobrodu "Gange", o Božiću 1932'. Novosti 13 (13 January 1933): p. 5.

Novak, Grga (1933b) 'Paris starog svijeta – Aleksandrija. Aleksandrija u prosincu 1932'. Novosti 15 (15 January 1933): p. 11.

Novak, Grga (1933c) 'Po tragovima Kleopatre. Aleksandrija, 30. prosinca 1932'. Novosti, 22 (22 January 1933): p. 9.

Novak, Grga (1933d) 'Kairo – Egipatski velegrad, njegovo lice i naličje, Kairo 5. siječnja 1933'. Novosti 24 (24 January 1933): p. 10.

Novak, Grga (1933e) 'U Kairskoj čaršiji i ramazanskoj noći, Kairo, u siječnju 1933'. Novosti 25 (25 January 1933): p. 11.

Novak, Grga (1933f) 'Dva grada Sunca – dva Heliopolisa. Heliopolis, u siječnju 1933'. Novosti 28 (28 January 1933): p. 8.

Novak, Grga (1933g) 'K piramidama. Posljednji ostatak velegrada Memfisa. Gizeh, u siječnju 1933', Novosti 38 (7 February 1933): p. 12.

Novak, Grga (1933h) 'Keops, Kefren i Mikerin. Kod piramida, u siječnju 1933'. Novosti 46 (15 February 1933): p. 8.

Novak, Grga (1933i) 'U šumi stupova drevnih hramova. Luksor, 4. veljače 1933'. Novosti 53 (22 February 1933): p. 9.

Novak, Grga. (1933j) 'U gradu boga Sunca. Meleui, u veljači 1933'. Novosti 77 (18 March 1933): p. 16.

Novak, Grga (1933k) 'Na obali Nila uz muslimanski gradić i veliku prošlost. U Luksoru, u veljači 1933'. Novosti 83 (24 March 1933): p. 4.

Novak, Grga (1933l) 'Na starom obratniku u Asuanu. Asuan, u veljači 1933'. Novosti 91 (1 April 1933): p. 5.

Novak, Grga (1933m) 'Na jezeru koje pokriva hram Izide. Asuan-barage, u veljači 1933'. Novosti 103 (12th April 1933): p. 16.

Novak, Grga (1935) 'Novo putovanje Jadranske straže. Grčka i Egipat. 30 juna–16 jula 1935'. Jadranska straža XIII.6: pp. 233–39.

Novak, Grga (1945) U zemlji faraona. Zagreb.

Nazor, Vladimir (1942) Iz Splita do piramida. Zagreb.

Schaschel, Jakob (1863) Bilder aus dem Oriente aufgenommen während einer Reise nach Aegypten, Nubien, Sudan in Jahren 1853 und 1854. Unpublished manuscript. Karlovac, Gradski muzej, inv. no. KP-460.

Schaschel, Jakob (2003) Bilder aus dem Oriente aufgenommen während einer Reise nach Aegypten, Nubien, Sudan in Jahren 1853 und 1854. Karlovac: pp. 21–116.

Šašel, Jakov (2003) Slike s Orijenta nastale tijekom jednog putovanja u Egipat, Nubiju i Sudan godine 1853. i 1854. Karlovac: pp. 172–256.

Škrtić, Antonija (2008) 'Slikarski opus Jakova Šašela – The paiting works of Jakov Šašel'. In: Kočevar, Sanda (ed.), Jakov Šašel (1832-1903). Karlovac: pp. 18–29.

Škrtić, Antonija (2012) 'Šašelove Slike s Orijenta: *iz prakse Gradskog muzeja Karlovac*', Muzeologija 48/49, pp. 50–55.

Tomorad, Mladen (2003a) *Egipat u Hrvatskoj, egipatske starine u hrvatskoj znanosti i kulturi*. Zagreb, Barbat.

Tomorad, Mladen (2003b) '*Zagrebačka egipatska mumija i lanena knjiga*'. *Meridijani* 77: pp. 54–59.

Tomorad, Mladen (2015) 'The Ancient Egyptian Antiquities in Institutional and Private Collections in Croatia' in: Tomorad, Mladen (ed.), *A History of Research into Ancient Egyptian Culture conducted in Southeast Europe*. Oxford, Archaeopress: pp. 51–52.

Tomorad, Mladen (2016) 'Foundation of the Ancient Egyptian Collections in Croatia: Travellers, Private Collectors and the Genesis of the Collections (1800–1920)' in: Hudakova, Lubica (ed.) *Egypt and Austria IX*. Wien: pp. 325–40 and 405.

Newspapers & Periodicals

Staroegipatska civilizacija vol. II: Uvod u egiptološke studije. Zagreb.

Tomorad, Mladen & Štimac, Ivana (2016) 'Visualizing Egypt in the Collection of the Archaeological Museum in Dubrovnik and the Newspaper/travel Reports Published by Grga Novak between 1933 and 1945' in: *Egypt and Austria X: Visualizing the Orient: Central Europe and the Near East in the 19th and 20th Centuries*, ur. Júnová Macková, Adéla-Storchová, Lucie-Jún, Libor. Prague 2016: pp. 229–44.

4

Tycoons on the Nile:
How American Millionaires brought Egypt to America

Susan Allen

Unlike the great museums of Europe, which acquired their monumental Egyptian collections in the first half of the 19th century through the activities of agent-entrepreneurs such as Salt, Belzoni and Drovetti, America was a 'Johnny Come Lately', preoccupied by its own internal affairs. It was not until after the end of the American Civil War in 1865 that newly wealthy Americans had the means to travel and collect, and to found and fund the great museums and institutions that today house the Egyptian collections of America.

It is not that Americans were unfamiliar with ancient Egypt: the Egyptian Revival movement, which began after the Napoleonic Expedition to Egypt (1798–1801), led to many public buildings and cemeteries being designed in an Egyptian (or 'Egyptianizing') style, with pylons, winged scarabs, and obelisks. Early French, German and Italian expeditions produced lavishly illustrated books such as the *Description de l'Egypte*. The first copy of this work in America was given to the Harvard University Library in 1822, and it influenced the monumental pylon gateway of the Mt Auburn Cemetery in Cambridge, Massachusetts, designed by Jacob Bigelow (1832).[1]

Economic conditions in the United States were much altered after the American Civil War (1860–65). The country was transitioning to an industrial economy, particularly in the northern states that had won the war. Vast new fortunes were being made in railroads, manufacturing, steel, oil and finance, and the American museums founded at this time benefited greatly.[2] The so-called 'Robber Barons' of what came to be known as the 'Gilded Age' were intent on acquiring the best the world could provide and that money could buy for their museums, and building grand Beaux-Art buildings to house them. They realized that, as a new nation and a power on the world stage, America lacked both monuments and a cultural and artistic history. These however, could be easily acquired and imported from elsewhere.

The first major Egyptian monument to come to America was the obelisk of Thutmose III, now known as Cleopatra's Needle, which was removed from

Fig 4.1 William Henry Vanderbilt Jr. After Gorringe, Egyptian Obelisks.

Alexandria in 1880. The idea of bringing an ancient Egyptian obelisk to America was first floated in 1869 by a prominent New York newspaper editor, Henry Hurlburt. He revived the idea in 1877 and, after lengthy negotiations by the US Consul General, Elbert E. Farnum, the Khedive Ismail Pasha agreed to make a gift of the obelisk to the city of New York. Hurlburt had already secured the financial support of William H. Vanderbilt (Fig.4.1), the enormously wealthy railroad magnate.[3] It was felt that, as the new world power, America needed an obelisk to match those in Paris (erected 1833) and London (erected 1878).[4]

The removal of the obelisk, its transport to New York and erection in Central Park behind the newly-built Metropolitan Museum of Art would not have happened without the brilliant naval engineer Henry H. Gorringe, who designed a structure for turning and lowering the obelisk (Fig.4.2). This was prefabricated and shipped to Alexandria. Gorringe then had to overcome numerous obstacles, both logistical and political, to bring the obelisk safely ashore at New York in July 1880.[5] It took 112 days to move the obelisk from the banks of the Hudson River to Central Park where it was returned to the vertical in January 1881 before a public unveiling the following month.

The first Americans to begin long-term scholarly and archaeological work in Egypt were Charles Edwin Wilbour (Fig.4.3) and Theodore M. Davis. Both were self-made men who acquired their fortunes in sometimes less than ethical ways under the infamous 'Boss Tweed' of New York (1858–72). When the 'Tweed ring' collapsed, Wilbour went abroad in 1874 and studied Egyptology in Paris and Berlin.[6] For the last 20 years of his life he spent each winter in Egypt, first accompanying Gaston Maspero on the antiquities service steamer and then in 1886 on his own *dahabiyya*, *The Seven Hathors*, which served as his working base. Never an excavator, he focused on copying inscriptions, freely sharing his discoveries with other scholars, and on collecting. Unfortunately, he chose not to publish his research. After his death, in 1896, his library and collection were presented by his family to the Brooklyn Museum in 1916.[7]

Theodore Davis (Fig.4.4) was a more ambitious and complicated man than Wilbour, making his fortune by speculating in mining and banking. He survived the downfall of the 'Tweed ring' and profited greatly from cleaning up some of its mess, even surviving a Congressional investigation. By 1877, aged 39, he had made enough money to be, in the words of his biographer John Adams, 'a true tycoon on the Nile'.[8] Davis retired to Newport, Rhode Island, in 1882, building a grand 'cottage' on the ocean, spending his winters in Europe and summers in Newport,

Fig 4.2 Lowering the Obelisk in Alexandria. From Gorringe, Egyptian Obelisks.

which had become a gathering place for Boston intellectuals, whose company he found stimulating.

Davis's ambition and intellectual curiosity led him first to art collecting and, after a bout of pneumonia, to a trip to Egypt in the winter of 1887. He met up with Wilbour, began collecting Egyptian antiquities, and by 1896 had commissioned the building of his own *dahabiyya, The Beduin*. He befriended many young archaeologists, including Howard Carter and Percy Newberry. Eventually, in 1901, the millionaire turned from collector to excavator. He obtained a concession for the entire Valley of the Kings, hired a young British Egyptologist, Harold Jones, to supervise the excavation, and began

Fig 4.3 Charles Edwin Wilbour. Frontispiece from Travels in Egypt (December 1880 to May 1891) letters of Charles Edwin Wilbour, Brooklyn Museum 1936. Brooklyn Museum, Wilbour Library of Egyptology.

Fig 4.4 Theodore Montgomery Davis. The Metropolitan Museum of Art, Egyptian Expedition Image.
© The Metropolitan Museum of Art.

a remarkable string of discoveries that would include the royal tombs of Thutmose IV, Hatshepsut, Yuya and Tuya (Fig.4.5), KV55, Horemheb, and a dozen others. So successful was he in clearing the Valley of the Kings through long-term, systematic excavation that when he stopped digging there in 1914, the Valley was thought to be exhausted (by everyone except Howard Carter).[9]

Davis was also willing to commit substantial funds to publishing the results of his excavations. To document his work, he employed the artist Joseph Lindon Smith as well as the photographer Harry Burton, who would go on to a long and successful career with the Metropolitan Museum of Art's

CHAIR WITH CUSHION.

Fig 4.5 Chair from the tomb of Yuya and Tuya.
After Davis, The Tomb of Iouiya and Touiyou.

Egyptian Expedition and as the photographer for the tomb of Tutankhamun. Davis published his discoveries in a lavish series of six large-format volumes, with colour illustrations, between 1904 and 1912.[10]

After Davis's death, the probate of his will turned into a fiasco, involving fraud and bribery by his nephew. But in 1930, his paintings and Egyptian collection (both purchased, and also from his share of the excavation division) were finally transferred to the Metropolitan in New York, where they are prominently displayed in the New Kingdom galleries.[11]

Concurrent with Davis's solo work in the Valley of the Kings, American museums and universities saw the advantage of excavations in Egypt to fill their new galleries. The situation in Egypt had changed since the early 1800s. Mariette and Maspero had founded the Egyptian Museum in Cairo and begun excavations to fill its galleries. They also organized the Antiquities Service, which now issued permits for excavation, allowing for the division of finds. This was a powerful incentive to American museums.

The American museums hired trained Egyptologists and archaeologists to organize large-scale excavation and documentation programmes at multiple sites. Many of these men had worked with or had been influenced by the British excavator William Matthew Flinders Petrie, who pioneered a new, more scientific, methodology of careful excavation and recording of everything found – pottery, skeletons, and humble broken bits such as stonemason's mallets. Petrie also pioneered the idea of raising funds from private individuals and institutions to support his work. Many American museums were subscribers to the Egypt Exploration Fund, in London, and they received a share of the antiquities discovered by Petrie and others. For major subscribers, these could be quite significant additions to their collections, such as reliefs and a sarcophagus from the temple of Mentuhotep-Nebhepetre in Deir el-Bahri now in the Metropolitan Museum of Art.[12]

The first American to support scientific excavation in Egypt to the benefit of a museum was Phoebe Apperson Hearst, founder of the Phoebe Apperson Hearst Museum of Anthropology and Archaeology at the University of California, Berkeley, who hired George Andrew Reisner (Fig.4.6) in 1899 to begin excavations in Egypt.[13] Reisner excavated at a number of important cemetery sites in Upper Egypt and began working at Giza in 1903.

From the very beginning he documented the work and the finds with photography, and the Museum of Fine Arts, Boston, houses more than 45,000 glass-plate negatives from these early excavations as well as his later work in Nubia and Giza.[14] In the early years it was Reisner himself who often took the pictures. Later, he trained several Egyptian photographers, who worked for him for more than 25 years. The photographs provide an irreplaceable documentation of his excavations; the Giza negatives have been digitized for the Giza Archives website,[15] and the negatives from Nubia and other Egyptian sites have now been almost entirely digitized and will in the future be linked to the MFA collections database.

Fig 4.6 George Andrew Reisner. Courtesy of the Museum
of Fine Arts, Boston.

Though her funding for these excavations ceased in 1905, Hearst continued to fund the publication of the excavation reports for the large, multi-period cemetery site of Naga ed-Deir—an important scientific contribution.[16]

Fortunately for Reisner, support of the excavations both in Egypt and later Nubia was continued by donors to the Museum of Fine Arts, Boston, and enabled the joint Museum of Fine Arts–Harvard University Egyptian Expedition to bring a wealth of Old Kingdom and Nubian material to Boston.

Not to be outdone, the Metropolitan Museum of Art in 1906 established the Department of Egyptian Art, with the support of J. Pierpont Morgan (Fig.4.7). The Department enticed Albert

Fig 4.7 John Pierpont Morgan at Khargeh. The Metropolitan Museum of Art, Egyptian Expedition Image.
© The Metropolitan Museum of Art.

M. Lythgoe, Reisner's assistant and curator at the Museum of Fine Arts, Boston, and his student Herbert Winlock away from Boston to head the new department and establish what would become a multi-part excavation and recording programme, which included digging at Lisht, Thebes, Wadi Natrun, Hierakonpolis and el-Khargeh Oasis, as well as a Graphic Section that recorded tombs and temples.

Morgan himself was a supporter on the ground as well as financially. In 1909, he began to make inspection trips to Egypt to visit the excavations and even commissioned his own steamer in 1911 from Thomas Cook, which he named *The Khargeh*, after a site he had particularly enjoyed visiting. He was also directly involved in the design of new galleries for the finds coming from Egypt, insisting that electric lights be installed to improve the visitor experience. In

Fig 4.8 Edward Stephen Harkness. The Metropolitan Museum of Art, Egyptian Expedition Image. © The Metropolitan Museum of Art.

1912, Morgan saw to the construction of a large excavation house at Thebes.[17]

The Metropolitan Museum benefited handsomely from 30 years of excavation in Egypt, acquiring a collection of Middle and New Kingdom art matching the quality and depth of Boston's Old Kingdom and Nubian collections.

Morgan fell ill in Egypt in 1913, and after his death, another trustee, Edward S. Harkness (Fig.4.8), became the principal supporter of the museum's expeditions. Harkness was the son of an early partner of John D. Rockefeller and a friend of Albert Lythgoe. Having inherited a huge fortune, he became a professional philanthropist. He funded the acquisition and installation of the Old Kingdom tomb of Perneb from Saqqara in 1913, which was sold to the Metropolitan Museum by the Egyptian government, and he contributed $200,000 towards the purchase of the Carnarvon Collection in 1926.[18] Perhaps his best-known gift was William, the blue faience hippopotamus figurine dating to the Middle Kingdom, which became an icon of the museum.[19]

Harkness made several trips up the Nile to visit the excavations, and in 1921 purchased a movie camera and arranged for the expedition's photographer, Harry Burton, to come to Hollywood in 1924 to be trained on it. A trove of reels of the excavations in progress

Fig 4.9 James Henry Breasted. Courtesy of the Oriental Institute of the University of Chicago.

that Burton and Lythgoe took in Thebes between 1922 and 1925 were found in the 1980s in a cupboard at Harkness's Long Island estate and have been transferred to new film stock.

Not to be outdone by Boston and New York, James Henry Breasted, (Fig.4.9) of the University of Chicago, conceived a project to copy 'all the inscriptions of Egypt and publish them', a project that he felt could be accomplished in 10–12 years by a team of six in a nine-month season at a cost of $10,000 a year (Fig.4.10).[20] In 1905, Breasted secured funding for the research from John D. Rockefeller Jr (Fig.4.11), whose fortune vastly surpassed those of other early supporters of work in Egypt, and who was the younger son of John Sr, one of the founders of the university.

Fig 4.10 Epigraphers recording at Medinet Habu. Courtesy of the Oriental Institute of the University of Chicago.

Breasted emphasized the role that photography would play in his new modern method of epigraphy, proposing to use modern photographic equipment for both its accuracy and efficiency. With a large-format camera the inscription was photographed head-on, eliminating distortion. A print was then made and the copyist—now called an epigrapher—annotated his readings, corrections, etc., directly on the print. This eventually evolved into what was called the Chicago House method, after the university's base in Luxor, where an artist drew the outlines of the reliefs and inscriptions directly on the photographic print. The print was then bleached away leaving the outline drawing to be collated by the epigrapher.[21]

Fig 4.11 *John Davison Rockefeller Jr. WikiCommons.*

Daniel Burnham, the noted architect of the 1893 Chicago Columbian Exposition, which was built adjacent to the new University of Chicago campus, is quoted as saying 'Make no small plans'.[22] Breasted certainly subscribed to this and in 1919 he founded the Oriental Institute at the university to study the rise and development of ancient civilizations. In 1924, he established the Epigraphic Survey of Egypt, which continues to operate to this day, and in 1930, the new Oriental Institute and Museum opened, largely designed by Breasted. By the time of his death, Breasted had raised almost $12 million from Rockefeller in support of projects and research.

Conclusion

Modern-day Egyptologists and archaeologists may fault their predecessors for their emphasis on monuments, élite cemeteries and inscriptions. Scholars, such as Winlock, thought in broad or macro terms. Winlock's goal was to reconstruct the history and civilization of ancient Egypt from excavations. Certainly, these excavators had the luxury of well-furnished dig houses, consistent funding and the ability to be in the field for extended periods. Much of their work has been published, though often by their successors.

Today's archaeologists focus more on the unseen and the micro level, bringing new scientific tools and methods such as C-14, magnetometry, ground penetrating radar, and satellite imagery to look for evidence of changes in the landscape and environment. Research focuses on cultural markers such as 'food ways' through the analyses of fauna and botanical evidence, and the health of the ancient population. It now takes longer to excavate a site, with many fewer workmen and more specialists, and with more tightly organized and limited excavation programs. While the early excavators thought in terms of reconstruction of the monuments, the emphasis now is on their conservation and protection from both human and natural forces.

The goal is still to recover the remains of ancient Egypt, to preserve and disseminate them both to donors and to the public at large. Anyone can read about current excavations on museum and university websites, view them in progress in television documentaries, visit reconstructions based on the recovered data and even walk virtually through an ancient Egyptian temple. However, none of them entirely removes the need for digging down carefully through layers of debris and searching for nearly invisible clues in the quest to unearth ancient Egypt.

Endnotes

1   Oliver, 2014: p. 121. Linden, 2007: pp. 210–16
2   Both the Museum of Fine Arts Boston and the Metropolitan Museum of Art were founded in 1870.
3   D'Alton, 1993: pp. 12–15
4   D'Alton, 1993: p. 9. The French had removed an obelisk of Ramses II from the Luxor Temple in 1831, while the British had taken the fallen mate of the New York obelisk to London in 1877.
5   Gorringe, 1882. D'Alton, 1993
6   Wilson, 1964: pp. 101–09
7   Bierbrier, 2012: pp. 440–41; Capart, 1936: pp. vii–xi
8   Adams, 2013: p. 186
9   Adams 2013: p. 302
10 Davis et al, 1904–12
11 Adams, 2013: pp. 307–14.
12 MMA accessions 06.1230 and 07.230
13 Thomas, 1995: pp. 56–58
14 Der Manuelian, 1992
15 http://www.gizapyramids.org
16 Reisner et al. University of California Publications. Egyptian Archaeology, Vols. 1–5 (1905–30), Berkeley, California
17 Strouse, 1999: pp. 608–09 and 633–36
18 Tomkins, 1970: pp. 139–40
19 MMA 17.9.1, http://metmuseum.org/art/colleciton/search/544227
20 Abt, 2011: pp. 117–18
21 Abt, 2011: pp. 281–301
22 Burnham (1907) quoted in: Charles Moore (1921). *Daniel H. Burnham, Architect, Planner of Cities.* Vol. 2, Chap. XXV 'Closing in 1911–1912': p.147

Bibliography

Abt, Jeffrey (2011) *American Egyptologist: The Life of James Henry Breasted and the Creation of His Oriental Institute.* Chicago and London, The University of Chicago Press.
Adams, John M. (2013) *The Millionaire and the Mummies: Theodore Davis's Gilded Age in the Valley of the Kings.* New York, St Martin's Press.
Bierbrier, M. L. (ed.) (2012) *Who Was Who in Egyptology*, 4th revised edition. London, The Egypt Exploration Society.

Capart, Jean (ed.) (1936) *Travels in Egypt [December 1880 to May 1891]: Letters of Charles Edwin Wilbour*. Brooklyn, Brooklyn Museum.

D'Alton, Martina (1993) *The New York Obelisk or How Cleopatra's Needle Came to New York and What Happened When It Got There*. New York, The Metropolitan Museum of Art/Abrams.

Davis, Theodore et al. (1904–12) *Excavations: Bibân el-Molûk*. London, Constable.

Gorringe, Henry H. (1882) *Egyptian Obelisks*. New York, published by the author.

Linden, Blanche M. G. (2007) *Silent City on a Hill: Picturesque Landscapes of Memory and Boston's Mount Auburn Cemetery*. Amherst and Boston, University of Massachusetts Press.

Oliver, Andrew (2014) *American Travelers on the Nile: Early U.S. Visitors to Egypt, 1774–1839*. Cairo and New York, The American University of Cairo Press.

Reisner, George Andrew et al (1908). *The Early Dynastic Cemeteries of Naga ed Der*. Berkley, University of California Press.

Strouse, Jean (1999) *Morgan, American Financier*. New York, Random House.

Thomas, Nancy. 'American Institutional Fieldwork in Egypt 1899–1960', pp. 49–75, in *The American Discovery of Ancient Egypt: Catalogue* (1995) Nancy Thomas (ed.). Los Angeles, Los Angeles County Museum of Art and American Research Center in Egypt.

Tomkins, Calvin (1970) *Merchants and Masterpieces: The Story of the Metropolitan Museum of Art*. New York, E. P. Dutton.

A Bostonian in Egypt at the Dawn of Photography

Andrew Oliver

Henry B. Humphrey of Boston, 30 years old, arrived in Alexandria, Egypt, on 15 November 1839, and expressed his first vision of the city upon landing in words that many European and American travellers had used and would write again and again in their journals and published memoirs:

> It would be difficult for any one who lives at all among the things of this world to discern of the departed glory of Egypt when first entering this fallen city.... ambling donkeys, loaded camels, dirty half naked, two eyed and one eyed Arabs... swarms of flies, yelping dogs, and apprehensions of the plague.... I groped my way for some distance through narrow streets totally forgetting what I had come for and that there were such things as obelisks, pyramids and ruined temples.'

What Humphrey did not realize, and did not know during his time there, was that he had arrived only 11 days after the first photographers to reach Egypt. Following the presentation by François Arago at the Académie des Sciences in Paris in mid-August 1839 of the process perfected by Louis-Jacques-Mandé Daguerre, any number of entrepreneurs acquired the equipment and chemicals necessary to make daguerreotypes and set off on their travels. In the autumn of 1839 two photographers arrived in Egypt. One was Frédéric-Auguste-Antoine Goupil who came with his colleague and teacher, the well-known painter Horace Vernet.[1] The other was Pierre-Gustave Joly de Lotbinière, a Swiss-born Quebecois. By coincidence, both photographers arrived in Alexandria from the Greek island of Syra on 4 November aboard the same steamer, the French 'pacquebot' *Rhamses.*

Goupil published an account of his trip to Egypt with Vernet, in 1843.[2] Joly kept a journal, now in his archives in Quebec, which was only published in 2010.[3] Henry Humphrey also kept a journal, but that has never been published. It is owned by the Massachusetts Historical Society in Boston, and is the source for much of the narrative in this article.

Let us start by asking who was Henry Humphrey? And along the way ask how his visit to Egypt compared with visits by other Americans of the day, not to mention the far greater number of Europeans, including hundreds of British who were passing through Egypt each year on their passage to India.

Henry Benjamin Humphrey was born in Boston in October 1809, the seventh generation of Humphreys in America. His five times great-grandfather on his father's side had came from England to Dorchester, near Boston, in 1643. His mother's family had settled in Massachusetts even earlier, in 1630. He attended school in Boston but did not go to Harvard College. Instead, after first apprenticing with a firm of importers and dry goods merchants, he formed a mercantile partnership with John H. Pearson.[4] Approaching 30, and having made a small fortune, he decided to travel abroad. He left Boston on 19 April 1839, by the local steamer *Rhode Island* for New York via Stonington, and then on 2 May he took passage on the packet ship *St. James* from New York bound for London. Travelling with him from Boston was Joseph Langdon, a merchant who had long been a resident of Smyrna in Turkey, where he had married the daughter of an Anglo-Swiss merchant and now had several young children.[5] It is likely that Langdon persuaded Humphrey to travel at least as far as Turkey, if not in fact all the way to Egypt.

In any event, after visiting London, Humphrey went to Hamburg, Amsterdam, Leiden, Rotterdam, Brussels, Cologne, going up the Rhine to Koblenz, to Mainz and Frankfurt. In the Natural History Museum in Frankfurt, he saw the remarkable collection brought from Egypt, Nubia, and the Red Sea by Eduard Rüppell, a native of Frankfurt who was in Egypt and Nubia from 1822 to 1825.[6] Then he went on to Baden-Baden, Zurich, Berne, and Lyons – going to church and the opera everywhere.

Humphrey reached Marseilles on 1 September. From there he took passage on the French steamer *Scamandre* for Malta, where he changed to the steamer *Tancred* and went via Syra to Smyrna. Arriving there on 23 September, he saw, among others, Joseph Langdon, his travelling companion from New York to London. From Smyrna Humphrey went to Constantinople for several weeks, meeting everybody, seeing everything. Finally on 8 November, 'having received an invitation from Captain Ford of the Turkish steamer *Peki Sherket*[7] to take passage with him to Alexandria, it being a special voyage to convey the Persian Princes & suite, I accordingly accepted & in a hurried manner settled my bills and took leave of my numerous friends.'

At one o'clock, Humphrey and two fellow European passengers boarded a caique to go out to the steamer. And he added in his diary:

> After waiting an hour for the arrival of the Princes the steamer got under weigh & in a few moments bid adieu to Constantinople upon its seven hills & the last sound which struck my ear was the Allah [muezzin] heard from the minarets calling all the faithful to prayer. The party consists of one Prince who was formerly a King of Persia, but supplanted and dethroned by a nephew; he with two brothers & a young man, first cousin to the present King accompanied by about 40 noblemen, slaves, eunuchs, &c. Their appearance is very imposing in the different vagaries of costumes. Their manner of eating is rather beastly, the food being conveyed to the mouth by their fingers, & using rich embroidered napkins. Had the pleasure of playing a game of draughts with one of them. He was not particular which way he moved. They are making a pilgrimage to Mecca to visit the tomb of Mahommed.

The Prince, Hulagu Mirza, dethroned by a nephew, was now living in exile in Constantinople to avoid imprisonment or death.[8] With these passengers in mind, Captain Ford needed English-speaking support, so he invited Humphrey to come along as his guest, joining two other westerners aboard. They stopped briefly in Smyrna, where Humphrey did some banking, and where Mr Lee, a member of an English expatriate merchant family in Smyrna, joined them, and then steamed on to Alexandria.

In the course of his stay in Egypt, into March 1840, Humphrey reported meeting ten fellow Americans, ten continental Europeans, and more than 30 British travellers. But he never said a word about the two photographers who, by the time he arrived, had set up their equipment.

He had two companions in Egypt: Thomas Weir and Captain J. B. Petre. Weir was a Scotsman whom he had met in Constantinople and had come with him on the steamer via Smyrna to Alexandria. Humphrey first met Petre – surely John Berney Petre – in Cairo around 27 November. All three travelled on the Nile together with Humphrey's dragoman, Hassan.

On 28 November, two weeks after he arrived in Egypt, Humphrey met George Gliddon, the young British-born American consul in Cairo, to whom he had letters of introduction from Mr Churchill in Constantinople and Joseph Langdon in Smyrna. The same day, he met Henry Abbott, the British self-styled doctor, and a man long resident in Egypt, whom everyone went to see, and who at the time was secretary of the Egyptian Society – 'a rendezvous for travellers' founded in 1836 that possessed a modest library. That very evening, Humphrey went to the theatre to see an Italian comedy. During his time here, he saw all the sights of Cairo in the company of various English and continental travellers.

On 1 December, Humphrey saw his first fellow American, namely George Sumner of Boston, who had just returned from Thebes and was afflicted with the eye disease ophthalmia. When Humphrey was first in Smyrna in October, he had heard about Sumner from Joseph Langdon who 'told me that Sumner, son of the late sheriff Sumner [Charles Pinckey Sumner, sheriff of Suffolk County, Mass.] was supposed in Constantinople to have been employed by the Russian government as a spy & letters were received in Smyrna to that effect.' Travelling with Sumner was David Bushnell whom Humphrey met several days later, 'a gent from Ohio... an odd fish & green from the wilds of Kentucky.' Bushnell is known to those who study graffiti of Europeans on Egyptian monuments as one who left a disfiguring signature and the date 14 November 1839 in the Rock Tombs at El Kab. Some days later, Sumner took Humphrey to a tailor, who had made him an American flag, to have one made for Humphrey.

George Sumner should not be confused with his more famous older brother Charles, who ultimately became a Senator from Massachusetts and a noted abolitionist. Charles Sumner had sailed for Europe only two months before George, and had spent three years studying in Paris and elsewhere. George left on a cargo ship in March 1838 bound via Denmark for St Petersburg. After several months of meeting people including the Czar, he left for Moscow, the Crimea, Odessa, Constantinople and Smyrna. Sumner's high level contacts in Russia probably accounted for the unlikely rumour that he was a spy. Now in the autumn of 1839 he was in Egypt, where he would remain until mid-March 1840. Unlike his brother Charles, who returned home in 1840, George Sumner remained abroad for more than a decade.[9] No diary of Sumner's eastern tour is known to exist.

In the evening of 5 December, Humphrey met another fellow countryman, Stebbins June, 'an American from New York who is out in pursuit of zoological subjects. He has already a beautiful female giraffe in Mr. Gliddon's charge.'

While in Cairo, before setting forth on the Nile, Humphrey saw a number of British travellers who were about to ascend the Nile just as he was, among them a Mr Leighton and Mr Drummond travelling together, and Mr Worsley and Mr Mundy. He also met a group of Englishmen waiting for the steamer from Suez to Bombay, among them Captain Smyth of the Bengal Engineers, Colin MacKenzie of the Madras Service and George Alexander Bushby, secretary to the government of India, not to mention Patrick Francis Robertson of the house of Turner & Co, Canton, and Joseph M. Smith of Canton, both of whom were travelling all the way to China. And indeed all of these travellers and many besides, 48 in total, took passage on the steamer *Berenice* from Suez and arrived in Bombay on 10 January 1840.[10]

In addition to British travellers, Humphrey met the classical archaeologist, Peter Wilhelm Forchhammer.[11] He missed seeing the Hon. George and Mary Georgina Dawson-Damer – she wrote an account of their trip – who had arrived in Cairo from Suez on 30 December, after Humphrey had left on his Nile excursion, and had left Alexandria for Malta on 25 January, before his return.[12] He also missed seeing the departure of the host of pilgrims, including the Persian princes, for Mecca on 28 December.

On 9 December, after hoisting their national flags, American and British, Humphrey and his two companions, Weir and Petre, set forth on their Nile excursion. Humphrey tells us what he was reading at the time. Just before leaving Cairo, he spent the best part of a day going through Conder's *Egypt*, and once underway he read Lord Byron. Every American traveller to the Mediterranean read Lord Byron.

At the opening of the New Year, Humphrey set down some private thoughts:

> What mingled emotions of pleasure and pain fill my heart on the commencement of another year of my pilgrimage on earth. Alas! How checkered & various have been the scenes through which I have been permitted to pass by an all seeing, pervading & merciful providence. In the deepest humility to I bend down to seek forgiveness for past follies and offenses & render thanks for all blessings & do pray for a continuance not only for myself but for all mankind. Bless and preserve all those to whom I am more closely allied & bring me to the close of another year better fitted & proper to enjoy what may be left in store for me.

The next day, 2 January, they arrived at Dendera and visited the ruins. There Humphrey saw the name of Lowell carved into a stone with the date 'Sept 16 1839', a name he knew to be that of the Rev. Dr Charles Lowell.[13] In Constantinople, Humphrey had seen Lowell's name in his hotel register with a mid-July date, so it cannot have been a total surprise to see his name here.

While they were at Dendera, Humphrey missed seeing the photographer Pierre-Gustave Joly de Lotbinière who went up the Nile, unlike his fellow photograper Goupil – who remained in Lower Egypt. In his diary, Joly says he left Thebes on 1 January, taking eight days to return to Cairo. He probably passed Dendera on or about 2 January. Regrettably, no American writes of meeting Joly, but he is well remembered in the published diary of the English traveller, the Hon. Mrs Dawson-Damer. She says that she met him first in Athens when she and her husband were on their way to Constantinople with Lord Alvanley[14]– there she calls him merely Mr. de L— and she met him again after he had reached Cairo from Thebes. On 10 January she wrote, 'We found our Athens acquaintance, Mr. J. de L—, who has just arrived from Thebes, with a series of beautiful daguerrotypes of all the principal monuments.'[15] And Joly himself wrote in his diary,[16] '*Je rencontrai aussi au Caire le colonel Damer qui arrivait de Jérusalem par le désert.*'

By 4 January, Humphrey and his companions reached Thebes where they spent several days. On 7 January, he wrote in his diary, 'Started early in the ferry boat taking donkeys & crossed over the river where after landing rode on to the ruins of Medinet Habu & spent several hours there & chiselled my name on one of the propylons.'

His name[17] can still be read there: HB Humphrey/Jan 7 1840/Boston/USA

They travelled as far south as Abu Simbel which they reached on 23 January, and where, as on every day on the Nile, Humphrey wrote several pages in his diary, beginning and ending as follows:

> Moored alongside of the small temple of Ebsamboul at twelve o'clock last night. On looking out of my cabin window at day break the first object which presented itself to me were six colossal statues cut into the rock of sandstone which are said to represent Rameses II and his queen. After breakfast proceeded on shore with guide & candles to examine the interior. My expectations have been more than fully realized. It is certain a most astonishing monument of the great conception of the ancient Egyptians.... At 3 o'clock I rose to depart (my comrades having already regained the boat), feeling some compunction of conscience for having chiselled my name upon the fine proportioned calf of Rameses' queen. Having made such slow progress for the past two days without incidents of any sort that it had accustomed me a certain dullness of spirits which I am happy to record are entirely removed today by a sight of the noblest monument of antiquity which is to be seen on the Nile.

Only part of his inscription[18] remains today: HB H[]/BO[   ]/U.S.A/1840

While on the Nile, especially above Luxor, Humphrey continued to meet travellers, British and American. On 24 January, at Dehr, after starting downstream, he was hailed by George Gliddon, who was now travelling with Anthony C. Harris, a British collector and archaeologist resident in Alexandria. It was on this trip that Gliddon and Harris found one of the famous boundary stelae of Akhenaton.[19] (Gliddon says he kept a diary: where is it now?) On 27 January, he saw the English duo, Robert Tassell and his son also named Robert. Tassell's letters to his daughter in the form of a journal are preserved in the Middle East Centre at St Anthony's College, Oxford.[20]

On 29 January at Philae, Humphrey saw Fairfax Catlett of Virginia and his wife Esther Ann of New York (Fig.5.1).[21]

Fig 5.1 Esther Catlett, Oil on canvas, c. 1838. Photograph courtesy Carlsen Gallery, Inc., Freehold, New York.

Fairfax Catlett, Yale class of 1829, had married Esther Ann Laverty in May 1838, and now, a year and a half later, they were on an extended European tour and had reached Egypt. Humphrey said that he was 'in bad health being afflicted with pulmonary affection'. Some days earlier, on 23 January, the Catletts were seen at Luxor by Henry Edward Fane who, returning to England from Bombay, had left the steamer at Cossier, a port on the Red Sea, and had come overland to Luxor in order to see the sites on the Nile.[22] A little over a week later, at Abu Simbel, the Tassells met up with the Catletts and travelled with them *in tandem* nearly all the way back to Cairo.

Also at Philae on 29 January, the same day that Humphrey had met Fairfax Catlett and his wife, he climbed one of the propylons, after copying the famous French inscription, and wrote in his diary:

> While on the top of the propylon I saw an English boat and four travellers [sic] appear among the ruins. On descending I found my companion Petre in conversation with one of them who happened to be an acquaintance of his & to whom I was introduced, Mr. Thomas. He accompanied us to our boat & enjoyed an hour's agreeable chit chat over a bottle of claret, enjoying at the same time a fine Spanish cigar which was really a luxury.

Mr Thomas was travelling with three Austrians, one of them Count Koller (Culla, as Humphrey spells it), secretary of the Austrian Embassy in Berlin, his brother and a third Austrian. (I am unable to identify Mr Thomas.) 'Count Koller' is surely Baron August von Koller (1805–83) who served as counsellor in a number of European embassies. His brother was either 29-year-old Wilhelm or 27-year-old Alexander, sons of the then late Franz Freiherr von Koller, one of the commissioners who accompanied Napoleon to Elba,[23] and an enlightened gentleman who had formed great collections of Greek vases (now in Berlin) and Egyptian antiquities (now in Leipzig).

A few days later, on 2 February, further downstream at Kom Ombos, Humphrey met James Ewing Cooley of New York and his wife Louisa, who were travelling together with Stephen Olin, president elect of Wesleyan College in Connecticut. Stebbins June, the animal tracker, was their guide. Louisa Cooley was an Appleton, and one of her brothers had sailed from New York for London with Humphrey back in May 1839. Cooley wrote his own account, which was published by his wife's father Daniel Appleton, but since he turned his story into a parody of travel and an attack on the habits of everyone he met he cites no one by their real name.[24] This is the book which prompted a scornful 20-page review by George R. Gliddon, who was then the former American Consul in Cairo.[25]

Stephen Olin also published an account, and in that he mentions meeting Humphrey:[26] 'At 7 o'clock this evening we met a downward bound boat with the American flag flying at her missen-mast, and the English at her stern. Mr. Humphreys [sic], of Boston, an affable Scotch gentleman, and an English military officer were on board, with whom we passed an agreeable hour about a mile below the passage of the river through the pass called Hadjar of Jebel Silsily.'

Where fellow Americans were met in the course of their travels, what were the subjects of their conversations? Olin was a recent widower, and in one of his travel accounts he reports that the Lowell family was with him in Naples in May 1839 at the time his wife had died. In Trieste in November 1839 he had seen the Lowell family on their return from the East.[27] And while in Trieste Olin had also seen the Catletts, as well as Professor Moore of Columbia College, all three bound for Egypt. More likely than not they traded stories of the Americans they had met along the way.

On 5 February, back in Luxor, Humphrey encountered five boats with European travellers: namely Mr St Leger (the *touriste anglais* seen by the photographer Joly de Lotbinière);[28] John Shae Perring, the pyramid expert, and his wife Elizabeth;[29] Rev. Henry Formby travelling with Benjamin Clarkson and a Mr Worsley;[30] Mr Thomas, Baron Koller, his brother, and a third Austrian whom he had seen at Philae; and Messrs Drummond and Leighton whom he had seen in Cairo in November.

In addition, Humphrey encountered the young John Saville Lumley travelling with his two brothers. They were the sons of Lord Scarborough: two letters Lumley wrote to his father are preserved in the Nottinghamshire Record Office. Humphrey saw them several times on the Nile from 7 to 20 February. Continuing downstream to Asiout, Humphrey wrote this in his diary for 11 February: 'Shortly after sundown two boats hove in sight passing up the river which on saluting, the first proved to be English: Mr. Moreland, Lady & child, the other American, Mr. N. F. Moore of New York who moored his board a short distance beyond us. Called aboard & spent a half hour very agreeably.'

The American was Nathaniel Fish Moore of New York, whom Stephen Olin might have mentioned to him some days earlier. Moore, Professor of Greek and Latin at Columbia College, had recently been appointed head librarian at the College and now at the age of 57 was celebrating this appointment by taking an extended trip abroad. It was not his first trip: some years earlier he had travelled around Europe for nearly two years, and before leaving on that trip Moore had had his portrait painted by the American artist Henry Inman (Fig.5.2).[31] In 1842, soon after his return to New York, Moore was elected the eighth president of Columbia College.

Fig 5.2 Nathaniel Fish Moore, by Henry Inman, 1836. Columbia University, New York, Avery Architectural and Fine Arts Library.

Regrettably, while he was in Egypt, Humphrey missed meeting Edward Joy Morris of Philadelphia, who also published an account of his travels.[32] Morris had left Cairo for his Nile excursion with a Venetian gentleman, a Mr L., on 27 December, some two and a half weeks after Humphrey. He reached Dendera on 11 January and Assuan by 18 January. He was back in Luxor at the very end of January and returned to Cairo on 18 February. There, he reported in his diary that he just missed meeting Mr E. J. Morris of Philadelphia who had left to travel across Sinai. In fact, while on the Nile, Humphrey and Morris cannot have been far from one another because Lord Alvanley, one of the Arden brothers, who had travelled with the Dawson-Damers to Greece and Constantinople, and was also known to the photographer Joly de Lotbinière, was on his way up the Nile at the same time, and was seen by Humphrey and Morris only one day apart. Humphrey saw his boat – without actually meeting him – at Dehr on 24 January, Morris saw him at Esneh on 25 January. Humphrey did not meet a Scottish gentleman and his wife who were seen by his fellow American Mr Morris, which was a pity because Morris said that they had a complete set of the *Description de l'Égypte* on board their boat.

Humphrey was back in Cairo on 18 February, after two months and a week on the Nile.

The Cooleys, Stebbins June, and Stephen Olin arrived a few days later having gone as far south as Aswan. In Cairo, Humphrey spent a little over two weeks conducting banking business and purchasing supplies necessary for the desert journey across the desert to Suez, Sinai and St Catherine's monastery, and beyond to Palestine. He left on 6 March together with one of his former companions, Thomas Weir, and his dragoman Hassan. In Suez, they met the Rev. Henry Formby and his companion Benjamin Clarkson, whom they had seen earlier on the Nile at Luxor. Arriving at St Catherine's monastery on 15 March, they realized that they had been preceded by a large party of travellers: Robert Tassell and his son, Mr Thomas and his three Austrian companions (Baron Koller, his brother and a friend), the Cooleys and Stephen Olin, a Mr Carrington travelling with Olin, and an Italian gentleman, apparently the Venetian companion of Edward Joy Morris, Mr L., now on his own, and whom Humphrey names as Mr Levy – although this does not sound very Venetian. Despite letters of introduction from the Greek convent in Cairo, the monks were completely surprised and did not know where to put them. Some had to vacate their own rooms to house them. And contrary to custom, the monks could provide only bread, dates, olives, dried fish and water, but no meat because it was Lent.

On 18 March, eight of their party opted to go to Gaza and from there to Jerusalem instead of taking in Petra. They included Mr Thomas and his three Austrian companions, the Cooleys, Stephen Olin, and the Venetian, Mr Levy. But discussion among themselves that evening persuaded the eight to change their minds and stay with the others, namely Humphrey and his companion, Mr Weir, the Tassells (father and son), the Rev. Henry Formby and his companion Benjamin Clarkson, and Mr Carrington. As a result, the entire party left St Catherine's monastery for Aqaba.[33] Arriving there on 24 March, they found Edward Joy Morris of Philadelphia camped on the beach, about to depart for Gaza. Morris went with them, for a second time, to Petra. This large party of 16, not counting servants, left Aqaba on 27 March, and arrived at Petra a few days later, after admiring along the way the oleanders, wild fig, capers and eagles screaming overhead. They marvelled at the site for several days and then moved on to Hebron and Bethlehem, reaching Jerusalem in time for Holy Week. Humphrey was sick for the whole of week. In Jerusalem, Humphrey learned that Carrington's servant's name was Paul – perhaps Paolo Nuzzo who had travelled some years earlier with the American John L. Stephens.

After visiting Baalbec but not Damascus, Humphrey left Beirut on 21 May on the Austrian steamer *Seri Pervis* together with the Americans Nathaniel Fish Moore, the Catletts, Stephen Olin and several British friends, all bound for Smyrna. Once there, he took off his Turkish clothes and through his friend Langdon arranged to take daily lessons in French. One of his teachers was an American, Asa Giles Alexander (Yale class of 1836), who went on to spend the rest of his life as a teacher in Smyrna. He saw several fellow Americans who had been travelling in Egypt: within days of his arrival he met John S. Miller of Philadelphia and Daniel Low of New York and Low's daughter Anna.[34] On 9 July, Humphrey saw Low and his daughter again on their return from Constantinople.

In mid-August, Humphrey went on board one of the French steamers to see three more Americans – Mr Lewis of Connecticut and Messrs Preston and Dehon of Virginia, who had been travelling together in Egypt.[35] Otherwise, Humphrey spent the entire summer – June to September – in the polite company of American and British expatriate merchants and officers of the United States Mediterranean squadron, dining out, going to the opera, travelling in the country, and occasionally having a *'pic-nic'* with friends. Humphrey had no wish to go home, but nor had he any other business to keep him in Smyrna.

Humphrey next travelled through parts of Greece, and arrived in Valletta in Malta in mid-December. Freed from the lazaretto on 20 December, Humphrey remained in Valletta for two months. There, he hob-nobbed with everyone of importance, and met people passing through Malta to points east and west. He met Messrs Oliver and Colt off the steamer *Megara* from Marseilles before they took the steamer *Great Liverpool* to Alexandria. Oliver was Thomas Oliver of Baltimore, who had gone to Paris with his wife, three children and two nannies and was now leaving them there to go to Egypt with his nephew John Oliver Colt of Paterson, New Jersey. One of Thomas Oliver's elder brothers, Henry, by then long deceased, had gone to Egypt 12 years earlier, in 1829.[36] Humphrey met two more Americans coming from Alexandria on the return trip of the *Great Liverpool*, Messrs Kennik and Aymar. Kennik was probably William Kennik, who had obtained a passport the previous August. Aymar was either Augustus or John Q. Aymar Jr., 22-year-old twins from a wealthy New York merchant family, who had left New York together about 17 May 1840.[37] It is not known which one visited Egypt.

As Humphrey's diary ends, on 28 February 1841, he says he is about to go to Sicily. He stayed abroad over two more years, probably spending much of the time in Paris. Why otherwise had he been learning French in Smyrna, if not to socialize in Paris? Moreover, he says that travelling with him from Greece to Malta in December had been Comte Olivier de la Rochfoucaud[38] who had given him 'many important memorandums for my guidance on arriving in Paris'. Yet we known nothing about his time there.

At last, in June 1843, he returned home to New York from London bearing, as newspapers put it, 'despatches from our Minister at the Court of St James to the Government at Washington'.[39] A year later, in July 1844, he was in Saratoga, in up-state New York, where he had his silhouette cut by the French artist Auguste Edouart – a silhouette now in a portfolio at the Metropolitan Museum of Art (Fig.5.3).[40] I have been unable to find his image in a photograph or any portrait in oil.

Humphrey had obviously become acquainted with diplomatic personalities in Washington, as well as in European capitals, because in February 1846 he was nominated by President James K. Polk 'to be Consul for the port of Alexandria, in Egypt', to succeed Alexander Tod (who was John Gliddon's son-in-law).[41] He was confirmed by the Senate in April. This was a splendid honour following what had started out six years earlier as a wide-ranging tour and long residence in Europe.

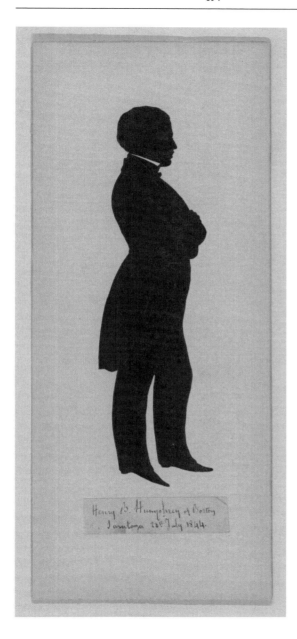

Fig 5.3 Henry B. Humphrey. Silhouette by Auguste Edouart, 1844. Cut paper. 21 x 57.5 cms. The Metropolitan Museum of Art, 50.602.625. Bequest of Glenn Tilley Morse 1950.

Before continuing, we should consider the careers of the other Americans whom Humphrey met in Egypt. George Sumner remained abroad in western Europe for another decade, travelling widely but calling Paris his home, meeting and corresponding with men of science and letters. He returned to the United States in 1852. His travelling companion, David Bushnell of Ohio, disappeared from the record. Fairfax Catlett was afflicted with a pulmonary 'affection' (*sic* – as Humphrey noted). In any event, it is clear that he had consumption (tuberculosis) and this prompted him and his wife Esther Ann to return to Egypt seeking relief in the dry air. Sadly, he died in Cairo in 1843. The Cooleys returned to New York with a baby girl and James published what many considered then and still do today, a rather foolish account of their tour, but more importantly, he resumed his business as a bookseller and auctioneer. Stephen Olin, travelling with the Cooleys, and president elect of Wesleyan College in Middleton, Connecticut, returned to assume this position. A widower, he remarried in 1843 and remained at Wesleyan until his death in 1851. Stebbins June, their companion on board and guide, who had come to Egypt to capture giraffes, maintained his career as a man of the menagerie, bringing wild animals to the United States, and working for a concern that ultimately became P. T. Barnum's circus. Nathaniel Fish Moore became president of Columbia College in 1842 but resigned in 1849. He travelled abroad again in 1851, and was fascinated by demonstrations of photography at the Crystal Palace Exhibition in London, taking up photography himself and producing both fine landscapes and portraits, a fair number of which survive in the archives of Columbia University Library. Edward Joy Morris, whom Humphrey missed seeing on the Nile, but caught up with on their trek to Petra, entered public life. He was a member of the Pennsylvania House of Representatives (1841–43), served briefly in the US Congress, was Chargé d'Affaires in Naples (1850–53) and served again in the US Congress (1857–61); then, owing to a long interest in the Mediterranean, he was appointed by Abraham Lincoln to be Minister Resident to Turkey, a position he held until the end of the decade.

Now what about the opportunity offered to Henry Humphrey? In April 1846, three months after Humphrey was confirmed as Consul for Alexandria, James Buchanan, then Secretary of State, wrote to him granting his request to delay his departure for 60 days owing to an alarming illness in the family.[42] And in fact one of his sisters, Oriens Turner Humphrey (named after their mother), died in Cambridge on 18 September 1846. Yet there was another more profound change in his personal life. On an unknown date, he married Pastora Elizabeth Mason of Thomaston, Maine. Humphrey's diary reveals that this was not a new attachment: on two pages, he lists the addressees of 40 letters he wrote beginning in England in June 1839 and carrying on to Cairo in March 1840: in addition to those to his two brothers, his former partner (John H. Pearson) and other business colleagues, the name P. E. Mason appears seven times. In the end, Humphrey declined the appointment to go to Alexandria on the grounds that the post was not raised from Consul to that of Consul-General. Was that a genuine or specious reason? Consider this: when his successor Daniel S. Macauley took the position on 31 October 1848,[43] and arrived in Alexandria in February 1849, his title was Consul-General.

Instead of a diplomatic career, Henry moved to Thomaston and spent much of the rest of his life focusing on his wife and their fine house. The house, built in the late 1790s, was demolished around 1939, but photographs give a fine idea of its stately three-storey façade. He was clearly a leading citizen of the town. In August 1851, Thomaston appointed him chair of a committee to 'cause a block of granite, marble, or limestone to be prepared and send on for the Washington monument in the national capital'.[44] Some 200 other communities, societies, masonic lodges, states, and even foreign capitals, were doing the same.[45] The stones are still visible on the inside of the Washington monument, inscribed with the names of their donors. Local records say that Humphrey was a prominent Freemason, a member of the volunteer fire department and a member of the Artillery Company, and that when parading with the Artillery Company, he usually wore a Turkish military uniform. It was perhaps to add to the splendour of his uniform that he acquired from Tiffany in New York in 1863 an elaborate sword, a ceremonial weapon which figured recently in a sale of historic edged blades and firearms.[46] This can have been only one of many unusual acquisitions. Early in 1867, he was appointed as commissioner from Maine to the Paris Exposition of that year;[47] on this occasion, he gave a farewell banquet for his friends in Boston before leaving for Paris.

During his life, Humphrey formed an outstanding collection of books, more a private library than the careful acquisition of rare volumes. In a mention of activities in Thomaston during 1859, his library is cited as containing 3,000 volumes, far out numbering the holdings of the Ladies School and the Female School that, respectively, had some 400 and 800 books.[48] Humphrey's library was sold in Boston at a notable auction in 1871, where more than 11,000 volumes in over 3,400 lots raised a grand total of $25,873.84 (the equivalent of $500,000 today).[49] One of the works in the catalogue was Stephen Olin's two-volume account of the 1840 trip he had made in Egypt and elsewhere in the East in which, as we noted earlier, he and Humphrey had met. One volume of this very copy was recently offered for sale in Gloucester, Massachusetts, with a gilded stamp of Henry B. Humphrey, giving his name within a wreath with two angels above and a lyre flanked by anchors below; and in addition a note in his hand: 'Dr. S. Olin was a fellow-traveller with me in Egypt, Palestine, and Syria. He deceased at Middleton, Conn. August 16, 1851, H.B.H..'[50] More than ten years later that trip clearly still meant much to him.

According to the introduction of the 1871 auction catalogue, the books were in Newport, Rhode Island, already a fashionable New England town, where the Humphreys also owned a house. Indeed, a newspaper reported that their house was at the corner of Bull and Broad Streets.[51] Henry Humphrey died in Newport early the following year, 1872, and is buried in Mount Auburn Cemetery in Cambridge, Mass. After his death, his widow lived on in Newport, but little is known of her life there apart from a record that in 1879 she became a shareholder in the venerable Redwood Library, one of the oldest private subscription libraries in the United States.

Pastora Elizabeth Humphrey died in June 1889 and was also interred in Mount Auburn Cemetery. A year later, in 1890, a miniature portrait of herself done by Alvan Clark, perhaps at the time of her marriage, was lent to an exhibition in Newport.[52] In 1892, the first item in her will was announced: a bequest of $10,000 to Harvard College to establish the Henry B. Humphrey scholarship fund.[53] In addition, she left six paintings to the Redwood Library (one of which, a portrait of Abraham Lincoln is still there). And she left her diamond-studded jewellery to various in-laws; among the items was a 'diamond locket set in black with my late husband's likeness and hair inside' which was left to Henry's three married sisters *in seriatim* and then to their descendants. The sisters were Mary Ann, Caroline Amelia, and Elizabeth Louisa, married respectively to Francis W. Welch, Joseph Dorr, and Frederick Spelman Nichols, and who, by the time of Pastora's death, had all had children and grandchildren. Henry's two brothers, Francis and Benjamin, predeceased his widow, left no children, and are not named in her will. One of Pastora's executors was Joseph Dorr, the husband of Henry's middle sister; the other was William J. Swinburne, a long-time Newport resident, whose wife Mary Ann was born in Thomaston and must have been a friend of long standing. The number of legatees meant that the estate would go in many directions. The diary from which much of this account has been drawn was acquired in the book trade by the Massachusetts Historical Society in 1957. Where it was between the late 19th century and then is not known. More information about Henry Humphrey's life surely lurks in the record but it has yet to be found.

Endnotes

1   Michèle Hannoosh (2016) 'Horace Vernet's 'Orient': photography and the Eastern Mediterranean in 1839, part I: a daguerrean excursion', *The Burlington Magazine* clviii: pp. 264–70; M. Hannoosh (2016) 'Horace Vernet's 'Orient': part II: the daguerreotypes and their texts', *The Burlington Magazine* clviii: pp. 430–39.

2   F. Goupil-Fesquet (1843) *Voyage d'Horace Vernet en Orient*, Paris. Engravings made from his daguerreotypes were published in *Excursions Daguerriennes. Vues et monuments les plus remarquables du Globe*. Paris, 1842.

3   Jacques Desautels, Georges Aubin, Renée Blanchet, eds. (2010) *Voyage en Orient (1839–1840). Journal d'un voyageur curieux du monde et d'un pionnier de la daguerreotype*, Quebec. Aquatints made from his daguerreotypes were published in Hector Horeau (1841), *Panorama d'Égypte et de Nubie avec un portrait de Méhémet-Ali*, Paris.

4   *The New England Historical and Genealogical Register*, Vol. 27, 1873: pp. 197–98. *Memorial Biographies of the New-England Historic Genealogical Society*, VII, 1907: pp. 18–19.

5   Joseph Langdon (1799--1870), Tom Rees (2003) *Merchant Adventurers in the Levant: Two British Families of Privateers, Consuls and Traders 1700–1950*. Stawell, Somerset: pp. 114–16. The French artist Charles Gleyre, travelling with the American John Lowell in 1834, did a watercolor of 'Madame Langdon', an image now in the Lowell collection at the Museum of Fine Arts, Boston: William Hauptman, *Charles Gleyre 1806-1874*, Princeton, 1996, Vol. 2: p. 98. fig. 173.

6   Eduard Rüppell (1794–1884) (1829) *Reisen in Nubien, Kordofan und den Peträischen Arabien*. Frankfurt.

7   The *Peki Sherket* (Powerful messenger), formerly the *Phocéen*, had been acquired by the Sultan in 1837 from the French: Daniel Panzac (2012) *La marine ottoman. De l'apogée à la chute de l'Empire*. Paris: p. 295.

8   Briony Llewellyn (2003) 'David Wilkie and John Frederick Lewis in Constantinople, 1840: an artistic dialogue', *The Burlington Magazine*, 145: pp. 624–31. I am grateful to Briony Llewellyn for bringing her article, with illustrations of the prince in question, to my attention and to her and Charles Newton for providing additional details and descriptions of the prince.

9   Robert C. Waterston (1880) 'Memoir of George Sumner', *Proceedings of the Massachusetts Historical Society* xviii: pp. 189–223. George Sumner contributed at least one letter to American newspapers recounting his travels: *The Friend: a Religious and Literary Journal*, Jan. 9, 1841, reprinting a letter dated 'Grand Cairo, March 15, 1840'. Letters of George

Sumner, *Proceedings of the Massachusetts Historical Society* 46, 1912–13: pp. 341–70, but none from Egypt.

10 *Asiatic Journal and Monthly Register* n.s xxxi, (January–April). London, April 1840: p. 397, listing their names.

11 Peter Wilhelm Forchhammer (1801–94) travelled in Italy, Greece, Asia Minor and Egypt, 1838–40.

12 The Hon. Mrs. G. L. Dawson Damer (1841) *Diary of a Tour in Greece, Turkey, Egypt and the Holy Land*, 2 vols. London.

13 Charles Lowell (1782–1861), Harvard class of 1800, was travelling with his wife Harriet and one of their daughters, Rebecca Russell Lowell (1809–73). Lowell and his family left Boston May 1837, returning home summer 1840: 'Charles Lowell', *Memorial Biographies of the New England Historic Genealogical Society*, Vol. 4, Boston, 1885: pp. 134–69 (tour on pp. 158–63). No diary is known to exist, but Lowell published an account of one part of the tour and comments on several parts in [Charles Lowell], 'Sermon XLVII, Jerusalem' and 'Notes to the Sermon on Jerusalem and Syria' in: *Sermons: Chiefly Pratical*, Boston, 1855: pp. 341–62. For part of the time, Major Thomas Best Jervis (1796–1857) travelled with them: *Proceedings of the Massachusetts Historical Society,* April 1898: pp. 191–92.

14 William Arden, 2nd Baron Alvanley (1789–1849), noted bachelor and spendthrift.

15 Dawson-Damer, *Diary of a Tour*, Vol. 2: p. 199.

16 *Voyage en Orient (1839–1840)*: p. 212.

17 Roger O. De Keersmaecker (2006) *Travellers' Graffiti from Egypt and the Sudan, V Thebes. The Temples of Medinet Habu*, Mortsel, Antwerp: p. 35.

18 Roger O. De Keersmaecker (2012) *Travellers' Graffiti from Egypt and the Sudan, additional volume. The Temples of Abu Simbel*, Mortsel, Antwerp: pp. 60 (place and date) and 152 (his fragmentary name). On the last day of 1842, a British traveller read his name, still fully legible, and that of one of his companions, T. Weir 1842, at Abu Simbel: diary of R. Bremner in the Beinecke Rare Books and Manuscripts Library at Yale University, Ms Osborn d159: p. 194.

19 Andrew Oliver (2014) *American Travelers on the Nile. Early U.S. Visitors to Egypt, 1774-1839*. Cairo: pp. 263 and fn 49.

20 I am grateful to David Kennedy for providing me with typescript copies he had made of Mr Tassell's letters.

21 Portrait of Esther Ann Catlett, oil-on-canvas, probably done on the occasion of her marriage. Reproduced by courtesy of Carlsen Gallery Inc., Freehold, New York where it figured in an auction in 2005.

22 Henry Edward Fane (1842) *Five Years in India... and Journey overland to England*, London, Vol. 2: p. 280. Anthony Sattin (1988/2011) *Lifting the Veil; Two Centuries of Travellers, Traders and Tourists in Egypt*. London: pp. 74–76.

23 Constant von Wurzbach (1864) *Biographisches Lexikon des Kaiserthums Oesterreich*, Vol. 12. Vienna: pp. 339–43.

24 James Ewing Cooley (1842) *The American in Egypt with rambles through Arabia Petraea wnd the Holy Land during the years 1839 and 1840*. New York.

25 [George R. Gliddon], *Appendix to 'The American in Egypt'*. Philadelphia, 1842.

26 Stephen Olin (1843) *Travels in Egypt, Arabia Petræa, and the Holy Land*, 2 vols. New York.

27 Stephen Olin (1853) *The Life and Letters of Stephen Olin, D.D., LL.D.* New York, Vol. 1: pp. 267 and 345.

28 Probably Anthony R. St. Leger of Waterford, Ireland, whose name, 'A. R. St. Leger', was seen cut at Abu Simbel by the British traveller R. Bremner in 1842 (diary in the Beinecke Rare Books and Manuscripts Library at Yale University), Ms Osborn d169: p. 194.

29 Patricia Usick (2001) 'A Portfolio and Diaries Belonging to J. S. Perring', *Göttinger Miszellen*: pp. 180 and 103–06. Perring's manuscript diary survives but has not yet been published.

30 Henry Formby (1843) *A Visit to the East; Germany and the Danube, Constantinople, Asia Minor, Egypt, and Idumea*. London – in which he names no one and, for an Englishman, is uncharacteristically dismissive of Egypt.

31 Portrait of Nathaniel Fish Moore by Henry Inman, oil-on-canvas, 1835. Reproduced, courtesy of Columbia University. And see Benjamin I. Haight (1874), *A Memorial Discourse on Nathaniel F. Moore, LL.D., sometime President of Columbia College, New York. Delivered at the request of the Alumni, January 14, 1874 in the College Chapel*. New York.

32 Edward Joy Morris (1842) *Notes of a Tour through Turkey, Greece, Egypt, Arabia Petraea, to the Holy Land, including a visit to Athens, Sparta, Delphi, Cairo, Thebes, Mr. Sinai, Petra, &c.*, 2 vols. Philadelphia.

33 Baron Koller published an account of the trip to Aqaba: 'Extract from Baron Koller's Itinerary of his Tour to Petra describing an Inland Route from Mount Sinai to Akabah', *Journal of the Royal Geographical Society*, xii, 1842: pp. 75–79.

34 Daniel Low (1792–1867) had left New York with his daughter in early November 1838; they returned home in November 1840. Virtually nothing is known of their European tour.

35 George Richards Lewis (1809–53), Yale 1829, a prominent citizen of New London, Connecticut; Thomas Lewis Preston (1812–1903), University of Virginia 1833, and Theodore Dehon (1816–87). In a letter Preston wrote to Lewison on 16 April 1844, he recalled among other things the time they spent together travelling (Library archives, University of South Carolina, Columbia, SC).

36 Oliver, Andrew (2014) *American Travelers on the Nile. Early U.S. Visitors to Egypt, 1774-1839*. Cairo: pp. 124–25.

37 Augustus James Musson Aymar (1819–91) and John Quereau Aymar, Jr. (1819–43), twin sons of Benjamin Aymar.

38 Alexandre Marie Joseph Ernest Olivier de la Rochfoucaud (1797–1885).

39 *The Daily Atlas*, Boston, Mass. 3 June 1843.

40 50.602.625. Bequest of Glenn Tilley Morse, 1950.

41 *The Daily Union*, Washington, DC, 3 April 1846.

42 Letter preserved in the Hay Library at Brown University, Providence, Ms.51.22, gift of Wallace G. Maxon.

43 John Bassett Moore, ed. (1909). *The Works of James Buchanan*, Vol. 8. Philadelphia: pp. 227–29.

44 Cyrus Eaton (1865) *History of Thomaston, Rockland, and South Thomaston, Maine*, Hallowell, Vol. 1: pp. 425.

45 Judith M. Jacob (2005) *The Washington Monument. A Technical History and Catalog of the Commemorative Stones* (the stone from Thomaston is cited on p. 69).

46 Rock Island Auction Company, 29 April–1 May 2016, lot 181; previously illustrated in *True Magazine*, August 1958.

47 *Daily Evening Traveler*, Boston, 23 January 1867.

48 Eaton (1865) *History of Thomaston,....,* Hallowell, Vol. 1: p. 439.

49 *Catalogue of the Valuable Library of Henry B. Humphrey, Esq. To be sold by auction on Tuesday, May 9th 1871 and Following Days in the Library Salesroom of Leonard and Company, Boston,* Cambridge 1871. John Thomson of Bartleby's Books, Washington DC found a copy for me to acquire, fully annotated with prices and buyers' names, and the personal copy of Lawrence Rhoades, the compiler of the catalogue, and with his bookplate.

50 Offered by Dogtown Book Shop, Gloucester, Massachusetts in the summer of 2016. Bob Ritchie of the shop kindly sent along a fine image of the gilded stamp.

51 *Evening Post,* New York 6.22.1870: 'The Villas at Newport, who occupy them'.

52 Theodore Bolton (1921) *Early American Portrait Painters in Miniature.* New York: p. 25.

53 *The Harvard College Catalogue* 1892–93, Cambridge, Mass., 1892: p. 216.

Edward Robinson, Eli Smith and Their Travels in Search of Biblical Geography

Susan Cohen

In 1838, and again in 1852, the American biblical scholar Edward Robinson (Fig.6.1) and the American missionary Eli Smith travelled together throughout the Middle East in order to map the world of the Bible. Carrying only compasses, a thermometer, telescopes, measuring tapes and their Bibles for reference, Robinson and Smith travelled from Egypt through Palestine, in search of historical sites and geographic features that could help provide physical evidence to illustrate the biblical landscape of the Protestant religious past. Using Smith's knowledge of Arabic, and the descriptions, landmarks and accounts of sites, routes and battles, etc. in the biblical text, together with deductive reasoning based on comparative linguistics, contemporary knowledge and religious belief, Robinson and Smith essentially created a new academic discipline – biblical historical geography. In so doing, these travellers played an integral role in shaping how future generations of scholars would examine the ancient biblical world, how they would map it and the ways in which they would present this world to the public.

Introduction

In the first half of the 19th century, Congregationalist minister Edward Robinson (1794–1863), a professor at Andover Theological Seminary, together with Presbyterian minister and missionary Reverend Eli Smith (1801–57), himself a former student at Andover, travelled the length and breadth of the Levant from Egypt and Sinai through Palestine to Lebanon, taking notes and making observations concerning Biblical Geography. Their first visit, in 1838, took place over a span of two and a half months, and resulted in the production of Robinson's first two-volume work, *Biblical Researches in Palestine*, which achieved nearly instant scholarly acclaim as well as immense public popularity, reprinting in 11 editions, and earning Robinson a gold medal from the Royal Geographic Society in 1842 (Lipman, 1989: pp. 29–30) (Fig.6.2). The second, shorter, visit in 1852 resulted in a further publication, which although an independent work, was also produced as the third volume of the series.[1] These publications related modes and means of travel in the Near East, the travellers' impressions of the land and its peoples and their attempts to identify the 'real' location of as many biblical sites and events as possible. In so doing, these two travellers inaugurated the modern tradition of research into the geography and topography of the Bible. This created the inception of the academic tradition of biblical geography, while also promoting a sort of Protestant 'religious tourism' (Dìaz-Andreu, 2007: p. 149), which combined travel to sites of biblical and historical import with the language of scientific exploration, with both steeped heavily in American biblical literalism.[2]

Fig 6.1 Photograph of Edward Robinson

The travel: methods and means

After Robinson's arrival in Egypt from Europe via steamer, the two travellers set about the traditional European/American process of hiring servants, acquiring provisions, and so on. The first part of their travel involved trekking through Sinai 'for some thirty days', and Robinson devoted considerable time in the opening section of the first volume to describing the preparations taken for such a journey, including detailed accounts of their tent, water-skins, the provisions needed for that period of time, plus 'all the numerous smaller articles which are essential to the traveller's progress and health, even if he renounces all expectations of convenience and comfort' (Robinson, 1874a: p. 34).[3]

For accommodation, the travellers chose a large tent with a single pole, and used large pieces of painted canvas to spread on the ground under their mattresses. During the day, the mattresses were rolled up in the canvas. Their provisions consisted primarily of rice and biscuits, and later in the journey, they also added flour that was baked into unleavened bread (Robinson, 1874a: p. 35). Meat ('flesh') was obtained from local inhabitants along the way, and their other staples included coffee, tea, sugar, butter, dried apricots, tobacco and wax-candles. Robinson described the dried apricots as a 'luxury in the desert' and observed that 'a timely

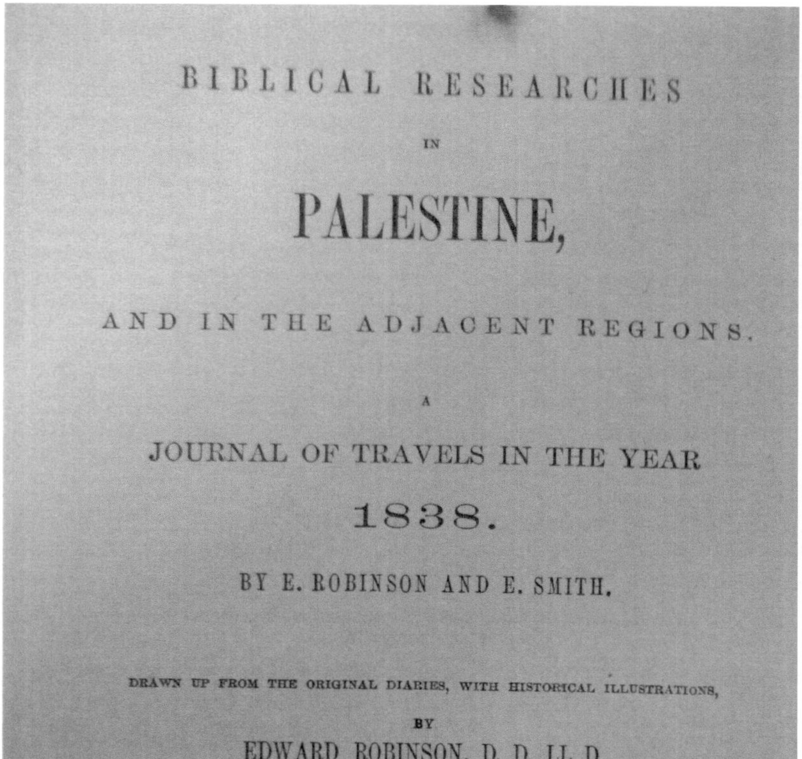

BIBLICAL RESEARCHES

IN

PALESTINE,

AND IN THE ADJACENT REGIONS.

A

JOURNAL OF TRAVELS IN THE YEAR

1838.

BY E. ROBINSON AND E. SMITH.

DRAWN UP FROM THE ORIGINAL DIARIES, WITH HISTORICAL ILLUSTRATIONS,

BY

EDWARD ROBINSON, D. D. LL. D.

PROFESSOR OF BIBLICAL LITERATURE IN THE UNION THEOLOGICAL
SEMINARY, NEW YORK.

WITH NEW MAPS AND PLANS.

IN TWO VOLUMES.

VOL. I.

ELEVENTH EDITION.

BOSTON:
PUBLISHED BY CROCKER AND BREWSTER,
No. 51 WASHINGTON STREET.
LONDON—JOHN MURRAY.
1874.

Fig 6.2 Cover page of the 1874 edition of Biblical Researches in Palestine.

distribution of coffee and tobacco among the Arabs is an easy mode of winning their favour and confidence' (Robinson, 1874a: p. 35).

After some deliberation, Robinson and Smith also armed themselves with two old muskets and a pair of old pistols that Robinson freely admitted they had little intention of actually using (Robinson, 1874a: p. 35).[4] Unlike many travellers of an earlier era, Robinson and Smith remained in European clothing, although they did adopt the red tarbush at times, as well as carrying cloaks to use and disguise their appearance from local people travelling close by or passing at a distance, although the need for this dissimulation never arose (Robinson, 1894a: p. 36).

Finally, the travellers hired two Egyptian servants (the expedition was also accompanied by a number of other individuals who remain unnamed, and mostly unmentioned, in the narrative), and acquired three dromedaries and five camels. Once across Sinai, other means of transportation included horses and/or mules.

The different animals used for transport play a crucial role in understanding how Robinson and Smith reckoned distance, viewed topography and their subsequent identification and localization of sites and places of key events mentioned in the Bible. Throughout their travels, distance was measured by time, and calculated in increments of hours. Accordingly, the actual amount of distance covered during one hour varied significantly, depending on the type of animal being used for transport as well as the nature of the terrain being covered (Robinson, 1874a: p. xv). Robinson and Smith determined distance based on calculations of the general average of travel speed with different animals, which, according to Robinson, 'has been found most correct and convenient' (1874a: p. xv). (Table 1). Throughout the narrative, then, the distances between biblical sites that enabled Robinson and Smith to find areas of biblical action, so to speak, were based upon these averages, together with a judicious consultation of those ancient sources deemed most accurate and reliable by the travellers, as discussed further below. Taken together, the subjective acceptance of sources, combined with the average of the speed over ground of different quadrupeds, helped to lay the basis for establishing the geography of the Holy Land.[5]

One Hour by Camel	One Hour by Horse / Mule
2 geographical miles	2.4 geographical miles
2 1/3 Stat. M.	2 ¾ Stat. M
2.5 Roman miles	3 Roman miles
1/3 German miles	3/5 German miles

Table 1: Comparative chart of distance covered by different animals as measured by Robinson and Smith during their travel.

Of more significance for Robinson and Smith, however, beyond the items required for sustenance and various animals used for transport, were the additional resources they used to elucidate biblical geography. The first trip in 1838 had not initially been planned as a survey, and thus the travellers' equipment (in a list that has since been enshrined in the history of Near Eastern archaeology's self-narrative) (e.g. Bliss, 1906: pp. 194–95; Williams, 1999: p. 218) consisted solely of a surveyor's compass, two pocket compasses, a thermometer, telescopes and measuring tapes (Robinson, 18974a: p. 32). Added to this list, and arguably the most significant item, both from Robinson and Smith's perspective, as well as that of their audience and generations of later scholars, were their Bibles, in English and 'in the original tongues' (Robinson, 1874a: p. 32).

Robinson and Smith also carried with them a small library of other books published by earlier travellers and scholars, consisting of Reland's *Palestina*, which, according to Robinson, was 'next to the Bible... the most important book for travellers in the Holy Land'. (1874a: pp. 32–33), Raumer's *Palästina*, Burckhardt's *Travels in Syria and the Holy Land*, the English compilation from Laborde's *Voyage de l'Arabie Petrée*, and the *Modern Traveller in Arabia, Palestine, and Syria* (Robinson, 1874a: p. 33). Robinson and Smith also possessed a copy of Laborde's 'Map of Sinai and Arabia Petraea', and Berghaus' 'Map of Syria', praised by Robinson as 'the best undoubtedly up to that time, but which was of little service to us in the parts of the country we visited' (Robinson, 1874a: p. 33). While in Jerusalem, these sources were augmented by access to the works of Josephus, and also 'of several travellers' (who sadly remain unnamed in Robinson's account). For Robinson, these literary resources provided sufficient background and supplemental information for his travels and observations, although he also noted that, should he undertake the journey again, he would add 'a compendious History of the Crusades, and the volumes of Ritter's *Erdkunde*, containing Palestine in the second edition' (1874a: p. 33). Thus, in 1838, well-equipped, well-organized, and armed with basic surveyor's tools, a small library, and a compendious knowledge of Scripture and history in keeping with their background, time and station, Robinson and Smith set off on their travels throughout the Levant and 'discovered' – so to speak – biblical topography and geography.

The travel: Reason and Rationale

Robinson chose to present his narrative in journal format, combined from the daily notes of both travellers, so that the reader might follow their 'processes of inquiry' (1874a: p. viii) regarding everything they saw and all the places they visited. As such, the volumes included personal observations and narrative as well as discussions of historical, topographical and biblical points. This format was chosen so 'as to exhibit the manner in which the Promised Land unfolded itself to our eyes, and the processes by which we were led to the conclusions and opinions advanced in this work' (Robinson, 1874a: vii). As a result, the narrative presented the travellers' personal ideas, approaches, thoughts and musings so that the reader – although removed in time and space – would be able to follow the course of travel as closely as possible, and thereby experience it more directly, rather than if he or she were simply presented with a final summary of the results (Robinson, 1874a: p. viii).

In this way, the travels of Robinson and Smith provide a sense of discovery and wonder – places are described on different days, at different times and in relation to different concepts, knowledge and experience. The cumulative effect, therefore, is as Robinson intended – new discussions of places already visited are presented over the course of reading through the volume; only at the conclusion of each section or segment of travel does the reader then possess the full information relating to places, peoples, sites and ideas as did Robinson and Smith.

In addition to the personal narrative, and by far the more important component of the travels for later scholarship, however, was the focus on biblical history, topography, toponymy and geography. To Robinson, like many of his contemporaries in Europe and America, the Holy Land was a place already well known through religious upbringing; in many cases, particularly in America, the biblical place names and geography of the past were better known than those in the present (Cohen, 2014). While an American might not know the location of sites in the contemporary Middle East or bring to mind a map of the region as it existed in the mid-19th century, the geography and locales of the ancient world, and particularly the ancient biblical world, were part and parcel of his (and more rarely her) educational upbringing. As Robinson himself noted:

> As in the case of most of my countrymen, especially in New England, the scenes of the Bible had made a deep impression upon my mind from the earliest childhood; and afterwards in riper years this feeling had grown into a strong desire to visit in person the places so remarkable in the history of the human race. Indeed in no country in the world, perhaps, is such a feeling more widely diffused than in New England; in no country are the Scriptures better known, or more highly prized. From his earliest years the child is there accustomed not only to read the Bible for himself; but he also listens to it in the morning and evening devotions of his family, in the daily village-school, in the Sunday school and Bible-class, and in the weekly ministrations of the sanctuary. Hence, as he grows up, the names of Sinai, Jerusalem, Bethlehem, the Promised Land, become associated with his earliest recollections and holiest feelings. (1874a: p. 31.)

While fuelled by a genuine interest in the contemporary landscape, Robinson's and Smith's goal to uncover the location of historical/biblical places and sites received further impetus from their unequivocal faith and staunch American Protestant literalism (Williams 1999). Robinson's study of the geography and topography of the region was fuelled by the signal concern to separate 'real' facts from 'the mass of topographical tradition, long since fastened upon the Holy Land by foreign ecclesiastics and monks, in distinction from the ordinary tradition or preservation of ancient names among the native population' (Robinson, 1874a: pp. viii–ix). To Robinson, this 'mass of topographical tradition' – often established by myth and legend, together with the distortion provided by centuries of religious interpretation – was clearly to be differentiated from the 'truth' as gleaned from a strict and literal reading of the biblical text itself (Robinson, 1874a: p. ix). As a result, this juxtaposition of 'tradition' and 'truth' derived from Robinson's vehement anti-Catholicism and fervent American Protestantism shines strongly throughout the travelogue and accompanying commentary (Lipman, 1989: p. 37; Williams, 1999: *passim*).

For example, Robinson noted that many locations and the religious traditions associated with them were:

> for the most part brought forward, by a credulous and unenlightened zeal, well meant, indeed, but not uninterested; so all the reports and accounts we have of the Holy City and its sacred places, have come to us from the same impure source. The fathers of the church in Palestine, and their imitators the monks, were themselves for the most part not natives of the country. With few exceptions they knew little of its topography; and were mostly unacquainted with the Aramaean, the vernacular language of the common people. They have related only what was transmitted to them by their predecessors, also foreigners; or have given opinions of their own, adopted without critical inquiry and usually without much knowledge. The visitors of the Holy Land in the earlier centuries, as well as the crusaders... looked upon Jerusalem and its environs, and upon the land, only through the medium of the traditions of the church. (Robinson, 1874a: 252.)

As a result of this presumably uncritical, and in Robinson's view, unacceptably Catholic and superstitious, perspective, 'there has been grafted upon Jerusalem and the Holy Land a vast mass of tradition, foreign in its sources and doubtful in its character; which has flourished luxuriantly and spread itself out widely over the western world' (Robinson, 1874a: p. 253). From this, therefore, the inescapable – to Robinson – conclusion was that 'all ecclesiastical tradition respecting the ancient places in and around Jerusalem and throughout Palestine, IS OF NO VALUE, except so far as it is supported by circumstances known to us from the Scriptures, or from other cotemporary [sic] testimony' [Robinson, 1874a: p. 353, original italics and emphasis].

Needless to say, neither Robinson, Smith, nor any of their Protestant contemporaries perceived the clear irony present in these statements. To them, while the Catholic tradition was steeped in superstition and remained doubtful in character, by contrast Robinson's work was devoid of bias, religion, and religious superstition—instead, he was conducting modern and objective science in conjunction with a firm knowledge of 'Truth' provided by the Protestant religious lens. This conviction is made abundantly clear, not only by Robinson's statement 'As I have no interests to subserve but those of scientific and religious truth, so I have no fears as to the result' (1874b: p. 204), but by the effusive praise heaped upon his work by like-minded contemporaries: 'His simple, single aim was to give the exact sense of the sacred writers, unprejudiced by dogmatic assumptions or preconceived theories' (Smith and Hitchcock, 1863: p. 6).

The issue of subjectivity surrounding 'truth' in religion, or any questions regarding accuracy, historicity and use of the biblical text as a viable source for understanding the past clearly never entered Robinson's mind (Smith and Hitchcock, 1863: p. 86; Williams, 1999: *passim*). While the 19th century also saw the development of the discipline of biblical criticism, most notably in Germany, of which J. Wellhausen's famous *Prolegomena* represents one of the best known iterations, this method of biblical analysis generally was considered anathema in many British and American circles, and particularly so in the American seminary tradition that nurtured Robinson and Smith (Brown, 1969; Williams, 1999). In fact, part of the American Protestant tradition of emphasis on literalism, and the efforts to establish topographic and toponymic 'truth' developed as attempts to refute these challenges to biblical veracity. The 'hard' data of geography helped to serve as a counter to the insidious insinuations of biblical criticism that suggested that while the land and places mentioned in the sacred text might be real enough, the events and history played on them might not have taken place precisely as described, or, in some cases, occurred at all (Cohen, 2014). Significantly, Robinson's emphasis on direct experience of the biblical landscape, together with the conviction that the ancient landscape could be found in the contemporary one, resulted in a positivistic tradition of examining, describing and mapping the region through the lens of Protestant literalism, an approach which influenced both contemporary European and American views of and claims to the ancient Near Eastern world and the academic disciplines that developed from them (Long, 2003:pp. 134–35).

The Travel: Conjecture and Conclusions

While Robinson's impressions of Jerusalem have become part of the standard lore of studies of that city's history, his travels to and accompanying discussions of Megiddo and Jericho, both cities of considerable biblical fame, represent perhaps the quintessential examples of the travellers' achievements and illustrate their particularized religious perspective towards their undertaking. While Megiddo possesses considerable notoriety as the site of biblical Armageddon (Rev. 16:14), it also figured prominently in the Old Testament's presentation of the histories of ancient Israel, starting with the actions of the legendary King Solomon (e.g., I Kgs. 9:15) and as the location of the death of King Josiah at the hand of the Egyptian pharaoh Neco (II Kgs. 23:29). Likewise, Jericho stands out as the most famous example of the ancient Israelite conquest of the 'Promised Land' of Canaan (Josh. 6).

Regarding Megiddo, Robinson wrote that, while travelling across the plain, with the sites of Tanaach and Lejjun in view: 'we could not resist the impression, that the latter [modern Legio] probably occupies the site of the ancient Megiddo...' (1874a: p. 329). This deduction, first made in 1838, was based on a variety of reasoning drawn from examination of the biblical account and the later Christian authors Eusebius and Jerome, both of whom passed Robinson's criteria for reliability over and by comparison with other, more 'superstitious' religious traditions. Robinson's reasoning was as follows: i) both Eusebius and Jerome mentioned the distance between Taanach and Legio as being approximately 3–4 Roman miles; ii) Megiddo is rarely cited 'in Scripture' except in conjunction with Taanach, so this implied their proximity to one another (Robinson, 1874a: pp. 329–30); iii) the battle between Deborah and Barak (Judges 5–6) took place on the plain of Taanach near 'the waters of Megiddo'; iv) Megiddo therefore gave its name to the valley or low plain near the Kishon River, and v) both Eusebius and Jerome mentioned the plain of Legio as related to the plain near Megiddo (Robinson, 1874a: p. 330). Thus, to Robinson, 'all these circumstances make out a strong case in favour of the identity of Legio and Megiddo; and leave in my own mind little doubt upon the point' (Robinson, 1874a: p. 330).

This initial impression was then further confirmed in the minds of the two travellers during their visit to the same region in 1852 when, while standing on top of Tell el-Mutsellim (which actually is the site of ancient Megiddo) looking out over the plain, Robinson recounted feeling as though he was looking out at the scene of the 'great battle' between Deborah and Barak. He remarked, 'The Tell would indeed present a splendid site for a city; but there is no trace, of any kind, to show that a city ever stood there' (Robinson ,1874b: p. 117). Thus, while standing on top of the site he sought in order to gain a better vantage point to find it, Robinson reiterated the conclusion that Legio was the site of ancient Megiddo (Robinson, 1874a: pp. 328–30), and noted that this second visit to the region only strengthened that conviction (Robinson, 1874b: p. 118).[6]

In a similar vein, the travellers' descriptions of their impressions of their peregrinations around the region of Jericho also present a mix of deductive logic based on biblical and classical sources, together with their own views and convictions regarding biblical tradition regarding the site. As with Megiddo, Robinson's description of what would eventually be identified as the ancient site of Jericho – 'a high double-mound, or group of mounds, looking much like a tumulus, or as if composed of rubbish, situated a mile or more in front of the mountain Quarantana' (1874a: p. 555) – did not yet have the benefit of later knowledge concerning the processes of tell formation that would determine that these mounds were the remains of ancient sites (Bliss, 1906: p. 206; Blakely, 1990). While Robinson noted that these mounds were 'covered with substructions of unhewn stone; and others of the same kind are seen upon the plain towards the southwest' (1874a: p. 555), he then devoted his time and energy to attempting to identify where the ancient site of Jericho could instead have been located. He wrote, 'Here then are traces of ancient foundations, such as they are; but none which could enable us to say definitively: This is the site of ancient Jericho. Around the fountain, where we should naturally look for its position, there is nothing which can well be referred to any large or important building; nothing, in short, which looks like the ruins of a great city, with a vast circus, palaces, and other edifices' (Robinson, 1874a: p. 556).

To Robinson, this was frustrating; although he acknowledged that the stones of earlier buildings might have been taken to aid in the construction of later ones, he seems never to have made the connection between ruins and cities, complaining that 'yet nevertheless, one would naturally expect to find some traces of the solidity and splendour of the ancient city' (Robinson, 1974a: p. 564). Finally, as a means of attempting to explain the failure definitively to locate such an important and significant city from biblical antiquity where it 'should' have been, Robinson reverted to an explanation based in scriptural lore rather than the physical landscape, suggesting that perhaps 'the site of the later Jericho may have been changed in order to evade the curse' (1874a: p. 565), referring to Joshua 6:26.[7] Here again, biblical literalism combined with scientific observation to produce conclusions that were quite credible for their time and place and reveal also the overwhelming focus on scriptural veracity.

These examples of Jericho and Megiddo illustrate the amalgamation of internal logic, biblical tradition and deductive reasoning coupled with personal observation and religious conviction that characterized Robinson's and Smith's travels and their methods of geographic and toponymic identification. While their efforts were only partially successful, largely because the geological and archaeological knowledge to identify the location of ancient city sites in the mounds dotting the landscape had not yet been realized (Bliss, 1906; Blakely, 1990), they set the stage for future scientific endeavours in Palestine. Thus, although the story of Robinson and Smith standing on top of Megiddo while looking for Megiddo has become famous – or infamous – within historiographic tradition regarding knowledge and exploration in the ancient Near Eastern world, simultaneously Robinson remains enshrined as 'the father of biblical geography'.

Conclusion

On the surface, there is little of note in the actual travels of Robinson and Smith that would distinguish them from many of their contemporaries. Here were two American ministers, travelling together in a fairly unremarkable way throughout the 'orient' in a period when American and European visits to the region, if not entirely common or trouble-free, were certainly less arduous and less exotic than that undertaken by their predecessors even a mere few decades earlier. What makes these travels by Robinson and Smith so significant, then, is their approach to the study of ancient topography and geography of the biblical world, and the significance and weight attributed to their discoveries, both by their contemporary readership (e.g., Hitchcock and Smith 1863), and by later scholars in the academic traditions that they influenced, helped to form, and, in the case of biblical geography, have received the credit for creating. Robinson and Smith's travels pioneered new approaches to the understanding of the geography of the ancient biblical world in a way that married the American Protestant concern with biblical literalism and veracity with the search for 'hard' physical data – creating an approach that helped to develop and still helps to drive the modern disciplines of ancient Near Eastern geography and archaeology as well as influence modern perspectives on the history, geography and cartography of the modern Middle Eastern world.

Endnotes

1   The full titles of the works are: *Biblical Researches in Palestine and Adjacent Regions: A Journal of Travels in the Year 1838* and *Later Biblical Researches in Palestine and Adjacent Regions: A Journal of Travels in the Year 1852.*

2   Travel to religious sites in the Holy Land existed of course long prior to the rise of this type of Protestant touring; pilgrimage to sites in Palestine can be traced to the late 4th century AD, beginning with the visit to Jerusalem and surrounding regions by Helena, mother of Constantine, in her attempts to locate the 'true cross', the place of Jesus' crucifixion and other key locations integral to the development of Christian theology. Protestant 'religious tourism', however, moved beyond simple visitation of sites for devotional purposes by incorporating an element of historical verification and reasons of exploration into the mix (Davis, 1996; Long, 2003; Dìaz-Andreu, 2007).

3   Citations from Robinson's account in this paper have been taken from the 11th and final edition of both volumes: *Biblical Researches in Palestine and Adjacent Regions: A Journal of Travels in the Year 1838.* 2 vols, 11th ed. Boston: Crocker and Brewer; and *Later Biblical Researches in Palestine and Adjacent Regions: A Journal of Travels in the Year 1852.* 11th ed. Boston: Crocker and Brewer.

4   No information is given regarding the make and/or model, and it may be asked how proficient a Congregationalist seminary professor and a Presbyterian missionary might be in the use of either weapon.

5   Although it was not uncommon to use transport animals as means of measuring distance over the landscape, this method of reckoning becomes more subjective when used to extrapolate distance between two as yet unknown points from antiquity as described in earlier sources which themselves might be of uncertain historicity.

6   A similar situation occurred regarding the biblical site of Ai (Williams, 1999: p. 239).

7   In this passage, Joshua says, 'Cursed of the Lord be the man who shall undertake to fortify this city: he shall lay its foundations at the cost of his first-born, and set up its gates at the cost of his youngest'.

Bibliography

Blakely, J. A. (1990) *Historical Geography and Its Impact on the Analysis and Publication of Excavated Ceramics in the British and American Traditions of Palestinian Archaeology.* Unpublished dissertation. University of Pennsylvania.

Bliss, F. J. (1906) *The Development of Palestine Exploration. Being the Ely Lectures for 1903.* New York, Charles Scribner's Sons.

Brown, J. (1969) *The Rise of Biblical Criticism in America, 1800–1870.* Middletown, CT, Wesleyan University.

Cohen, S. (2014) Mapping the Z-axis: early archaeological engagement with time and space in the ancient Near East. *Bulletin of Historical Archaeology* 24: pp. 1–13. http://dx.doi.org/10.5334/bha.2413

Davis, J. (1996) *The Landscape of Belief. Encountering the Holy Land in Nineteenth-Century American Art and Culture.* Princeton, Princeton University Press.

Díaz-Andreu, M. (2007) *A World History of Nineteenth-Century Archaeology. Nationalism, Colonialism, and the Past.* Oxford, Oxford University.

Lipman, V. D. (1989) *Americans and the Holy Land through British Eyes: 1820–1917.* Jerusalem, The Self Publishing Association.

Long, B. (2003) *Imagining the Holy Land. Maps, Models, and Fantasy Travels.* Bloomington, IN, Indiana University.

Robinson, E. and E. Smith (1874a) *Biblical Researches in Palestine and Adjacent Regions: A Journal of Travels in the Year 1838.* 2 vols. 11th edition. Boston, Crocker and Brewer.

Robinson, E. and E. Smith (1874b) *Later Biblical Researches in Palestine and Adjacent Regions: A Journal of Travels in the Year 1852.* 11th edition. Boston, Crocker and Brewer.

Smith, H. B. and R. D Hitchcock (1863) *The Life, Writings, and Character of Edward Robinson, D.D., L.L.D.* New York, Anson D. F. Randolph.

Williams, J. G. (1999) *The Life and Times of Edward Robinson: A Connecticut Yankee in King Solomon's Court.* Altanta, GA, Society of Biblical Literature.

The Boston Green Head:
Tales of a much-travelled ancient Egyptian sculpture[1]

Lawrence M. Berman

One of the great masterpieces in the Egyptian collection of the Museum of Fine Arts (MFA), Boston, USA, is a small portrait head of an old man with a shaven head, broken from a statue, and in greywacke, a fine, hard, dark grey-green stone (Fig.7.1).[2] Although it is only 10.5 cm high (a little over 4 in), the head makes a monumental impression.[3] The features are wonderfully life-like and individual. Most remarkable is the sense of skin and bone, the bumps and shallows of the skull, the heavy arched brows, and roundness of the eyeballs set deep in their sockets, the delicacy of the lids, the prominent cheekbones, hollow cheeks and slightly saggy jowls.

The only clue to the subject's identity is his coiffure, or rather, the lack of one. Although not all priests appear shaven-headed in Egyptian sculpture, most statues and reliefs of shaven-headed men represent priests.[4] The top of the back pillar preserves the name of the Memphite funerary deity Ptah-Sokar. And that is all. When complete, the inscription would have

Fig 7.1 The Boston Green Head – Head of a Priest – Egyptian, Late Period, Dynasty 30 (380-332 BCE). Graywacke, 10.5 x 8.5 x 11.3 cms. Museum of Fine Arts, Boston, Henry Lillie Pierce Fund, 04.1749.

included, at the very least, the subject's name and occupation. As it is, for lack of anything better, the piece is known worldwide as the Boston Green Head, after the colour of the stone and the place where it now resides. Under that name it has become world famous.

The head has, moreover, a fascinating modern history. Discovered in 1857 by Auguste Mariette at the Saqqara Serapeum, it entered the collection of the notorious Prince Jérôme Napoléon (nephew of Napoleon I and first cousin of Napoleon III), who kept it in his Pompeian House in Paris. It came to the MFA in 1903 via Edward Perry Warren, the Bostonian expatriate collector who transformed the museum's department of classical art from an assembly of plaster casts to America's premiere collection of Greek and Roman originals.

In 1857, Prince Napoleon Joseph Charles Paul Bonaparte

Fig 7.2 Hippolyte Flandrin (1809-1864), Napoleon Joseph Charles Paul Bonaparte, 1860, oil on canvas, 117 x 89 cms. Musée national du Château du Versalles, inv. no. RF 1549. © RMN-Grand Palais / Art Resource, New York. Photograph: Hervé Lewandowski.

(Fig.7.2), known in Parisian circles by his nickname 'Plon-Plon', announced his intention of travelling to Egypt. For the passionately pro-French Muhammad Said, Viceroy of Egypt, the prince's visit was an historical event. The son of Muhammad Ali was determined to receive the nephew of Napoleon I in a manner befitting the occasion. In 1855, Archduke Ferdinand Maximilian, brother of Emperor Franz Joseph I of Austria, had paid a state visit to Egypt. Maximilian was an avid art collector, so as a gift Said had allowed him to take home his pick of the national antiquities collection in the Citadel. He could do no less for Prince Napoleon, a collector as well. He would also send the prince up the Nile and who better to guide him than Auguste Mariette, the young French Egyptologist who just a few years before had made one of the great finds in the history of Egyptology, the Serapeum of Memphis and the catacombs of the sacred Apis bulls, and had sent some 6,000 antiquities to the Louvre?

On the recommendation of his childhood friend Ferdinand de Lesseps, who had just received the concession to build the Suez Canal, Said summoned Mariette back to Egypt to prepare for the impending visit and to form a collection to uncover in the presence of His Imperial Highness: 'Every step of the visiting prince was to sprout antiquities, and to assure a fertile crop and to save time, Mariette was to proceed upriver, dig for antiquities and then bury them again all along the route'.[5] Mariette jumped at the chance. Said gave him a government steamer, letters to all the provincial governors ordering them to provide manpower for his excavations and a bodyguard. Mariette started digs simultaneously at Giza, Saqqara, Abydos, Thebes and Elephantine.[6]

The prince, meanwhile, took his time. On 18 October, his aide-de-camp, Colonel Camille Ferri Pisani, wrote to Mariette that the prince was still determined to go to Egypt but had not yet set the date of departure. People began to joke about it: 'Prince Napoleon is resolved to go to Egypt', so they said, 'the moment the Luxor obelisk [in the Place de la Concorde] goes back'.[7] Finally, on 31 January 1858, Ferri Pisani wrote that 'important considerations' compelled the prince to cancel the trip he had set his heart on.[8]

Mariette, who dreamed of establishing an Egyptian antiquities service and museum, had the brilliant idea that the prince might appreciate a few souvenirs of the trip upon which he had set such store but was forced to cancel. The Pasha was happy to comply. The delighted prince asked Mariette to convey his thanks to Said. Even more importantly, the prince let the viceroy know that 'should His Royal Highness wish to ask France for the assistance of a scholar to establish an Egyptian museum, the French government would certainly not recommend any other man but [Mariette]'. As a result, on 1 June 1858, Said appointed Mariette *mamur al-antiqat,* or *directeur des monuments historiques de l'Egypte et du musée.*[9] A coloured drawing by Théodule Devéria (1831–71), a promising young Egyptologist from the Louvre, who was sent to in Egypt

Fig 7.3 Théodule Charles Devéria (1831-1871), Portrait of Auguste Mariette, 1859, coloured pencils on tan paper, 35 x 23 cms. Museum of Fine Arts, Boston, gift of Mrs. Horace L. Mayer, 1978.571.

Fig 7.4 Gustave Boulanger (1824-1888), Rehearsal of 'The Flute Player' and 'The Wife of Diomedes' in the Atrium of Prince Napoleon's Pompeian House in Paris in 1860, 1860, oil on canvas, 83 x 130 cms. Private Collection. © RMN-Grand Palais / Art Resource, New York. Photograph: Daniel Arnaudet.

in 1858 as Mariette's assistant, shows him in 1859, a year after he became director of antiquities (Fig.7.3).[10]

Meanwhile, Prince Napoleon's Egyptian collection arrived in France. Among the choice objects was the little green head of a priest. And the prince had just the place to put it: his newly built Maison Pompéienne (Pompeian House), at 18, avenue Montaigne.[11] The plan was based on the so-called Villa of Diomedes in the Via dei Sepolcri outside the walls of Pompeii, though Diomedes (or whoever lived there) would have been surprised at the accommodations imposed by the Parisian climate and the habits of Parisian society.[12] Facing the street, an Ionic portico doubled as a porte-cochère; inside, as in a Roman house, the principal rooms opened off an atrium complete with central pool and pierced ceiling above, glassed over to afford protection from the weather, and presided over by a togate figure of Napoleon I. The walls were decorated with imitation Pompeian wall paintings, interspersed with pictures by Jean-Léon Gérôme and Gustave Boulanger in the latest Néo-Grec style.[13]

The spirit, as well as the look of the house, is captured in a painting by Gustave Boulanger showing actors from the Comédie Française rehearsing *The Flute Player*, a play by Emile Augier (Fig.7.4).[14] The painting is based on an actual event, the painter having dropped by during a dress rehearsal. The actual performance took place in 1860, in the presence of Napoleon III and Empress Eugénie.

The Green Head appears in print for the very first time in an 1859 article by Ferri Pisani in the very first issue of the *Gazette des beaux-arts* somewhat misleadingly entitled, 'Egyptian Bronzes from the Collection of Prince Napoleon', as the article covers the whole collection.[15] There, its setting is described:

> The statues, sphinxes, and lions adorn the gardens and avenues of the house; the steles are arranged along the walls of that unique and charming room, whose moveable floor contains a pool capable of holding sixty cubic meters of hot water, which so strongly excites the curiosity of visitors; finally, the bronzes and small objects are displayed in a large vitrine on one side of the Picture Gallery, opposite the Greek temple of Mr. Hittorf, the pastels of Maréchal and the Marat of David, beside the large Cimmerian canvases of Pils and Vernet.[16]

Quite an eclectic assortment! And again, we know just what it looked like. A page in the weekly paper *L'Illustration* shows two engravings superposed. The upper one depicts the Picture Gallery converted into an ancient theatre for the performance of Augier's *The Flute Player*.[17] The room is filled with men in frock coats and women in crinolines. We see the guests from behind as they sit facing the stage. One can just make out Jacques-Louis David's *Death of Marat* hanging on the wall on the right.[18] On the opposite wall, next to Horace Vernet's vast Crimean War canvas, *The Battle of the Alma,* is the vitrine; somewhere in there is the Green Head.[19]

Prince Napoleon finally did go to Egypt in 1863 to inspect the work on the Suez Canal, of which he was an outspoken supporter. Mariette took him up the Nile; the steamer *Menchiéh* was luxuriously outfitted for his imperial pleasure.[20] It was summer, however, and very hot. 'Plon-Plon' hardly left the boat, rising from his apathy only to see the inscription carved on the entrance pylon of the temple of Isis on the island of Philae commemorating the French victory over the Mamluks: 'Year 6 of the Republic, 15 Messidor [1 July 1798], a French army commanded by Bonaparte landed at Alexandria. Twenty days later, the Army having put the Mamluks to flight at the Pyramids, Desaix, commanding the first division, pursued them beyond the cataracts, where he arrived 18 Ventose of Year 7 [3 March 1799].'

Someone had hacked out the words 'French army' and 'Bonaparte'. An indignant 'Plon-Plon' had them re-carved before his eyes, saying, '*On ne salit pas une page d'histoire*' (One does not defile a page of history).[21]

We next see the head, again in the *Gazette des Beaux-Arts,* eight years later in an article by French Egyptologist Charles Lenormant on the Egyptian antiquities on display in the 'Egyptian Temple' designed by Mariette as the pharaonic component of the Egyptian display at the Paris Universal Exposition of 1867.[22] In the 'Egyptian Temple', Mariette vowed to 'do for Egyptian art what Prince Napoleon has done for the art of Pompeii'. Although illustrated on the first page of the article, the head is neither identified by a caption nor mentioned in the text. Although it is amusing to picture the Green Head exhibited alongside the statue of the scribe Ka-Aper, often referred to as Sheikh el-Beled, and the jewels of Queen Ahhotep, as far as we know, the Green Head was not exhibited at the fair.[23]

Meanwhile, the prince had begun to tire of his antiquities. In 1866, he put the Pompeian House up for sale. When his friends heard about this, a group of them got together to buy the house and its contents, including the art collection.[24] They tried operating it as a museum and charging for admission, but the novelty soon wore off and the enterprise failed. The sale of the Prince's antiquities took place at the Hôtel Drouot, Paris, 23–26 March 1868.[25] Egyptian antiquities comprised 222 lots: bronzes, scarabs, funerary figurines, terracottas, jewellery, weapons and statuary in stone. The Green Head is conspicuously absent.

Indeed, it is not the least mysterious thing about the Green Head and its whereabouts are entirely unknown from 1867, when it last appeared in the *Gazette des Beaux-Arts*, until 30 December 1903, when it arrived at the Museum of Fine Arts, Boston.

Where was it for those 36 years? We may never know. It is exactly the sort of object to appeal to a collector of refined taste, someone not primarily interested in Egyptian art, whose main interest lay in other areas. It is significant, therefore, that the Green Head, arguably the finest Late Egyptian portrait sculpture in any museum, was acquired by the MFA from the same man who sent to Boston the finest specimens of Greek and Roman art ever before seen in America.[26]

The son of a highly successful paper manufacturer, Edward (Ned) Perry Warren grew up in Boston's Beacon Hill neighbourhood surrounded by paintings, porcelain, and bric-a-brac. Although Boston was the centre of the Aesthetic Movement in America, it was not aesthetic enough for Ned, so after graduating from Harvard he went to New College, Oxford, as an undergraduate again, to study Classics. It was there that he found his calling in life.

For Warren, the Classical Greek ideals of beauty, nobility and manliness, were embodied in Classical Greek art. Greek art was a religion to Warren, and collecting Greek art for America, which for him meant Boston, became his mission: 'We are doing', he wrote, 'the work most needed of all works, supplying eventually the terrible gap that exists in this new continent, the absence of that which delights the eye and rests the soul'.[27]

In 1890, he found the house of his dreams, 'huge, old, and not cheap', as he described it, in the town of Lewes in East Sussex, England.[28] A photograph of Warren, his partner John Marshall and an unidentified companion in the garden of Lewes House, shows Warren holding a Roman statue of Mercury he and Marshall sold to the MFA in 1895 (Fig.7.5).

Within a short time Warren succeeded in attracting to Lewes House, as it was called, some half a dozen like-minded homosexual or bisexual young men, mostly Oxford graduates, who lived completely off his largesse.[29] Some, like Marshall, helped with the collecting, others with running the household; others were not much help at all. Life at Lewes House was an odd combination of princely grandeur and monastic austerity.[30] The men sat around a richly carved oak Tudor table on pews salvaged from an old church in Lancashire. The

Fig 7.5 Edward Reeves (1824-1905), Edward Perry Warren and John Marshall with Statue of Mercury, 1890s, photograph. © Edward Reeves, Lewes, Sussex, England.

setting lacked a tablecloth and seat cushions, let alone rugs or curtains, but the men ate and drank well from old silver and fine china. Art was everywhere, and not just antiquities. Lucas Cranach's *Adam and Eve* – now in the Courtauld Collection – hung in the dining room; an over-life-size marble version of Auguste Rodin's sculpture of a man and woman embracing, *The Kiss*, stood in the coach house for years.[31] Warren placed the Rodin on loan in the town hall at Lewes, but it made the Lewesians uncomfortable, so they returned it; it is now in the Tate Britain.

It is easy to see how a connoisseur of portraits of noble Romans of the Republican period, noted for their brutal realism[32], would appreciate the Green Head. So well does the head stand alone as a portrait, it is easy to forget that it once had a body. The Green Head likely belonged to a striding or kneeling figure holding a *naos*, or shrine, containing the image of a deity, one of the most common types of Egyptian statue in the Late Period. An excellent example, complete except for the feet and base, is the statue of the priest Sematawy in the British Museum.[33] So different is the treatment of head and body that they might belong to different sculptures. Whereas the head is skilfully modelled to reveal the underlying bony structure of the skull, Sematawy's ankle-length, wraparound skirt completely masks the contours of his body. A superbly delineated head has been set on top of a chunky, nondescript lump.

This discrepancy was jarring to early connoisseurs. Even someone as knowledgeable about Egyptian art as Gaston Maspero, Mariette's successor as director of antiquities in Egypt, could write, 'Our museums contain examples of these disconcerting statues, in which the feebleness of the body is in such striking contrast to the truth of the face.'[34] What if the Green Head had a body like Sematawy's?

In her discussion of the statue of Sematawy, Edna R. Russmann makes the point that

Classically oriented collectors of the nineteenth and twentieth centuries prized Egyptian Ptolemaic portrait heads like this because they looked so 'Roman'.... These Eurocentric collectors considered the bodies of the Egyptian statues to detract from the classical quality of their heads, with the consequence that today the great majority of Ptolemaic portrait heads lack their bodies. Some were broken off in modern times to make them more marketable.[35]

But I don't think that's what happened to the Green Head. According to Ferri Pisani, the head was found with a hoard of bronze statuettes in the foundations of the funerary chapel of an Apis bull built by Apries, who reigned 589–570 BCE. There are two issues with this. First, the burial chambers of the Apis bulls in the 26th Dynasty (664–525 BCE) were not built upon the sand surface; they were excavated in the bedrock. Mariette did not find his bronzes there, in the Greater Vaults, he found them outside: beneath the pavements, by the enclosure walls, and along the unpaved road that led north to the Sacred Animal Necropolis and the catacombs of the Mothers of Apis (Fig.7.6).[36] Second, no art historian today would date the Green Head to the 6th century BCE; since the 1960s, the choice has been between the 4th century BCE (Dynasty 30) and the 2nd century BCE (Ptolemaic Dynasty).[37]

Fig 7.6 Plate 4 from Auguste Mariette, Choix de monuments et des dessins découverts ou executes pendant le déblaiement du Sérapeum de Memphis (Paris, 1856).

A look at the Sacred Animal Necropolis, excavated by British archaeologists in the 1960s and 70s and incomparably better documented than the Serapeum, is instructive. The Serapeum and the Sacred Animal Necropolis functioned as one big sacred landscape and developed *in tandem*. Caches of bronzes were found in the Sacred Animal Necropolis as well. Most were found close to the enclosure wall of the Main Temple, either below the foundations or in construction debris against the wall.[38] In one instance, mixed in with the usual bronze statuettes of deities were statues of kings and officials made of wood, stone and faience.[39] All had been broken or damaged in some way. The absence of the missing portions of the damaged statues indicates that they were already broken when buried. None of the objects could be dated by style or inscription later than the 30th Dynasty (360–343 BCE), which is consistent with the archaeological evidence that the deposit was found under pavement of Ptolemaic date. Few had any clear connection with the Sacred Animal Necropolis though some have inscriptions that suggest they originated in one of the shrines of ancient Memphis. Supposing they had been damaged during an attack on the city and then buried in the sacred precincts as a pious gesture and also to save them from further damage, the most likely occasion, given the history of the site and the date of the latest pieces, would have been the Persian invasion of 343 BCE, which put an end to the 30th Dynasty. The Persians enjoyed an odious reputation in Egyptian tradition.[40] The Greek historian Diodorus Siculus (fl. 60–30 BCE) tells us that the invaders demolished the walls of the most important cities and plundered their shrines.[41] The temples themselves bear witness to this, both at the Sacred Animal Necropolis and the Serapeum proper, where the reconstruction work of the early Ptolemies suggests that the buildings of the 30th Dynasty rulers had been defaced.[42]

An analogous scenario can be envisioned for the Green Head. The mention of the Memphite god Ptah-Sokar on the back pillar suggests only that the statue originated in the Memphite area but not necessarily the Serapeum. I suggest that the priest's statue stood in a temple that was looted by the Persians in 343 BCE, when the statue was broken. The head, salvaged by the priests, was later buried in the sacred precinct of the Serapeum during the restoration work that followed the ouster of the Persians by Alexander the Great, together with a group of bronzes, of which some bore the name of Apries.[43] Mariette might well therefore have assumed that all of the objects dated to Apries' reign.

Of course, this is just speculation, but it agrees with the historical record as well as the archaeological evidence, and also helps us to decide between the two dates proposed for our priest by art historians. Perhaps now this masterpiece of Egyptian sculpture, having come spatially to rest, may now come temporally to rest as well.

Endnotes

1   This article has been adapted from my book, *The Priest, the Prince, and the Pasha: The Life and Afterlife of an Ancient Egyptian Sculpture* (Boston, MFA Publications, 2015).

2   Often misidentified as basalt, schist or slate, the stone is graywacke from the Wadi Hammamat quarry in the Eastern Desert, about halfway between the Nile and the Red Sea on the Koptos-Quseir road; see Barbara G. Aston, James A. Harrell, and Ian Shaw, in Paul Nicholson and Ian Shaw, eds., (2000). *Ancient Egyptian Materials and Technology*. Cambridge: Cambridge University Press: pp. 57–58.

3   When complete, the figure was probably represented standing or kneeling. If standing, the figure would have been about 28 in (71 cm) high; if kneeling, about 17½ in (44 cm) high, to which one would have to add from 1½ to 2 in for the height of the integral base. Based on a classic grid of 18 squares from the browline to the soles of the feet for a striding statue and 11 squares for a kneeling statue. The head measures about 3 in (7.5 cm) from the browline to the junction of the neck and shoulders, equal to 2 squares.

4   Out of 24 statues of priests in Bernard V. Bothmer with Herman de Meulenaere and Hans Wolfgang Müller, *Egyptian Sculpture of the Late Period 700 B.C. to A.D. 100*, exh. cat. (Brooklyn, The Brooklyn Museum, 1960), only six have shaven heads, but out of seven shaven-headed statues only two are not priests. Shaven-headed priests: nos. 14 (Mentuemhat in relief, Kansas City 48–28/2); 56 (Padebehu, Brooklyn 60.11 and Vatican 167), 66 (Family stele, Edinburgh 1956.134); 81 (Ankhpahkhered, son of Nesmin, MMA 08.202.1); 83 (Userwer, head in Brooklyn 55.175, body in Cairo JE 30864); 99 (Prophet of Horemheb, Academy of the New Church Museum, Bryn Athyn, PA). Shaven-headed but not priests: nos. 65 (Psamtiksaneith, Cairo CG 726), 74 (relief of Thaasetimu, royal secretary, Brooklyn 56.142). In bronze statuary, shaven-headed priests predominate in all periods: Barbara Mendoza, *Bronze Priests of Ancient Egypt from the Middle Kingdom to the Graeco-Roman Period*, BAR International Series 1866 (Oxford, Archeopress, 2008): pp. 25–27.

5   H. E. Winlock (1924). 'The Tombs of the Kings of the Seventeenth Dynasty at Thebes', *Journal of Egyptian Archaeology* 10: p. 259.

6   Emmanuel de Rougé (1858). '*Une lettre écrite d'Egypte par M. Mariette*', *Comptes-rendus des séances de l'Academie des Inscriptions et Belles-Lettres*, 2e année, pp. 115–21.

7   H. Wallon (1883). *Notice sur la vie et les travaux de François-Auguste-Ferdinand Mariette-Pacha*, Paris, Institut de France: p. 39.

8   Wallon, *Mariette-Pacha*: p. 90.

9   Donald M. Reid (2003). *Whose Pharaohs? Archaeology, Museums, and Egyptian National Identity from Napoleon to World War* I. Berkeley, University of California Press: p. 100.

10 MFA 1978.571; William Kelly Simpson (1974). 'A Portrait of Mariette by Théodule Devéria', *Bulletin de l'Institut français d'archéologie orientale* 74: pp. 149–50.

11 Marie-Claude Dejean de la Batte, '*La maison pompéienne du prince Napoléon avenue Montaigne*', *Gazette des Beaux-Arts*, Ser. 6, Vol. 87 (April 1976): pp. 127–34; Curtis Dahl, 'A Quartet of Pompeian Pastiches', *Journal of the Society of Architectural Historians* 14, no. 3 (Oct. 1955): pp. 4–6.

12 The so-called Villa of Diomedes in the Via dei Sepolcri outside the city walls.

13 Gerald M. Ackerman, 'The Néo-Grecs: A Chink in the Wall of Neoclassicism', in June Hargrove, ed., *The French Academy: Classicism and Its Antagonists*. Newark, University of Delaware Press: pp. 168–95.

14 Versailles, Musée National du Château; *The Second Empire 1852–1870: Art in France under Napoleon III*, exh. cat. (Philadelphia, Philadelphia Museum of Art, 1978): pp. 259–60, no. VI–12.

15 C. Ferri Pisani, 'Bronzes égyptiens *tirés de la collection du Prince Napoléon*', *Gazette des Beaux-Arts* 1 (1859): p. 281; Berman, *The Priest, the Prince, and the Pasha*: p. 93. The illustration of the head shows it reversed, and is none too flattering, as the piece (labelled 'head of a eunuch') sits flat on its break resting at an odd angle, so the head appears to be tilted up and slightly to one side.

16 Ferri Pisani. '*Bronzes* égyptiens': pp. 271–72.

17 Berman, *The Priest, the Prince, and the Pasha*: p. 91 http://gallica.bnf.fr/Search?ArianeWireIndex=index&p=1&lang=EN&f_typedoc=images&q=pompeienne

18 This painting, a studio copy of David's celebrated painting of 1793, is now in Versailles, Musée National du Château. The original is in Brussels (Royal Museums of Fine Arts of Belgium).

19 The painting by Vernet, now in the Musée Fesch, Ajaccio (Corsica), shows Prince Napoleon in the right foreground on horseback commanding his tropps: http://www.musee-fesch.com/index.php/musee_fesch/Collections/Peintures-du-XIXe-siecle/La-bataille-de-l-Alma

20 Gaston Maspero, Mariette's successor as head of antiquities, gives this account of the boat in *Egypt: Ancient Sites and Modern Scenes* (London, T. F. Unwin, 1910): p. 6.

> From 1881 to 1886, the period of my first sojourn in Egypt, a steamboat, the *Menchieh*, was put at my disposal. She was better known to the riverside population by the name of Nimro Hadachere, No. 11. She was a flat-bottomed brigantine, provided with an engine of a type archaic enough to deserve a place in the Museum of Arts and Crafts. From 1840 to 1860 she had regularly performed the journey to and fro between Alexandria and Cairo once a month. She was then invalided on account of old age, but was again put into working order for the visit of Prince Napoleon to Egypt in 1863. In 1875 she was presented to Mariette, and after a long period of inaction, descended to me, and I made my journeys in her for five years. My successors, however, did not preserve her, and on my return I found a princely old dahabieh, the Miriam, which I have used ever since.

http://scholarship.rice.edu/jsp/xml/1911/9293/761/MasEgyp.tei-timea.html#index-div1-N1030E

21 Gaston Maspero (1904). *Notice biographique sur Auguste Mariette (1821–1881)*. Paris, Ernest Leroux: p. 138.

22 François Lenormant, 'L'antiquité à l'Exposition universelle: L'Egypte (deuxième article)', *Gazette des Beaux-Arts* 23 (1867): p. 31.

23 Similarly, Prince Napoleon's bronze Osiris-Iah appears on the first page of the first article in the installment though it is not mentioned in the text either; François Lenormant, 'L'antiquité à l'Exposition universelle: L'Egypte (premier article)', *Gazette des Beaux-Arts* 22 (1867): p. 549.

24 Arsène Houssaye (1891). *Les Confessions: Souvenirs d'un demi-siècle 1830–1890*, Vol. 5. Paris, E. Dentu: pp. 173–74.

25 *Catalogue d'une collection d'antiquités par M. Fröhner, conservateur-adjoint des musées impériaux* (Paris, 1868); http://gallica.bnf.fr/ark:/12148/bpt6k6524839t.r=Fr%C3%B6hner.langEN

26 I am here inspired by the words of Bernard B. Bothmer: 'It is significant that the man who brought to America the finest Greek sculpture of the Classical period in the Western Hemisphere, the Boston companion piece to the "Ludovisi Throne," should also have acquired by far the best Ptolemaic portrait sculpture owned by any museum in any country.' Bothmer, de Meulenaere, and Hans Wolfgang Müller, *Egyptian Sculpture of the Late Period*: p. 138: For the 'Boston Throne' (MFA 08.205), see http://www.mfa.org/collections/object/three-sided-relief-151033

27 Osbert Burdett and E. H. Goddard (1941). *Edward Perry Warren: The Biography of a Connoisseur*. London, Christophers: p. 333.

28 Burdett and Goddard, *Edward Perry Warren*: p. 122.

29 The principal characters are discussed by David Sox (1991). *Bachelors of Art: Edward Perry Warren and the Lewes House Brotherhood*. London, Fourth Estate.

30 For life at Lewes House, see Burdett and Goddard, *Edward Perry Warren*: pp. 128--34, 139–50 and 257–58.

31 Burdett and Goddard, *Edward Perry Warren*: p. 259. The Cranach is now in the Courtauld Gallery, London; see http://courtauld.ac.uk/gallery/collection/renaissance/lucas-cranach-the-elder-adam-and-eve. Warren placed the Rodin on loan in the town hall at Lewes, but it made the Lewesians uncomfortable, so they returned it; it is now in the Tate Britain; see http://www.tate.org.uk/art/artworks/rodin-the-kiss-n06228/text-catalogue-entry.

32 A fine example is the marble head of a bald old man that Warren sold to the MFA in 1899, MFA 99.343; Berman, *The Priest, the Prince, and the Pasha*: p. 147.

33 British Museum EA65443; Berman, *The Priest, the Prince, and the Pasha*: p. 131. http://www.britishmuseum.org/research/search_the_collection_database/search_object_details.aspx?objectId=152570&partId=1&orig=%2fresearch%2fsearch_the_collection_database%2fmuseum_number_search.aspx&numpages=10&idNum=65443&currentPage=1

34 G. Maspero, *Art in Egypt* (London, William Heinemann, 1921): pp. 252–53.

35 Edna R. Russmann (1921). *Eternal Egypt: Masterworks of Ancient Art from the British Museum*, exh. cat. London, British Museum Press: pp. 253–55.

36 Christiane Ziegler, 'Une découverte inedited de Mariette: les bronzes du Sérapeum', *Bulletin de la Société française d'egyptologie* 90 (1981): p. 31.

37 For the 4th century BC: W. Stevenson Smith, *The Art and Architecture of Ancient Egypt*, revised with additions by William Kelly Simpson, Pelican History of Art (New Haven and London, Yale University Press): p. 247; Jack A. Josephson, 'Egyptian Sculpture of the Late Period Revisited', *Journal of the American Research Center in Egypt* 34 (1997): pp. 18–20; Josephson, O'Rourke, and Fazzini, 'The Doha Head': pp. 226–28. For the 2nd century BCE: Bothmer, Meulenaere, and Müller, *Egyptian Sculpture of the Late Period*; Robert S. Bianchi et al., *Cleopatra's Egypt: Age of the Ptolemies*, exh. cat. (The Brooklyn Museum, 1988): pp. 140–42, nos. 45–46; Russmann, *Eternal Egypt*: p. 39, fig. 26; Olivier Perdu, in *Le Crépuscule des Pharaons: Chef-d'oeuvres des dernières dynasties égyptiennes*, exh. cat. (Paris, Musée Jacquemart-André; Brussels, Fonds Mercator, 2012): pp. 90–93, nos. 33 and 34.

38 Elizabeth Anne Hastings, *The Sculpture from the Sacred Animal Necropolis at North Saqqara, 1964-76* (London, Egypt Exploration Society, 1997): p. xxxiii (6).

39 Hastings, *Sculpture from the Sacred Animal Necropolis*: pp. xxxii–xxxiii (4).

40 See Alan B. Lloyd, 'The Egyptian Attitude to the Persians', in *A Good Scribe and an Exceedingly Wise Man: Studies in Honour of W. J. Tait,* ed. A. M. Dodson, J. J. Johnston, and W. Monkhouse, GHP Egyptology 21 (London, Golden House Publications, 2014): pp. 185–98.

41 Diod. 16.51.2–3. Diodorus of Sicily, *The Library of History VII: Books XV.20-XVI.65,* trans. Charles L. Sherman, Loeb Classical Library (Cambridge, Mass, Harvard University Press; London, William Heinemann, 1963): pp. 381–83.

42 H. S. Smith, 'Saqqara, Nekropolen, SpZt', *Lexikon der* Ägyptologie (Wiesbaden: Otto Harrassowitz, 1972–92), 5: pp. 420–21.

Observations, Adventures and Scandals: East India Company Officers on the Red Sea and in the Syrian Desert 1776–81

Janet Starkey

During the late 1770s to the early 1780s, several East India Company officers based in Madras travelled across the Middle East, including the Scottish hydrographer Alexander Dalrymple FRS (1737–1808) appointed in 1759 (Fig.8.1); Colonel James Capper (1743–1825), from Londonderry, appointed in 1773 (Fig.8.2); and Eyles Irwin (?1751–1817), an Irish poet born in Calcutta, and appointed in 1767 (Fig.8.3 and Fig 8.5).

Traditionally, there were two major routes for travel between England and India: one via the Cape of Good Hope, a journey that took at least six months; and another overland via Antioch to Aleppo and across the Great Syrian Desert to Basra, then by ship to Bombay. A further option between India and England was explored in the mid-18th century: up the Red Sea to Suez, across the Eastern Desert to Cairo, along the Nile to Rosetta and then Alexandria to catch a boat heading for Europe.

Fig 8.1 Alexander Dalrymple (1737-1808). Attrib. c.1765 John Thomas Seton. © National Museums of Scotland.

In the 18th century, European ships were prohibited from entering the Red Sea and the Sublime Porte issued several firmans reiterating this prohibition in severe terms. Yet the East India Company continued to trade intermittently in coffee at

Fig 8.2 James Capper (1743-1825) and his daughter. John Russell. © Christ Church, Oxford.

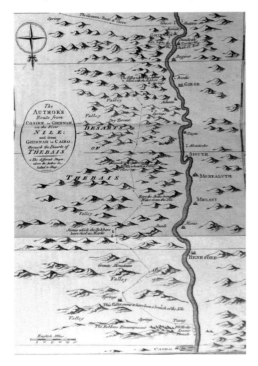

Mocha and, by 1763, had established a factory there. By 1762, when Carsten Niebuhr sailed down the Red Sea, there was an East India Company factory in the entrepôt of Jiddah.[1] Warren Hastings (1732–1818) (Fig.8.4), Governor-General of Bengal from 1773 to 1785, saw possibilities of trade between Bengal and the Red Sea and campaigned to develop the shorter Suez route to Europe. In 1773, in Cairo, the explorer James Bruce was granted permission by the Mamlūk regent of Ottoman Egypt, Muhammad Bey Abū al-Dhahab (1735–75) for the British to trade via Suez. Bruce alerted Hastings who began to send ships from Bengal to Suez. In March 1775 John Shaw, sent by Hastings, negotiated an agreement in Cairo to enable East India Company ships to use the Suez route. George Baldwin (1743/4–1826) (see p.152, below), previously a Levant Company factor, became the East India Company agent in Cairo in 1775. By January 1776, Baldwin had facilitated the transit of despatches from India by the stoop HMS *Dolphin* (which, with HMS *Swallow* had sailed around the world under Samuel Wallis and Philip Carteret in 1766–68).

Furthermore, the significance of a fast route by sea or land for transmitting intelligence between Europe and India was appreciated by Sir Eyre Coote (1726–83) (Fig.8.6), who returned to India as Hasting's commander-in-chief in 1779. Alexander Dalrymple, Capper and

Fig 8.3 Eyles Irwin's map of part of his route in Egypt.

Eyles Irwin were thus encouraged to explore the feasibility of various alternative routes. The *Swallow* reached Suez by 8 January 1777, but its three passengers Dalrymple, Capper and C. (?Charles) Dighton, were detained by custom officials for several days until George Baldwin intervened. The travellers arrived in Alexandria by 19 January 1777. In a letter, Dalrymple described the overland journey from Suez to Alexandria via Cairo. He then crossed the Mediterranean by boat leaving Alexandria on 30 December 1777, followed the Turkish coast in poor weather, arriving in Marseilles on 25 March and, after 20 days' quarantine there, he reached Calais on 19 April and was in London by 22 April 1777. Dalrymple, after travelling from

Fig 8.4 Warren Hastings (1732-1818). Tilly Kettle. © National Portrait Gallery, London.

Fig 8.5 George Baldwin at Vienna in Autumn 1780 (1744-1826). Lithograph by J(oseph) Bouvier. © National Portrait Gallery, London (NPG D11274).

Fig 8.6 Lt-Gen Sir Eyre Coote (1726-1783). Attrib. Henry Robert Morland. © National Portrait Gallery, London.

Madras to London in 1777, produced a report entitled 'Correspondence with India via Suez' in which he estimated that the trip from Bengal to Suez would take 40 days, with a further 88 days via Alexandria, Trieste or Venice, that is, a total of seven weeks. Yet Dalrymple also observed that the Sublime Porte (the Guardians of the Holy Places) was hostile to any scheme that would only benefit the local beys.

In response to correspondence from Coote, Capper produced his *Observations on the Passage to India, Through Egypt: Also By Vienna to Aleppo and From Thence By Bagdad and Directly Across the Great Desert to Bassora. With occasional remarks on the adjacent countries, an account of the different stages, and sketches of the several routes on four copper-plates* (London, W Faden, 1785), in which he assessed the various routes.[2] It comprises several journals, including two by Baldwin, that are full of fascinating local detail and numerous hints for the travellers in the region. In his *Observations*, Capper outlined the problems of organizing times of sailing during the year, for the passage up the Red Sea was little known to Europeans and 'is rendered extremely dangerous by rocks and shoals and the wind'. Ships' captains needed to take note of the direction of prevailing winds, for the north part of the Red Sea has persistent north-west winds of 7–12 km/h. The rest of the Red Sea and the Gulf of Aden are subjected to regular and seasonally reversible winds associated with the monsoon seasons, as Capper described: 'If they can to embark at Gedda time enough to avail themselves of the Khumseen wind which blows southerly from the end of March to the middle of May and conveys them in less than a month back again to Suez the vessels from India must also quit Gedda so as to be out of the streights [sic] of Babelmandel before the end of August.'[3]

Eyles Irwin's rather poetic travel account, published in 1787, was aptly entitled *Series of Adventures in the Course of a Voyage up the Red Sea*.[4] Irwin also published several volumes of rather bad poems about Arabia, the Nile, the desert and so on, along the lines of:

> and on thy furthest sandy shore
> Which hears the Red Sea's billows roar
> May Commerce smile her sails unfold
> And change thine iron age to gold

Irwin's account reads like a *Boy's Own* pastoral adventure, reminiscent of *The Arabian Nights* – tales also recommended by Capper to his readers as embodying life there. About Irwin's *Adventures*, *The Critical Review* began:

> The author Mr Eyles Irwin seems to be an active and spirited young man of good sense and understanding with a tender and benevolent heart who has performed the disagreeable talk allotted him by his masters the East India Company with great zeal and intrepidity, met with many hair-breadth scapes and braved innumerable dangers amongst a set of unlettered barbarous and perfidious savages through dangerous and uncultivated desarts [sic] hitherto unknown to the European traveller... That insatiable curiosity and love of the marvellous and astonishing, which is implanted

in our natures, is never so agreeably flattered as by discoveries of unknown tracts, and the relation of strange and perilous adventures; voyages and travels, therefore, especially if written by men of credit, and character are generally read with more avidity than books of any other kind.[5]

Leaving Madras in January 1777, Irwin entered the Red Sea by the straits of Bab al-Mandab; then arrived at Mocha and then was driven onto the Arabian coast and to the Gulf of Suez but 'by the treachery of the Arabs' was carried to Qusayr, a port in Upper Egypt. He then travelled 120 miles with the caravan for Qena on the Nile across the Eastern Desert, was 'carried by other treacherous guides to Banute', and eventually reached Qena on 18 September 1777. This was followed by a journey through the deserts of Thebais during which he met a band of robbers, travelled along the banks of the Nile and saw the Pyramids. He arrived and explored Grand Cairo, where he stayed with George Baldwin; then embarked for Alexandria, where he met Baldwin's agent, Signor Brandi, and embarked on the *Cleopatra*, a French ship commanded by Mr Calvi, for which journey Irwin paid a fee of 133 crowns. He reached Marseilles on 8 October 1777.

Like Capper and Dalrymple, Irwin was able to provide much useful information about the routes they took and the peoples they met. Given that Irwin endured terrible experiences in al-Qusayr and Qena, it is surprising that Capper wrote in favour of the route. Furthermore, Capper gives no indication that he shared his journey to Alexandria with Dalrymple. In fact, it is hard to work out from Capper's descriptions that he travelled up the Red Sea rather than towards India, and he even suggests that it would be quite within reasonable limits to take only 59 days for the journey. Likewise, Irwin made no reference to Capper's journey by the Syrian desert.

There was a much more pressing reason for Dalrymple, Capper and Irwin to travel through the Middle East, however, than to simply identify possible routes to India and the hazards travellers might encounter. All three desperately needed to inform the East India Company Court of Directors, in London of the house arrest of Lord Pigot (1719–77) (Fig.8.7) the Governor of Madras, at the Garden House, on 24 August 1776, by a large

Fig 8.7 George Pigot, Baron Pigot (1719-1777). George Willison. © National Portrait Gallery, London.

faction of the Madras Council under George Stratton (1733–1800), who later became an MP. Basically, Pigot had wanted to reinstate the Thuljaji, Rajah of Tanjore (1738–87), in southern India, to the financial detriment of Mohammad 'Ali Khan Wallajah (1717–95), the Nawab of Arcot, and his creditors in the Madras administration. A minority of councillors – Dalrymple, John Maxwell Stone and Claud Russell – were suspended from office and increasingly harassed by the majority.[6]

Eventually, Pigot secured a place for Dalrymple in October 1776 on the sloop HMS *Swallow*, under the command of Captain John Panton, so that Dalrymple could report to the Company's Court of Directors, in London. Pigot sent duplicate copies of his despatches to London via a French frigate, *l'Etoile*, and another set with Captain Robert Wood, Mayor of Madras, on the *Grenville* which arrived in Plymouth by 25 April 1777. Capper, who sided with the majority, using the excuse that he needed to return to England on urgent family business, also managed to secure a berth on the *Swallow* and carried despatches from the Majority Council. As a Madras merchant, John de Fries, wrote to Robert Palk, a previous Governor of Madras:

> 1776, October 10th, Madras. 'This goes by the *Swallow*, which is to put the letters ashore at Suez, to be forwarded from thence to Grand Cairo and Alexandria and so to Europe, and may probably be the first advice that you will receive of the revolution that happened in the Government of this settlement on 24th August last. Mr Dalrymple goes with Lord Pigot's packet, and Colonel Capper with the Nabob's, by whom I send this.'

Dalrymple, a stubborn man of great integrity, was first employed by the East India Company in 1759. Previously, he had commanded an East India Company ship to survey the China Sea, made a treaty with the Sultan of Sulu, Sharapud-Din (*r.*1789–1808), and established a settlement on Balabangan, now an Batavian island. He had also been the Royal Society's candidate to lead the Transit of Venus 1769 expedition (1768–71) that was eventually led by Captain James Cook. On the *Swallow*, Dalrymple kept a maritime log on his journey from Madras having borrowed a chronometer from Captain Abercromby of the *Grenville* – from 14 October 1776 (off Sri Lanka) to 10 January 1777, when they reached Suez, where he sketched some of the Red Sea harbours.

North-westerly winds in the Red Sea lengthened their passage from Madras to Suez by three months. Dalrymple, Capper and Dighton were detained for several days by custom officials under instructions from Ibrahim Bey in Cairo, until Baldwin intervened. On 19 January 1777, Dalrymple despatched a letter to the Company's Court of Directors (unbeknown to Capper) from Alexandria that was received overland in London on 17 March 1777, along with other relevant despatches. In this letter, Dalrymple also described the overland journey from Suez to Alexandria via Cairo. They left Alexandria on 30 January 1777, followed the Turkish coast in poor weather (with Dalrymple producing sketches and charts) and arrived in Marseilles on 25 March. After 20 days' quarantine there, Dalrymple (and no doubt Capper) reached Calais on 19 April and was in London by 22 April 1777. In London, Pigot's plight was met with alarm by the Court of Directors and the matter was raised in Parliament. Unsurprisingly perhaps, neither Capper nor Dalrymple ever mentioned the other in their missives and publications.

Meanwhile, in Madras, other Company officers were keenly sensitive to the wrong done to Pigot. Claud Russell and other friends, including Eyles Irwin, Pigot's secretary the Hon. Edward Monckton (1744–1832) of Somerford Hall, Staffordshire,[7] and William Burke (1729–98), a putative cousin of Edmund Burke MP, objected strongly to Pigot's treatment by the rump Madras Council under George Stratton. In an attempt to carry on as normal during the winter of 1776–77, 'the Mount became the gayest place on the Coast', when Monckton, Claud Russell and John Maxwell Stone all gave 'uncommonly splendid balls' for Christmas, New Year's Day and Twelfth Night.[8]

> Mr Russell made a grand entertainment of cards and supper at the Mount, both at Christmas and on New Year's Day, and put up a handsome *pandal* [drapped pavilion]. Most of the civil servants, some of the officers and the principal English and Armenian residents were present. Mr Stratton found himself deserted on those occasions, as everyone went to visit Lord Pigot.[9]

Several were suspended by the majority, including Eyles Irwin, Dalrymple, Maxwell Stone and Claud Russell. Aiming to explain the situation to the Court of Directors in person and carrying a bundle of despatches, Eyles Irwin sailed from Madras for Suez in early January 1777 on the 'snow' *Adventure* (a square rigged vessel with two masts) under the command of Captain Bacon. After many adventures and a journey of 11 months, Irwin arrived in London in the autumn 1779 to find that he had been reinstated in his post as superintendent of the company's grounds within the bounds of Madras.

On 11 June 1777, John Whitehill (1735–?), chief at Masulipatam, who was on leave in London, was instructed to travel to Madras, with orders for Lord Pigot's immediate reinstatement. Whitehill's journey back to India was extraordinarily speedy. Dalrymple had reported in his letter from Alexandria that it might be possible to send a reply back to Madras rapidly via vessels from Marseilles to Alexandria and then by the *Swallow*, which had remained in Suez as several sailors had the scurvy, and the winds might be favourable. Whitehill left London on 13 June, travelled to Alexandria and on to Cairo in a month (instead of the normal two), over the desert to Suez and the Red Sea and then joined the *Swallow* under the command of Captain Panton in Mocha then to Madras. The sea journey took 59 days to Bombay instead of at least 78, a record that remained for many years.

The situation Whitehill encountered when he arrived in Madras on 31 August 1777 was far worse than he expected. Pigot had been dead for three months. Stratton had moved Pigot from the relatively pleasant atmosphere of the Garden House, one mile south west of Fort St George, to the fort itself. On 28 April, as his health deteriorated,

Pigot was returned to the Garden House, while still under house arrest. On 11 May 1777, Pigot died and his secretary Edward Monckton immediately demanded an inquest. Following its verdict, a charge of wilful murder was brought against the majority and all council members were recalled to London. Those senior members of Madras Council who were responsible for Pigot's mistreatment, George Stratton, Henry Brooke, Charles Floyer and George Mackay, were suspended on 31 August 1777. Russell and Stone left Madras in October 1777 on the *Egmont* via the Cape of Good Hope and arrived home after a journey of seven months. George Stratton and Henry Brooke eventually left Madras, arriving in Suez on 11 March 1778, a month after the news of Pigot's death reached London. In April 1779, Pigot's brother, Sir Hugh Pigot (1722–92) raised the matter in the House of Commons, but it was not until 27 May 1780 that the Court 'resolved that Messrs Russell, Dalrymple, Stone and Lathom, having come home in pursuance of the Resolution of the General Court, in 1777, to have their conduct inquired into, and no objection having been made in so long a time, nor appearing against their conduct, should be again employed in the Company's Service.'[10] There, under pressure from Dalrymple and Hugh Pigot MP, the majority were tried for murder at the King's Bench in February 1780 but escaped with a £1000 fine imposed on 10 February 1780 (equivalent to £150,000 in 2013), and were allowed to return to India. Floyer was appointed Chief of the Guntoor Circars in southern India, but Brooke and Stratton left the service in 1782. On the other hand, Dalrymple, Stone and Russell were all exonerated.

Of course, there is also a romantic twist to the tale. In 1775, Lord Pigot's two natural daughters, Leonora (c1761/4–1829) and Sophy/Sophia Pigot (c.1757/60/63–1800) had accompanied their father, Lord Pigot, Dalrymple and Claud Russell on the *Grenville*, captained by Abercromby, and reached Madras after a very tedious and uncomfortable passage of nine months (during which Dalrymple maintained a meticulous logbook). On his death, Pigot left his daughters in the unfortunate position of being in Madras without a guardian. Leonora and Sophia's dates of birth are vague and it has been suggested their mother was Leonora Jane Jackson, *née* Hepburn (1738–61), wife of a Robert Jackson 'employed in the Country service' – but she died in Madras probably before Leonora was born. More likely, as Howard Fry states, their mother was Indian.[11] The sisters, Sophia and Leonora, received great wealth through their father's will, as he had acquired a vast fortune in India, which included precious stones.[12] Although Dalrymple was besotted with Sophia, it was Monckton who married her on 14 March 1776, six months before Dalrymple's voyage on the *Swallow*. She brought with her a dowry of at least £20,000. Claud Russell had been planning to marry Leonora even before her father was arrested. He eventually married her in St Mary's Church, where her father had been buried five months previously. Not wanting to leave Leonora alone in Madras, a marriage settlement was drawn up on 16 October 1777 between 'Claud Russell, *esquire of Fort Saint George, Coromandel Coast, East Indies*' and Leonora Pigot.[13] She was then about 16, and had inherited a fortune estimated at around £20,000. The marriage took place in haste on the day before they both embarked on the *Egmont* bound for London. They arrived in Britain about 20 May 1778, and on *28* August 1780 Claud Russell finalized the marriage agreement.[14] Dalrymple never married, but remained devoted to Sophia and a close friend of the Russells and Moncktons until his death in 1808. [15] In his will, Dalrymple left a portrait of himself to Leonora, an Astronomical Quadrant of six inches radius made by John Bird to Claud, and to Sophia he bequeathed 'pearl ear rings and cross and rose set round with diamonds' (which Dalrymple had been given by the Sultan of Sulu).[16] Dalrymple was not the only person who admired Sophia: while travelling back across Egypt; Eyles Irwin in *Eastern Eclogues*, dedicated a poem in praise of her.

> SELIMA: or, THE FAIR GREEK.
> Scene: A Seraglio in Arabia Felix,
> TIME: NOON
> To the Hon. Mrs. S. Monckton.
> FAST by the vale that bosoms Sennaa's pride,
> By streams meander'd, and with shades supply'd;
> Shades, which the boughs of breathing spices throw,
> And streams that through eternal verdure flow;
> Where in one form the seasons shine confest,
> And blend to rule o'er Araby the blest;
> A mansion, pervious to no prying eye,
> Adorns the mead, and lifts its head on high:

Afterwards...

Eventually, they all, apart from Dalrymple, returned to India. Claud Russell returned to Madras in 1781 accompanied by his new wife but also by his brother, Patrick Russell MD FRS, who famously rewrote *Natural History of Aleppo* (1756)[17] by their half-brother, Alexander Russell MD FRS (1714–68), and published his new edition in 1794.[18] The immensely valuable accounts by Alexander and Patrick of their sojourns in Aleppo and their medical research are the subject of several recent publications.[19] Patrick also published a series of pioneering works on the natural history of India.[20] Dalrymple was appointed Company Hydrographer in 1779, and then to the Admiralty from 1795 until 1808. Between 1779 and 1794, he produced almost 550 plans and charts of harbours, navigational memoirs and 45 coastal views as well as 50–60 books and pamphlets of nautical instruction to aid East Indies navigation, based on the study of logs and journals in the Company's archive.

In response to Hastings and Coote's instructions, Capper produced a fuller account entitled *Observations* in which he described various routes between England and India that could be used. In the autumn of 1778, Capper left London, reaching Madras on 8 February 1779, taking five months and two days on his journey from Leghorn to Bombay.[21] He crossed the Great Desert to Basra with Major Thompson from Aleppo, Mr Dighton, Jean Cadeo (his French *valet de chamber*) and his cook Babeck from Aleppo. Also travelling with them were Mr Shaw's Armenian servant, 80 armed Arabs, ten of them being shaykhs, 60 camels with 31 loads plus another 19 camels accompanied by 19 Bedouin carrying tents, water and provisions; a Jewish merchant with 30 camels carrying grain; plus two strong camels who took it in turns to carry a *howdah*. Capper took the overland route 'to explore the feasibility of opening a new channel for transmitting intelligence between Europe and India, returning to Madras via Aleppo, the Arabian desert, and Basrah' and included an account in his *Observations*. According to the *Gentleman's Magazine* (1784), Capper's account of the Syrian Desert crossing to Basra in 1778 'is in general as dry as the Desert itself, though an account of the soil wind weather &c that occurred every day or the antelopes, ostriches etc. that they saw, may be interesting at the time, or to those who pursue the same route, it affords little amusement to others. Nothing remarkable seems to have happened.' He was never reimbursed for the expenses he incurred during his extensive travels and in a resentful memorial he criticized the East India Company's corrupt civil management. While nothing really eventful occurred, he did meet a party of 10,000 Bedouin 'irreconcilable enemies' to whom he paid a tribute of one chequin[22] for every camel carrying merchandise. His book also includes two journals by George Baldwin about travelling between Constantinople and Aleppo and a return journey from Constantinople to Vienna. In India, Capper resumed his post of comptroller-general of the army in Madras and became an authority on winds and monsoons. He resigned in 1791 to pursue his interests in meteorology and local agriculture in South Wales.

Eyles Irwin also returned to India by land with despatches from the Directors of the India Company to the Governments of Bombay and Madras that were 'too important to admit of delay consequently they were entitled to every attention, exertion and support which the Company's agents had in their power to bestow.' In a Supplement to his *Adventures*, he vividly described his escapades. He left London on 26 October 1780, crossed to Ostend and went on to Brussels, through the Tyrol and arrived in Venice, where he boarded a vessel on 14 November, but its captain and crew abandoned ship, so he returned to Venice, then crossed stormy seas to Latachea on the coast of Syria, continued to Aleppo (19 March), then went across the Great Syrian Desert to Baghdad, reaching Basra on 7 May, Bombay on 29 May 1781, and arriving in Madras in early June.

Irwin continued to write poems. For example, on 13 May 1781 he wrote an 'Ode to the Persian Gulf' on a voyage to Muscat.

> FAIR Gulf! whose undulating wave
> Is by the annual torrent swell'd,
> Which Tygris and Euphrates pour,
> When pressing Eden's banks to lave,
> By ruin'd Babylon impell'd,
> They join, and haste to kiss thy shore.
> "What tuneful shell may sound thy fame?

Thy Sadi and thy Hafez mute,
And all thy glory set in dust:
Yet shalt thou live with Ammon's name;
A Cyrus was thy golden fruit,
And Zoroaster, wife and just!
Deep in thy rocky bosom laid,
Quickens the embryo pearl apace,

Irwin, 'a painstaking and conscientious administrator', was then appointed Superintendent of Tinnevelly and Madura; married Honor Brooke, a cousin of the insurgent Henry Brooke in 1778; returned home in 1786; was superintendent of the East India Company's affairs in China from 1792, and retired from the service in 1794. Apart from more volumes of mediocre poems based on his Oriental reminiscences, Irwin wrote and produced *The Bedouins, or Arabs of the Desert. A Comic Opera in three Acts* that was performed for three nights at the Theatre Royal, Dublin, in 1802. Celebrating the hospitality and generosity he received during his adventures, Irwin's main character Abdullah was modelled on Osman Abu ʿAli, a benevolent Bedouin he knew in Upper Egypt.

And what of the East India Company's hopes of having a Suez route? Egypt slid into chaos after the death of Abu al-Dhahab in 1775. As Irwin described in a postscript, by August 1779, Bedouin raids on caravans of goods being transported from British ships between Suez and Cairo had got out of hand. Political instability combined with outbreaks of the plague and Ottoman distrust of foreign ships in the Red Sea, brought an end to the British attempt to open up Suez to European and Indian trade until the 1830s.

Endnotes

1   Carsten Niebuhr (1776; Amsterdam: S. J. Baalde, 1780) *Voyage en Arabie et en d'autres Pays circonvoisins*; id., *Travels through Arabia and other countries in the East,* transl. Robert Heron. (2 vols. Edinburgh, R. Morison, 1792).

2   James Capper (1783) *Observations on the passage to India, through Egypt; also to Vienna through Constantinople and Aleppo, and from thence to Bagdad, and across the Great Desert to Bassora.* London, W. Faden et al.

3   Capper, *Observations*, xv.

4   Eyles Irwin, 'Series of Adventures in the Course of a Voyage up the Red Sea: on the coasts of Arabia and Egypt; and of a route through the desarts [sic] of Thebais, in the year 1777.... ; and of a route through the desarts [sic] of Arabia, by Aleppo, Bagdad, and the Tygris to Busrah, in the years 1780 and 1781.' in *Letters to a Lady, &c.* (London, J. Dodsley, 1787).

5   *The Critical Review* 49 (1780): p. 405.

6   For a brief summary of Claud Russell's life, refer to Maurits Van den Boogert, 'Patrick Russell and the Republic of Letters in Aleppo', in Alistair Hamilton, Maurits Van den Boogert and Bart Westerweel (eds) (2005) *The Republic of Letters and the Levant*. Leiden, Brill: pp. 223–64; Janet Starkey, Examining Editions of *The Natural History of Aleppo*:

Revitalizing Eighteenth-Century Texts', PhD Thesis (University of Edinburgh, 2013) and Janet Starkey, *The Scottish Enlightenment Abroad: the Russells of Braidshaw in Aleppo and the Coromandel Coast* (Leiden: Brill), in press., forthcoming.

7 From the time George Monckton joined the Company as a Writer in Madras in 1762, he knew Lord Pigot in India. Monckton retired from India in 1778 and became MP for Stafford from 1780 to 1812.

8 H. D. Love (1913) *The Vestiges of old Madras*. London, John Murray, iii: p. 118.

9 Chokappa Chetti, one of the 'Company's merchants' in Madras, to Robert Palk, in Historical Manuscripts Commission (1922) *Report on the Palk manuscripts in the possession of Mrs Bannatyne, of Haldon*, Devon, London, HMSO: p. 311.

10 *European Magazine* 42 (1802): p. 326.

11 Pigot's long-term mistresses included Mrs Catherine Hill in Shropshire, who probably brought the sisters up after Pigot brought them to England in 1764. Pigot never married but had many other illegitimate children, including Amelia and George Wood; Elizabeth Surry; Harriet Sneed; Mary Green (c.1772–1852); Major George Pigot (1772?–1830), who migrated to South Africa; General Richard Pigot (1774–1868), a colonel in the 4th Dragoon Guards, and Sir Hugh Pigot KCB (1775/6–1857), Admiral of the White. Howard T. Fry (2013) *Alexander Dalrymple and the Expansion of British Trade*, London, Routledge: p. xxv.

12 The sisters did not inherit the 'Pigot Diamond' (c.47.38 carat) that Pigot probably brought back to England in 1764. The largest diamond in Britain, it was bequeathed to Pigot's siblings, Sir Robert (1720–96) and Sir Hugh (1722–92), and his sister Margaret (Fisher). It was eventually purchased by the Albanian ruler ʿAlī Pasha (1740–1822) who deemed it unlucky and ordered it to be crushed after he was fatally wounded.

13 Payne, BL, IOC, Orme Mss, 28 (11 March 1758), quoted in E. F. Gollannek, 'Empire Follows Art' PhD Thesis (University of Delaware, 2008): pp. 261–63.

14 Lee Family of Hartwell D-LE/4. Yorkshire Deeds; Copy Marriage Settlement D-LE/4/43 16 October 1777. D3074/B/2/1-2, 28 August 1780, *Declaration of Trust with bond Edward Monckton/Claud Russell on his marriage.*

15 George Barker to Robert Palk, in Historical Manuscripts Commission (1922) *Report on the Palk manuscripts in the possession of Mrs Bannatyne, of Haldon*, Devon, London, HMSO: p. 314.

16 Fry, *Alexander Dalrymple*: p. xxvi.

17 Alex.[ander] Russell, MD (1856 [1756]) *The natural history of Aleppo, and parts adjacent, containing a description of the city and the natural productions of its neighbourhood*. London, Andrew Millar.

18 Alex.[ander] Russell, MD (1794) *The natural history of Aleppo, and parts adjacent, containing a description of the city and the natural productions of its neighbourhood*. Second edition, revised, enlarged and illustrated with notes by [his half-brother] P.[atrick] Russell, 2 vols. London, G. G. and J. Robinson.

19 Maurits Van den Boogert (2010) *Aleppo observed*. Oxford, Oxford University Press/Arcadia Library; Philip Mansel (2016) *Aleppo: the rise and fall of Syria's great merchant city*. London, I.B. Tauris; Janet Starkey, *The Scottish Enlightenment Abroad* (Leiden: Brill), in press., forthcoming.

20 Patrick Russell's works on Indian natural history include his Preface to William Roxborough's *Plants of the coast of Coromandel* (London, [W. Bulmer], 1795): pp i–vi; *An Account of Indian Serpents Collected on the Coast of Coromandel* (London, George Nicol,

1796); *An Account of Indian Snakes collected on the coast of Coromandel* 2 vols (London, The East India Company, 1803); *Descriptions and figures of two hundred fishes* (London, G. and W. Nicol, 1803); *An Account of Indian serpents, collected on the coast of Coromandel* (London, Shakespeare Press, 1805); *A continuation of an account of Indian serpents containing descriptions and figures from specimens and drawings* (London, The East India Company, 1801 [1809])

21 From 29 September to 2 October 1778, he travelled from Leghorn to Latichea; 1–4 November 1778 from Latichea to Aleppo; 10 November–18 December 1778 across the Syrian Desert.

22 Cf. A sequin: a gold coin of the Venetian Republic.

Bibliography

Capper, James (1783) *Observations on the passage to India, through Egypt; also to Vienna through Constantinople and Aleppo, and from thence to Bagdad, and across the Great Desert to Bassora.* London, W. Faden et al.

Fry, Howard T. (2013) *Alexander Dalrymple and the Expansion of British Trade.* London, Routledge.

Gollannek, E. F. 'Empire Follows Art': Exchange and the Sensory Worlds of Empire in Britain and Its Colonies, 1740–1775, PhD thesis (University of Delaware, 2008).

Historical Manuscripts Commission (1922) *Report on the Palk manuscripts in the possession of Mrs Bannatyne, of Haldon, Devon.* London, HMSO.

Irwin, Eyles (1787). 'Series of Adventures in the Course of a Voyage up the Red Sea: on the coasts of Arabia and Egypt; and of a route through the desarts of Thebais, in the year 1777.... ; and of a route through the desarts of Arabia, by Aleppo, Bagdad, and the Tygris to Busrah, in the years 1780 and 1781.' in *Letters to a Lady, &c.* London, J. Dodsley.

Love, H.D. (1913) *The Vestiges of old Madras.* London, John Murray.

Mansel, Philip (2016) *Aleppo: The Rise and Fall of Syria's Great Merchant City.* London, I.B. Tauris.

Niebuhr, Carsten (1780) *Voyage en Arabie et en d'autres Pays circonvoisins.* Amsterdam, S.J. Baalde.

Niebuhr, Carsten (1792) *Travels through Arabia and other countries in the East*, transl. Robert Heron. 2 vols. Edinburgh. R. Morison.

Russell, Alex.[ander] MD (1856 [1756]) *The natural history of Aleppo, and parts adjacent, containing a description of the city and the natural productions in its neighbourhood.* London. Andrew Millar.

Russell, Alex.[ander] MD (1794) *The natural history of Aleppo, containing a description of the city, and the principal natural productions in its neighbourhood*, 2nd edition, revised, enlarged and illustrated with notes by [his half-brother] P[atrick] Russell, 2 vols. London, G. G. and J. Robinson,.

Russell, Patrick (1795) Preface to William Roxburgh's *Plants of the coast of Coromandel.* London, [W. Bulmer], i: pp. i–vi.

Russell, Patrick (1796) *An Account of Indian Serpents Collected on the Coast of Coromandel.* London, George Nicol.

Russell, Patrick (1803) *An account of Indian snakes collected on the coast of Coromandel*, 2 vols. London, The East India Company.

Russell, Patrick (1803) *Descriptions and figures of two hundred fishes*, London, G and W Nicol.

Russell, Patrick (1805) *An account of Indian serpents, collected on the coast of Coromandel*, London, Shakespeare Press.

Russell, Patrick (1801 [1809]) *A continuation of an account of Indian Serpents containing descriptions and figures from specimens and drawings* [with a memoir of the life and writings of P. Russell – Appendix]. London, the East India Company.

Starkey, Janet, (2013) 'Examining Editions of *The Natural History of Aleppo*: Revitalizing Eighteenth-Century Texts', PhD Thesis, University of Edinburgh, online.

Starkey, Janet, (in press) *The Scottish Enlightenment Abroad: the Russells of Braidshaw in Aleppo and the Coromandel*, Leiden, Brill.

Van den Boogert, Maurits (2005) 'Patrick Russell and the Republic of Letters in Aleppo', in Alistair Hamilton, Maurits Van den Boogert and Bart Westerweel (eds), *The Republic of Letters and the Levant*. Leiden, Brill: pp. 223–64.

Van den Boogert, Maurits (2010) *Aleppo observed*. Oxford, Oxford University Press/ Arcadia Library.

An Artist Recovered from Anonymity: Antoine van der Steen – 'Un peintre du Bosphore', a Discoverer of the Midas Monument and Lieutenant-fireworker in the Bombay Artillery

Brian J. Taylor

In 1994 and 2011, paintings of Constantinople and its environs in Sweden's Von Celsing Collection of Ottoman Art at Biby – now in the Orientalist Museum at Doha, Qatar – were identified as the work of the 18th-century Dutch landscape artist Antoine van der Steen (?–1782) or attributed to him. Signed and dated letters written in French found in 2011 and 2012, two each in the National Archives in The Hague, and in the Von Celsing Collection, indicate that van der Steen was artist-in-residence at the Swedish embassy in Constantinople between 1768 and 1771 and perhaps for several years either side. In addition, and contrary to previous research, van der Steen and the English entrepreneur and former consul George Baldwin (1744–1826) can now be identified as the first Europeans, in 1780, to discover the Midas Monument in Turkey's Phrygian Highlands.

This new information has necessitated a reappraisal of the life and work of Antoine van der Steen, who is sometimes referred to as Jan van der Steen. Yet, there are shortcomings in our knowledge of this obscure artist: his date and place of birth, nationality, and his training – if any. He may have been affiliated to a northern Dutch school of painting (Scheen Jr, 1981: p. 495), specializing in city, land and riverscapes.

But there also remains the enigma as to why the artist, ostensibly untrained militarily – and surely a pre-requisite for such a posting – on arrival at Surat, in India, became an officer in the Bombay Artillery. A comprehensive list of officers who served in the regiment from its foundation in 1749 records that Anthony Vandersteen died, cause unspecified, on 31 October 1782.

What's in a name?

Variously known as Antoine van der Steen, Jan van der Steen, Anthony Vandersteen, A. Steen and even A. van der Heen (an error in differentiating between 'S' and 'H'), van der Steen was initially referred to as '*een schilderij van den Hollandschen schilder*' (Van Woensel, 1789: pp. 83–84) and later as Jan van der Steen, a Dutch artist who subsequently anglicized his name to Stone (van Eijnden and van der Willigen, 1817: p. 188; Scheen, 1970: p. 388).

Fletcher, in describing the Von Celsing Collection refers to the large and magnificent set of view paintings and drawings by the Dutchman, Jan van der Steen (Fletcher, 2011), although the two letters found associated with the same collection are signed A. van der Steen. Similarly, the letters in the National Archives in The Hague are signed Antoine van der Steen, while the artist is referred to in a list of officers of the Bombay Artillery as Anthony Vandersteen (Spring, 2005: p. 74).

It has been assumed that Antoine van der Steen is of Dutch descent, but without his date and place of birth, his nationality must remain in doubt because in the 18th century the Netherlands was divided into the United Provinces in the north and the Austrian Netherlands in the south, incorporating most of modern Belgium. Therefore, 'van der Steen', thought to be a common surname throughout the Netherlands at this time, could have been northern or southern Dutch, a distinction of relevance, perhaps, in speculating on the early life of the artist.

Previous research – before 1995

Most of the initial information on Antoine van der Steen seems to have been derived from a near contemporary of his, the Dutchman Pieter van Woensel (1747–1808), physician, adventurer and travel writer whose biographical account of van der Steen (Van Woensel, 1789: pp. 83–84), and probably based on secondary sources, cannot be relied upon. Nevertheless, it has been reiterated, with additions, by R. van Eijnden and A. van der Willigen (1817: p. 188), P. A. Scheen (1970: p. 388) and P. A. Scheen Jr. (1981: p. 673) who collectively suggest that van der Steen was a Dutch painter who was active between 1750 and c.1784 and worked in and around Constantinople but then travelled overland to Oost-Indie between 1750 and 1760 with a party of Englishmen. (It is suggested that those authors using the term 'Oost-Indie' were referring to the eastern half of the Indian subcontinent, notably Bengal or the East Indies.) There, he anglicized his name, joined the East India Company and became an artillery officer before dying in Bengal before 1784, perhaps even well before 1784 (van Eijnden and van der Willigen, 1817: p. 188).

In 1968, in an unpublished thesis on George Baldwin and British interests in Egypt, (Zahlan 1968: p. 88) referred to Baldwin as having left Constantinople on 11 May 1780, 'accompanied by van der Steen, a Dutch painter'. Zahlan also mentions a report (FO78/1) by Sir Robert Ainslie, the English ambassador (1776–94) in Constantinople to the Earl of Hillsborough dated 17 May 1780, in which Ainslie refers to the English entrepreneur George Baldwin leaving the city on 11 May 1780, accompanied by Vandersteen, a Dutch artist, bound for Aleppo, Basra and India. Zahlan (1968: p. 88) also recounts, briefly, an attack on Baldwin's party by robbers and the loss of some of the baggage, but there are no further references to van der Steen or the 'wondrous building' he and Baldwin discovered on their journey through Turkey's Phrygian Highlands.

In August 1994, following a visit to the Celsing Estate at Biby, near Stockholm and an interview with Fredrik von Celsing, Mansel (1995: pp. 218 and 465) reported seeing 'twenty-five hypnotizing (but unsigned) panoramas of the Golden Horn, the city, the palaces and boats of the Bosphorus and, above all, the blue and green kiosks and gilded pavilions of Sa'adabad, of which they are the best visual record'. Forming part of the Von Celsing Collection of Ottoman Art, these paintings, suggested Mansel (1995: p. 218), may have been by the same artist ('A. Steen') who dedicated some drawings of Constantinople to Monsieur Gustaf de Celsing, resident and envoy at the Swedish embassy in Constantinople from 1747 to 1770 (Theolin, 2001: p. 192). The paintings were probably executed prior to 1770, before Ulric succeeded his brother, although Gustaf remained in Constantinople until 1773 (Germaner and Inankur, 2002: p. 28).

New research – 1995 to present

In 2001, Theolin (2001: p. 63) referred to the Von Celsing Collection as 'a unique Turkish collection from the eighteenth century' and one of 'major historical and cultural significance' – even though most of the paintings were anonymous, attributed to European or local artists and probably dated to the mid 1700s. Because of the anonymity of most of the paintings at this time, the works of van der Steen were not referred to here, but there are several references to him in a substantive account of the history of the Collection by a number of distinguished art historians (Adahal and others, 2003). However, references to van der Steen mainly reiterate the often inaccurate statements of previous researchers and add very little to an account of the life and work of this artist.

In 2011, in his catalogue of the Von Celsing Collection of Ottoman art at Biby (comprising 121 paintings), Sotheby's director Andrew Fletcher, in reviewing the same landscapes seen by Mansel in 1994, identified most of them as being the work of 'Jan van der Steen' whom, he states, died in Bengal before 1784. The identifications were based on a signature and date (1771) hidden beneath the frame of one of the oils (Fletcher Catalogue No. 25). Several other paintings in the same genre were either attributed to Jan van der Steen or affiliated to the 'School of Constantinople, 18th century.'

In addition to the paintings, several letters were discovered in a hitherto unopened travel chest brought back to Sweden by Ulric Celsing in the 1780s. One of these, addressed to '*Son Excellence*' (Gustaf Celsing Jr) was written by 'A. van der Steen' from Pera and dated 30 September 1768, while two other letters, also addressed to 'His Excellency' were written by fellow artist Francis Smith (fl. 1763–79) from Naples and signed and dated 6 October 1770 and 20 February 1771. In the second of his letters, Smith commends 'Monsieur van der Steen' as a very skilful painter who would no doubt produce an excellent collection of views of Constantinople. The two letters dated 1768 and 1771 indicate van der Steen was based in Constantinople between these dates and probably residing there both earlier and later as artist-in-residence at the Swedish embassy.

In 2012, and in honour of 400 years of diplomatic and trade relations between Holland and Turkey, the Amsterdam Museum held an exhibition entitled 'The Chamber of the Levantine Trade – Dutch Merchants and the Ottoman Sultans' in which three paintings by van der Steen were displayed. All three were probably given to the Directorate of Levant Trade (1625–1826) by diplomat Joost Frederik Tor (born c1740; Koene, 2013: p. 99) following his sojourn in Constantinople and the Ottoman Empire in the second half of the 18th century. Earlier (1789), one of these paintings (SK-A-2056), a view of Constantinople from the Swedish embassy at Pera, was reproduced as an engraving by Tor's friend Pieter van Woensel to illustrate (facing p. 84) his '*Aanteekeningen, gehouden op eene reize door Turkijen, Natolien, de Krim en Rusland, in de jaaren 1784-89*'. The other two paintings represent views of the Bosphorus with the aqueduct of Justinian in the distance (SK-A-2054) and of the Dardanelles showing a fort (SH-A-2053) – one of several built on either side of the Strait – and a ship firing a shot. All three paintings were dated 1770–80 by the Rijksmuseum.

Also in 2012, two more letters signed Antoine van der Steen and dated 13 June and 22 August 1780 were discovered in the National Archives in The Hague (Eveline Sint Nicolaas, personal communication). Written from Aleppo in Syria and addressed to the Dutch ambassador, Baron de Haeften (1729–1800), in Constantinople, they allude to the artist's reason for going to India, the need for secrecy and his determination to continue on the journey after the party was attacked near Antioch and Baldwin had returned to Constantinople.

Antoine van der Steen – 'un pientre du Bosphore'

In the second half of the 18th century, a few Dutch artists sought employment at one or more of the European embassies based in Constantinople. Among them was Johan Raye (1737–1823) who became attaché to the Dutch ambassador Willem Gerrit Dedel (1765–68) at the Palais de Hollande, and accompanied him on his travels (Spanbroek, 1765). During his sojourn in Constantinople, Raye produced several coloured drawings of the city and its environs and of Ambassador Dedel being presented at court (Hoenkamp-Mazgon, 2002: pp. 73 and 75; Raye 1987, fig. 25) in a conventional format established earlier in the century by Jean-Baptiste Vanmour (1671–1737).

Another Dutch artist and probably a contemporary of Raye was Antoine van der Steen who stayed at the Palais de Suede for several years. Alas, nothing is known about van der Steen's early life – his place and date of birth and whether he was self-taught or trained professionally as a member of one of the trade and craft guilds flourishing in the Netherlands from the first half of the 17th century and which, in some instances, developed their own style of painting. However, there are no records in the surviving archives to suggest van der Steen was a member of the Archief Delft (Rene Liefaard, personal communication), the Guild of Saint Luke in Haarlem or the Confrerie Pictura (Suzanne Laemers, personal communication).

Furthermore, and unlike Raye (Raye, 1987), nothing is known about when and how van der Steen journeyed to Constantinople. It has been suggested he worked in and around the city c.1750 (Scheen, 1970: p. 388; Scheen Jr., 1981: p. 495) and then travelled overland to India between 1750 and 1760. However, the recent discovery of signed and dated letters in the Von Celsing archives and an item of correspondence (FO78/1) between Ambassador Sir Robert Ainslie and the Earl of Hillsborough dated 17 May 1780 indicate that in the unlikely event of van der Steen having undertaken two similar journeys, the earlier dates must be discounted in favour of a period between the mid 1760s and 1780 – after which the artist left Constantinople for India.

Van der Steen's known oeuvre indicates that he was a landscape artist who worked mainly in and around Constantinople where he took advantage of the elevated position of the Swedish embassy at Pera to paint a number of panoramas of the city as it looked in the second half of the 18th century, a hilly and sprawling metropolis of 7–800,000 people living in houses built of wood and plaster, but often with fine views of the sea (Baltimore, 1767: p. 38-9). (Fig.9.1)

Of the 25 paintings in the Von Celsing Collection alluded to by Mansel (1995: p. 218) as being the work of 'A. Steen', these have since been catalogued by Fletcher (2011) and subdivided by him into 21 by 'Jan van der Steen', three attributed to Jan van der Steen, one engraving after Jan van der Steen and six paintings representing the 'School of Constantinople, 18th century'. The paintings are mainly oil on canvas together with watercolour on paper and ink and wash on paper, some of the watercolours probably representing preparatory works for a number of the

Fig 9.1 Constantinople from the Swedish embassy at Pera with the Topkapi Palace (at centre) and imperial caiques on the Bosphorus. Oil painting (SK-A-2056) by Antoine van der Steen c1770-1780.
© Rijksmuseum, Amsterdam.

larger canvases. Although several paintings assigned by Fletcher to the 'School of Constantinople, 18th century' may be the work of van der Steen, they cannot be confidently identified as such because they are damaged (Andrew Fletcher, personal communication).

Among the Von Celsing Collection are three panoramas of the city and its suburbs taken from the Asian side of the Bosphorus. Painted from slightly different perspectives, prominent and familiar landmarks such as the Topkapi Palace, the Genoese Tower and the Blue Mosque can be seen as well as the ubiquitous Bosphorus, replete with sailing vessels of all sizes. Two of these 'cityscapes' are referred to in a letter the artist wrote to Gustaf Celsing Jr. on 30 September 1768, in which he informs his patron that while the '*deux vues*' are nearly finished, he would like to be advised on where to place the dervishes (Fletcher, 2011: p. 47).

Several more paintings in the collection are also large in scale and represent further examples of Mansel's 'hypnotizing panoramas' (Mansel, 1995: p. 218). These include a view of the Sultan's palace of Besiktas (Beshik-Tash) beside the Bosphorus with the Sultan's barge in the foreground, a painting attributed to Jan van der Steen and 'securely' dated to pre-1780 (Fletcher, 2011: p. 38) because it excludes the Valide Sultan Dairesi or the Queen Mother's apartment built in 1780 and which Antoine Melling later included in his work (Melling, 1809–19; Fletcher, 2011: p. 38).

The Dolmabahce Palace of its day, the Besiktas Palace was, like most if not all of the buildings in Constantinople at the time, built of wood and constructed piece-meal as a collection of waterfront units or yali-kiosks.

Alas, waterfront palaces such as that at Besiktas did not last very long and were replaced by a succession of new buildings in the European style that were not always approved by visitors to the city. For example, Julia Pardoe, who arrived in Constantinople in 1835, thought the new palace at Besiktas, built for Sultan Selim III, was the most extensive 'but decidedly the least picturesque and elegant' of the waterfront palaces (Pardoe, 1850: p. 1).

Another grand palace represented in the Von Celsing Collection is that of Sa'adabad or the 'Palace of Eternal Happiness', built for Sultan Ahmed III in 1721 and reconstructed in 1723 following a rebellion. Situated where two streams known as the Sweet Waters of Europe run through meadows down to the sea, this palace represented, probably more than any other, a conscious attempt by the ruling Ottomans to mimic European classical architecture (Artan, 2006, 465), notably French classical architecture and garden design. Perhaps it is no coincidence that prints of Versailles form part of the library at Topkapi (Mansel, 1995: p. 180).

Hence at Sa'adabad, there were parterres, rococo-style water features, rows of espalier trees and elegant walkways between lakes, but there was also a number of typical Ottoman features that appealed so much to Mansel when he first saw the paintings of Sa'adabad in the collection, namely 'the blue and green kiosks and gilded pavilions' (Mansel, 1995: p. 218), suggest this particular royal residence must have represented the epitome of the golden age of waterfront palaces in the 18th century.

Of course, the Bosphorus, the 'pulse' of Constantinople, features in several paintings by or attributed to van der Steen (Fig.9.2) while others, including one signed and dated 'Steen f 1771', depict, in the far distance, the tiered aqueduct attributed to the Byzantine Roman emperor Justinian and his architects Anthemis and Isidorus (*c*.538 AD). One of many supplying water to Constantinople, the aqueduct (approx. 240m long and 35m high) is best seen (Fletcher Catalogue No. 26) spanning the valley of Ali Bey Kouy (White, 1846: p. 24) near the Sweet Waters of Europe, having conveyed water from several sources near the village of Belgrade and a large reservoir farther downstream before eventually debauching into a *taksim* (reservoir) at Egri Kapou (Edrehi 1855: p. 17) erected by Emperor Constantine.

In other paintings by van der Steen, members of the Ottoman court including the Grand Vizier are shown encamped in the shade cast by some trees, extensive gardens are seen beside the shores of the Bosphorus, and Tarabya (or Therapeia), a resort on the eastern shore of the Upper Bosphorus, is also represented as a watercolour on paper – probably a preparatory work for an oil on canvas showing the same view.

Because of its location and the 'pure' air associated with the Upper Bosphorus (believed to be an antidote to epidemics such as cholera and plague), Tarabya

Fig 9.2 The Bosphorus seen from Beykoz (at northern end of the waterway) with the aqueduct of Justinian in the distance. Oil painting (SK-A-2054) by Antoine van der Steen c1770-1780. © Rijksmuseum, Amsterdam.

was a favourite summer vacation for the well-to-do of Constantinople, especially those from the Greek Orthodox ruling class, who sailed their *kayiks* and *sandals* (rowing boats) and built their wooden palaces or yale beside the blue waters of the Bosphorus, jostling for position with the imperial palaces.

Alas, the original wooden yale beside the Bosphorus have gone or are all but gone, many of them having burned down, including the old estate at Tarabya (1911). Therefore, van der Steen's paintings represent postcards from the past by one who, because of his hitherto anonymity, was not considered by Boppe (1911) to be one of his *'peintres du Bosphore'* even though his patron, Gustaf Celsing, was said to be, like Gustaf Celsing Sr., *'particulierement attaché a etudier l'Orient'* (Boppe, 1911: p. 152).

Many of van der Steen's images of buildings beside the shores of the Bosphorus are detailed and finely drawn and suggest that, like Antoine Melling, he may have had some training in architectural or technical draughtsmanship or the use of a camera obscura. It is not known whether the Celsings were directly involved in the choice of subject matter that van der Steen depicted or whether the artist was allowed complete freedom of expression, but on at least one occasion (letter from van der Steen to his patron dated 30 September 1768), van der Steen, while regretting the fact bad weather had prevented him from going out into the countryside to draw, expressed the view that he hoped he would have the honour of going with His Excellency to Belgrade to do some drawing.

The Forest of Belgrade, situated 15km northwest of Constantinople, was a favourite location for those wishing to escape from the plagues and the oppressive heat of the city in the spring and summer months, and a popular venue for artists. Many Europeans and wealthy Ottomans had houses there where they could enjoy views over the Black Sea and the Bosphorus (Eveline Sint Nicolaas, 2003: p. 19).

Antoine van der Steen and art patronage in Constantinople in the second half of the 18th century

In the second half of the 18th century, during van der Steen's sojourn in Constantinople, the diplomatic quarter of Pera (Beyoglu), situated high up above Galata on the European side of the Golden Horn and with extensive views over the city, represented a prime location for the European embassies and their staff and an ideal situation for artists – and as some embassies were close together or even adjacent to one another along the Grande Rue de Pera, an *esprit de corps* often developed that enabled artists to get to know one another and in some instances share the same patron. Some ambassadors (for example, the Comte de Choiseul-Gouffier and Sir Robert Ainslie) sought to record their time spent in the exotic east by employing an artist-in-residence who was commissioned to produce a portfolio of paintings and drawings which not only depicted a colourful Constantinople and its environs but also represented other parts of the vast Ottoman Empire and its peoples.

Thus the French artist (of Flemish origin) Jean-Baptiste Vanmour (1671–1737) worked for the French ambassador, the Marquis du Ferriol (in post 1699–1711), a number of French envoys and the Dutch ambassador Cornelis Calkoen[1] (in post 1727–44) while two other French ambassadors, the Comte de Vergennes (in post 1756–68) (Murphy, 1982), and the Comte de Choiseul-Gouffier (in post 1784–92) employed Antoine de Favray and Louis-François Cassas who lived and worked at the French embassy in 1762–71 and 1784–86, respectively (Mansel, 1996: p. 48).

Le Comte de Choiseul-Gouffier also employed the artist Jean-Baptiste Hilair (or Hilaire) both before and during his tour of duty. The English ambassador Sir Robert Ainslie, one of the longest serving of the European diplomats based in Constantinople (1776–94) paid for the services of the Italian-trained artist Luigi Mayer and his wife Clara Bartholdi (c.1750–1803) who 'resided' at the embassy from about 1786 to 1794 (Newton, 2007: p. 32; Taylor, 2013: p. 172) but then left to accompany Ainslie on his return journey to England. Sometime prior to 1780, van der Steen was also a member of Ainslie's household (FO78/1) before being 'debauched out of my family' by George Baldwin at the onset of their journey to India. Evidently, Ainslie felt aggrieved that Baldwin had had the audacity to poach the artist without, presumably, coming to a gentleman's agreement on this matter.

Either by employing an artist-in-residence or by collecting the works of others, or both, patrons based in Constantinople often acquired considerable private collections like that of the Von Celsing family from Sweden. Begun by Gustaf Celsing Snr. (1679–1743), a student of oriental languages and secretary at the Swedish legation based in Constantinople between 1709 and 1714, his interest and aptitude for collecting works of art were carried on by his sons Gustaf Jr (1723–89) and Ulric Celsing (1731–1805) who, together, served the Swedish embassy as secretaries, residents and ambassadors between 1745 and 1780, and who sent back to Sweden more than 100 pictures from Constantinople (Mansel, 1996: p. 48).

Representing one of the greatest assemblages of Ottoman art in the 18th century, the Celsing brothers not only bought paintings, but were patrons to the Dutch landscape artist Antoine van der Steen between 1768 and 1771 and probably for several years either side. Also patronized by the Celsing brothers, but on a more tenuous and less satisfactory basis was the English water colourist Francis Smith (fl. 1763–79) who, based on the evidence of the two letters he wrote, was very dilatory in complying with his patron's wishes.

However, unlike fellow landscape artists Louis-François Cassas and Luigi Mayer who travelled extensively throughout the Ottoman Empire (Llewellyn, 1989: p. 36; Taylor, 2013), van der Steen does not appear to have travelled far beyond the environs of Constantinople and so his oeuvre is limited. While he may have been content to paint in and around the city, a letter he wrote from Aleppo on 13 June 1780 to Baron de Haeften, the Dutch ambassador in Constantinople, points to some serious underlying causes, to unspecified 'discomforts' he complained about that prevented him from travelling, including travelling to other countries that he had 'desired for so long'. Hence his eagerness to join George Baldwin on his trip to India.

Furthermore, and unlike Antoine de Favray (1706–98), who lived in Constantinople between 1762 and 1771, van der Steen only incorporated people in his foregrounds and may not to have been attracted, like Favray, 'by female subjects depicted in the vain glorious flash of their adornments' (Degiorgio and Fiorentino, 2004: p. 108). Similarly, and unlike, for example, de Favray and Johan Raye, van der Steen's style may not have been particularly suited to official portraiture involving, for example, audiences with the Sultan and Grand Vizier that usually coincided with the arrival and departure of a European ambassador. Hence, the anonymous portraits of Ulric Celsing in audience with the Grand Vizier and Sultan Abdulhamid I (Fletcher, 2011) and of Gustaf Celsing being received by Sultan Mustafa III, perhaps prior to his departure from Constantinople in 1773 (Gürçağlar, 2003: p. 11, fig. 4) almost certainly cannot have been painted by van der Steen. Instead, it has been suggested the portrait of Gustaf Celsing was produced by a local or Levantine artist (Gürçağlar, 2003: p. 11).

The 'missing years' – 1771-80

Between a reference to van der Steen in a letter written by Francis Smith to Ulric Celsing at the Swedish embassy on 20 February 1771 and Steen's departure for India with George Baldwin in May 1780, nothing so far is known about his whereabouts. It is possible that between these two dates van der Steen was still in the employ of the Swedish embassy – hence the views of Constantinople and its environs (Mansel, 2012: pp. 51 and 54) dated c1770–80 by the Rijksmuseum, while 'A View of the Dardanelles' (Fig.9.3), another painting in the museum, has also been given the same 'blanket' date.

However, there is no doubt van der Steen was in Constantinople in 1780 because in an item of correspondence (FO78/1) between the English ambassador, Sir Robert Ainslie and the Earl of Hillsborough dated 17 May 1780, Ainslie says, with irony, that 'the famous Mr Baldwin departed from this Place in the most secret manner on the 11th Inst, accompanied by a Dutch Painter named Vandersteen whom he debauched out of my family. I am informed they took the road of Aleppo, with intention to proceed to Bassora and embark for India.' Ainslie knew of this route because in 1779, following in the wake of Col. James Capper and party who made the journey in a 'light caravan' in 1778 (Grant, 1937: pp. 176–78), Ainslie sent two English officers with some official dispatches to Bombay via Mesopotamia by way of Aleppo and Bassora (Hoskins, 1924: pp. 309–10; Furber, 1951: p. 124). In addition, in a letter addressed to the Dutch ambassador from Aleppo and dated 13 June 1780, van der Steen mentions having left 'Mr the ambassador of England' with Baldwin for India.

Fig 9.3 The fortified Dardanelles, formally known in classical antiquity as the Hellespont. Oil painting (SK-A-2053) by Antoine van der Steen c1770-1780. © Rijksmuseum Amsterdam.

The two items of correspondence imply that sometime between 1771 and 1780, van der Steen was a member of Ainslie's household, possibly as an artist-in-residence at a time (before c.1786) when the artist Luigi Mayer (c.1750–1803), often associated with Ainslie throughout his long period in office (1776–94), was working in Sicily, initially for Ferdinand IV, King of Naples and the Two Sicilies and then for the Prince of Biscari (Taylor, 2013: p. 163).

Nevertheless, there is no evidence at present to indicate van der Steen painted for Ainslie because when the ambassador's entire estate was auctioned by Christie's (Christie's, 1809), all the drawings and paintings were by that 'Ingenious Artist' Mayer. Furthermore, when fine arts consultant Mark Donnelly (personal communication) conducted a routine probate evaluation of the estate of the late Ainslie Sandilands, a descendant of Sir Robert Ainslie through his sister's family, no paintings other than those by Mayer were recorded.

Moreover, and unlike Luigi Mayer who was paid a stipend by Ainslie (Llewellyn, 1990: p. 10), there is no evidence that van der Steen was similarly employed, although by the second half of the 18th century, when the diplomatic service became 'professional', the Foreign Office began paying salaries to a few personnel other than the head of a mission (Geoffrey Berridge, personal communication).

The Phrygian Highlands and the Midas Monument

The 'famous Mr Baldwin' (Fig.9.4) referred to earlier was George Baldwin (1744–1826), an English entrepreneur who was at various times, a factor with the Levant Company, a consul in Cyprus, an agent of the East India Company and one who often acted independently as a private merchant intent on developing and shortening trade and communication routes between India and Egypt via Suez – rather than the longer overland route via the Arabian Peninsular, the Euphrates/Tigris 'corridor', Aleppo, Anatolia and Constantinople. According to Ainslie (FO78/1), Baldwin was also 'considerably indebted at Bombay to the unfortunate People who he persuaded to engage in the Trade to Suez' and one of the purposes of the journey was to visit 'his incensed Creditors in India'.

Single minded, ambitious, far-sighted, well-travelled in the Levant, and with a knowledge of Arabic, Baldwin was often at loggerheads with many of his contemporaries, especially with Sir Robert Ainslie, who viewed Baldwin as the proverbial political and economical fly in the ointment, a pesky and persistent irritant whose spirit and

staunch belief in himself and ideas for the future prosperity of the Levant – and George Baldwin – remained undaunted despite the ambassador's often belligerent opposition, for Baldwin had, by promising immense profits, persuaded creditors in England and India to advance him money and pay him a commission for enhancing the prospects of re-routing the Indian trade via Egypt.

In 1773, Baldwin, who had been consul in Cyprus from 1771, resigned and travelled to Egypt intent on proceeding from there to India. His plans miscarried (Marlowe, 1971: p. 23) but then, after returning to England for a short while, he hastened back to Egypt to renew his efforts to expedite his grand design, having received encouragement from two sources. Firstly, the East India Company commissioned Baldwin to act as their agent in Cairo (Hoskins, 1924: p. 305) in order to facilitate what was later referred to as 'a regular intercourse between England and the British Possessions in the East Indies through

Fig 9.4 Enterprising diplomat George Baldwin at Vienna in Autumn 1780 (1744-1826). Lithograph by J(oseph) Bouvier. © National Portrait Gallery, London (NPG D11274).

Egypt' (Love, 1852: p. 343). Secondly, Mehmed Bey, governor of the province of Tirja in Upper Egypt, promised Baldwin that if ships could be brought from India to Suez, he (Mehmed) would 'lay an aqueduct from the Nile to Suez' (Baldwin, 1801: p. 4), thereby enabling vessels to pass directly from the Red Sea to the Mediterranean.

In 1780, following a series of embittered meetings in Constantinople between Ainslie and Baldwin to discuss the importance of expediting trade between India and Egypt via Suez, the relationship between the two men became so volatile (with each accusing the other of cowardice and deviousness) that Baldwin, in a fit of pique, left Constantinople in a hurry and set out once more for India via Aleppo, leaving behind his teenage wife, Jane Maltass, otherwise referred to as 'the pretty Greek', in the care of Richard Willis, a friend and fellow merchant.

To accompany him on his journey, Baldwin enlisted the help of Selim Aga, a Tartar guide, Emin Aga, Baldwin's servant Matthew, an unnamed Armenian, two post boys called Serugees and the artist van der Steen who is inexplicably not named as such in Baldwin's account (Baldwin, 1785) but referred to instead as 'Mr...', a painter by profession', 'my friend the painter' or just plain 'Mr...'. The reason for this omission is not known.

We now know that in 1780, van der Steen was a member of Ainslie's household (FO78/1) and may have been a resident for some time. Furthermore, as artist-in-residence at the Swedish embassy, van der Steen, unbeknown to the Celsings (and Ainslie), may have entertained a long-held but unfulfilled latent ambition to travel more widely. And so, when the opportunity came to join Baldwin on his journey to India, the artist accepted, albeit with apologies and expressions of remorse to Ainslie for his clandestine behaviour. Van der Steen's task was presumably to produce a pictorial record of the venture.

Having purchased a firman from the Ottoman Porte, the journey began at 7.00 am on the morning of the 11 May with a boat trip across the Hellespont to Scutari where post horses were obtained (Baldwin, 1785). In order to cross Anatolia from there, several west-east routes were available to Baldwin, some of which utilised the Euphrates–Tigris corridor before reaching Basra or Bassora at the head of the Persian Gulf. For example, one trek followed approximately the configuration of Turkey's northern coastline before extending southwards via Amasya, Tokat and Diyarbakir to Mosul, the so-called 'great junction' of the caravan routes, before taking the riverine road (the Tigris and Euphrates) to Baghdad and beyond.

However, Baldwin decided that in order to reach Aleppo and then Basra, he would travel diagonally across Anatolia in a south-easterly direction towards Konya and Adana, a route incorporating some of the western extremities of the Silk Road emanating from China. Disguised as tartar couriers (messengers of the Sultan) to avoid any undue hostility, and lightly armed, they made good progress, travelling between three and four miles an hour between post houses located approximately a day's travel apart (i.e. about 15–30 km, where fresh mounts were obtained and the travellers could rest after many hours in the saddle).

Of the many wonders that they saw during what Baldwin described as a 'journey of adventures', the most spectacular of all were the weird rock formations produced by the processes of weathering and erosion (and human activity) on the relatively 'soft' volcanic rocks. There were temple and tomb-like edifices with façades in a classical Greco-Roman style, often decorated with inscriptions written in a language no one in the party could comprehend – but there is nothing in Baldwin's account of the journey to suggest van der Steen was invited to draw one of these carved rock faces or indeed any other aspect of the scenery.

But then, while travelling in the Phrygian Highlands in the vicinity of post house number seven, at 'Cofruff Bafha'or 'Cosruff Basha', they were told of a 'wondrous building' on which Frank (European) characters had been inscribed – and which, said Baldwin (Baldwin, 1785: p. 108), had 'been erected before the Turks had driven the Infidels (Ghiaours) from the country. Because the 'wondrous building' was an hour's ride from the post house, Hadgee Mustafa, the Menzel Aga of Cosruff Basha, offered to lend Baldwin some horses and act as guides – and so Baldwin and van der Steen mounted up and followed the old Turk.

The Phrygian Highlands, a roughly triangular area bounded by the modern cities of Afyon, Eskisehir and Kutahya, rose steeply above the valley floors in a series of incised plateaus criss-crossed by ancient aqueducts and surmounted by the ruins of ancient towers. But these were not what the Aga had in mind. Instead, he led them to a projecting spur and there showed them an amazing monumental façade (later said to be 20m high; Perrot and Chipiez, 1892: p. 83) resembling a huge house or temple front that far exceeded all the other monuments they had seen on the journey so far. (Fig.9.5)

Constituting what may have been his only drawing on the journey thus far, van der Steen's illustration (Capper, 1785: facing p. 108) shows the frontage of a 'building' composed of vernacular and Greco-Roman elements such as a pedimented roof crowned by an akroterian comprising two inwardly curving volutes (the middle ground between the volutes appears to have been destroyed) as well as rafters decorated with lozenges and, most conspicuous of all, an overall geometrical pattern of interconnected, labyrinthine polygons similar to that found on furniture from Gordion (Berndt-Ersoz, 2006: p. 104), the capital of Midas's kingdom, but probably representing a more advanced design.

At ground level in the centre of the façade, van der Steen drew what looked like a door or niche which might have been occupied by a tomb; he also recorded, on the sides and upper part of the roof, several inscriptions, but Baldwin was astute enough to resist any attempt to interpret their significance or that of the monument itself, and instead concluded that it must have been 'a work antecedent to the classical institutions in architecture; but regular, sublime, and bold' (Baldwin, 1785: p. 109). Van der Steen's drawing appears to be unsigned and undated.

Before 1780, a few Europeans had travelled in the Phrygian Highlands in the first half of the 18th century but only two, Paul Lucas (1664–1737) and Jean Otter

Fig 9.5 '... *he told us also of a wondrous building in the neighbourhood of the place, on which Frank characters were inscribed' (Baldwin, 1785, p.108). Drawing of the Midas Monument by Antoine van der Steen, 1780.* © *British Library (145.b.13).*

(late 1730s), appear to have come close to the façades now referred to as the Midas Monument (Lucas in 1705 and Otter in 1738 [Otter 1748]). Both passed through Eskisehir (spelled either 'Eskicheror' or 'Eski-Chehre'), but only Lucas (1712) has left a full account of the area he visited and the inscriptions he transcribed, all of which indicate that whereas he saw and reported on many interesting antiquities, the Midas Monument, the most magnificent of all Phrygia's rock-cut faces, was not among them.

It seems reasonable to suggest that unknown to them at the time, Baldwin and van der Steen were the first western Europeans to discover the Midas Monument, an attribution often ascribed by others (for example, Ramsay, 1888: p. 30; Perrot and Chipiez, 1892: p. 65 and Haspels, 1971: p. 28) to the antiquarian and topographer William Martin Leake (1777–1860) who, says Haspels (1971), 'had beginner's luck' when he came across it with Brigadier General Koehler and others on 27 January 1800 (Leake, 1824: p. 22) and brought the monument to the attention of the world.

General Koehler or Leake made a sketch (Leake, 1824: p. 20; Wagstaff, 1987, fig. 5) of the monument – referred to as the monument of Doganlu – while Archdeacon Carlyle, Professor of Arabic at the University of Cambridge, and Leake studied the inscriptions; these, they deduced, were not written in pure Greek but in a dialect associated with the Phrygians. However, on reading the words 'to King Midas' on one of the uppermost inscriptions, Leake (1824v31) suggested the monument was erected in honour of a Phrygian king of the Midaian family – several of whom were named Midas. It was Leake and his fellow travellers, therefore, who were the first to recognize the historical significance of the monument, but W. M. Ramsay (1851–1939), traveller and New Testament scholar who earlier referred to the whole settlement as 'Midas-city' (Ramsay, 1888: p. 25), thought the artwork here and elsewhere in Phrygia probably developed under the influence, or in imitation of, Syro-Cappadocian or 'Hittite' art (Ramsay, 1888: p. 3) and, because of its uniqueness, that the 'Midas-necropolis' would be, 'were there nothing else in Phrygia....worth the journey' (Ramsay, 1882: p. 16). Ramsay also recommended (Ramsay, 1889: p. 156) that the 'Midas-tomb' was important enough in the history of art to justify the expense of an accurate drawing. However, because van der Steen's drawing was not known to Ramsay, it was not included in the theologian's censure.[2] The Midas settlement or 'Yazilikaya' settlement was later excavated in the 1930s and 1940s (Haspels, 2012; Ozarslan, 2010: p. 13) by the French Archaeological Institute based in Istanbul and in the 1990s by the Eskisehir Museum.

One of the reasons, even the principal reason, why the discovery of the Midas Monument by George Baldwin and van der Steen has been overlooked hitherto is because Baldwin's account of their journey was incorporated within another travel account published in the same year, namely the third edition of James Capper's *Observations On The Passage To India, Through Egypt: Also By Vienna Through Constantinople To Aleppo, and From Thence By Bagdad, and Directly across the Great Desert, to Bassora*. Baldwin's account occupies pages 97–158 and is indicated in the omnibus title by the phrase 'Constantinople to Aleppo'. Also incorporated in Capper's narrative is an account of Baldwin's return journey from Aleppo to Constantinople and his journey with his wife to Vienna. Colonel James Capper, an employee of the East India Company, travelled the Great Desert route from Basra to Aleppo in 1778 (Grant, 1937: p. 176) in order to report on the suitability of this short passageway to India, and thought that Baldwin's account of his journey, although 'written in haste', provided valuable insights into the manners and customs of the peoples of Anatolia and as such supplemented Capper's own observations.

The age of the Midas Monument is not known with certainty but most of the other decorated façades in the area have been dated to the middle of the 6th century BCE – as opposed to a date of 800–550 BCE for the step monuments. As to the true purpose of the monument, this is still a matter of some dispute despite many years of research.

For example, it has been suggested the monument represents:

    i.   a shrine to the Mother Goddess Cybele (in which case, the niche or false door at ground level may have contained a likeness of the deity (Whiting, 2001, 449)

    ii. a 'remarkable statement of Lydian presence at Midas City' and a link between the Lydian dynasty, Phrygian royalty and cult tradition (Berndt-Ersoz, 2006, 89)

    iii. a cenotaph to 'keep green the memory of a mythic ancestor' (Perrot and Chipiez, 1892, 86) and eponymous hero or, as expressed slightly differently

    iv. a posthumous dedication to Midas as a 'heroized or deified king' (Munn, 2006, 77).

Shortly after returning from the monument, but before setting off on their journey, the belief among the peoples of the east that all Franks (western Europeans) were either doctors or conjurors (Baldwin, 1785: p. 111) was put to the test when van der Steen, at Baldwin's behest, 'having something more intense in his phiz', was asked if he would check Hadgee Mustafa's pulse to ascertain that he was well. To this end, Baldwin handed the artist some rhubarb (thought to be a useful herbal antidote to a wide range of 'disorders') to 'cool' the old man's blood, a remedy that evidently proved effective for the Turk responded to the treatment before bidding farewell to the travellers.

By the time van der Steen is referred to again in Baldwin's narrative, the party had ridden more than 1,000 miles, some of it by the light of the moon, and the first part of their journey to India (from Constantinople to Aleppo) was almost over. However, near Antioch, the party was attacked by four horsemen and in the ensuing mêlée, Selim Aga was shot in the head and died where he fell. Emin Aga was mortally wounded; a sabre struck him 'close under his eyes and the blade ran down to the socket of his jaws', severing half his face, and Baldwin was shot in the arm. Two horses were also killed, but the two post boys and Baldwin's servant Matthew (replete with the leader's carbine) managed to escape and van der Steen also survived unharmed. When, however, the artist was later found by three 'kaffars', who were guarding an iron bridge, and three Delahia or cavalry soldiers, who had witnessed the attack from the opposite side of the river, he was half naked, frightened and unaware he was among friends.

Although the party was now in a state of some disarray, Baldwin decided to carry on to Aleppo, a journey of some two days, where a surgeon could be found to treat his arm and so, with Baldwin's arm in a sling, they mounted up and made their way, via a river crossing, to Salkin (Salqin), the 21st post house on the route. Here, a barber-surgeon examined Baldwin's arm and finding no fracture, filled the open wound with a mixture of honey, melted butter, salt and ground onions before binding up the arm and counselling Baldwin to be reconciled to his fate.

Once Baldwin had been dealt with, the barber surgeon attended to Baldwin's 'friend', the artist van der Steen, who was given a shave to 'get rid of so much of his ghastliness' (Baldwin, 1785: p. 143). Thereafter, van der Steen is not referred to again, but we know the party finally arrived in Aleppo on 27 May 1780, after a journey lasting 17 days. Due to the additional professional skills (Baldwin, 1785, 144) of Dr Adam Freer (1747–1811), who served as physician (*c.*1771–81) with the Levant Company (Janet Starkey, personal communication), Baldwin eventually recovered the use of his arm and, as a result, was able to complete the drafting of his account retrospectively. However, he decided to abandon his attempt to reach India, perhaps because after the attack, a portmanteau evidently containing most of the important papers was never found, even though Baldwin undertook a diligent search of the area and had the temerity to confront the thieves themselves.

And so, Baldwin, adopting a slightly different route, returned to Constantinople where he was reunited with his young wife and together, they returned to England via a Grand Tour of Europe (Ingamells, 1997: p. 43), whereas van der Steen presumably remained in Aleppo only long enough to plan the next stage of the journey to India.

Having lived and worked abroad for 41 years and visited many countries including Egypt, Syria, Cyprus, Greece and Turkey, George Baldwin compiled a modest collection of *objets d'art* referred to as 'Mr Baldwin's Museum' (Baldwin, 1810; Baldwin and Bouvier, 1810). When the contents of the museum were auctioned by Cauty's on 8 and 9 May 1828 (Cauty, 1828), there were cameos and intaglios as well as bronzes, busts and cabinets together with a portfolio containing some 'Lithographic Drawings of heads, seven parcels of drawings of heads and quantities of lithographic plates', but nothing to suggest any of this artwork was by van der Steen. Similarly, when two 'booklets' about the museum were privately published in 1810, the only plates were of Greek and Roman engraved gemstones by T. Bouvier together, perhaps, with some stones from Asia Minor (Martin Antonetti, personal communication).

Some questions, however, remain to be answered; namely, was van der Steen's drawing of the Midas Monument the only one undertaken on the journey through Anatolia?; where is the original now?; were other drawings by van der Steen lost when Baldwin's portmanteau was stolen in the mêlée near Antioch?; and where was Baldwin's Museum or cabinet of curiosities located? (According to the *Gentleman's Magazine*, his collections were sold at Christie's). Further research and serendipity may eventually provide some of the answers.

Van der Steen leaves Aleppo for India 1780

Having survived the attack on Baldwin's party, van der Steen was determined to continue the planned journey to India. However, before doing so, he wrote from Aleppo to Baron de Haeften, the Dutch ambassador in Constantinople, the two highly important letters discovered in the National Archives in The Hague (Eveline Sint Nicolaas, personal communication). In lieu of an account of van der Steen's journey between Aleppo and Basra, both letters, catalogued as 'Legatie Turkije, No. 774', provide some valuable information on the state of mind of the writer, his aspirations, the likely route taken and the time of year.

In the first of these letters, dated 13 June 1780, van der Steen refers to the fact that in order to keep Baron de Haeften well informed, he had written 'a detailed and rather long account' (not yet found) of the journey between Constantinople and Aleppo which he had forwarded via Mr Willis, probably Richard Willis (1724–80), an English merchant with the Levant Company and a friend of George Baldwin.

Also in the letter, van der Steen regrets his role in the clandestine arrangements concocted between him and George Baldwin that were thought necessary to hide from Sir Robert Ainslie several salient facts, namely his long-held wish to travel – and to travel to countries 'desired for so long' and the need to take advantage of his friendship with Mr Baldwin, who would, once they were in India, be 'worth all the letters of recommendation'. Furthermore, van der Steen refers to the fact that prior to the attack on Baldwin's party, the travelling had acted as an opiate in helping him recover from the discomforts he evidently complained about in Constantinople – indeed, 'everything was for the best' until, that is, the attack.

In the second letter, dated 22 August 1780, van der Steen refers to the attack on Baldwin's party, Baldwin's search for the missing papers and his return to Constantinople, the help received from Nicolass van Maseyk, the Consul des Pays-Bas (in post 1763–84) regarding letters of recommendation to the governor of Surat and of his desire to continue the journey on his own ('*Il m'a laisse seul pour continue Mon Yoyage*' [?Voyage]).

A reference in his letter dated 13 June to 'when going through the desert' suggests that on leaving Aleppo, van der Steen intended, in the middle of summer, to travel overland utilizing either the 'Little Desert Route' via Baghdad and the Tigris–Euphrates 'corridor' or the longer 'Great Desert Route' which led directly to Basra (or Bassora) at the head of the Persian Gulf, a distance of approximately 765–780 miles. Usually undertaken by camel, the Great Desert Route took between 24 and 38 days (Grant, 1937: p. 171), during which time the traveller spent all of it in the open desert. Some of the vicissitudes of travelling between Aleppo and Basra in 1780–81 are described by Eyles Irwin (?1751–1817), an employee of the East India Company who undertook what might have been a similar journey approximately a year later (Irwin, 1787: p. 281). There is no known account of van der Steen's journey between Aleppo and Basra, but two published narratives probably replicate some of the conditions he experienced. The first of these, by Eyles Irwin, has already been referred to. The second, undertaken by 'a gentleman' in 1780, can be found as an appendix in Lusignan, 1783: p. 225–59.

At Aleppo, the northern terminus of the overland route, van der Steen needed to arrange his travel for the next stage of the journey to India, a stage made dangerous by the presence there of nomadic and often hostile Arab tribes who preyed upon the vulnerable traveller. Camels, derived mainly from Basra (Irwin, 1787: p. 281), were frequently in short supply, especially following the departure of the Basra Caravan when more had to be fetched from Basra and Damascus to meet the demand.

Thereafter, van der Steen had to decide between several choices: he could travel alone with one or more Arab guides for company, join the twice yearly 'merchant' caravan – timing here was essential – or he could elect to travel with one of several smaller and faster 'light' caravans that operated a more frequent but irregular service. Then, once in Baghdad, the traveller had the option of either continuing the journey by camel or, as with Irwin, taking a boat or boats (the so-called 'Baghdad Boats' such as takanahs, shaykhas or ghrabs) to Basra and thus avoid some of the fatigues and dangers of the Great Desert.

As it would have been foolhardy for van der Steen to have travelled to Basra alone, it seems likely that, as referred to by others (for example, Van Woensel, 1789: p. 83–84; van Eijnden and van der Willigen, 1817: p. 188 and Scheen, 1970: p. 388), he joined a small caravan which included a number of English employees of the East India Company who, like other travellers in the area, became 'increasingly persuaded of the greater relative advantage' of this land route to India (Grant, 1937: p. 160).

During the journey between Aleppo and Basra, van der Steen may have had an opportunity to purchase some feathers of the Arabian ostrich (referred to in his letters to Baron de Haeften dated the 13 June and 22 August) he had promised as a gift to Madame de Haeften – as *Struthio c. syriacus* (now an extinct species) once roamed over the whole of the Syrian Desert 'right up to the banks of the Euphrates' (Carruthers, 1922: p. 473). Several contemporaneous accounts confirm the presence of this ostrich in the area in the last few decades of the 18th century – including traveller, writer and employee of the East India Company, Eyles Irwin who, *en route* to India in 1780–81, came across a nest of 'not less than 15 eggs' at a location between 190 and 228 miles south of Aleppo (Irwin, 1787: p. 304). Similarly, when Colonel James Capper was travelling between Aleppo and Basra in 1785 (in the service of the East India Company), he reported seeing ostriches on two occasions, including a group of six (Capper, 1785: pp. 191 and 200) while G. A. Oliver, when travelling through the 'Arabian Euphrates desert' in 1797, observed ostriches 'in greater numbers than usual but a long way off' (Mosenthal and Harting, 1877: p. 29), as well as others 23 miles south of Deir-ez-Zur beside the River Euphrates. Unfortunately, because *Struthio c. syriacus* had superior feathers compared with the larger African species, it was ruthlessly hunted for its plumes (Shanawany, 1999: p. 12) but managed to survive into the middle of the 20th century before becoming extinct.

Following his arrival in Basra, van der Steen may have continued his journey to India overland, but it is much more likely he boarded a ship bound for Surat in Gujarat. At this time, Basra, where the East India Company had established a permanent factory in 1763–64, was just recovering from the after-effects of the Ottoman-Persian War (1775–79), the siege of the city by the Persians and its capture by the Ottomans. However, and despite the turmoil, there were probably enough ships, including East India Company ships or those owned by the Chalabi family (Abdullah, 2001: p. 62), to take van der Steen to Surat – for he carried with him letters of recommendation to the governor there from Baron de Haeften and

Nicolaas Van Maseyk. Surat was an important trading post on the Gulf of Cambay and the location of several factories established by the English, Dutch, French and Portuguese. Among the most important of the Indo-Arab ships trading between Basra and western India were those owned by the Chalabi family, especially after the late 1750s when the Dutch East India Company (Vereenigde Oost-Indische Compagnie) virtually withdrew most of its fleet from the Persian Gulf [Abdullah, 2001: p. 28], following intense competition from the English.

Surrounded by an outer wall seven miles in circumference pierced by 12 gates, and an inner wall for additional protection, Surat represented an outpost of the Bombay Army (Moor, 1801: p. 73) and a bustling harbour and commercial centre that must have presented as colourful a spectacle to van der Steen as it obviously did to fellow artist James Forbes (Forbes, 1834: p. 150). Thus, when Forbes visited Surat in the early 1770s, he referred to 'bazars filled with costly merchandize; picturesque and interesting groups of natives on elephants, camels, horses and mules; strangers from all parts of the globe, in their respective costumes ... European ladies in splendid carriages (and) Asiatic females in hackeries, drawn by oxen ... and the motley appearance of the English and nabob's troops on the fortifications'.

Van der Steen and India – Pieter van Woensel and previous research

The earliest account of van der Steen is by Dutchman Pieter van Woensel (1747–1808), physician, adventurer and travel writer (Van Woensel, 1789: p. 83–84). Thus, he reported that 'Heer Van Der Steen, a strange passenger' had travelled overland from Turkey to 'Oost-Indie' in the company of several Englishmen, changed his name to Mr Stone, became a lieutenant of artillery in the service of the East India Company and died in Bengal. Subsequently, the essence of van Woensel's brief biography was, with some additions, reiterated by others. Van Woensel's own plans to visit India were abandoned when he and his fellow travellers reached Baghdad.

Although the lives of van der Steen and Van Woensel overlapped, they were not contemporaries and it is unlikely they met because while van der Steen was in Constantinople and then India (*c.*1768-82), van Woensel was studying medicine at the University of Leiden (1768–71), visited Russia (1771–78), Holland (1778–84), Izmir (1784) and Constantinople (1784) – where he spent 18 months – and then travelled on horseback across Anatolia before arriving in the Crimea later in the year (Bakker, 2008: p. 179).

What van Woensel has written would seem to have been derived from one or more sources including, perhaps, the Dutch ambassador Reinier, Baron de Haeften who took up his duties in 1778 and who was aware, as a correspondent of the artist, of his intention to travel to India – which he did two years later. However, a more likely source and a friend of van Woensel's at the Dutch Embassy in Constantinople was Joost Frederik Tor (Schmidt 1998). Between 1765 and 1778, Tor served as second secretary (van Spanbroek, 1765: p. 17) to Ambassador Willem Gerrit Dedel (in post 1765–68), private secretary (together with Gaspard Testa) to Frederik Gijsbert van

Dedem (in post 1785–1808) and proxy ambassador or chargé d'affaires (Koene, 2013: p. 99) between 1776 and 1778, following the death of Frederik Johan Robert van Weiler (Hoenkamp-Mazgon, 2002: p. 80). Tor was, therefore, based in Constantinople at about the same time as van der Steen.

Furthermore, as a diplomat and in particular as acting ambassador, Tor would doubtless have made it his duty to get to know about other Dutch nationals working for the diplomatic service and based in Constantinople, including the Swedish embassy which was located nearby in Pera. In addition, Tor, as a friend of van Woensel, was ideally placed to bring back to the Directorate of Levantine Trade in Amsterdam the large panorama of Constantinople by van der Steen which Van Woensel had used to illustrate an account of his own journey (Van Woensel, 1789: fig. facing p. 84) as well as two further but smaller paintings by the artist.

In 1779, Tor returned to the Netherlands (Koene, 2013, 99) and then resided in Venice between 1781 and 1783 before returning to Constantinople as private secretary (in 1785) to Ambassador van Dedem for whom he wrote what has been described as a 'minor masterpiece', namely an account of Van Dedem's journey from Marseille to Constantinople via Malta and the Greek islands (Tor, 1785).

It is intriguing to speculate on whether Tor and perhaps de Haeften were van Woensel's only sources of information on van der Steen or whether there were others who contributed to a veritable potpourri of fact and fiction. However, recent research proves van der Steen did indeed travel to India and following his arrival at Surat in north-western India, became an artillery officer, not with the Bengal Army but with the Bombay Artillery that recorded his death under the name 'Anthony Vandersteen'[3] on 31 October 1782 (Spring, 2005: p.74).

Van der Steen – the soldier

Soon after his arrival in Surat, and having forsaken the relative material comforts and security of a residency at the Swedish embassy in Constantinople, van der Steen embarked on a life-changing experience when he became a junior officer in the Bombay Artillery, a regiment within the Bombay Army that managed military matters in western India on behalf of the East India Company at a time when the Dutch East India Company was in decline following fierce competition from the English. The English military establishment regarded the Bombay Army as a 'reinforcing army' and so many of the actions in which it took part were in the south and east of the country (Butalia, 1998: p. 136). However, although the harbour and dockyard at Bombay were strategically important to the British, the site was unpopular because of the surrounding marshland and malarial climate (Howard, 2010: p. 216) that probably led to the death of combatants including, perhaps, van der Steen.

All previous biographical accounts of van der Steen mention his volte-face from artist to military officer, but no one has suggested why he exchanged 'the paint brush for the sword'. What motivated such a radical transformation and how well prepared was he to undertake his new role?

Certainly, it was not unusual for a foreign national to join one of the three British armies (Bengal, Bombay and Madras) based in India. Indeed, in some instances, foreign mercenaries and indigenous Indians (sepoys) often outnumbered their British counterparts in wars against the French, when success often depended on the army's European-manned artillery and its sepoys (Bryant, 2000: p. 12, footnote).

Most, if not all of van der Steen's fellow recruits would have been trained in England at the Royal Military Academy at Woolwich, whereas he must have arrived either untrained in the use of firearms or trained during an as yet unknown stage in his career. The fact he was promoted twice within a year (Spring, 2005: p. 74) suggests that prior to his arrival in Surat, he had served either in the military or at sea as, for example, a *scheepskorporaal* (see Coda).

Van der Steen's choice of regiment may also have been influenced by the fact that shortly after Baldwin's party had left Constantinople, they encountered Captain James Smith of the Bombay Artillery (Baldwin, 1785: p. 99) who was attacked *en route* to London via Basra and forced to flee before being rescued by Baldwin who put him on a boat bound for Constantinople and the safe haven of Sir Robert Ainslie's embassy.

As an artillery officer, van der Steen would have lived a highly-disciplined life bound by a rigorous set of standing orders and regulations (Moor, 1801). Furthermore, his duties may have been both defensive and offensive, i.e. he may have been deployed to defend one of the many garrisons under the aegis of the Bombay Army, or he could have joined his fellow combatants on the battlefield.

The list of officers who served in the Bombay Artillery refers to 'Anthony Vandersteen' (Spring, 2005: p. 74) as 'from sergt., Lfw. 19 June 1781. d. 31 Oct. 1782'.[4] Unlike some of the others listed, there is no reference to his service record and no mention of him (either as Vandersteen or Stone) in the East India Military Calendar (Philippart, 1823–26). However, between 1780 and 1782, van der Steen may have been involved in the first of the Anglo–Maratta Wars (1774–83) or the Second Anglo–Mysore War (1780–84) between the Sultanate of Mysore (Hyder Ali) and the East India Company. In the summer of 1782, in this latter campaign, company officials in Bombay sent six battalions of additional troops under Major William Abington to Tellicherry (Thalassery) in an attempt to raise the siege (1779–82) there. The war ended in stalemate with the Treaty of Mangalore (1784), whereby both sides restored their conquered territories and liberated their prisoners.

Van der Steen – Views of North-western India, 1780–82

Although the Bombay Army 'served' a wide area of west, southern and even eastern India, A. van der Steen seems, from the time he joined the Bombay Artillery to his death in 1782, to have painted only in the Bombay/Surat area – where he produced five known watercolours, all of them dated to 1782.

The watercolours are all landscapes and represent views of the indented coastline west of the Western Ghats. The Ghats form a backdrop to a series of 'tranquil' scenes seemingly far removed from any war-like activity, although forts occur in all the paintings; while in the foregrounds are boats as well as camels and other animals and both Indians and Europeans, the European men probably including soldiers from the forts. Where women and children are depicted, they are shown being protected by a parasol from the glare of the sun. It is not known whether these watercolours were executed while van der Steen was on military manoeuvres and quietly making topographical drawings for surveillance purposes, or acting out his alter ego.

Four of the watercolours are housed in the India Office Records at the British Library. Signed and dated, they were formally attributed by Mildred Archer to the amateur (sic) artist A. Van Der Heen (fl. 1782) because the artist's signature was misread (Archer, 1969: p. 228–29). Subsequently overlooked by Kattenhorn (1994, vii), the four watercolours have since been reassigned by J. P. Losty to van der Steen (see Losty in Galloway, 2012: pp. 102–06, fig. 35) and as such have added to the artist's oeuvre besides being some of the earliest views of north-western India.

The watercolours represent three views of Thana (Fig.9.6) seen from Bombay Harbour and a fourth of Surat observed from across the River Tapi (or Tapli). The fort of Thana, built by the Portuguese on the island of Salsette in 1730 and then modified by the Marattas (who added two wall towers) was in a desolate state

Fig 9.6 View of a European field station beside a fort in north-western India, perhaps Thana Fort on the island of Salsette. The fort was constructed by the Portugese in 1730 and completed by the Mararthas. Watercolour by Antoine van der Steen, 1782. Copyright The British Library Board. (WD 1060)

when amateur artist James Forbes (1749–1819), formerly a writer with the East India Company, visited the site in 1774 (Forbes, 1834, 284–85). Forbes (1834: p. 147) also visited Surat, situated on the south bank of the River Tapi, with its venerable Indian castle and the factories and garden houses of the English, Dutch, French and Portuguese settlements beside the river, the Dutch factory occupying the site of 'the most regular and best-built mansion' (Forbes, 1834: p. 151).

A fifth watercolour by van der Steen, signed and dated 1782, annotated on the reverse side and auctioned by Christie's in 2006 (Losty in Galloway, 2012: pp. 102–06, fig. 35) shows a view of Bombay and the black town of Dungeree (Dhongri) from the Mazagan (Mazagaon) Hill, which was a fashionable place to live in the late 18th century. Bombay Castle and Fort George are among the other locations referred to. The port of Bombay was then represented by a number of islands and while the process of land reclamation to connect them had begun, the task was not completed until 1882.

Hitherto, James Forbes (in 1782) and James Wales (in 1791–92) have been credited with being 'the first to make drawings of the Bombay islands systematically on the spot and not from their imagination' (Rohatgi, 1997: p. 58, and figs. 4 and 11; Godrej, Rohatgi 1989: p. 128, fig. 76) but van der Steen's five watercolours referred to here must also be recognized as significant (Losty in Galloway, 2012: pp. 102–106). Van der Steen may also have been one of the earliest, if not the first, professional Dutch artist to visit and portray the Indian subcontinent in the 18th century.

Coda

It is not yet known why Antoine van der Steen joined the Bombay Artillery. This is an obvious question to ask about someone known, if known at all, as a landscape artist, but a question also open to much conjecture.

In wars against the French and the Marathas in India, the English depended heavily on artillery to win their battles so when recruits arrived from Europe to join one of the three English armies resident in India, the artillery always had the first choice in preference to all other corps (Moor, 1801, 51), while other recruits were drawn from the armed ships. For van der Steen to have arrived in Surat in the latter half of 1780 and then to have been promoted twice by June 1781 suggests that on arriving in India, he was already experienced in the use of firearms (as has been alluded to elsewhere, for example, Adahl, 2003: p. 233) – but if this was indeed the case, where and when did he acquire this knowledge?

Since van der Steen was an artist-in-residence at the Swedish embassy in Constantinople from at least 1768, his military experience must predate his arrival there and could have been gained either as an infantryman or as a *scheepskorporaal*, i.e. naval corporal, on board a ship of the Dutch East India Company, where he would have been responsible for maintaining the ship's weapons as well as assisting the master-of-arms in his duties.

One such *scheepskorporaal* was Anthonij van der Steen from Bruges (Durme, 2007–08: p. 154) who, between 1751 and 1761 (when he was 'repatriated'), made the second of two voyages, during the course of which he visited the Cape of Good Hope, a victualling station *en-route* to other outposts of the Dutch Empire. But thereafter, nothing is known of the remainder of the voyage except that Anthonij returned safely. This second voyage by Anthonij van der Steen took place at about the same time as the artist Antoine van der Steen was (according to Scheen, 1970: 388 and Scheen Jr, 1981) travelling overland from Constantinople to India accompanied by some Englishmen. Other sources closer chronologically to van der Steen (for example, Woensel, 1789: pp. 83–84; van Eijnden and van der Willigen, 1817: p. 188) refer to the same journey but omit any dates.

Between 1750 and 1760, there is only one western traveller, John Carmichael, who recorded his journey from Aleppo to Basra (Carmichael, 1751) and no one, other than Carmichael, an employee of the East India Company based in Bombay, who then travelled on to India in a west to east direction. The merchant caravan Carmichael joined (Carruthers, 1928: p. xxxiii) included seven Jews, 'about twenty Turks, thirty-three Christians, merchants and passengers' (Grant, 1937: p. 144), but there are no specific references to any Englishmen, Dutchmen, or to van der Steen.

There is no written record to support the suggestion that van der Steen undertook such a journey over such a long period of time unless the dates represent a gross generalization to cover a journey undertaken in stages including one or more passages by sea.

Alternatively, van der Steen could have spent most if not all of those ten years at sea as did his namesake Anthonij van der Steen and it is tempting to suggest that the artist and the *scheepskorporaal* were one and the same person – like, for example, Johannes Rach (1720–83), an employee of the Dutch East India Company, who was an artist as well as a gunner and 'fireworker extraordinary' (De Silva and Beumer, 1988: p. 460).

There are, of course, counter-arguments to the notion that the two Dutchmen are one and the same person. For example, if van der Steen had previously acquired a knowledge of firearms why did he fail to stand his ground, along with Selim Aga, Emin Aga and Baldwin when the party was attacked by four horsemen – unless, of course, he was unarmed. Instead, according to Baldwin, van der Steen fled 'the contrary way' (Baldwin, 1785: p. 140). Furthermore, if van der Steen did spend the years 1750–60 at sea with the Dutch East India Company, there is no pictorial evidence known at present to indicate where he might have travelled to, for example, the Dutch settlements at the Cape of Good Hope, Ceylon (Sri Lanka) and Batavia (Indonesia) – unlike Rach who, setting out for the Dutch East Indies in 1762, produced hundreds of topographical drawings of Batavia, although he did not always sign his work, thus making subsequent authentication difficult (De Silva and Beumer, 1988: p. 460).

Militarily the link between the two men seems feasible, but is still a conjecture that awaits the results of further research.

Acknowledgements

This paper has benefited considerably from correspondence and discussions with Eveline Sint Nicolaas, Curator in the Department of History at the Rijksmuseun, Amsterdam; Suzanne Laemers, Curator of Early Netherlandish Painting, Netherlands Institute for Art History, The Hague; Andrew Fletcher, Head of Auction Sales and Senior Director, Old Master Paintings, Sotheby's, London; Dr Philip Mansel, historian; Dr Laban Kaptein of the Netherlands, independent research scholar; Paul Carlyle, National Archives, Kew, London; John Falconer, British Library, London; Birgitta Kurultay, Swedish Research Institute, Istanbul; Professor Geoffry R. Berridge, University of Leicester, UK and Martin Antonetti, Smith College, Northampton, Massachusetts, USA.

I should also like to thank Madame Mireille Rohart (Paris) and Margaret Stones (Uppingham, UK) for translations, John Foster (Monmouth, UK) for books and my daughter Dr Clare L. Taylor for her editorial advice.

Endnotes

1. Although Fletcher (2011: p. 7) has stated the three view paintings 'by van der Steen were bought or commissioned by Calkoen' and formed part of his collection, this contradicts what is known about the ambassador, namely that he left Constantinople in 1744 and died in 1764, shortly before he was due to take up a second posting (Sint Nicolaas, 2012: p. 71).

2. Van der Steen's drawing of the Midas Monument can be compared in detail with examples from the 19th century – like the stylized version by General Koehler (Leake, 1824: facing p. 21) or Martin Leake (Wagstaff, 1987: fig 5), together with those by Texier (1838: p. 416), Steuart (1842) and Perrot and Chipiez (1892). In the last named, the 'false door' was drawn by E. Guillaume.

3. There is no artillery officer named A. Vandersteen or Steen listed in the Bengal Army while a John Stone (Dodwell and Miles, 1838: p. 14–15) who is cited, was in service (1764–78) when van der Steen was almost certainly residing in Constantinople, possibly as a member of Sir Robert Ainslie's household and at a time when Ainslie's 'other' artist, Luigi Mayer, was based in Sicily (Taylor, 2013: pp. 163–64). However, it is possible that on arriving in India, van der Steen anglicized his name in order to facilitate communication with his fellow combatants, especially the predominantly English officer class.

4. A Lfw or Lieutenant fireworker was a junior officer rank below that of Second Lieutenant. For details on the conditions of service in the Bombay Army in the second half of the 18th century, including the dress code for a lieutenant fireworker, see Moor, 1801. The duties of officers of the Company of Artillery included having a knowledge of 'the manner of serving and firing all sorts of pieces of Artillery, whether designed for the throwing of shot, shells, stones, grenades, carcasses or other fireworks... and in making (of) batterys or breastworks, as also the manner of making intrenchments... etc' (Butalia, 1998: p. 132).

Bibliography

Adahl, K. (2003) *Landskapsmalningarna i Bibysamlingen*. In *Minnet av Konstantinopel den osmansk-turkiska 1700-talssamlingen pa Biby*. Atlantis.

Abdullah, T. A. J. (2001) *Merchants, Mamluks and Murder - the Political Economy of Trade in Eighteenth-century Basra*. Albany, State University of New York Press.

Archer, M. (1969) 'Amateur artists' in *British Drawings in the India Office Library*.Vol.1. London, HMSO.

Artan, T. (2006) 'Arts and architecture' in *The Cambridge History of Turkey, Vol. 3. The later Ottoman Empire, 1603-1839*. Ed. Suraiya N. Faroqhi. Cambridge, Cambridge University Press.

Bakker, R. (2008) *Reizen en de kunst van schrijven: Pieter van Woensel in het Ottomaanse Rijk, de Krim en Rusland, 1784-1789*. Doctorate thesis, University of Leiden, Leiden.

Baldwin, G. (1785) 'A Journey from Constantinople to Aleppo', pp. 97–158 in Capper, J. (1785) *Observations on the passage o India, through Egypt: Also by Vienna through Constantinople to Aleppo, and from thence by Bagdad, and directly across the Great Desert, to Bassora. With occasional remarks on the adjacent countries, an account of the different stages, and sketches of the several routes on four copper plates. Third Edition, with alterations and additions*, 3rd edition, with alterations and additions, London, Faden, Robson and Sewell.

Baldwin, G. (1801) *Political Recollections Relative to Egypt - with a Narrative of the Ever-memorable British Campaign in the Spring of 1801*. London, W. Bulmer and Co.

Baldwin, G. (1810) *Baldwin's Museum - Issues 1-6*. Privately printed.

Baldwin, G., Bouvier, T. (1810) *Baldwin's Museum. Sixty lithographs of Gems by T. Bouvier with Lithographic Letter-press*. Privately printed.

Baltimore, F. G., Baron. (1767) *A Tour to the East, in the Years 1763 and 1764. With Remarks on the City of Constantinople and the Turks. Also Select Pieces of Oriental Wit, Poetry and Wisdom*. London, Richardson and Clark.

Berndt-Ersoz, S. (2006) *Phrygian Rock-Cut Shrines: Structure, Function and Cult Practice*. Leiden, Koninklijke Brill NV.

Boppe, A. (1911) *Les peintres du Bosphore au dix-huitieme siecle*. Paris, Librairie Hachette etc.

Bryant, G. J. (2000) 'Indigenous mercenaries in the service of European imperialists: the case of the Sepoys in the early British Indian army, 1750–1800', *War in History*. Vol 7, Issue 1, pp 2–28, Sage Publications

Butalia, R. C. (1998) *The Evolution of the Artillery in India - from the Battle of Plassey (1757) to the Revolt of 1857*. India, Allied Publishers Limited.

Capper, J. (1785) *Observations On The Passage To India, Through Egypt: Also By Vienna Through Constantinople To Aleppo, And From Thence By Bagdad, And Directly Across The Great Desert, To Bassora - with Occasional Remarks on the adjacent Countries, An Account of the different Stages, And Sketches of the several Routes on four Copper Plates. The Third Edition, with Alterations and Additions*. London, W. Faden.

Carmichael, J. (1751) *A Journey from Aleppo over the Desert to Basserah, Oct.21, 1771*. Also as an appendix to Vol.1 of J. H. Grose's *Voyage to the East Indies*, London, 1772.

Carruthers, D. (1922) 'The Arabian ostrich', *Ibis*.

Carruthers, D., ed. (1929) *The Desert Route to India, being the journals of four travellers by the Great Desert Caravan Route between Aleppo and Basra, 1745-1751*. The Hakluyt Society, Second Series, LXIII.

Cauty. (1828) *A Catalogue of the very Valuable and Interesting Museum of the late Geo. Baldwin, Esq., Consul-General of Egypt, Collected during the Various Peregrinations Made by that Distinguished Individual, over Cyprus, Syria, Egypt, Greece, and other Countries, during a Period of 41 years, Being between the Years 1760 and 1801*.

Christie's. (1809) *A Catalogue of the Very Valuable and Entire Collection of Drawings, and Paintings in Oil, of Sir Robert Ainslie, Bart. The Whole of Which were Executed by that Ingenious Artist, Mayer, Also, a Few Marbles*. Sale of 10–11 March 1809.

Christie's. (2006) 'A. van der Steen (active 1782). A view of Bombay and the black town Dungeree (Dhongri) taken from Mazagan (Mazagaon) Hill lettered with a key to the topography, signed, inscribed with a key and dated' in *Sale of Books, Maps and Photographs Relating to Travel in Asia including China Trade Paintings*. 13 July, lot 18.

Degiorgio, S., Fiorentino, E. (2004) *Antoine Favray (1706-1798). A French Artist in Rome, Malta and Constantinople*. Valletta, Malta, Fondazzjoni Patrimonju Malti.

Dodwell E., Miles, J. S., eds. (1838) *Alphabetical List of the Officers of the Bengal Army with the Dates of their Respective Promotion, Retirement, Resignation, or Death, whether in India or in Europe from the Year 1700 to the Year 1834 Inclusive, Corrected to September 30, 1837*. London, Longman, Orme, Brown, and Co.

Durme, M. van. (2007–2008) *Zuid - Nederlanders in dienst van de Verenigde Oost - Indische Compagnie Tweede helfe achttiende eeuw*. Thesis, University of Ghent, Ghent.

Edrehi, I. (1855) *History of the Capital of Asia and the Turks: together with an account of the domestic manners of the Turks in Turkey*. Vol. I. Boston, Reprinted for Isaac Edrehi.

Eijnden, R., van der Willigen, A. (1817) *Geschiedenis der Vaderlandsche Schilder kunst, sedert de helft der XVIII eeuw*. Vol. II. Haarlem.

Fletcher, A. (2011) *Sotheby's Catalogue of 'The Von Celsing Collection of Ottoman Art at Biby'*. Privately published.

Forbes, J. (1834) *Oriental Memoirs: A Narrative of Seventeen Years Residence in India*. Vol. 1. London, Richard Bentley.

Furber, H. (1951) 'The overland route to India in the seventeenth and eighteenth centuries' *Journal of Indian History* 29.2: pp. 105–33.

Germaner, S., Inankur, Z. (2002) *Constantinople and the Orientalists*. Istanbul, Isbank.

Godrej, P., Rohatgi, P. (1989) *Scenic Splendours - India through the Printed Image*. London, The British Library.

Grant, C. P. (1937) *The Syrian Desert: Caravans, Travel and Exploration*. London, A. & C. Black Ltd.

Gürçağlar, A. (2003) 'The diplomatic trinity: ambassadors, dragomans and the Porte', *Journal of Translation Studies*, 13.

Haspels, C. H. E. (1971) *The Highlands of Phyrigia: Sites and Monuments*. In two volumes. Princeton, Princeton University Press.

Haspels, C. H. E. (2012) *Midas City Excavations and Surveys in the Highlands of Phrygia - I am the last of the travellers*. Edited by Dietrich Berndt and others. Istanbul, Archaeology and Art Publications.

Hoenkamp-Mazgon, M. (2002) *Palais de Hollande te Istanboel Het ambassadegebouw en zijn bewoners sinds 1612*. Amsterdam, Boom.

Hoskins, H. L. (1924) 'The overland route to India in the eighteenth century', *History (The Journal of the Historical Association)* 9.36: pp. 302–18.

Howard, S. (2010) *A new theatre of prospects: eighteenth-century British portrait painters and artistic nobility*. Two volumes. PhD thesis, University of York.

Ingamells, J. (1997) *A Dictionary of British and Irish Travellers in Italy, 1701-1800*. New Haven and London, Yale University Press.

Irwin, E. (1787) *A Series of Adventures in the Course of a Voyage up the Red-Sea on the Coasts of Arabia and Egypt, and of a Route through the Desarts of Thebais in the year 1777; with a Supplement of a Voyage from Venice to Latichea; and of a Route through the Desarts of Arabia, by Aleppo, Bagdad, and the Tygris, to Busrah in the Years 1780 and 1781* in *Letters to a Lady*. Vol. II. London, J. Dodsley.

Kattenhorn, P. (1994) *British Drawings in the India Office Library*. Vol. III. London, The British Library.

Koene, B. (2013) *Schijngestalten. De levens van diplomaat en rokkenjager Gerard Brantsen (1735-1809)*. Verloren, Hilversum.

Leake, W. M. (1824) *Journal of a Tour of Asia Minor, with Comparative Remarks on the Ancient and Modern Geography of that Country*. London, John Murray.

Llewellyn, B. (1989) *The Orient Observed. Images of the Middle East from the Searight Collection*. London, The Victoria and Albert Museum.

Llewellyn, B. (1990) Luigi Mayer, Draughtsman to his Majesty's Ambassador at the Ottoman Porte. *Watercolours, Drawings and Prints* 5.4: pp. 9–13.

Losty, J. P. (2012) *Indian Miniatures and Courtly Objects* by F. Galloway. Exhibition catalogue. New York, Leslie Feely Fine Art.

Love, H. D. (1913) *Vestiges of Old Madras, 1640-1800: Traced from the East India Company's Records Preserved at Fort St. George and the India Office, and from other Sources*. In four volumes. Vol. III. London, J. L. Murray for the Government of India.

Lucas, P. (1712) *Voyage du Sier Paul Lucas, fait par ordre die Roy dans La Grece, l'Asie Mineure, La Macedoine et L'Afrique. Tome 1. Contenant la Descripion de la Natolie, de la Caramanie, and de la Macedoine*. Paris.

Lusignan, S. (1783) *A History of the Revolt of Ali Bay, Against the Ottoman Porte, Including an Account of the Form of Government of Egypt; together with a Description of Grand Cairo, and of Several Places in Egypt, Palestine and Syria; to which are added, a Short Account of the Present State of the Christians who are Subjects to the Turkish Government, and the Journal of a Gentleman who Travelled from Aleppo to Bassora. By S. L.* London, James Phillips for the author.

Mansel, P. (1995) *Constantinople: City of the World's Desire, 1453-1924.* London, John Murray.

Mansel, P. (1996) 'Art and diplomacy in Ottoman Constantinople', *History Today,* August: pp. 43–49.

Mansel, P. (2012) 'A Dutch treat', *Cornucopia* 47: pp. 48–54.

Marlowe, J. (1971) *Perfidious Albion – the Origins of Anglo-French Rivalry in the Levant.* London, Elek Books.

Melling, A. I. (1809–19) *Voyage Pitoresque de Constantinople et des Rives du Bosphore,* 3 vols. Paris, Strasburg and London.

Moor, E. (1801) *A Compilation of all the Government and General-Government-General-Brigade and Garrison Orders-Minutes of Council-Commands of the Hon. Company-or Regulations, from whatever Authority Promulgated, from the Year 1750 to the 31st of July 1801, that are now in Force and Operating on the Discipline or Expenditure of the Bombay Army: the Whole Arranged According to Priority of Dates, Under Appropriate Heads etc Compiled from the Records of the Public Offices by Capt. Edward Moor.* Bombay.

Mosenthal, J. de, Harting, J. E. (1877) *Ostriches and Ostrich Farming.* Truber and Company.

Munn, M. (2006) *The Mother of the Gods, Athens, and the Tyranny of Asia: A Study of Sovereignty in Ancient Religion.* Berkeley, University of California Press.

Murphy, O.T. (1982) *Charles Gravier, Comte de Vergennes. French Diplomacy in the Age of Revolution, 1719-1787.* Albany, State University of New York Press.

Newton, C. (2007) *Images of the Ottoman Empire.* London, V&A Publications.

Otter, J. (1748) *Voyage en Turquie et en Perse, avec une Relation des expeditions de Tahmas Kouli-khan.* Vol. I. Paris.

Ozarslan, Yasemin. (2010) The Cultic landscapes of Phrygia. Thesis submitted to the Graduate School of Social Sciences of Middle East Technical University.

Pardoe, J. (1850) *The Beauties of the Bosphorus. Illustrated with a Series of Views of Constantinople and its Environs from Original Drawings by W. H. Bartlett.* London, Virtue and Co.

Perrot, G., Chipiez, C. (1892) *History of the Art of Phrygia, Lydia, Caria and Lycia.* London, Chapman & Hall.

Philippart, J., Ed. (1823–26) *The East India Military Calendar; Containing the Services of General and Field Officers of the Indian Army.* Vols. 1–3. London, Kingsbury, Parbury & Allen.

Ramsay, W. M. (1882) Studies in Asia Minor. The Rock-Necropoleis of Phrygia. Part 1., *Journal of Hellenic Studies* 3.

Ramsay, W. M. (1888) A Study of Phrygian Art. Part 1., *Journal of Hellenic Studies* 9: pp. 350–82

Ramsay, W. M. (1889) A Study of Phrygian Art. Part II., *Journal of Hellenic Studies* 10: pp. 147–89.

Raye, J. (1987) *Een levenslustig heer op reis naar de Orient. Brieven van Johan Raye, heer van Breukelerwaart 1764-1769. Van commentaar voorzien en bewerkt door dr. A.Doedens en L. Mulder*. Baarn, Bosh & Keuning nv.

Rohatgi, P. (1997) 'Early impressions of the Islands – James Forbes and James Wales in Bombay 1766-95. Part 1. Perceptions and observations', *Bombay to Mumbai – Changing Perspectives*. Eds. P. Rohatgi, P. Godrei and R. Mehrotra. Marg Publications.

Scheen, P. A. (1970) *Lexicon Nederlandse Beeldende Kunstenaars, 1750-1950*. Vol. II, M–Z. The Hague.

Scheen, P. A. Jr. (1981) *Lexicon Nederlandse Beeldende Kunstenaars, 1750-1880*. Vol. II, M–Z. The Hague.

Schmidt, J. (1998) *Perkoets naar Constantinopel; de Gezantschaperuis van Baron van Dedem van de Gelder naar Istanbul en 1785*. Zutphen, Walburg.

Shanawany, M. M. (1999) 'Origin and Evolution of the Ostrich'. In Food and Agricultural Organization of the United Nations, *FAO Animal Production and Health Paper* 144: pp. 5–14.

Silva, R. K.de, Beumer, W. G. M. (1988) *Illustrations and Views of Dutch Ceylon 1602-1796*. London, Serendib Publications.

Sint Nicolaas, E. (2003) 'The ambassador and the sultan', *An Eyewitness of the Tulip Era, Jean Baptiste-Vanmoor* by E. Sint Nicolaas, D. Bull, G. Renda and G. Irepoglu. Istanbul, Kocbank: pp. 9 –23.

Sint Nicolaas, E. (2012) The Curious Cabinet of Cornelis Calkoen, *Cornucopia* 47: pp. 58–71.

Spanbroek, J. A. M. van. (1765) *Le voyage d'un gentilhomme d'ambassade d'Utrecht a Constantinople en 1765. Presente et annote par Catherine Vigne*. L'Harmattan, reprinted 2007.

Spring, F. W. M. (2005) (compiled by): *The Bombay Artillery List of Officers Who Have Served in the Regiment of Bombay Artillery from its Formation in 1749 to Amalgamation with the Royal Artillery, with Dates of First Commissions, Promotions, Casualties, Also Appointments Held, War Services, Honours, and Rewards*. The Naval and Military Press Ltd. (based on an earlier edition published in 1902).

Steuart, J. R. (1842) *A Description of some Ancient Monuments with Inscriptions still existing in Lydia and Phrygia, several of which are supposed to be Tombs of the Early Kings*. London.

Taylor, B. J. (2013) 'Sir Robert Ainslie, Domenico Sestini and Luigi Mayer: a case of who went where, with whom and when', *Souvenirs and New Ideas –Travel and Collecting in Egypt and the Near East*. Ed. D. Fortenberry. Oxford, ASTENE and Oxbow Books.

Texier, C. F. M. (1838) *Tombeau de Midas, Asie Mineure. Descripion Geographique, Historique et Archéologique des provinces et des villes de la Chersonnese d'Asie*. Paris.

Theolin, S. (2001) *The Swedish Palace in Istanbul - a Thousand Years of Co-operation Between Turkey and Sweden*. Istanbul, Yaym Hazirlayan, Yapi Kredi Kultur Sanat Yaymcilik.

Tor, J. F. (1785) *Per koets naar Constantinopel; de gezantschapsreis van Baron van Dedem van de Gelder naar Istanbul in 1785*. Edited by J. Schmidt. Zutphen, Walburg Pers, 1998.

Wagstaff, J. M. (1987) 'Colonel Leake and the classical topography of Asia Minor'. Anatolian Studies, *Journal of the British Institute of Archaeology at Ankara*.

White, C. (1846) *Three Years in Constantinople; or, Domestic Manners of the Turks in 1844. In Three Volumes*. Vol. II. London, Henry Colburn Publishers.

Whiting, D. (2001) *Footprint Handbook to Turkey*. First Edition.

Woensel, P. van. (1789) *Aanteekeningen, gehouden op eene reize door Turkijen, Natolien, de Krim en Rusland in de jaaren 1784-1789*. Amsterdam, W. Holtop.

Zahlan, R. S (1968) George Baldwin and British Interest in Egypt, 1775–1798. PhD thesis, University of London, London.

Unpublished British State Papers from The National Archives, UK

FO78/1; C528623. Correspondence dated 17th May 1780, from Pera, Constantinople, from Sir Robert Ainslie (England's ambassador) to the Rt. Hon. The Earl of Hillsborough.

Unpublished letters

National Archives, The Hague (Ref. No. 1.02.20 – 774). Antoine Van Der Steen to the Dutch ambassador, the Baron de Haeften. from Aleppo, 22 April 1780.

National Archives, The Hague (Ref. No. 1.02. 20 – 774). Antoine Van Der Steen to Baron de Haeften, from Aleppo, 13 June 1780.

Von Celsing Collection. A. Van Der Steen to Son Excellence. From the Swedish embassy in Pera, Constantinople. 30 September 1768.

Von Celsing Collection. Francis Smith (fl. 1763–79) from Naples to Monseigneur, 6 October 1770.

Von Celsing Collection. Francis Smith from Naples to His Excellence, 20 February 1771.

Edmond G. Reuter:
A Life between Ancient Egypt and the Arts and Crafts Movement

Hélène Virenque

The History of Egyptology in the 19th century is full of discrete figures: supporting actors who worked with famous scholars, as draughtsmen, archaeologists or assistants, among other functions. My interest in Edmond Georges Reuter, his life and his career, was aroused during my research on the Swiss Egyptologist Édouard Naville. Reuter accompanied Naville as a draughtsman during his first trip along the Nile Valley in 1868–69,[1] yet very little was known about this Genevan artist.

Nevertheless, biographies and various documents, mainly private archives, both in Switzerland and France, have enabled me to discover other aspects of Reuter's life as well as some details of his later career.[2]

After his trip to Egypt, Reuter moved to England where he stayed for more than 20 years. There, he worked as an 'ornamentalist' at Minton's ceramics factory, and also took part in various publications and exhibitions of the Arts and Crafts movement, singularly through his collaboration with William Morris.[3] This paper offers an overview of Reuter's career in Switzerland, Egypt and England and shows how he managed to become the Swiss representative of the Arts and Crafts movement at the dawn of the 20th century.

Edmond Georges Reuter (Fig.10.1), son of Georges François Reuter, was born in Geneva in 1845.[4] Georges Reuter was curator

Fig 10.1 Portrait of Edmond Réuter dated 1903. (Courtesy of the Bibliothéque de Genève).

of numerous herbarium in the city. Being passionate about plants and flowers, he collected specimens throughout Europe and, from 1849 onwards, he was Director of the Botanical Garden of Geneva. The young Edmond must have been attracted by this family activity, as documents show that he drew flowers or floral patterns in most of his later creations. In 1867–68, he studied in Paris, at the École des Arts décoratifs where he may have attended lectures on plant ornamentation;[5] afterwards he went to work at the fabric factory of Dollfus-Mieg in Mulhouse (eastern France).

In 1868, Édouard Naville was planning to spend several months in Egypt and the young Egyptologist needed a draughtsman to copy the scenes on the walls of temples. Naville hired Reuter for the journey, his first to the Nile Valley. The two men explored the country, travelling in a *dahabiyya* from Cairo to Wadi Halfa and back over a period of seven months (November 1868 to May 1869). Naville's travel accounts show that, although they did not become friends, the two men worked well together, with Reuter making the best use of his drawing skills by copying Egyptian reliefs and hieroglyphics for Naville, particularly those at Abydos and Edfu.[6]

In parallel to this academic work, Reuter also drew his own sketches, offering us a more personal account of his feelings and impressions about Egypt. Painted in a small but unpublished sketchbook containing around 35 illustrations, that is still kept by his family, his watercolours show a diversity of Nile landscapes and antique temples.[7] One sketch, dated '*Dimanche 21 mars 1869*', shows the '*maison appartenant au gouvernement français, et habitée par Lady Gordon, Louxor*' (Fig.10.2). This house, known

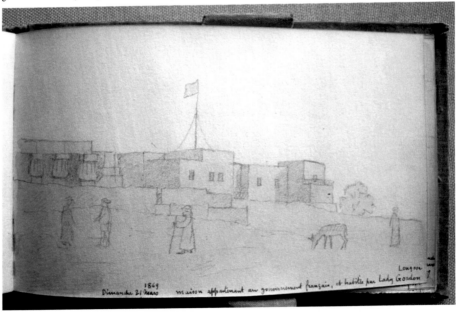

Fig 10.2 Watercolour of Luxor from Réuter's sketchbook of his trip to Egypt (21st March 1869). (Private Collection).

as the Château de France, was built on the sanctuary of the Luxor temple. Many famous scholars and travellers throughout the 19th century stayed there when they came to Egypt. Lucie Duff-Gordon herself lived there from 1864 until her death in July 1869 near Helouan. Since her family and Naville's were acquainted, Naville and Reuter paid her a visit during their stay in Luxor.[8] The aspect of the house, as Reuter sketched it, with its square walls and with the French flag on the roof, is well documented thanks to drawings and descriptions made by travellers.[9]

In addition to illustrations of the Egyptian landscape, in the last pages of his sketchbook, Reuter also copied ornamental patterns from medieval buildings. Furthermore, he painted watercolours of columns, reliefs and cartouches that were used, after he returned home, by a Swiss colleague for his lectures on the history of ornamentation.[10] True to his interest in botanical subjects, Reuter also drew large watercolour plates of flowers, comparing the original plant to their ancient Egyptian stylized interpretation (Fig.10.3). Eventually, he used some of his sketches to create larger watercolours, still for personal purposes (Fig.10.4).

Back in Geneva, Édouard Naville and Edmond Reuter did not maintain contact. However, their respective careers involved both of them continuing to work on

Fig 10.3 'Fleur naturelle du Lotus Nymphea bleu, double grandeur naturelle d'après Redouté' and 'Fleur conventionelle de Lotus d'après une empreinte faite à Karnak' drawn by Réuter. (Courtesy of the Bibliothéque de Genève).

Fig 10.4 Temple or Luxor, watercolour by Ed. Réuter, January 1870. (Private Collection).

British projects: from 1882 onwards, Naville became an important member of the Egypt Exploration Society, while Reuter moved to London in 1870, where he was appointed as an art teacher at the National Art Training School (now the Royal College of Art). Reuter also worked as a designer for the well-known Minton's Art Pottery studio that had been established in Kensington, in premises near the School.[11] The French designer Léon Arnoux was then the renowned art director at Minton's and his reputation attracted other French and continental artists to migrate to England and work with him. Following a fire at Minton's in 1875, the studios were not rebuilt in London and Reuter moved to the main factory at Stoke-on-Trent, where he remained until 1895.[12] Reuter wrote hundreds of letters to his family relating to his life in England, adding small sketches from time to time that represented, among other things, a self-portrait or a view of the smoky chimneys of Stoke-on-Trent, which illustrated the nickname given to the city – 'the Potteries' – because of the large number of coal-fired kilns operated by the many successful factories there such as those of Minton and Spode (Fig.10.5).

Known as a silent and modest worker, Reuter was also a very versatile designer. He was paid to decorate pottery, tiles, vases and dinner services, but in his spare time he also produced illuminated manuscripts, painted tapestries, furniture, watercolours, paintings, vessels in metal, carved wooden door-panels, curtains and more. His art was

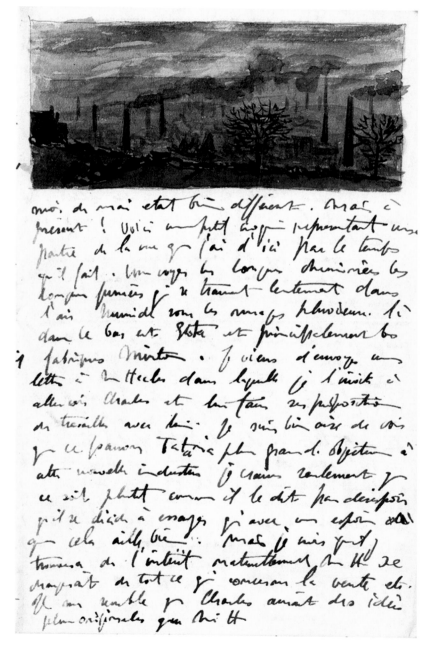

Fig 10.5 Details of letter by Réuter to his family, dated Stoke-on-Trent May 1879. (Private Collection).

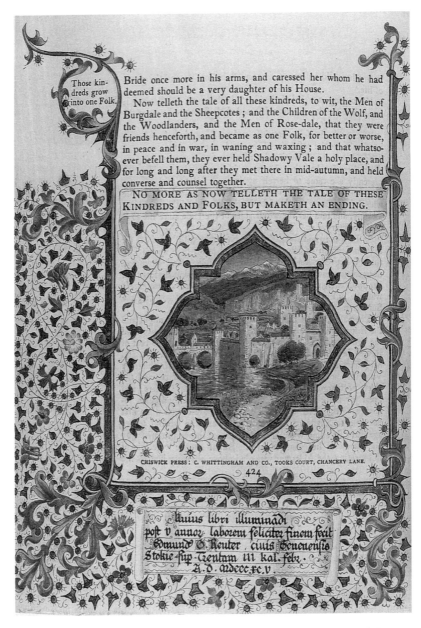

Fig 10.6 Illuminated page drawn by Edmond Réuter for William Morris' The Roots of the Mountains,
dated 1895. From The Library of William Foyle, Part III, English literature and manuscripts, travel books:
Christies auction catalogue, London, 12-13 July 2000, page 287.

influenced by, among others, John Ruskin, the Pre-Raphaelite painters, and William Morris, but Reuter experimented with medievalism long before he had any contact with the ideas of the Arts and Crafts movement. Morris appreciated his work and asked him to illuminate several of his books; the highlight of which must have been the work for the fantasy romance *The Roots of the Mountains*.[13] According to a Latin inscription written by Reuter within the manuscript, the five-year-long task of illuminating the book was 'a happy labour completed in 1895' (Fig.10.6). Reuter also submitted his work to the annual London displays of the Arts and Crafts Exhibition Society, in order to show his skills in illumination as well as in carving decorated panels.[14]

In parallel, Reuter continued to be influenced by orientalism, at least in his decoration of ceramic wares. This first showed itself during the late 1870s in a number of illustrations he made for Minton, in which he further developed his passion for flowers. He also designed oriental furniture, thus contributing to the wider interests of the factory for using such motifs in manufactures of all types. At the same time, Reuter also worked for his friend Lawrence Birks of Birks Rawlins & Co. The pieces Reuter produced show he had mastered perfectly the popular 'Persindo Porcelain', painted with decorative elements from Persian, Indian and Japanese Art.

The will to work independently, together with the recognition of his skills by numerous English publications, may have encouraged Reuter's return to Geneva in 1895, where he worked on commissions for the Genevan bourgeoisie until his death in 1917. His works in various formats – ceramic ware, watercolours, tapestries and carved wooden-panels – were regularly shown in local exhibitions, such as that of 1898. Reuter travelled around Switzerland, and once visited Italy where the castles and seaside views he saw may have inspired some of the melancholic and fantastic landscapes (Fig.10.7). He also drew book illustrations in his collaborations with Swiss authors.

As I have found during my research into the life and works of Edmond Reuter, hundreds of works that show the impressive abilities of this artist are held in collections throughout Europe, and yet he may have considered himself as nothing more than an artisan. It is through the influence of his family, and his travels in Egypt with Naville, that Reuter was able to mix Oriental and Mediterranean impressions into his own style of plant ornamentation, a talent quickly recognized by the leading exponents of the Arts and Crafts movement.

"MELANCHOLY LANDSCAPES," NO. 3   BY E. G. REUTER

Fig 10.7 'Melancholy landscapes, No 3'. Undated. After The Studio, vol 30, 1904, page 358.

Endnotes

1 D. van Berchem (1989). '*L'Égyptologue genevois Édouard Naville. Années d'études et premiers voyages en Égypte*'. Genève; M. Patané (1993). '*Les dessins de Edmond G. Reuter retrouvés*', *Göttinger Miszellen* 137: p. 107–11; Éd. Naville, J.-L. Chappaz (2012). *Voyage en Égypte (1868-1869), suivi de, Histoire de l'égyptologie (1892)*, CSEG 11. Geneva.

2 Reuter married Susanne Céret in 1880, but they never had children. Correspondence, pictures, and a sketchbook are kept by the descendants of his sister. I would like to thank Valentine Frei-Dégallier, Nicolas Dégallier and Pado Mutrux for giving me access to their family archives and for authorization to use some unpublished material for this article. No letters from Egypt have so far been found.

3 R. Mobbs (1912). 'A Swiss artist: Edmond G. Reuter', *The Studio*, Vol. 55: p. 290–97.

4 J. Briquet (1940). *Biographies des botanistes à Genève de 1500 à 1931*; *Bulletin de la Société botanique Suisse*, Vol. 50A: p. 398–405.

5 Family archives indicate that he went to the School of Victor Ruprich-Robert (1820–87), an architect close to Viollet-le-Duc who actually taught composition and ornamentation, then majored in plant ornamentation at the École royale de dessin et de mathématiques (now the École nationale supérieure des Arts décoratifs). A biography of Victor Ruprich-Robert can be found online: http://www.inha.fr/fr/ressources/publications/publications-numeriques/dictionnaire-critique-des-historiens-de-l-art/ruprich-robert-victor.html (accessed 30 Oct.16).

6 See for example Éd. Naville (1870). *Textes relatifs au mythe d'Horus recueillis dans le temple d'Edfou et précédés d'une introduction*, Geneva-Basel, where at the bottom of the scenes appears Reuter's initials: 'EGR'.

7 A small number have already been published in Patané, 1993.

8 Van Berchem, 1989: p. 65; Naville, Chappaz, 2012:, p. 87 and 92.

9 S. Weens (2015). '*La Maison de France: grandeur et décadence sur le toit du temple de Louqsor*', *Memnonia* 26: p. 185–200, pl. 26-29.

10 Some are kept at the Centre d'iconographie genevoise (Bibliothèque de Genève).

11 G. W. Rhead, Fr. Al. Rhead (1906). *Staffordshire Pots and Potters*. London: pp. 354–55 and 360–61.

12 Minton's archives are not yet inventoried. Therefore, it has not been possible to learn more about his position.

13 Reuter met Morris at the 1889 Arts and Crafts Exhibition and made several illuminated pages for the Kelmscott Press, see R. Coupe (2002). *Illustrated Editions of the Works of William Morris in English*. Delaware-London: pp. 222–23; W. Morris (1996). *The Collected Letters of William Morris, Tome III, 1889-1892*. Princeton: pp. 422–23.

14 See for example, Arts and Crafts Exhibition Society (ed.), *Catalogue of the second exhibition*, [London], 1889, pp. 110–11, 114, 201–02 and 241 – available online: https://archive.org/details/ACESExhib02AAD19801798 (accessed 30 Oct.16).

Guilty or Innocent? The Buckingham vs. Bankes Libel Trial of 1826

Don Boyer

The early 19th-century English traveller and adventurer William John Bankes spent almost five years visiting and recording ancient sites in the Levant. He was in Egypt and Nubia for much of this time, but he also visited Palestine and Syria. While in Palestine, in early 1816, he made a short side trip to Jerash (Jarash) and Umm Qais (Gadara) east of the Jordan, in the company of James Silk Buckingham. The trip proved to be historically interesting but was otherwise unremarkable in the context of his other travels; however, there were unexpected ramifications. These surfaced three years later following the publication of a prospectus of a book on Buckingham's travels in the Middle East that included a lengthy section on the trip to Jarash and Umm Qais.[1] This triggered an angry response from Bankes, then in Egypt, who distributed a letter accusing Buckingham of, among other things, using Bankes' notes and plan of Jarash, and culminated in Buckingham bringing a libel case against Bankes four years later. After a three-year delay, the libel case came to trial in October 1826, ten years after the Jarash–Umm Qais trip, and resulted in Buckingham being awarded £400 in damages. The trial preparations and its aftermath attracted considerable press attention at the time, but there has been little modern commentary.[2] Buckingham's subsequent publications and actions implied that he considered his win at the libel trial had largely disproved Bankes' accusations. Briggs & Co. had paid the costs of his return trip from Egypt to India, but separate allegations that lengthy delays on this 12-month long trip constituted a breach of trust with Briggs & Co were never satisfactorily resolved.

A review of the available evidence has identified unpublished documents in the Bankes archive at the Dorset History Centre at Dorchester (DRC) that casts new light on the attribution of guilt and innocence in the libel case and on the veracity of Buckingham's justifications in connection with the alleged breach of trust with Briggs & Co.

Brief background on Bankes and Buckingham

William John Bankes (1786–1855) came from a privileged background: born into a leading, wealthy Dorset family, he was affluent in his own right and heir to a fortune. He read Classics at Cambridge and was travelling in the Near East for pleasure and adventure. He had been the Tory MP for Truro in 1810 and, following his return from the Near East, was MP for Cambridge from 1822. He displayed the typical impatience and arrogance of his class, but despite confessing later to being indolent,[3] he did not fritter his time away. He travelled extensively throughout the eastern Mediterranean and the Near East between 1815 and 1820, and he became respected for his knowledge of Egypt and Nubia and his accurate drawings and watercolours. However, he published none of his travels, and consequently most of what we know of his accomplishments comes from his co-travellers.[4] His modern fame as an Egyptologist, artist and epigraphist comes from the research of largely unpublished archive material by authors such as Bowsher,[5] Lewis,[6] Sartre-Fauriat,[7] Sebba[8] and Usick.[9]

The background of James Silk Buckingham (1786–1855) was very different and his remarkable life repays a closer inspection. The following summary of his formative years comes from a biography by Turner.[10] The youngest son of a Cornish, seafaring family, he had a basic education and went to sea at the age of nine in a ship captained by his sister's husband.[11] The following years were full of adventures, including a spell in prison at Corunna. He briefly attended a naval academy, where he mastered nautical instruments, and while still in his teens became a Methodist and preacher. He married a neighbour's daughter at the age of 20 and attained command of his first merchant vessel the following year. Then he sailed in the Atlantic and the Mediterranean for the next six years. However, he was ambitious: leaving his wife and young family with relatives he departed England with debts of £500 to establish a trading business in Smyrna. The business failed, so he travelled to Egypt in 1813–14, visiting many ancient sites and 'hatching' financial schemes at every opportunity. But he did not leave Smyrna empty handed: while there he had met John Lee, the British Consul, who gave him an introduction to his brother, Peter Lee, the Consul in Alexandria.[12]

There were many other ambitious young men in the Near East at this time seeking their fortune, but Buckingham was a quick learner, well-driven and – more importantly – had realized the importance of good connections. He was charming and made many friends in his travels.[13] His befriending of the famous Swiss explorer John Ludwig Burckhardt (1784–1817) is typical. His introduction to Peter Lee had brought him into contact with other influential members of the expatriate community in Egypt at that time, and he exploited these connections to further his ambitions. This ultimately led to the souring of some friendships; his friendship with Burckhardt being just one example. Largely self-taught, he lacked the university education that marked the leading explorers in the region such as Burckhardt and Bankes, but he made up for this with resourcefulness and was driven to find opportunities to clear his debts and to re-invent himself as an explorer and author. An opportunity came in 1815, following the successful negotiation of a trading treaty with Mohammed Ali Pasha in Egypt on behalf of the merchant house of Briggs & Co. and himself, when an agreement was entered into with Lee, whereby Buckingham was to carry the treaty back to Bombay.[14] Thinking that the return to India by sea would involve a long delay, due to contrary winds, Briggs & Co. agreed to provide an unlimited letter of credit to cover costs of Buckingham's return trip to Bombay via Aleppo.[15] Buckingham published four books between 1821 and 1829, based on his adventures on this trip.[16] In the absence of a detailed, published critique of Buckingham's version of events on the trip, we have to rely on the version of events set out in his four travel books and his autobiography published immediately before his death. Turner's sympathetic biography mostly parrots Buckingham's published travelogue and is silent on contentious issues such as the arrangements made between Lee and Buckingham before the start of the return trip to India.[17]

Background to the court case

Bankes arrived in Egypt from Greece in 1815 and spent much of that year exploring Egypt and Nubia[18] before deciding to turn his attention to Syria.[19] While in Egypt, Bankes met traveller John Ludwig Burckhardt and the two became firm friends. Burckhardt had visited sites in Syria and the Decapolis in 1812 and had drawn maps of the places visited. Bankes was interested in seeing the same area and Burckhardt gave him a list of sites to visit.

Bankes left Cairo in late 1815 and arrived in Jerusalem on 2 January 1816, where he established himself at the Terra Sancta convent and set about making preparations for a trip to the Decapolis region, particularly Jarash (Jerash) and Umm Qais. Buckingham arrived in Jerusalem on 20 January 1816 and immediately sought a meeting with Bankes. The two men ended up sharing the same room at the convent. They visited several sites around Jerusalem together and Buckingham joined Bankes' planned expedition to Jarash and Umm Qais. The party of six set off on 28 January 1816, and reached Nazareth on 4 February. Disagreement over the precise nature of the arrangement made between the two men before departure, and the events that subsequently took place on the trip, were to be key points in the subsequent libel case that Buckingham brought against Bankes.

What triggered the libel trial?

On 2 October 1818, Buckingham included a lengthy prospectus of his forthcoming book *Travels in Palestine* in the first edition of his newly established *Calcutta Journal*. A copy of the published prospectus reached Egypt nine months later and came to Bankes' attention. Bankes was enraged when he saw the references to plans and descriptions relating to the eight-day trip from Jerusalem to Nazareth in 1816. On 12 June 1819, while in Thebes, Bankes wrote a scathing letter to Buckingham based on what he had seen in the prospectus (hereafter 'Letter'), accusing him of having copied and stolen material from Bankes while they had travelled together. He demanded retraction of the section in the book relating to the Jerusalem–Nazareth trip and return 'all that portion of the work advertised, that treats of a journey made at my expense and compiled from my notes'. The same day Bankes wrote to his father, enclosing a copy of the Letter. Around six months later, in late 1819,[20] an open copy of the Letter was sent with Mr Hobhouse to India. Bankes gave instructions for it to be shown to the British consuls in Aleppo and Bagdad, and to anyone Hobhouse wished to in India, with the intention of ruining Buckingham's reputation. The Letter took almost 12 months to reach Buckingham in India, arriving in Calcutta in June 1820. Buckingham delayed nearly three weeks before replying with a brief letter of rebuttal.[21] Buckingham did not comply with Bankes' demands regarding the book – apart from anything else the Jarash–Umm Qais trip with Bankes constituted about 30 per cent of the book[22] – and published it the following year. Buckingham considered that the distribution of the Letter constituted publication, and on his arrival in England from India towards the end of 1823 he brought a libel action against Bankes.[23] While Bankes had asked Hobhouse to distribute the contents of his Letter freely when he reached India, it is unclear as to how widely it was disseminated. Sebba suggests that it was;[24] however Buckingham himself later admitted that Hobhouse had shown the document to only a few people in Bombay before Buckingham saw it in Calcutta.[25] Buckingham himself effected a far more widespread distribution of the Letter by publishing it in the *Calcutta Journal* in August 1822;[26] thereby, inflaming the very libel that he accused Bankes of causing.

Bankes fumed over Buckingham's actions for several years. He was almost certainly the author of an anonymous criticism of Buckingham that was published in the *Quarterly Review* in 1822 in the guise of a review of *Travels in Palestine*. In this, among other things, he ridiculed Buckingham for thinking that the Jarash ruins were those of Pella rather than Gerasa; yet Bankes had thought the same during his 1816 visit and only changed his mind during his subsequent visits in 1818. Bankes also ridiculed Buckingham for thinking that Umm Qais was Gamala when in fact it is Gadara; yet Bankes – like Burckhardt before him[27] – had made the same mistake. These facts were all brought out the following year in a private publication by Irby and Mangles, who had accompanied Bankes on two trips to the area in 1818.[28]

Buckingham refuted the accusations contained in the Letter and the Quarterly Review in lengthy articles that appeared in the *Calcutta Journal* in August 1822 and in a 68-page appendix to his second book on his Near Eastern tour in *Travels among the Arab Tribes*, published before the libel trial.

There were several delays and adjournments in the proceedings leading up to the trial that delayed the hearing for three years. The first lengthy delay was the result of the court granting Bankes permission to bring two witnesses from the Near East; his servant, Antonio da Costa, and interpreter, Giovanni Finati. The need for Buckingham to send to Hobhouse in India for written confirmation of his actions in distributing Bankes' letter in Egypt and Syria caused a second major delay.

The trial was completed in a single day at the Court of the King's Bench in London on 19 October 1826. Buckingham had been fortunate to retain the brilliant Whig barrister Henry Brougham – later appointed Lord Chancellor – as lead counsel, who proved more than a match for Bankes' lead counsel, Mr Gurney.

What were Bankes' accusations against Buckingham?

Only four of the ten specific accusations in the Letter[29] were considered at any length at the trial. In a separate letter to Sir Evan Nepean dated 12 June 1819[30] Bankes also complained of Buckingham's ingratitude by failing to mention him in the prospectus. He was wrong, as Buckingham had acknowledged Bankes in the Preface to the prospectus[31] published in the *Calcutta Journal*, and also in many places in the text of *Travels in Palestine*. The accusations in the Letter were the basis for the libel case brought against him by Buckingham in 1823, and the most significant of these will now be examined in more detail.

The arrangements for the trip

Bankes and Buckingham were to disagree about just about everything that took place on the trip from Jerusalem to Nazareth. Finati's testimony at the trial confirmed that Bankes' arrangements for the trip from Jerusalem were well advanced before he met Buckingham. Bankes had arrived in Jerusalem on 2 January 1816. An undated, three-page aide-memoire in Bankes' handwriting in the DRC archives relates that the two men met for the first time in Jerusalem the day after Buckingham had introduced himself via a note delivered to Bankes in Bethlehem.[32] The aide-memoire also records that Bankes arranged for the hire and payment of two guides for the trip without any contribution or participation by Buckingham. The combined party of six set off on 28 January 1816: it comprised Bankes, his two servants (Giovanni Finati and Antonio da Costa) and two Arab guides, with Buckingham being the sixth member.[33]

Buckingham's role during the trip

The relationship between the two men on the trip – whether employer/employee as Bankes claimed – or a joint enterprise between two gentlemen as Buckingham claimed, became central to the libel case. Brougham argued that if it was a joint enterprise, then each was entitled to the product of their joint labours.[34] Buckingham is silent on the matter in *Travels in Palestine*, and the defence produced no written evidence to support Bankes' case. However, the aide-memoire also states that 'Mr B[Buckingham] begged to be permitted to accompany me offering to be of any use to me in his (power) by taking down any notes or memoranda or ascertain bearings for me. I consented to this specifying distinctly that there must be no publication on his part to this – of course there can be no witness the conversation passing only be between us two.'

The similarity of some of the wording of this passage in the aide-memoire with parts of the Letter suggests that Banks may have written it before the Letter. Bankes' position was supported at the trial by oral evidence given by Bankes' servant Antonio da Costa, although – as noted by Sebba[35] – Brougham effectively dismissed this evidence. Bankes' version of events is at least credible, whereas Buckingham's claim that Bankes 'invited and pressed me for his own advantage, as he could not speak a word of the language'[36] is not; for in Giovanni Finati, Bankes appears to have had a far more experienced interpreter to cover this deficiency. Brougham claimed that Bankes' friendly letter to Buckingham, written at the end of February 1816, disproved the arrangements claimed by Bankes. This letter, written almost a month after the Jarash–Umm Qais trip, certainly showed that a friendship had grown between the two men by the time they reached Nazareth; but did not prove that this relationship existed at the start of the trip when the two men had only just met. Turner's later claim, that Bankes' letter 'cleared Buckingham of the charges of having been Bankes' hired servant'[37] is therefore flawed.

The plan of Jerash was constructed and noted by Bankes and copied by Buckingham

The defence produced plans compiled on Bankes' behalf by Charles Barry that compared Buckingham's plans and drawings of Jarash with those of Bankes drawn in 1816 and 1818, and Barry's plan drawn following his own visit to Jarash in 1819.[38] Buckingham acknowledged that he had copied Bankes' general plan of Jarash in Nazareth after the completion of their journey, but that he did so with Bankes' permission. Buckingham also claimed that, in any case, his published plan was not created from Bankes' drawing but from the measurements and notes taken on his solo visit one month later.

Buckingham offers three different explanations concerning his own published plan of Jarash. Version 1 was that it was a corrected version of the joint plan which was created (and copied) in early February: 'The plan of the ruins of Geraza, in the country of the Decapolis beyond the Jordan, is laid down also from actual observations, corrected by two subsequent visits to the spot; as well as the plans of particular edifices, amid the interesting remains of this ancient city.'[39]

Version 2 was that on 8 March he 'ventured out with my compass and note-book, to take sets of bearings for the correction of the plan of the city'.[40] Version 3, written on a footnote on the same page as Version 2, states that it was drawn entirely from information he collected in his later solo visit in March 'accompanied by a ground plan of the city, and many of its separate edifices, drawn entirely from the notes, bearings, and measurements taken by myself on this last occasion'. Buckingham apparently did not see the conflict between these statements or that his claim, that the information collected on his brief visit in March was more than the information they jointly collected over two days one month previously, would not stand scrutiny. He had arrived at Jarash in the dark on the evening of 7 March and left at noon on 8 March[41] – a total of six daylight hours on site.[42] It strains credulity that one man could map the entire city and make detailed measurements of many monuments in the space of six hours or less. In a letter written to Babington three weeks before Buckingham replied to Bankes' letter, he also claimed that his published plan was more accurate than the plan that he had copied from Bankes,[43] a claim repeated in his published response to the *Quarterly Review* article.[44] Charles Barry disputed this claim at the trial stating that while neither Bankes' plan nor Buckingham's plan was accurate, Buckingham's was the least accurate.[45] Buckingham's plan reflects his confused understanding of the layout of the site, which he acknowledged in *Travels in Palestine*.[46] The outline of the city walls on the 1816 plans by Bankes and Buckingham are both inferior to the wall outline on Burckhardt's plan constructed four years earlier.[47]

Buckingham had concealed from Bankes that he was already employed

Buckingham's version of the arrangement between himself and Peter Lee, the British Consul in Alexandria regarding his return trip to India is set out in letter he wrote to his friend Babington on 31 December 1820: 'Mr Lee...voluntarily offered to pay my way, on Brigg's and Co.'s account. No time was limited, no route was positively fixed, and no sum was named. It was generally understood that I should go as quickly and cheaply as I could, and that whatever the cost was I was to be repaid.'[48]

Buckingham also affirms that 'an unlimited letter of credit was given me on Mr. Barker, the Consul at Aleppo, the route by which I intended to go, although this was left open, to be determined as circumstances might direct' and that Lee had 'solicited' him to make the return trip to India by land,[49] but this cannot be verified as the full correspondence outlining the arrangement has not been published.

The issue of Buckingham's 'employment' by Briggs & Co. was raised at the trial, although the lack of proof surrounding the actual arrangements agreed with Lee in Alexandria means that it is a moot point whether or not the arrangements constituted employment. Brougham argued that the arrangement between Bankes and Buckingham could not be considered as employment, because Buckingham did not receive a salary for his services to Bankes. Brougham did not see the inconsistency of this argument and Buckingham's employment by Briggs & Co., where Buckingham did not receive a salary from Briggs & Co. either but there was a clear and acknowledged employment of his services.[50] This was not picked up by the defence, and was one of several opportunities foregone by the defence at the trial.

Bankes' accusation that Buckingham had kept his arrangement with Briggs & Co. secret prior to the trip was denied by Brougham, who claimed 'Mr Buckingham, Gentleman, denies most positively that he ever made a secret of his employment [to Briggs & Co.]... so far from Mr Buckingham having studiously concealed his employment, he openly and avowedly proclaimed his destination, and the object of his journey...'.[51] This denial directly contradicts Buckingham's earlier claim that he was 'not in any sense a servant of them or in their employ',[52] but the absence of hard evidence from either side meant that Bankes' accusation could not be proved.

Buckingham's reputation and character

Buckingham's stout defence of his reputation was a frequent feature of his publications and the plaintiff's case at the libel trial. Buckingham considered himself blameless, and his invariable response to criticism of his reputation was a lengthy burst of self-righteous indignation. But what exactly was this reputation that he sought to protect? At the trial, Brougham claimed that both Bankes and Buckingham held the social 'station' of 'gentleman'; the only difference between them being Bankes' wealth. This was a bold enough claim to make regarding their respective stations in life at the time of the trial – bearing in mind Buckingham's vastly improved circumstances over the previous five years in India, but a patently ludicrous assessment of his status on the trip with Bankes in 1816. Even Turner, Buckingham's sympathetic biographer, refers to him as 'a wandering sailor' on his arrival in Egypt,[53] but Usick's description of 'a hyperactive opportunist and adventurer'[54] is far more realistic. Buckingham had certainly done some travelling in Egypt but was only too aware that he lacked the education and Near Eastern experience of people like Burckhardt and Bankes and was simply not in the same league as these two travellers. So, in the context of the return trip to India, the accusations put forward by Buckingham's detractors – that he contrived to arrange things on the return trip for his own advantage – are consistent with his actual character and reputation at the start of the trip.

Three factors had contributed to the major improvement in Buckingham's fortunes on his return to India: the publication of *Travels in Palestine*, the minor celebrity status associated with his version of events of his return trip from Alexandria, and his establishment of the *Calcutta Journal* in 1818. Buckingham's considerable literary skills ensured the early success of the *Calcutta Journal*, but his constant criticism of the policies of the Indian Government and the East India Company ultimately lead to his banishment from India in 1823. His charisma combined with literary attacks on the Indian establishment attracted many friends and supporters in India, but his departure from India did not silence his detractors.[55]

The confidence and cocksuredness that marked Buckingham's younger days developed into something like narcissism during his return trip to India. Buckingham did not appreciate censure of any sort, and seemed genuinely perplexed when previous friends turned on him. While initially showing deference to Burckhardt and Bankes, Buckingham construed their later emnity towards him as 'a coalition of jealous enemies'. Burckardt's attacks on his character were through 'jealousy of my being able to give a better account of the countries east of the Jordan than himself', while Bankes' accusations were from 'from sheer envy, I believe, at my anticipating him in time, and giving a better account of the Hauran than he is likely to do'.[56]

Some conclusions from the trial

Bankes wrote the Letter to Buckingham in a rage and its contents were ill-considered. He was still in the same frame of mind five months later at Trieste when he asked Mr H. W. Hobhouse to take an open copy of the Letter for distribution in Syria and India. Bankes was criticized at the trial, and also in a biased article published in *The Times* in 1825,[57] that his libellous letter to Buckingham was based on a prospectus of Buckingham's book,[58] rather than the book itself; but such criticism overlooked two things. First, the prospectus was written in Buckingham's usual verbose style and was a substantial stand-alone document. The published prospectus occupied four columns and comprised chapter headings and a lengthy, comprehensive preface that gave the reader an excellent idea about the content of the book.[59] It could, therefore, be argued that it contained sufficient 'ammunition' for Bankes to draw the conclusions that he did. Second, one of the main purposes of the Letter was to get the offending material removed from the book *before* publication.

Bankes probably realized the problems he was going to have in proving the libel and played successfully for time, thereby effectively weakening Buckingham's position by causing him considerable expense and giving the defence time to get their case together; however, the time thus gained was squandered. Bankes had ample time before the trial to counter Buckingham's publication with a far better one of his own. He had the materials to achieve this, and even got Charles Barry to compile it, but it seems that Barry did not have the time to complete the work and Bankes was too indolent to do so himself.[60]

Bankes' weak position was exploited to the full in the well-argued case presented by Buckingham's lead counsel, a situation that was exacerbated by the indifferent performance of the defence's legal team. First, the defence failed to highlight certain failings of Buckingham character, especially the fact that he had been twice expelled from India and that libel cases had been brought there against the *Calcutta Journal*.[61] Second, they missed several opportunities to highlight deficiencies in the plaintiff's case: for example, to highlight that there was no written evidence from either side regarding the understanding between the two men on the Jarash–Umm Qais trip, that Bankes' correspondence demonstrating friendship with Buckingham post-dated the trip and was therefore arguably irrelevant, and the confusion over the issue of Buckingham's employment status.

Specifically, the defence failed adequately to prove three accusations considered to be important by the Chief Justice. First, that Burkhardt had described Buckingham in a letter as a 'villain'; second, that Buckingham could not distinguish between Ottoman and Roman architecture, and third, that Buckingham's character in Syria and Egypt was notorious. On the first count, Bankes appears to have been unlucky. Barker had forwarded Burckhardt's 'Paper "on Buckingham" in his own hand-writing' to Bankes in a despatch sent from Aleppo via Lord Strangford dated 11 November 1824.[62] It may not have been delivered, as there is no record of it in the

DRC Bankes archive: surely, if it had it would have been produced at the trial? The suggestion that Buckingham could not distinguish between Ottoman and Roman architecture was a silly accusation that was easy to disprove. The accusation of Buckingham's notoriety also failed, the Chief Justice noting that the views of one or two individuals did not sustain the claim of general notoriety.

Bankes had additional material that was critical of Buckingham's reputation: for example, Barker's comment on Buckingham in a letter to Lady Hester Stanhope dated 21 June 1816 that, if asked by Briggs & Co., his answers 'will ruin his character, with everybody who may become acquainted with his Syrian adventures'.[63] However, he was either unable or unwilling to present the letter at the trial – perhaps out of courtesy for the author and recipient; although, as we have seen, sections of the letter had already been published in *John Bull*.[64]

Other conclusions that can be drawn from the available evidence

The court found in Buckingham's favour, but the outcome did not fully satisfy him. In his summing up, the Chief Justice had highlighted several minor points that Bankes had proved. More importantly, from Buckingham's perspective, attention was drawn to several other far more important points where Bankes *may* have proved his justification. They included that the journey was taken at the expense of Banks and arranged before Bankes' meeting with Buckingham and that Buckingham either copied Bankes' 'notes or they were taken under Bankes' direction'. Buckingham's reaction was to publish a transcript of the trial proceedings (hereafter 'Law Report'); with lengthy footnotes providing amplification on commentary at the trial and correcting what he felt were 'deficiencies'.[65] This remarkable document included corrections to comments by his counsel and disagreements with some of the comments made by the Lord Chief Justice. For justification, he pointed to a letter written to *The Times* by Bankes' lawyers that questioned two points in an article which had been published by that paper the day before. Given that Buckingham had added more than 123 separate notes on wide-ranging topics to the verbatim transcript, this justification is hardly credible.

As noted above, no physical proof of Burckhardt's 'Paper "on Buckingham"' was presented at the trial; however, Buckingham admits to the document in a statement in the Appendix to *Travels among the Arab Tribes*.[66] We also know from a letter from Buckingham himself (Buckingham, 1825: p. 658) that Burckhardt referred to him in a letter as a 'rascal, scoundrel, liar and fool' (p. 658). So, while the Lord Chief Justice's precise judgement on this point was important in the overall libel judgement, we are left in no doubt as to Burckhardt's assessment of Buckingham's character.

There is no doubt that the material published by Buckingham on Jarash was largely collected during his two-day visit with Bankes from 31 January to 1 February 1816, and much of it was copied from Bankes' 1816 'Plan of the Ruins of Djerash'. Buckingham's counsel claimed that he was entitled to publish the jointly-collected material, but Buckingham insisted that the published material came solely from material collected on his later solo visit in March 1816. This is simply unsustainable in light of the obvious conclusions that much of it was clearly copied from Bankes' plan and, Buckingham's solo visit in March was so short that he did not have the time to do what he claimed. At the trial, Charles Barry also refuted Buckingham's claim that his plans were superior in accuracy to those by Bankes. The oversize scaling of the main monuments in Buckingham's published plan could be interpreted as a deception to make the plan appear different from the plan he copied from Bankes, but the defence did not raise this issue.

The alleged breach of trust with Briggs & Co.

The question as to whether Buckingham's actions on his return trip to India constituted a breach of trust under his agreement with Lee and Briggs & Co. was raised by the defence at the trial; however, as it was not an allegation made by Bankes in the Letter it did not form part of the decision on the libel. It was also an accusation levelled at Buckingham in Bankes' infamous (but anonymous) 'review' of *Travels in Palestine* published in the *Quarterly Review*,[67], and Buckingham himself raised the matter several times in various notes added to the trial transcript in the *Law Report*. The alleged breach of trust goes to the heart of Buckingham's honesty and integrity and therefore warrants closer scrutiny.

Buckingham's return travel route from India in 1816 is detailed in his four books. It took about 12 months and involved both land and sea travel (Fig.11.1).

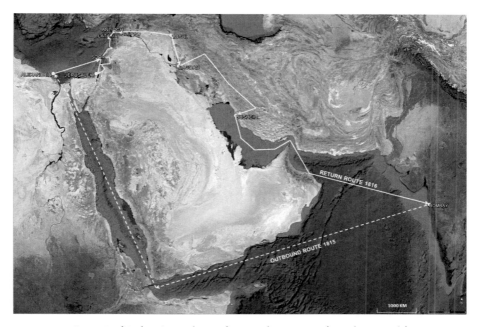

Fig 11.1 Buckingham's travel route from Bombay, 1815-16. (Map data: Google).

His explanation for the choice of the return route is given in his autobiography, where he states 'as the season for the southern passage [to India via the Red Sea] had just terminated,[68] and would require a long delay if we waited for its return, it was deemed best that I should make the journey to India overland, by way of Palestine, Syria, Mesopotamia, and Persia; and to this I readily consented.' His actual route to Aleppo included a two-and-a-half-month diversion through Palestine, east of the River Jordan and the Hauran and then a further two months travel to Aleppo. He had originally planned to travel from Aleppo to the Persian Gulf via the desert route,[69] but his actual route took him eastwards to Mosul and Baghdad over a period of more than three months (Fig.11. 2). Many of his decisions could not be independently verified, and therefore were open to other interpretations; especially where such actions impacted on his ability to complete his return journey 'as quickly and cheaply as possible'.[70] Four decisions account for most of the delays.

1. His landing at Soor after the storm while *en route* from Alexandria to Latachia and the subsequent abandonment of the sea journey.
2. Backtracking 170 km to the south to Jerusalem to obtain a firman, rather than advance his travels northwards directly into Syria.
3. Backtracking even further south to Kerak to access an alleged desert route to Baghdad.[71]
4. Spending two months visiting ruins in Persia *en route* from Mosul to the Persian Gulf.

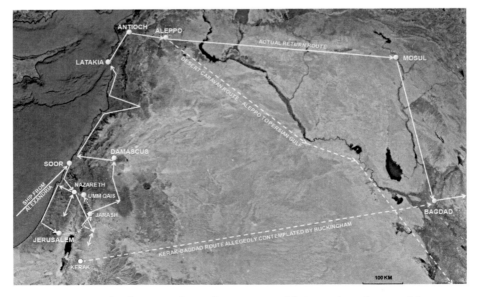

Fig 11.2 Buckingham's travel route from Soor to Baghdad, 1816. (Map data: Google).

In each of these cases, Buckingham tells us that the decisions were necessary because of local circumstances 'altogether beyond my control'.[72] On the face of it, this is a reasonable – if largely unprovable – explanation, given the local political instability and the inherent security risks to travellers at the time. But while Buckingham felt that his actions were fully justified, can we rely on his version of events? His detractors frequently implied dishonest conduct about his activities on his return trip to India, but are there real grounds for these claims? He brought some criticism on his head through inconsistencies in his explanations and, on occasion, he played fast and loose with the truth. His defence against imputations of dishonesty on his return trip to India brought by the Rev. Eli Smith in anonymous letters published in the *New York Observer* in 1839 serves to demonstrate the latter point. Buckingham objected to Smith's accusations and claimed that 'my conduct in this transaction [with Lee and Briggs & Co.] was approved... and in the Court of the King's Bench in England, the writer of an anonymous article in the *Quarterly Review*,... was convicted of making the same base insinuations... and the accumulated costs of three years protracted proceedings, making 6,000 pounds sterling...'.[73] Despite being delivered with conviction, Buckingham's claims were all false: the 'transaction' and the article in the *Quarterly Review* were not part of the libel case and the £6000 in costs related to the combined costs from the libel trials of John Murray, Henry Bankes, and William Bankes and not William Bankes alone.[74]

There are many occasions where the judgement of Buckingham's actions and justifications may be a matter of opinion, but one case of deliberate misrepresentation stands out in the evidence. It occurred during Buckingham's stay with Mr Claudius Rich, the consul in Baghdad, in late August–early September 1816 and is to be found in a copy of a letter to Barker, the consul at Aleppo, dated 29 November 1816.[75] The two men had not met previously, and there appears no reason to doubt that Rich's views were an honest account of Buckingham's behaviour. Rich stated that Buckingham had 'behaved him self well under my roof... and with great modesty & apparent candour of his situation & prospects'. He added '*He stated however in the most positive manner that he was travelling entirely at his own expense, and that Messrs' Lee & Co had not advanced him a farthing either for this journey or a former one in Egypt.*' [author's emphasis] Given the events in the journey up to that point, this statement is manifestly a misrepresentation.

These instances show that Buckingham sometimes got his facts wrong and that at least on one occasion there is evidence of a deliberate misrepresentation. It does not necessarily negate all his assertions regarding his return journey, but it does cast a shadow on their veracity. John Barker, the consul at Aleppo – and a one-time friend and admirer – was less charitable. Before departing Aleppo for Mosul on 25 May 1816, Buckingham had left letters with Barker for onward transmission to Lee and Briggs & Co. Buckingham tells us that they contained responses to 'angry reproaches' in letters he had received from Lee in Alexandria regarding unnecessary delays in his return trip to India.[76] Barker was incensed at Buckingham's expectation that

Barker would add his imprimatur to the explanations Buckingham had given in the letters for the delays in the journey, and complained bitterly in a long letter to Lady Hester Stanhope dated 21 June 1816. Sections of Barker's letter had actually been published in the *John Bull* newspaper in Calcutta;[77] however, their damning effect had been mitigated by them being 'unattested and unauthenticated'. Confirmation of the existence of a copy of this letter in Barker's hand in the DRC Bankes archive now removes any justification for this mitigation.[78] Barker's scathing comments on Buckingham succinctly expose the flaws in Buckingham's version of key events on his return trip to India. The key entry is as follows:

> That B [Buckingham] should abuse the confidence, squander the money, and sacrifice the interests of his benefactors to the vanity of becoming an author, or to the expectation of great profit from his Book, is all very natural, because we meet a rascal at every step; but can we reconcile with his appearance of being a man in his senses, the attempt he has made to impose upon our judgements these long rapsodical [*sic*] Epistles, in almost every line of which there is either a bare-faced falsehood too gross to deceive any body or wilful misrepresentation and exaggerations as easily detected. To bring himself to believe that by such inventions he can justify his conduct to Briggs & Lee he must have taken them for complete idiots. But the strongest proof of his own folly is, his expectation that I should come forward and vouch for the truth of the Tempest which threw him on the coast at Soor & deterred him, tho' a sailor, to continue his voyage as he had been enjoined to Latachia! That the direct road from that place to Aleppo is Antioch!! That the excursion from Tripoli to the Cedars, Balbeck, and Homs could... be performed in five days!!!! That the Buyurdi [firman] he got from Haim for Jerusalem could not have been equally procured, or would have proved ineffectual for Leida, Bairut, Tripoli & Latachia. That Assalt or Karak is a place from which a European can go to Bagdad without any money for the journey, or the means of subsisting when he got there... Oh! I retract my opinion of his abilities being superior to those of Mr Bankes and am quite ashamed that I could have for one moment made the comparison or believed him to possess common sense.'
> (Underlined text denotes original emphasis).

The letter is a systematic demolition of the key justifications for Buckingham's return trip itinerary and on his integrity and reputation. It is all the more significant because of Barker's consular status, and because there had also been a genuine friendship between Barker and Buckingham: Barker had held Buckingham's abilities in high esteem – even superior to those of Bankes. In the end, the letters to Lee and Briggs & Co. were despatched without any comment from Barker. A friendly letter had been sent by Barker to Buckingham just ten days prior,[79] and the sudden turnaround in Barker's view of Buckingham may have been triggered by the realization of the 'absurdity' in Buckingham's letters to Briggs & Co.

Brougham's introduction at the trial included a claim that Buckingham had only considered publishing a book on his travels on his return to India, where he was encouraged to do so by some residents.[80] Presumably, this was designed to support

Buckingham's notion that he was not using the trip as a means to gather material for a forthcoming book. However, Brougham's claim was not true, as there is evidence in a letter from consul Barker to Lady Hester Stanhope[81] that shows that Buckingham was considering the publication of the book by the time he had reached Aleppo and had mentioned it in letters to Lee and Briggs & Co.[82]

Concluding Points

A review of Buckingham's statements in connection with his intentions on the return trip to India has proved inconclusive. Buckingham claimed that 'the first *idea* of publication' arose on 23 March 1816 in Damascus and that Bankes suggested it.[83] We also learn that Buckingham mentioned a book at Aleppo in his correspondence with Lee and Briggs. The question, therefore, is not so much whether it was ever his intention to use the trip for this purpose, but when he decided to do so, and to what extent this affected his judgement on decisions made on the trip that resulted in extensive delays to his itinerary.

The fact that Buckingham used at least part of the trip to gather material for his book immediately throws into question the reasons for key decisions such as the landing at Soor and his two-and-a-half-month tour of Palestine and east of the Jordan River: but proves nothing. His two-month extended tour of sites in Persia on his way from Baghdad to Bushier in the Persian Gulf is more readily explained, as this occurred after he had mentioned his book in correspondence and there was arguably less need to disguise his actions if that was his intention. We know that Buckingham had planned a trip to Jarash and Syria as early as 1813,[84] so it is possible that he had been planning a publication before the trip with Bankes. Lee, Briggs and Barker all disbelieved Buckingham's explanations for the trip delays: Barker's letter to Lady Stanhope demolishing Buckingham's credibility makes his position very clear, and Briggs' decision to cancel the letter of credit implies he felt totally deceived. Buckingham's misrepresentation to Rich at Baghdad demonstrates that he was capable of subterfuge regarding his intentions, but not the extent to which this was applied.

No firm conclusion can, therefore, be drawn regarding Buckingham's justifications for the trip delays, other than he was not entirely honest in his claims about them. It is also impossible to draw firm conclusions as to whether Buckingham's actions did constitute a breach of trust without the ability to analyse all the correspondence and agreements between Buckingham, Lee and Briggs & Co. for the duration of the trip, and very little of this material appears to have been published.

The allocation of true guilt and innocence in the case is not straightforward, as neither party was blameless. Bankes has been criticized for launching his accusations at Buckingham based on the prospectus for the forthcoming book alone, but it is argued that there was enough information in the very comprehensive prospectus to give Bankes an excellent idea of what was in the book. Bankes lost the case because neither ill-considered claims against Buckingham's character and abilities nor key accusations of plagiarism and theft could be proved. An important accusation was that Burckhardt had accused Buckingham of being a 'villain' in a letter, but no proof of the letter was presented by the defence at the trial. There is no doubt that the letter existed and Bankes was unlucky in that it appears that he may not have received the proof – a copy of Burckhardt's letter in Burckhardt's own hand – that had been sent to him by Barker from Aleppo. Proof of this accusation would have been a telling, but not fatal, blow against Buckingham. The accusations of plagiarism and theft were the most important points from Bankes' perspective: this may have distracted him from appreciating the importance of his attacks in Buckingham's reputation, and contributed to his defeat at the trial. But the uncertainty of proof in many accusations was cold comfort to Buckingham, as it meant that his position was not fully exonerated either, and he lost no time in trying to correct this unfortunate outcome by publishing a transcript of the trial with commentary with an explanation of these 'deficiencies'. Buckingham was also fortunate that accusations of his alleged breach of trust with Briggs & Co. were not on the court's agenda because his position on this issue was weak.

Analysis of the available evidence shows that both Buckingham and Bankes were unreliable in their claims and accusations from time to time, and there is at least one clear case of misrepresentation by Buckingham. Buckingham's self-righteous indignation in defence of his behaviour on his return trip to India was probably genuinely felt. However, he was a narcissist, and the reputation that he was defending was a self-created illusion rather than a true reflection of his persona in 1816. With one exception, his justifications for the delays on the return trip to India were plausible but difficult to prove; however, they certainly did not convince three people who were closely involved – Lee, Briggs and Barker. The exception is his alleged pursuit of the desert route from Kerak to Baghdad, which was a thinly disguised excuse for a side trip to the Amman area and a return to Damascus via Jarash. Had Briggs' instruction cancelling Buckingham's letter of credit reached Aleppo and Baghdad in time, the outcome of the trip would likely have been very different, with all the attendant implications for Buckingham's later career.

For all its perceived deficiencies, the trial result was the making of Buckingham's subsequent career. He had come a long way from the poor, enthusiastic adventurer seeking his fortune in Cairo 13 years earlier. The trial outcome was a great advertisement for his books, and legitimized his position as an experienced Near East traveller. It also assisted his on-going legal dispute with the East India Company and the Indian Government that was to continue for many years. His travelling experiences provided the material for his emerging career as a public speaker and allowed him to expound his reformist views on a growing range of subjects that included the East India Company, free press, anti-slavery and temperance. He was a garrulous public speaker, giving more than 3500 public lectures across Britain and overseas over a ten-year period. While Buckingham enjoyed a long and active career after the trial, the proceedings had raised question-marks against his character that occasionally resurfaced in public. Buckingham was always quick to refute them, but his detractors in India refused to be silenced and continued to criticize him for years after his win against Bankes in 1826. The hectoring tone of his replies was perhaps a throwback to his early preaching days. A voluminous writer, he adopted a ponderous writing style that was aptly summarized by a contemporary.[85] While essentially travelogues, his books have enriched the corpus of historical and archaeological knowledge of the southern Levant, and his first book provides much of the known record of the trip from Jerusalem to Nazareth with Bankes in early 1816.

Bankes lost the kudos of being the first to publish details of his travels in the Decapolis. However, he could have easily rendered Buckingham's published material on Jarash and Umm Qais less irrelevant by publishing the far more accurate material that he had collected during two subsequent expeditions to Jarash in 1818 before the trial. The final plans and drawings of this work on Jarash were, in fact, compiled and prepared for publication by Charles Barry in 1820, but the project was never completed. It seems that Barry did not have the time to finish the job, and Bankes was too indolent to do so – although Bankes was still contemplating publication as late as 1830. It appears that the attempt to discredit Buckingham in the lead up to the libel trial was, in the end, a higher priority for Bankes than the publishing of his far more accurate work. As a result, the detailed information collected in 1818 lay hidden for about 180 years.[86]

The conduct of the three-year trial proceedings was costly in monetary terms for Bankes, but there seems to have been little lasting damage to his reputation and, in this, he was no doubt insulated by his wealth and position. Bankes was returned as MP for Marlborough in 1829 and to Dorset in 1832, ironically for part of that time being in parliament at the same time as Buckingham, who was returned as MP for Sheffield in 1832.

Endnotes

1   The prospectus was published in the first edition of the *Calcutta* Gazette on 2 October 1818. The book, (Buckingham, 1821) is hereafter cited in the text as *Travels in Palestine*.
2   The most comprehensive coverage is that by Sebba (2009: pp. 135–39) and Usick (2002; pp. 72–75).
3   Thompson, 2015: p. 183.
4   Buckingham, 1821; 1825 [hereafter cited in the text as *Travels among the Arab Tribes*]; Finati, 1830; Irby & Mangles, 1823. W. J. Bankes was the translator of Finati, 1830, and footnotes imply that he also contributed some content to that publication, and Sebba (2009: p. 73) found evidence that Bankes collaborated in the publication by Irby and Mangles.
5   Bowsher, 1997.
6   Lewis, 1997; 2001; 2007; Lewis, Sartre-Fauriat & Sartre, 1996.
7   Sartre-Fauriat 2001; 2004a, 2004b; Sartre-Fauriat & Sartre, 2007.
8   Sebba, 2009.
9   Usick, 1998; 2002.

10 Turner,1934: pp. 35–64.

11 Turner, 1934. See also the two-volume autobiography by Buckingham (1855).

12 *Ibid.*: p. 71.

13 He was described by one contemporary as being 'endowed with a remarkable speciousness of manners, and possessing the art of making himself agreeable to no common extent'. (The East India Company, 1829, May: p. 370.

14 We only have Buckingham's version of the nature of these arrangements, as no copies of any correspondence have been published. He claimed, among other things, that the actual route to be taken was 'left open, to be determined as circumstances might direct' (Buckingham, 1825: p. 600).

15 'As our voyages by the Red Sea [from India to Egypt], however, had been so long and tedious, and as the season for the southern passage had just terminated, and would require a long delay if we waited for its return, it was deemed best that I should make the journey to India overland, by way of Palestine, Syria, Mesopotamia, and Persia; and to this I readily consented.' (Buckingham, 1855, Vol. 2: p. 421).

16 Buckingham, 1821, 1825 1827, 1829.

17 Turner, 1934.

18 See Usick, 1998; 2002.

19 See Lewis et al., 1996; Sartre-Fauriat, 2004b.

20 Buckingham, 1826, hereafter cited in the text as *Law Report*: pp. 24–25.

21 Buckingham's reply to Bankes is dated 22 June 1820 (Buckingham, 1825: p. 619), but three weeks before (3 June) Buckingham had written to his friend Babington in London saying he had just received Bankes' letter.

22 The trip from Jerusalem to Nazareth only took up eight days of the eight-week trip, but eight chapters are dedicated to it. Fifty pages are devoted to Jarash (Gerasa): they include a ground plan of the city and the major structures and detailed plans of the two theatres, two temples, two baths and a 'Corinthian Temple' (church).

23 Buckingham, 1825: p. 599.

24 Sebba, 2009: p. 136.

25 Buckingham, 1825: p. 619, footnote.

26 *Ibid.*: p. 618.

27 Burckhardt, 1822: p. 271.

28 Irby & Mangles, 1823.

29 Buckingham, 1825: pp. 618–19.

30 DHC D/BKL HJ1/99.

31 Buckingham, 1821: p. xxii.

32 DHC D/BKL HJ1/97. Buckingham noted that the two met on 20th January 1816 (*Ibid.*: p. 182).

33 Buckingham incorrectly claimed that Bankes' party comprised four people only (Buckingham, 1825: p. 619.

34 Buckingham, 1826: p. 16.

35 Sebba, 2009: p. 138.

36 Buckingham, 1826: p. 8

37 Turner, 1934: p. 144.

38 DHC Bankes archive reference D/BKL HJ IIIA 18a, b, c; HJ IIIA 38a, b, c; HJ IIIA 39a, b. c (Boyer, 2015: p.41).

39 Buckingham, 1821: pp. xxi–xxii.

40 *Ibid.*: p. 132.

41 *Ibid.*: pp. 126–32.

42 In note 48 on page 47 of the trial transcript Buckingham admits to having worked for five hours on the site. This is consistent with his entries in *Travels among the Arab Tribes*, but inconsistent with a comment in the Appendix to this book, where he states 'I made a third visit to Jerash,...; and being unmolested through the whole of the day, had an opportunity of making a new and more detailed plan of the town generally, besides plans of the separate edifices, with bearings of all the principal points, and memoranda of every useful particular..'(Buckingham, 1825: p. 620).

43 *Ibid.*: p. 620.

44 *Ibid.*: p. 607

45 Buckingham, 1826:, p. 66.

46 Buckingham, 1821: p. 394 footnote.

47 Boyer, 2015: p. 45.

48 Buckingham, 1825: p. 630.

49 *Ibid.*: p. 600.

50 Buckingham, 1826: p. 13.

51 *Ibid.*: p. 13.

52 Buckingham, 1825: p. 647.

53 Turner, 1934: p. 73.

54 Usick, 2002: p. 56.

55 A lengthy article written in the *New Scots Magazine* (What is to be done with India, 1829, Sept.: p. 182), three years after the libel trial, contains a savage and well-argued case against Buckingham's reputation in India.

56 Buckingham, 1825: p. 622.

57 Dated 6 June 1825 (Sebba, 2009: pp. 136–37).

58 Notably in *The Times* newspaper of 6t June 1825 (Sebba, 2009: p. 137).

59 The preface was 17 pages long in the published book. Buckingham himself described the prospectus as 'being almost an exact copy of the preface to the work itself, giving an outline of the whole journey performed' (Buckingham, 1826: p. 27, footnote 12).

60 Boyer, 2015: p. 44.

61 Kling, 1976: p. 29, n. 1.

62 DRC D/BKL: HJ 1/244.

63 DHC D/BKL: HJ/1/53.

64 Buckingham, 1825: p. 649.

65 Buckingham, 1826: p. 84.

66 Buckingham, 1825: p. 664.

67 It was contained in a lengthy footnote in the article in volume 52 of the *Quarterly Review* (*Ibid.*: p. 607).

68 This may not be strictly true, as a southerly passage is possible in the northern half of the Red Sea as far as 18°N from November to March (Delaney et al., 2016), from where the coastal caravan route could be followed to Yemen. From around May, ships could then catch the south-west monsoonal winds to India.

69 Buckingham mentioned in a letter to Bankes dated 30 April 1816 (DHC D/BKL: HJ 1/46) that he intended to visit Palmyra on his way to Baghdad, but later claimed that this was not possible as he could not find a guide to take him (Buckingham, 1825: p. 649).

70 Letter to Babington, 31 December 1820 (Ibid.: p. 630).
71 A look at the planned route in Fig. 2 proves the lie of Buckingham's claim regarding this route. The fact that he left his baggage with Bankes to be sent on to Damascus and took no money (Buckingham, 1825: p. 647) also shows that it was a fiction that provided him with an excuse to visit Amman and sites nearby.
72 Ibid.: p. 600.
73 Buckingham, 1840: p. 24.
74 Buckingham, 1834: p. 26.
75 DHC D/BKL: 1/62.
76 These 'angry reproaches' included 'writing to me in Syria as to the deviation from the straight line which I appeared to him to have made, and reproaching me with what to him appeared unnecessary delay, I defended my conduct by showing the necessity that had occasioned it' (Buckingham, 1825: p. 654). Lee's letters were sent before Mr Brigg's return to Alexandria. On seeing Lee's letters to Buckingham, Briggs sent a courier to Aleppo cancelling Buckingham's letter of credit and instructing that any funds advanced to Buckingham were to be recovered from him (Ibid.: p. 630). The courier died en route, and the letter was never delivered. News of Brigg's actions reached Baghdad only after Buckingham had left for Persia.
77 Ibid.: p. 649.
78 DHC D/BKL: HJ/1/53.
79 Probably the 11 June 1816 (Ibid.: p. 648).
80 Buckingham, 1826: p. 10.
81 DHC D/BKL: HJ/1/53.
82 'That B [Buckingham] should abuse the confidence, squander the money, and sacrifice the interests of his benefactors to the vanity of becoming an author, or to the expectation of great profit from his Book, is all very natural, because we meet a rascal at every step', (Ibid.).
83 Buckingham, 1825: p. 304.
84 Letter to Babington dated 3 June 1820 (Ibid.: p. 619), where he states 'the Hauran generally, and consequently one of its principal cities, Jerash, was long contemplated as the subject of my examination, I need only refer to a letter from Mr. Burckhardt... dated December 13, 1813'.
85 'He is afflicted with an abominable incapacity of retention, and seems to imagine that everything that can be said should be said, and then everything which has been written should be repeated. His account of the transaction [forthcoming libel case with Bankes] is one eternal recitation of documents, and reiteration of charges and arguments.' (Mr. W. Bankes and Mr. Buckingham, 1825: p. 1).
86 Boyer, 2015, 2016.

Bibliography

Bowsher, J. (1997) 'An early nineteenth century account of Jerash and the Decapolis: the records of John William Bankes', Levant 29: pp. 227–46.

Boyer, D. D. (2015) The relative contributions of William John Bankes and Charles Barry to the early plans of Gerasa/Jarash (Jordan): evidence from the Bankes and Barry archives. In N. Cooke & V. Daubney (eds.), Every Traveller Needs a Compass:

Travel and collecting in Egypt and the Near East (pp. 33–53). Oxford, Oxbow Books/ ASTENE.

Buckingham, J. S. (1821) *Travels in Palestine, through the Countries of Bashan and Gilead, East of the River Jordan: including a visit to the Cities of Geraza and Gamala, in the Decapolis*. London, Longman, Hurst, Rees, Orme & Brown.

Buckingham, J. S. (1825) *Travels Among the Arab tribes Inhabiting the Countries East of Syria and Palestine: including a journey from Nazareth to the mountains beyond the Dead Sea, and thence through the Plains of the Hauran to Bozra, Damascus, Tripoly, Lebanon, Baalbeck, and the Valley of the Orontes to Seleucia, Antioch, and Aleppo. With an appendix, containing a refutation of certain unfounded calumnies industriously circulated against the author of this work, by Mr. Lewis Burckhardt, Mr. William John Bankes, and the Quarterly Review.* London, Longman, Hurst, Rees, Orme, Brown, & Green.

Buckingham, J. S. (1826) *Verbatim Report of The Action for Libel in The Case of Buckingham versus Bankes, Tried in The Court of King's Bench.* London, R. Carlile.

Buckingham, J. S. (1827) *Travels in Mesopotamia.* London, H. Colburn.

Buckingham, J. S. (1829) *Travels in Assyria, Media, and Persia, including a journey from Bagdad by Mount Zagros, to Hamadan, the ancient Ecbatana, researches in Ispahan and the ruins of Persepolis, and journey from thence by Shiraz and Shapoor to the sea-shore. Description of Bussorah, Bushire, Bahrein, Ormuz, and Muscat, narrative of an expedition against the pirates of the Persian Gulf, with illustrations of the voyage of Nearchus, and passage by the Arabian Sea to Bombay.* London, H. Colburn.

Buckingham, J. S. (1834) *Parliamentary Enquiry into the Claims of Mr. Buckingham and the East India Company.* London, Charles Whiting.

Buckingham, J. S. (1840) *Public Address, Delivered by Mr. Buckingham, in Defence of His Lectures on Palestine Against the Criticisms of the Reverend Eli Smith, Published Anonymously in The New York Observer, in 1839: Delivered at the Lyceum of New York, on Wednesday, Jan. 1840.* New York, W. Molineaux.

Buckingham, J. S. (1855) *Autobiography of James Silk Buckingham: Including His Voyages, Travels, Adventures, Speculations, Successes and Failures, Faithfully and Frankly Narrated; Interspersed with Characteristic Sketches of Public Men with Whom He Has Had Intercourse, During a Period of More Than Fifty Years*, 2 vols. London, Longman, Brown, Green, & Longmans.

Burckhardt, J. L. (1822) *Travels in Syria and the Holy Land.* London, Murray.

Delaney, A., Neiswender, M. and Whitley, B. (2016) General Weather Conditions Year Round from the Red Sea and Across the Northern Indian Ocean. Retrieved from http://www.quay2yachting.com/zh/yachting-news-zh/124-general-weather-conditions-year-round-from-the-red-sea-and-across-the-northern-indian-ocean.html, accessed 28/09/2016

Finati, G. (1830) *The Narrative of the Life and Adventures of Giovanni Finati.* London, Murray.

Irby, C. L. and Mangles, J. (1823) *Travels in Egypt and Nubia, Syria and Asia Minor: during the years 1817 & 1818.* London, White & Co.

Kling, B. B. (1976) *Partner in Empire: Dwarkanath Tagore and the Age of Enterprise in Eastern India.* Berkeley & London, University of California Press.

Lewis, N. N. (1997) Johann Ludwig Burckhardt und William John Bankes: '*Die ersten neuzeitlichen Europäer in Petra*'. In *Petra: Antike Felsstadt zwischen arabischer Tradition und griechischer Norm.* Zaberns Bildbände zur Archäologie: pp. 5–13. Mainz, Zabern

Lewis, N. N. (2001) The anger of Lady Hester Stanhope: some letters of Lady Hester, John Lewis Burckhardt and William John Bankes. In S. Searight & M. Wagstaff (eds), *Travellers in the Levant: voyagers and visionaries,* ASTENE Conference 2001 (pp. 57–70). Durham, ASTENE.

Lewis, N. (2007) *A transcript of the journals written or dictated by W.J. Bankes during his journeys to and from Petra in 1818.* Croydon, Norman Lewis.

Lewis, N. N., Sartre-Fauriat, A, & Sartre, M. (1996) *William John Bankes: Travaux en Syrie d'un voyageur oublié. Syria* 73: pp. 57–100.

Mr. W. Bankes and Mr. Buckingham (1825, May) *The London Magazine and Review, May to August 1825*: pp. 1–11.

Sartre-Fauriat, A. (2004a) 'William John Bankes (1786–1855): *voyageur en Orient au début du XIXe siècle*' in *Colloque de l'Université de Dijon, Voyageurs et Antiquité classique, 25-26 octobre 2001*: pp. 135–44). Bordeaux & Beyrouth, Institut Ausonius.

Sartre-Fauriat, A. (2004b) *Les voyages dans le Hawran (Syrie du Sud) de William John Bankes (1816 et 1818).* Bordeaux & Beirut: Institut Ausonius/IFAPO.

Sartre-Fauriat, A., & Sartre, M. (2007) '*Le Voyage de William John Bankes en Carie (1817)*'. In *Scripta Anatolica, Hommages à P. Debord*: pp. 113-141). Bordeaux: Ausonius/Etudes, n°18.

Sebba, A. (2009) *The Exiled Collector. William Bankes and the Making of an English Country House.* Stanbridge, Dovecote Press.

The East India Company (1829, May) *The New Scots Magazine,* Vols. 1–2: pp. 368–76.

Thompson, J. (2015) *Wonderful Things: A History of Egyptology: 1: From Antiquity to 1881.* Cairo & New York, I.B. Tauris.

Turner, R. E. (1934) *James Silk Buckingham 1786-1855, A Social Biography.* New York, Wittlesey House.

Usick, P. H. (1998) *William John Bankes' collection of drawings and manuscripts relating to ancient Nubia,* 2 vols. PhD Thesis, University of London.

Usick, P. (2002) *Adventures in Egypt and Nubia: The Travels of William John Bankes (1786-1855).* London, British Museum Press.

Newspapers & Periodicals

'What is to be done with India?' (1829, Sept.). *The New Scots Magazine,* Vol. 2: pp. 169–84.

Thomas Legh of Lyme:
Travels in Greece, and the First Encounters with the Temples of Nubia

Robert G. Morkot

Dominating the Grand Staircase at Lyme Hall, Cheshire, is a dramatic portrait of a young moustachioed man in voluminous white trousers, a close-fitting shirt, embroidered jacket with hanging sleeves and turban, with a long dagger tucked into his sash. He stands beside his black horse, his left hand supporting a sabre, and is set against a glorious golden background. The subject is Thomas Legh (1792–1857), and his costume standard Ottoman dress: it could be the Turkish dress he bought in Istanbul. Painted circa 1820 by the young Manchester artist William Bradley (1801–57), it depicts the wealthy owner of Lyme soon after his return from a long journey through Russia, Syria, Palestine, Asia Minor and Europe. On this journey, he was one of the first Europeans in modern times to visit the site of Petra since its 'rediscovery' by J. L. Burckhardt in August 1812.

The portrait was painted after the journey of 1817–18, but already in 1812–14 Legh had travelled extensively in the Ottoman Empire. Following a time in Greece and the Aegean, and abandoning a tour through Asia Minor, Syria and Palestine because of the plague, Legh ventured to Egypt and Nubia. Accompanied by the Rev. Charles Smelt (c. 1785–1831) and their dragoman, Francis Barthow, the journey into Nubia went as far as Qasr Ibrim. Legh's *Narrative of a Journey in Egypt and the Country beyond the Cataracts* (based closely on Smelt's journal) was published in 1816 and is one of the first accounts of the temples of Lower Nubia. A second, considerably expanded, edition appeared the following year. Within a short time, there were many other travellers, which resulted in the 'opening' of the temple of Abu Simbel.

In the portrait's darker lower right, seated on the ground, is another young man wearing a much simpler style of Arab costume with a long shirt, belted at the waist: he looks upwards at Legh. Although bearded, dark-haired and darker-complexioned than the rosy-cheeked Legh, he is not from the Middle East, and is clearly not the Nubian slave boy acquired by Legh on his journey of 1813. The most obvious candidate must be Legh's dragoman and translator – and his companion on the long return journey from Petra through Syria, Turkey and Europe – the young Irishman, James Curtin (c.1796–1825).

By 1820, travels into northern (Lower) Nubia were becoming commonplace and those in search of more 'adventure' were forced further south to look for the fabled city of Meroe. These travellers' inability to read hieroglyphic texts, or even royal names, allied with extremely vague chronologies, posed questions about the antiquity of the Nubian monuments in relation to those of Egypt, and many travellers into the 1820s, and some such as George Hoskins in 1835, still followed the Classical tradition that Egypt derived its culture from the south.[1] Legh's account is therefore important, as his opinion of the monuments is unprejudiced by having seen Abu Simbel, a temple that came to overshadow all others, but also to act as an unfavourable comparator.

Thomas Legh of Lyme, MP, FRS, (1792–1857)

The Legh family was long-established in Cheshire and Lancashire with several branches and extensive land holdings. Thomas Peter Legh (1753–97) of Golborne, Lancashire, inherited Lyme Hall in Cheshire from his uncle in 1792.[2] Thomas Peter Legh seems to have been something of a rake: unmarried, he left seven children (three sons and four daughters) by seven different women. Of these, Thomas Legh was the eldest son and although a 'natural' (though illegitimate) son, his father ensured that the family's extensive estates in Cheshire and Lancashire passed to him, or, in default, to his brother. The four daughters were also recognized as legitimate members of the Legh family and married appropriately: one married an MP and became the mother of two bishops.

Thomas Legh inherited Lyme and other estates at the age of four. In June 1810, aged 17, he went up to Brasenose College Oxford, which he appears to have left without taking his degree (his father had stayed only a year, too). He was, however, created DCL in 1817. In 1824 Legh's rent roll was estimated at £27,000 a year and the family controlled the pocket borough of Newton, which returned two MPs. As the reviewer of his volume in the *Quarterly Review* commented, all Legh's exploration in Greece and Egypt was achieved before he reached the age of 21.

Legh travelled with the Reverend Charles Smelt – who was a little older, born about 1785. He had been a student at Christ Church, Oxford, from 1802 to 1812 (BA 1806, MA 1808). Smelt was later presented to the living of Gedling, Nottinghamshire by the Earl of Chesterfield and died in December 1831, aged 45, leaving a son and several daughters. Legh also acknowledges the help of his friend Dr MacMichael whom, we learn from a footnote to the 1817 edition of the *Narrative*, also accompanied him on the tour of Greece; although for how much of it remains unclear.[3] Legh's later travels also began in the company of MacMichael, and the Petra narrative, despite its important content, was appended to MacMichael's account of the journey from Moscow to Istanbul.

Son of a Shropshire Banker, William MacMichael (1784–1839) was a close contemporary of Charles Smelt and had also studied at Christ Church, Oxford, (going up in 1800 aged 16: BA 1805, MA 1807, B Med 1808), followed by Edinburgh University and St Bartholomew's Hospital. He was later appointed as Physician to George IV and William IV.

Athens and the Society of Travellers

In 1812, Legh, MacMichael and Smelt made a tour of Greece and Albania which is not detailed in the *Narrative*, ending with a more prolonged stay in Athens. While in Athens, they became involved with a group of architects and antiquarians who had already been resident for a couple of years, most having originally met in Rome from 1808 onwards. In 1810 (the year in which Napoleon designated Rome second city of the French Empire), the group left Rome, intending a tour of Greece and Asia Minor. From Otranto they crossed to Corfu in July, avoiding the British blockade of the French-held island and, in December, made Athens their base.[4] Lord Byron (who left Athens in April 1811) names them in letters, along with other British friends and acquaintances of his, some of whom were passing through and others who stayed for longer.[5]

The group referred to themselves as the Society of Travellers, 'the little company of adventurers', or 'the Friends'; but they also established the Philhellenes (Φιλέλληνες) and in November 1811 the Xeneion (Ξεινέιον) with restricted membership. In September 1813 they formed the Philomousos Hetaira (Φιλόμουσος Ἑταιρεία), that is 'the Society of Lovers of the Muses'.[6] With Athens as their base, they travelled around Greece, sometimes together, sometimes in smaller groups and with other visitors.

The leading figure was the architect Carl, Freiherr Haller von Hallerstein (1774–1817)[7] who went to Rome in 1808 where he met the others. The Danish architect, Peter Oluf Brønsted (1787–1842), from Copenhagen, went to Rome in 1806 to study the antiquities of Italy and Greece (later becoming chargé d'affaires at Rome 1813–26).[8] Of lesser significance due to his untimely death was George Heinrich Carl Koës (1782–1811), whose sister was engaged to Brønsted.[9] Otto Magnus, Freiherr von Stackelberg (1787–1837) from Reval (Tallinn) had been educated at Halle, Göttingen, and Dresden.[10] Stackelberg later took up residence in Rome, where he played a significant role in the development of archaeology in the city.[11] He also published an account of the excavations in the temples of Aphaia and Bassae. Stackelberg was a fine draftsman, and his portrait of Haller, drawn at Zante (Zakynthos) on 2 May 1814, is now in Munich.[12] The last of those who went from Rome, Jakob Linckh (1787–1841), was another artist: he took part in an excavation on Ithaca with Haller, Legh and Stackelberg about which there is not much detail.

Already in Athens when the others arrived was Georg Christian Gropius (1776–1850), who had been tutor to Wilhelm von Humboldt's children. He went to Asia Minor 1804,[13] and made drawings of antiquities for the Earl of Aberdeen. He acquired consular positions from several nations including Britain, remaining in Athens and playing an important role in the field of archaeology following the War of Independence.

The young British architects Charles Robert Cockerell (1788–1863) and John Foster (1787–1846) joined the group when they arrived in Athens. Cockerell had attended Westminster School with John Cam Hobhouse and had been in Constantinople with Hobhouse and Byron.[14] Altogether, this group had a wide range of connections through artistic, antiquarian and political circles throughout Europe.

In April 1811, Haller, Stackelberg, Linckh and Cockerell made the first of their significant discoveries, on the island of Aigina. Here, they excavated the sculptures from the temple of Aphaia, which were then sold to the Crown Prince of Bavaria (later King Ludwig I), having been restored in Rome in the workshop of the Danish sculptor Bertel Thorvaldsen. The Aigina marbles caused a sensation as they were the first Greek Archaic sculptures to be examined by Western European scholarship, and as such were strikingly different to the Roman originals and copies of Classical and Hellenistic sculpture that served as the ideal for the earlier 18th century and the influential writings of Winckelmann.

The Temple of Apollo Epikourios at Bassae

Following the removal of the Aigina sculptures to the island of Zante ready for auction, Gropius, Haller, Foster, Linckh and Cockerell, travelled around the Peloponnese and then into the northern Mani.[15] At Bassae, the group made their second major discovery when they uncovered some sculptures that had formed part of the temple's frieze. After sketching them, they covered them over, but resolved to return with permits to excavate.

Situated on a ridge of Mount Kotilion in the central Peloponnese, the temple of Apollo at Bassai (usually Latinized as Bassae in English), also known as Phigalia (the ancient city nearby), was important to early scholarship as the second century CE traveller Pausanias states that it was a work of Iktinos who was also the architect of the Parthenon.[16] Bassae was therefore ranked as a major structure and architectural model from the apogee of Greek Classical architecture.[17] The site had been known of, although rarely visited, since its 'discovery' by Joachim Bocher in 1765.[18] Among those who had visited were Robert Smirke (in 1802), William Gell (in 1804) and Edward Dodwell (in 1806).

The temple was the fourth constructed on the site since the 7th century BCE (hence 'Bassai IV'). It was begun around 429 BCE, with work continuing until 421 BCE or later.[19] It is architecturally significant for a number of reasons, notably the unique planning of the interior; the engaged Ionic colonnade and the earliest Corinthian capital known;[20] the distinctive form of the marble Ionic capitals;[21] and the sculptured internal frieze contrasted with an austere Doric exterior lacking both frieze and pediment sculpture.[22] In 1811, the outer Doric colonnade was still standing, but little of the interior above a couple of courses: the internal plan, however, was clear. Nothing remained of the pediments, only the lintels directly above the peristyle.

Legh saw Cockerell's sketches of the sculptures in Athens in May 1812, and with his companions visited 'Phigalia' the following month, but all was hidden and they dared not look for them. In the first edition of the Narrative Legh makes only a passing reference to the sale of the 'celebrated' frieze[23], but in the second edition he gives a long account of his visit to the site and the negotiations to acquire the sculptures, but without mentioning his own involvement.[24]

When we reached the spot, after a ride of two hours from the village of Andruzzena, it was difficult to resist the desire to lift up one of the blocks and catch a glimpse of the sculptured surface... For notwithstanding the brutal ignorance of the Turks, and their contempt for the beautiful specimens of ancient art, the recent extensive spoliation of the Temple of Minerva, and the eagerness shown on all occasions by travellers after Greek remains, had proved that as articles of merchandize, statues and inscriptions might be more valuable than oil, corn, or any other productions of the soil. Indeed, Veli Pacha had already begun to trade in these commodities...[25]

Legh's involvement was financial: funds were required for the costs of the excavation, and for the acquisition of the sculptures, and most of the artists lacked the ready money. Excavation necessitated negotiations with Veli Pasha, ruler of the Morea (and the son of Ali Pasha of Ioannina). An agreement was made between the 'Proprietors' who were Cockerell, Foster, Legh, Haller and Linckh. Legh and Foster advanced $3000 (two bills of £462 10s each) to pay Veli Pasha, and were to be reimbursed four sixths of this sum with 5 per cent interest per annum.[26] The plan to excavate also involved a plan to sell, and following the failure to acquire the Aigina sculptures, there was a determination that Britain should get them.

Having obtained the firman (grant) for excavation, the party consisted of Haller, Foster, Stackelberg, Linckh, Gropius and Brønsted. When the excavations at Bassae began on 9 July 1812, Legh and his companions had already left Greece, and Cockerell was in Sicily and Malta. The work took until the end of August to complete.

The excavation was carried out by permission of Veli Pasha on condition that half of what was found was given to him, despite the group asking to keep the frieze complete. Fortuitously for the excavators, a '*Caimacan*' (*qa'im-maqam*, deputy) from the Porte arrived ordering Veli to give up his government and retire to Thessaly: he quickly accepted £400 as his share, and left the entire collection of sculptures with the excavators.[27]

Haller made extensive drawings of the blocks, with plans that were to be the basis for the publications.[28] However, this was much delayed, due to Haller's early death: it was finally accomplished by Cockerell, working with a copy of Haller's drawings. As well as some fine watercolours of the temple in its landscape, Foster made an important series of drawings of the frieze slabs.

Leaving Athens in July, Legh's party sailed around the northern islands of the Aegean and landed in Asia to explore the Troad. Here, they learnt of the plague and were forced to abandon their plans of sailing to Bodrum (Halicarnassus), then travelling by land to Smyrna and thence to Istanbul, followed by a tour of Syria and Palestine[29]; they therefore sailed around the islands of the Aegean and returned to Athens. During this voyage, MacMichael made a collection of geological specimens that he later presented to the Geological Society. They spent three days 'excavating' near the temple of Apollo on Delos, but made no discovery of consequence 'nor were we able to carry off one of the numerous altars which are lying upon the adjoining island, called the Greater Delos'.[30]

Returning to Athens in September, where they passed another two months, they made 'some extensive excavations, and were fortunate enough to discover numerous vases, inscriptions, and bas-reliefs' in tombs 'at a short distance from the walls of the city on the western side of the road that leads to Thebes'.[31] A few of these were illustrated in the *Narrative*, and received an appendix in the 1817 edition. Three marble funerary monuments remain at Lyme Park, displayed in the Library.[32] Legh's volume also contains an engraving of a *pelike* and states that was in the possession of the Rev. William Wood of Fulham,[33] presumably a connection through Smelt or MacMichael. Strong suggests this may originally have belonged to Foster. It was acquired by the British Museum from a Sotheby's sale in 1895.[34]

Legh and his companions sailed through the Gulf of Corinth to Zante – a journey of five days – and the following day 'we had the pleasure of witnessing the arrival of the celebrated Frieze that had recently been discovered in the Temple of Apollo at Phigalia'.[35] The sale took place in Zante and the British Government paid £15,000 for the frieze, which sum was divided among the six 'Proprietors': a good profit for Legh on his investment.[36] The sculptures arrived in London in October 1815.

Following the sale of the Bassae frieze, Cockerell and others returned to Rome, where Cockerell spent a further two years. There are two portrait drawings of Cockerell by Ingres from this period: one is signed and dated by the artist '*Ingres à Messieurs Lynk et Stackelberg rome 1817*':[37] this portrait was in Stackelberg's possession until his death in 1837 and then in that of Linckh and his descendants. A companion double portrait is also dated 1817 and signed to 'Coquerel'. One of the pair is certainly Stackelberg, although the second is said not to be similar to other portraits of Linckh.[38]

Each of the 'Proprietors' of the Bassae frieze received a cast, to be delivered within two years of the arrival of the sculptures in London.[39] Thomas Legh's cast can be seen at Lyme, installed in the Bright Gallery, one of his additions to the house. Cockerell installed a set of casts in Oakly Park, Shropshire, where he made alterations for the Hon. Robert Clive.[40] In 1821, Cockerell included a cast of the Bassae frieze in the Dining Room (and a cast of the Parthenon frieze in the Drawing Room) of the Travellers' Club's temporary premises at 49 Pall Mall;[41] these were later transferred to the Library of the new club building in Pall Mall designed by Charles Barry in 1829.[42] Cockerell never became a true 'Greek Revival' architect,[43] but he did use the distinctive Ionic form of the Bassae capitals for the portico of his new Ashmolean Museum in Oxford (1841–45), where another cast of the frieze was installed.

To Egypt and Nubia

From Zante, Legh and Smelt returned to Malta, where they spent several weeks (including 20 days quarantine) before joining a merchant vessel for Alexandria on 21 November,[44] arriving in Boulac on 25 December (1812).[45] The *Narrative*[46] notes that 'Sheikh Ibrahim' (J. L. Burckhardt) was in Cairo and that they had been given a letter of introduction to him by the British Consul, Colonel Misset.

Legh and Smelt sailed for Upper Egypt in January 1813 'having engaged Mr. Barthow, an American, who had resided many years in the country'.[47] There are references to the works of Hamilton and Norden when they visited Beni Hassan[48] and to Denon in relation to Hermopolis.[49] On 26 January, they arrived at Siout (Asyut) which, Legh observes, had replaced Girgeh as the capital of Upper Egypt.[50] There, they met 'Sheikh Ibrahim' again:[51] he had travelled by ass and arrived at the same time if not slightly earlier. On 11 February, they reached Aswan.

Beyond the Cataracts

Legh states that 'the name of Nubia is given generally to that portion of the Valley of the Nile situated between Egypt and the Kingdom of Sennâr'.[52] He cites Costaz's work on Nubia, *Mémoire sur la Nubie et les Barâbras... Description de l'Egypte, par M. Costaz, Etat Moderne, tome i.* Costaz gives a list of villages above Philæ 'in which are introduced about ten names, that are purely imaginary'.[53] His own map is important as one of the first produced by someone who had sailed through Nubia (the first since Norden's), and was used by later travellers.

Legh gives reasons why Nubia was still 'unknown' to Europeans in 1813.[54] Although Europeans began to travel south of Cairo more frequently in the 18th century, increasing knowledge of the visible surviving monuments, the First Cataract of the Nile at Aswan was usually their stopping place because of the political situation. Following their conquest of Egypt in 1517, the Ottomans had extended their rule upriver to the Third Cataract and established Bosnian garrisons in strongholds at Aswan, Ibrim and Sai. Derr was the most important place in northern (Lower) Nubia and seat of the local rulers who actually controlled the region and paid some allegiance (and occasionally taxes) to the Ottoman representatives in Egypt.[55] Legh quotes William Browne on the 'war' between the Mamelukes of Upper Egypt and the 'Cashief' (*kashif*, district governor) of Ibrîm, which prevented travel from Egypt to Nubia.[56]

Travel through the Nile valley was, in practice, so difficult that the few Europeans who ventured south of Egypt usually took the northern part of the Darb el-Arbain road from Girgeh or Asyut through Kharga Oasis, rejoining the river at Dongola, or crossed the Eastern Desert to Abu Hamed.

One of the first Europeans to venture south of the First Cataract, in 1737–38, Frederick Norden (1708–42) sailed as far as Derr, but did not leave any detailed account of the monuments and was so concerned by his reception at Derr that he did not land anywhere else (hence the comment of Burckhardt – see p. 213). James Bruce had come back from Sennar across the desert from the Fifth Cataract, so had seen nothing of the Nubian Nile Valley: he had, however, recognized the site of Meroe in passing. Not long before, William George Browne (1768–1813) had used the Darb el-Arbain route to Darfur, but had not travelled along the Nile.

The French military invasion of Egypt in 1798 stopped at the First Cataract, as did the subsequent scholarly expedition. Legh refers to the first volume of the

Description de l'Égypte (1809), which has plans, views, and details of the temples of Philae and the Cataract region. Denon too, accompanying the military expedition, turned back at the Cataract and the travellers in the decade following did not venture further south.

In 1801, William Richard Hamilton, whose *Aegyptiaca* was published in 1809, which was a principal source for all travellers in the second decade of the century, had stopped at the Cataract. He was 'deterred from proceeding, by the accounts he there received of the difficulty of the roads, and the inhospitable disposition of the inhabitants'.[57] Legh also cites Hamilton's observation that the Mameluke beys had interests in keeping travel south of Aswan difficult in case they wanted to retreat there as a last resort, something that had actually happened between Hamilton's and Legh's journeys.

By 1813, the political situation in Egypt had changed: Muhammad Ali had acquired the *pashalik* in 1805, and his massacre of the Mamelukes at the Citadel in 1811 ensured his undisputed control of Egypt. The remaining Mamelukes fled south but, defeated at Ibrim, they were forced to retreat even further: the survivors established a new stronghold in Dongola, until ousted by Ismail Pasha's campaign of 1820–21. Northern Nubia – between the First and Second Cataracts – was now essentially independent, but maintained friendly relations with the Pasha. Nubia as far as the Second Cataract, and even beyond to the island of Sai, was accessible, in theory: the time had come for Europeans to 'explore' beyond the Cataract. Indeed, by 1817, the ascent to the Second Cataract was deemed 'perfectly easy'.[58]

In the first two decades of the 19th century, before the decipherment of hieroglyphics, the main sources of information on the history and culture of the region south of Egypt remained, as they were still for Egypt, the few Biblical references and the extensive writings of Greek and Roman authors and encyclopaedists. Many of the Classical writers had emphasised the similarities between *Aithiopia* and India – and some stories were transferred from one to another (gold-eating ants, being one). It was also widely believed that there had been strong religious and cultural influence from India on ancient Egypt: this connection was raised in a lengthy footnote in Legh's volume, and figures in the narrative of Henry Light[59] and the writing of Sergey Uvarov,[60] among many others.

Leaving their Swiss servant, Lavanchy, at Aswan with the baggage, Legh's small party set off with a Greek cook.[61] It was a straightforward sail south to Derr, the main centre of northern Nubia.

Giovanni Finati, accompanying William Bankes's first trip to Nubia in 1815, also with 'François' Barthow as dragoman, tells us that the 'native princes of Derr' who had taken power again following the retreat of the Mamelukes to Dongola, were three brothers said to be descendants of Bosnian soldiers.[62] The *kashif*, Hassan, 'spoke in terms of friendly recollection of Mr. Lee (*so*) and Mr. Smelt who had... paid him a visit some months before'.[63] This is not surprising, as Hassan had managed to part Legh from his 'sword with a Damascus blade worth about 500 piastres'.[64]

In 1820, Waddington and Hanbury were told by Hassan that 'the sword he then wore, was given to him by an Englishman, who received a slave in return for it, meaning Mr. Legh'.[65] This slave was 'a negro boy about ten years old'.[66] An extended footnote in the second edition of the *Narrative* adds more: the boy had been a slave to the wife of the ruler of Dongola but had been taken from there when he was six. Legh brought him back to England and comments that he 'is now living in the family of my friend, Mr. Smelt' and that 'he has nearly forgotten his own language, retains only a few Arabic words, but he speaks English well...'. Unfortunately, we are given no name: the boy's later history remains unknown.

Legh and his companions left their boats at Derr and then rode south to Ibrim.[67] Legh commented on the Mameluke destruction of Ibrim two years before: 'We remained at Ibrîm a few hours; and giving up the idea of proceeding to the second or great Cataract, which we were told was situated three days to the South, finally resolved to retrace our steps.'

Legh notes that since his return he had been informed by letter from Colonel Misset that 'Sheikh Ibrahim' had been able to penetrate almost as far as Moscho, 'the place where Poncet crossed the Nile on his route to Dongola and Sennâr'; that 'Captain Light, of the Artillery, whose acquaintance I had the pleasure of making at Malta, has also since visited Ibrîm: and I understand that Mr Bankes has succeeded in going still higher'.[68]

Light wrote that 'they mentioned, that at a place called Absimbal, on the west bank, a day and a half from Ibrim, there was a temple like that at Seboo; and another of the same sort at a place called Farras, three hours farther on the same side. I regretted that no more information was to be procured on this subject...'.[69]

The party now began the return journey. Unsurprisingly perhaps, remote as they were from any form of European society, they soon met someone they knew. Near Seboua, they saw 'two Arabs' on camels on the east bank and it turned out to be Sheikh Ibrahim with his guide: he was grateful for a mutton chop, even though from a 'lean and miserable sheep'.[70]

Burckhardt's own account records the date as February 27:

> I had here the pleasure of falling in with two English travellers, Messrs. Legh and Smalt [sic], and Captain Barthod (*so*), an American; I had already seen the two former at Cairo, and at Siout.... on reaching Assouan, [they] had hired a large boat to carry them up to Derr, from whence they had visited Ibrim, being the first Europeans who had reached that place, and examined the antiquities between it and the island of Philae; for Norden saw them only through his telescope![71]

Although not excessive vandalisers of monuments, Legh and Barthow left graffiti at a number of places: Qertassi, Amada, Dendur, Elkab, and at Thebes in the tomb of Ramesses VI (this one along with Smelt).[72]

The journey back was prolonged by their being detained at Minia because of plague in Cairo. Here, they meet Donald Donald (William Thomson) of Inverness

Fig 12.1 One of the two graffiti of Legh in the sanctuary of the temple of Amada.

who had been captured at the Battle of Rosetta: he had 'nearly forgotten his own language, had been circumcized and appeared reconciled to his situation'.[73] They also recount an adventurous visit to the crocodile catacombs near Manfalout. This is referred to later by Sir Frederick Henniker who went in search of the pits himself.[74] They waited six weeks at Alexandria before they could get to Malta, arriving back in England in November 1813.

The Temples of Nubia

Returning northwards, Legh provides more detail and comment on the temples. But, of course, there was a major omission: having stopped at Ibrim, Legh, Smelt and Barthow did not reach Abu Simbel. It was Burckhardt who was the first European in modern times to visit the temples (on 22 March 1813, on his return journey from Dongola) – and he nearly missed the Great Temple. As a result of Burckhardt's visit, news of the temples became available in Cairo, and soon spread further.

    Burckhardt recognized the colossal statues on the façade of the Small Temple as Osiris and Isis, and regarded the style of the relief sculpture of the interior as denoting 'high antiquity'. The head of one of the colossi of the Great Temple was 'approaching nearer to the Grecian model of beauty, than that of any ancient

Egyptian figure I have seen' and a work of the 'finest period of Egyptian sculpture'. He assumed from the hawk-headed figure (which he correctly took to be over the door) that the temple was dedicated to Osiris.[75]

Legh's *Narrative* provides a description of the temple of Derr with a comment on a figure with a hawk's head which they too interpreted as Osiris: this reflects the limited understanding of iconography reliant on the Classical writers. Osiris, Isis and Apis are the main deities known of and it is usually assumed that Osiris is being depicted.[76] Similarly, at Gerf Hussein they commented on the four seated statues in the sanctuary: 'We asked ourselves – Whom do they represent – Isis, Osiris, Apis, and Serapis?' Also at Dendur, they interpreted the offerings as being made to Isis and Osiris with hawk's head.[77]

They commented briefly on Amada, 'a fine temple'[78] and Debod.[79] At 'Dakki' (Dakka) 'The Propylon and Temple... are quite perfect, and the hieroglyphics are much better preserved than any we had seen above Essouan; they are in high relief', and the outside wall carried an inscription relating to 'Adrian'.[80] Kalabsha (Kalaptshi) had 'extensive ruins'. Dendur was 'a small temple in considerable preservation' and the 'hieroglyphics are relieved and sculptured in good style'. The decoration is described as 'common subjects: offerings to Isis and Osiris with hawk's head'.[81]

They found Wadi el-Sebua ('Sibhoi') one of the most imposing temples, with its colossal statues, sphinxes, two more colossi at the entrance to the temple, and square columns with engaged statues of 'priests' (actually Ramesses II) 'similar to those at the Memnonium':

> from what remains... we may declare this to have been a celebrated sanctuary, and well worthy of the admirers of Egyptian architecture... It is probably of an earlier date than those in Egypt. The walls are built in a ruder style, and the hieroglyphics, though bold, are but ill executed; the statues and sphinxes, however, will bear a closer examination: from the dress of the former, it is probable they are the representations of heroes. The period of the construction of these edifices is a matter of pure conjecture....[82]

They note the ruined village of Guerche (destroyed during the Mameluke retreat), 'opposite to which are the magnificent remains of Guerfeh-Hassan'. Of all the temples, Gerf Hussein impressed them the most: not an opinion shared by many later Egyptologists. Nor was it shared by one of the reviewers who considered it small when compared with some Egyptian temples. Later, Henniker commented on the *effect* of entering the rock-cut part of the temple, although is less flattering about the sculpture.[83]

The lengthy description compares Gerf Hussein with the Cave of Elephanta at Bombay and Legh cites J. Goldingham's description of that cave in *Asiatic Researches*, volume 4: 'Here we found an excavated temple that far surpasses anything we had witnessed above or below Essouan, and is indeed a stupendous monument of the labour bestowed by the ancients on their places of devotion.'[84] The court is again described as having columns with colossal statues of priests attached, 'rudely sculptured'; while inside were more pillars with statues of priests, leading to the sanctuary. A long footnote cites the Sanskrit scholar, Sir William Jones, who 'observes that the Ethiops of Meroë were the same people with the first Egyptians, and consequently, as it might easily be shewn, with the original Hindus.'[85] These ideas were current in the second decade of the 19th century, some derived from Greek and Roman writers, but as Sergey Uvarov commented: 'The English, by their labours in Bengal, have already ascertained, in a very authentic manner, various facts relative to the union and the points of relation which subsisted between ancient India and Egypt.'[86] Light recalls the incident of the 'Hindoo Sepoys' who immediately worshipped in the Egyptian temples on seeing the depictions of the Egyptian gods – proof indeed of the ancient connection.[87]

One element of their visit to Gerf Hussein omitted from the *Narrative* is the discovery of treasure! Burckhardt reports that on his visit to the temple at 'Gyrshe' the local sheikh begged him for half of the treasure that he had found, 'or at least, a handful... He shewed me the place where the Englishmen (Messrs. Legh and Smelt), who had been here before me, found, as he asserted, an immense treasure, with which they loaded their vessel; one of the peasants had seen the gold!'[88]

Their concluding appraisal of the Nubian temples is extraordinarily positive:[89]

> The excavated temple of Guerfeh Hassan, and the ruins of Dakki, and Kalaptshi, appeared to us to rival some of the finest specimens of Egyptian architecture. The same character of massive solidity is common to both, but, upon the whole, the stones which formed the walls of the Nubian temples did not appear to be so well wrought, nor so nicely joined together, as they are in those we had seen in Egypt. On the other hand, the style of execution in some of the hieroglyphics and other ornaments, indicates a degree of perfection in the arts which renders it difficult to discover their comparative antiquity.'

While they comment on the execution, they do not draw attention to the main issue in relation to the temples, the quality of the Nubian sandstone. Given that Wadi es-Sebua and Gerf Hussein are both very similar in architecture and decoration, and both date from the reign of Ramesses II, the 'rude' nature of the carving at Gerf Hussein is due almost entirely to the soft grainy stone. We can only speculate how they would have viewed the monuments if they had made it to Abu Simbel.

Published in 1816, the *Narrative*, although a fairly slim volume, provided Europeans with a map and the first detailed account of the temples that were visible in the Nile valley south of Aswan. The second edition, although reduced in size from quarto to octavo, has a considerably expanded text: the narrative of the Greek travels at the beginning is much longer and more detailed, and there are numerous inserted paragraphs and extended quotations throughout, the result being a text some 100 pages longer. In his Preface, Legh comments that 'to his fellow-traveller, the Rev. Charles Smelt, he is particularly indebted for the use of his Journal, from

Fig 12.2 Colossus of Ramesses II from the inner hall of the temple of Gerf Hussein.

which have been extracted many valuable notes and observations; and to the kindness of his friend Dr MacMichael his acknowledgements are due, for the assistance afforded him in arranging his *Memoranda* and preparing his *Narrative* for the press.'[90] The question therefore arises as to how much any of the published volume actually represents Legh's own thoughts and observations. Perhaps significantly, Legh's later account of his travels with Bankes, Irby and Mangles to Petra and the Dead Sea was published in his name, but was actually written up by MacMichael.

The notice in the *Quarterly Review* includes references to W. J. Bankes and a description of Abu Simbel (but without name) that had been included in a letter from Bankes to his father.[91] The *Edinburgh Review* is slightly critical in places.[92] The *Quarterly Review* and the *Monthly Review*[93] comment on the lack of illustrations. One copy in the British Library (owned by Sir Joseph Banks) does lack engravings, but the other 1816 edition (from the Royal Library) and the 1817 edition have the same illustrations ('T Legh delt'), although they appear in different places in the volume. A German edition appeared in Weimar in 1818.

The later edition contains appendices on the Greek vases and stelae and another giving an 'Itinerary through Syria by Sheikh Ibrahim' that Legh and Smelt were prevented from undertaking by an outbreak of the plague. A further addition is the 'Account of some fragments of "Thebaic" manuscripts on leather purchased by the author at the island of Elephantine; observations from the able pen of a friend, who has deeply studied the various branches of the antiquities of Egypt'. These were 17 leather rolls in Sahidic Coptic and translated by Thomas Young that were presented to the British Museum in 1817.

Legh's volume is referred to by a number of later travellers, and some clearly took the map, if not the book, with them. On 31 January 1819, halfway between Elkab and Edfu, John Hyde met with a group returning north – 'Wyse, Godfrey, Bailey and Barry'[94] – one of whom gave him a copy of Legh's map which was 'of great use to me'. Legh continued to be cited into the 1830s: Ludwig Heeren used the work in his description of the Nubian Nile Valley in one of the most extensive early discourses on Ethiopia and its role in the ancient world; as did Michael Russell in his synthetic study of 1833.[95]

Legh, Smelt and Barthow were soon to be followed by increasing numbers of travellers. In 1814, Captain Henry Light went as far as Ibrim: he tells us that he received information from James Silk Buckingham 'an English gentleman, who went as far as Dukkey [Dakka] a short time before me'. Light comments on the changes since Norden's visit and the places mentioned by him that are no longer spoken of, perhaps overwhelmed with sand, he suggests. Light seems to have had a particular interest in the ancient progress of Christianity and its links with Ethiopia. His volume, published in 1818, contained some attractive engravings of a number of monuments, from his own drawings.

Burckhardt's account became available in Cairo at some point after he returned from his second expedition across the desert to the Fifth Cataract and the Red Sea. It is detailed, although Burckhardt was not specifically interested in the antiquities. The publication came in 1819, after his death. William Bankes reached the Second Cataract in 1815, and speculated on whether the colossi at Abu Simbel were standing or seated, as indeed Burckhardt had. This, and his later travels, remained unpublished by him.

The post-Waterloo world saw significant changes in Egypt, and Muhammad Ali's policies brought many Europeans to Egypt to work. Giovanni Belzoni arrived in Egypt in 1815 with his wife and their 'servant' James Curtin; Colonel Misset resigned as consul due to ill health and was replaced by Henry Salt who soon engaged Belzoni. In the following years, half-pay army and navy officers and civilians arrived in ever-increasing numbers to travel.

Following his first failed attempt, Belzoni managed to enter Abu Simbel in August 1817, along with Charles Irby, James Mangles and Henry Beechey. They were soon followed by other travellers, such as Straton, Fuller and Bennet, and the Earl of Belmore's large party. Bankes finally gained entry the following year, and from 1818 onwards Abu Simbel dominated the Nubian 'tour': travellers sailed to the Second Cataract, generally visiting the rock of Abu Hamed, where many left their graffiti, and from which they could view the Cataract and look into the distant regions of Africa, musing on that (or on lunch). Then they would stop for a few days (if enthusiastic) at Abu Simbel. As a result, the other temples would be compared – and usually found wanting.

After Travelling

On his return from travelling in Greece and Egypt, and on reaching his 21 birthday, Legh became one of the MPs for the family's pocket borough of Newton in April 1814: from 1818, the second representative was Thomas Claughton, who was married to Legh's half-sister, Maria. Legh held the seat until the borough's abolition in the Great Reform Act of 1832.[96]

In 1815, Legh was an extra aide-de-camp to the Duke of Wellington at Waterloo, and in 1816, while still only 24, he was elected to the Society of Dilettanti. The following year, he was elected as a Fellow of the Royal Society, and he was also a founder member of the Travellers Club.

In 1817, following the death of Princess Charlotte, Legh and MacMichael went to Russia on an official mission. They travelled on, via Kiev, to Constantinople from where MacMichael returned to Britain. Legh bought Turkish dress in the city, possibly that which he wears in Bradley's portrait. Accompanied by a Greek servant called Nicolo, from Corfu, and a Tartar, Mustafa, Legh left in March via Rhodes and Larnaca for Jaffa. Arriving in Jersusalem, he found William Bankes who had gone beyond Legh's limit of Ibrim as far as Abu Simbel in 1815, and since then had been in Syria and Greece. He was returning to Egypt and finally entered Abu Simbel the following year. In Jerusalem, Legh and Bankes met the Naval captains Charles Irby and James Mangles who had assisted Belzoni in entering Abu Simbel some months beforehand. The group spent a month at Jerusalem, which included a surreptitious night-time dig at the 'tombs of the kings'. Then the Earl and Countess of Belmore with their large party (totalling 20) arrived from Egypt, closely followed by Bankes's dragoman, Giovanni Finati, who had escorted Sarah Belzoni and her 'servant' James Curtin.[97] Curtin expressed a desire to return to London, and Legh employed him as his interpreter: it was not a speedy return home.[98]

William Bankes, along with Irby, Mangles and Legh, and with the aid of Burkhardt's itinerary, set off in an attempt to reach Petra. Although the narratives give precedence to the gentlemen, they had their attendants. Legh was accompanied by Curtin, Mustapha the Tartar and Georgiolio, an Armenian who was in charge of his horses, having sent Nicolo with the baggage to Acre. They adopted Bedouin dress and Arab names (Legh was Osman). Following the successful expedition, the group returned north around the Dead Sea, before separating at Acre. Legh, accompanied by James Curtin, rode back via Jerash, Baalbek, Damascus, Palmyra, Homs, Hama, Aleppo, Antioch and Scanderoon, then over the Taurus to Iznik and on to Constantinople, before the journey across Europe back to London.[99]

Legh's account of the Petra journey was published as Chapter IV of MacMichael's narrative.[100] This solicited a comment from the reviewer who regarded its content as sufficiently important and interesting to merit separate publication. It also led to a sharp response from Bankes before he had seen the account.[101] Charles Irby and David Baillie (a university friend of Bankes and a financial sponsor of Charles Barry) attempted to smooth things over, noting that the account was slim and that it omitted all detail of Petra and deferred to Bankes and his (supposedly) forthcoming account. It seems that Legh had given the information (whether written or verbal) to MacMichael who had written it up himself.

Travelling done, Legh devoted himself to politics and his extensive estates. He carried out a major modernization of Lyme Park, placing the work in the hands of Lewis Wyatt. Legh gave some of his unproductive land to the expansion of

Fig 12.3 The south front of Lyme Park by Giacomo Leoni 1729-32, with the tower behind the pediment by Lewis Wyatt as part of his additions and modernisation for Thomas Legh in 1817.

Warrington and the new streets were named after his travels: Palmyra Square, Egypt Street, Cairo Street, Suez Street, and Pyramid Street.

Legh married first in 1829, but his wife died, aged only 20, shortly after giving birth to an only daughter. He married for a second time in 1843. In May 1857, Legh died at Milford Lodge, at Lymington, Hampshire: Lyme and the estates passed to his nephew.

Legh and many of the others he met on his travels continued to associate in London, most as founder members of the Travellers Club. Quite a few met up in Parliament, until – like Legh's – their pocket boroughs were abolished by the Great Reform Act of 1832.

By 1826, the Travellers Club had become yet another fashionable gentlemen's club without its original requirements and purpose. Legh was among the friends, along with Colonel Martin Leake and Captain James Mangles, to whom Sir Arthur de Capell Brooke suggested the creation of a new dining society, composed *solely* of travellers. Limiting the number to 40, the idea was to have a meeting once a fortnight. The first dinner was held at Grillion's Hotel in Albermarle Street (near John Murray's publishing house) in November 1826. At the second meeting, at Brunet's Hotel, Leicester Square, the society was formally constituted as the Raleigh Club. The original members included Legh and a number of those he had met on his travels: along with Leake and Mangles were C. R. Cockerell, the Earl of Belmore and his sons Viscount Corry and Henry Corry, and his half-brother Captain Corry RN, and William John Bankes. The first regular meeting was held on 7 February 1827, at the Thatched House Tavern, No. 74, St James's Street (also the home of the Society of Dilettanti). At the meeting of 24 May 1830, the formation of a Geographical Society of London was proposed, and Legh was one of its first members.[102] In 1819, Legh and Smelt were members of the Committee of the Africa Association and Legh was also involved in the 1838 fund to explore the sources of White Nile.[103]

Fig 12.4 Thomas Legh in Oriental dress, probably with James Curtin. Painted about 1819 by William Bradley. Lyme Park, Cheshire (National Trust) © Courtauld Institute of Art.

Within a short time, these early travels in Nubia radically expanded knowledge and opened the way to travellers further south still, to the northern Sudan and Meroe (the ambition of Bankes). They also began a process of challenging classical writers on the origins of Egyptian civilization, the connections with India and also the relative aesthetic merits of Egyptian and Nubian monuments.

Henry Light's summary – of Egypt and Nubia – probably strikes at one of the key issues for early travellers in the region:

> I felt they [the antiquities] wanted that charm or interest which is raised in other countries whose history is known, where the traveller ranges over the ground on which heroes and remarkable men, whose actions are familiar to him, once dwelt. But here, though treading the soil where sprang the learning, and genius, and arts, to which Europe has been indebted for its present superiority among nations; where the magnificence of ancient Egypt still remains to prove the existence of all these in perfection, he can only admire the – '*res antiquæ laudis et artis*', ['subject of ancient renown and art' – Vergil *Georgics*] without any sentiment of attachment to persons or times. He is lost in admiration, and has no idea but that of the sublime. A long night of oblivion has intervened, to cut off all but conjectures of their history.[104]

This succinctly presents the 'problem' for pre-decipherment travellers: Egypt's great renown was actually inaccessible – how did Sesostris, Psammuthis and the biblical Tirhakah relate to what was preserved and could be seen? As Uvarov commented, 'unfortunately a profound obscurity still hangs over the language, the history, and the monuments of Egypt.'[105] That was one of the key issues that Egyptology had to address after decipherment.

Legh's travels in Nubia are an important account of the monuments and of ideas about them before the significant changes that came in the 1820s. The question of how the temples relate to those of Egypt chronologically are still coloured by the idea that civilization was coming from the south, the Greek *Aithiopia*, to Egypt. The limited knowledge of which gods might be depicted is also a residue of the classical tradition. The links with India, soon to be exploded, were part of classical tradition and apparently supported by researches in India itself.

Legh is quite difficult to assess on a personal level because both narratives are indebted to Smelt and MacMichael as writers and editors. Yet Legh's continued interest in the Nile Valley and in geography suggests that we shouldn't dismiss him completely as just another young, rich chap off on exciting adventures in exotic places.

Endnotes

1   Morkot, 2013a.
2   Beamont, 1876: pp. 193–94.
3   Legh, 1817: p. 21.
4   Cooper, 1996a.
5   Eliot, 1968.
6   Cooper, 1996a: p. 13.
7   Bankel, 1986; Cooper 1996a: pp. 27–31.
8   Cooper, 1996a: pp. 16–17.
9   Cooper, 1996a: p. 26.
10 Cooper, 1996a: p. 26.
11 Dyson, 2006: pp. 30--31.
12 München Staatliche Antikensammlungen Inv.-Nr. 15106: p. 2; Bankel, 1986: p. 89.
13 Cooper, 1996a: p. 19.
14 Cooper, 1996a: p. 17.
15 Cockerell, 1903: p. 69–78.
16 Pausanias 8.41.7-10; 8.30.2–4; 8.388–89; Cooper, 1996a: pp. 383–84; on Ictinus: Cooper, 1996a: pp. 389–91.
17 Jenkins, 2006: pp. 130–50.
18 Constantine, 2011: pp. 203–04.
19 Cooper, 1996a: pp. 4–7.
20 Jenkins, 2006: pp. 137–38.
21 Cooper, 1996a: pp. 296–300.
22 Madigan and Cooper ,1992; Jenkins, 2006: pp. 143–49.
23 Legh, 1816: p. 2.
24 Legh, 1817: pp. 23–33.
25 Legh, 1817: p. 29–31.
26 Cooper, 1996a: p. 23.
27 Cockerell, 1903: p. 220; Legh, 1817: pp. 32–33.

28 Field Notebook of Haller von Hallerstein, Bibliothèque Nationale et Univérsitaire de Strasbourg MS 2723/11; Cooper 1996b, pls 81–113.

29 Legh, 1816: p. 1; 1817: pp. 2–3.

30 Legh, 1817: p. 19.

31 Legh, 1817: p. 22.

32 Strong, 1903.

33 Obit. *Gentleman's Magazine* 1841: Christ Church, Oxford 1786 at 17; BA 1790; MA 1793; BD 1801; student till 1814; sinecure Rector of Fulham 1811–41; vicar Fulham 1811–34; Rector of Coulsdon, Surrey 1830; Prebend of Canterbury 1834; d 11 Apr 1841.

34 Strong 1903, 358-9 n.10; BM Department of Greece and Rome, 1895,0831.1 from the Dipylon gate and attributed to the Villa Giulia painter.

35 Legh, 1817: p. 23.

36 Cooper, 1996a: pp. 23–24; Jenkins1992: pp. 77–81.

37 Ashmolean Museum 1998.179: Tinterow and Conisbee, 1999: pp. 217–18, no 75.

38 Musée Jensich, Vevey, Switzerland, Drawings Dept A437: Tinterow and Conisbee, 1999: pp. 218–20, no 76.

39 Jenkins, 1992: p. 79 and n. 19; for Haller's cast see Bankel, 1986.

40 Crook, 1972, fig 126; Watkin, 1999: p. 60.

41 Watkin, 1999: p. 56.

42 Watkin, 1999: p. 61 fig 7.

43 Crook, 1972: pp. 133–35.

44 Legh, 1816: p. 5; 1817: p. 37.

45 Legh, 1816: p. 18; 1817: pp. 56–57.

46 Legh, 1816: pp. 10–11; 1817: pp. 45–46.

47 Legh, 1816: p. 33 ; 1817: p. 78. On Barthow, see Oliver, 2014: pp. 42–43; Vivian, 2012: p. 56–72.

48 Legh, 1816: pp. 33-34; 1817: p. 86.

49 Legh, 1816: p. 35; 1817: p. 88.

50 Legh, 1816: p. 36; 1817: p. 90.

51 Legh, 1816, 37; 1817: p. 91.

52 Legh, 1816: p. 55; 1817: pp. 128–31.

53 Legh, 1817: p. 131.

54 Legh, 1816: pp. 46–47; 1817: pp. 110–14.

55 Adams, 1977: pp. 609–14; Jungfleisch 1946.

56 Legh, 1816: p. 47; 1817: p. 111.

57 Legh, 1816: p. 47; 1817: p. 111: Hamilton actually went as far as Debod, and reports that a very large temple was known to exist at Kalabsha further south.

58 *The Morning Post* (London, England), Sunday, 29 December 1817; Issue 14645.

59 Light, 1818: pp. xii–xiv and 113.

60 Ouvaroff, 1817.

61 Legh, 1816: p. 57; 1817: p. 133.

62 Jungfleisch, 1946; Finati, 1830, II: p. 78; see also Light, 1818: p. 72.

63 Finati, 1830, II: p. 79.

64 Legh, 1816: p. 73; 1817: p. 159.

65 Waddington and Hanbury1822: p. 19 note.

66 Legh, 1816, 73; 1817: p. 158.

67 Legh, 1816: pp. 75–79; 1817: pp. 164–69.

68 Legh, 1816: p. 79; 1817: pp. 169–70.
69 Light, 1818: p. 99; his footnote states 'mentioned by Mr. Belzoni, the artist employed by Mr. Salt, as Ybsambul, which he has described'.
70 Legh, 1816: p. 83; 1817: pp. 175–76.
71 Burckhardt, 1819: p. 16.
72 De Keersmaecker, 2001: pp. 3–4.
73 Legh, 1816: p. 129.
74 Henniker, 1823: p. 97. This incident was extracted from Legh's book and reported in *The Lancaster Gazette and General Advertiser, for Lancashire, Westmorland, &c.* (Lancaster, England), Saturday, 28 December 1816; Issue 811.
75 Burckhardt, 1819: pp. 88–92.
76 Legh, 1816: p. 81; 1817: pp. 172–73.
77 Legh, 1816: p. 62–63; 1817: pp. 142–45.
78 Legh, 1816: pp. 81-2; 1817: p. 173.
79 Legh, 1816: p. 58; 1817: p. 135.
80 Legh, 1816: p. 84; 1817: pp. 177–80.
81 Legh, 1816: pp. 62–63; 1817: pp. 142–45.
82 Legh, 1816: pp. 65–66; 1817: pp. 147–50.
83 Henniker, 1823: p. 154.
84 Legh, 1816: pp. 85–87; 1817: pp. 180–88.
85 Jones, 1793: p. 5. The volume was originally printed in Calcutta and reprinted in London 1796 and 1799. Jones refers to Classical tradition, but this was also the volume that contained Wilford's paper (see n.86).
86 Ouvaroff 1817: pp. 24–25 and Light, 1818: pp. xii–xiii. Ouvaroff's reference is to a paper by Lt Francis Wilford that appeared in *Asiatic Researches* 3 ('On Egypt and other countries adjacent to the Ca'li River, or Nile of Ethiopia, from the ancient books of the Hindus'. 1793: pp. 46–259, reprinted 1796 and 1799) that was later shown to be based on forged and manipulated texts.
87 Light, 1818: pp. xiii–xiv and 113.
88 Burckhardt, 1819: p. 109.
89 Legh, 1816: p. 94; 1817: p. 193.
90 Legh, 1817: p. viii.
91 *Quarterly Review* 16, no 31: pp. 1–27.
92 *Edinburgh Review* art vii: pp. 422–44.
93 December 1817: p. 337–47.
94 Hyde Journal: British Library Add Ms 42102, 67v.: These were (Sir) Thomas Wyse, (John) Godfrey, David Baillie, and Baillie's artist, (later Sir) Charles Barry; on their identities see Morkot, 2013b.
95 Heeren, 1832; Russell, 1833.
96 Fisher, 2009; Beamont, 1876: pp. 95–105 has various events out of order.
97 Finati, 1830, II: p. 220.
98 On Curtin, see Morkot, 2013c.
99 The gathering in Jerusalem and the Petra expedition were published by Irby and Mangles in 1823, based on Bankes's dictation; Finati and Bankes gave another account in Finati's *Narrative*: Bankes, 1830, II: pp. 222–94.
100 MacMichael, 1819: pp. 187–267.
101 Usick, 2002: pp. 72–73.

102 Markham, 1881.
103 The Committee of the Africa Association is listed in Burckhardt 1819; for the White Nile fund, see Schmidt, 2011: p. 214.
104 Light, 1818: p. 103.
105 Ouvaroff, 1817: p. 24.

Bibliography

Adams, William Y. (1977) *Nubia: Corridor to Africa.* Princeton, Princeton University Press.

Bankel, Hansgeorg, ed. (1986) *Carl Haller von Hallerstein in Griechenland, 1810–1817. Architekt Zeichner Bauforscher.* Berlin, Dietrich Riemer Verlag

Beamont, W. (1876) *A History of the House of Lyme (in Cheshire) compiled from documents of the Legh family of that house, and from other sources.* Warrington, P. Pearse, Sankey Street.

Burckhardt, John Lewis (1819) *Travels in Nubia.* London.

Cockerell, Samuel Pepys, ed. (1903) *Travels in Southern Europe and the Levant, 1810–1817. The Journal of C.R. Cockerell, R.A.* London, Longman, Green, and Co.

Constantine, David (2011) *In the Footsteps of the Gods. Travellers to Greece and the quest for the Hellenic Ideal.* London, Tauris Parke Paperbacks.

Cooper, Frederick A. (1996a) *The Temple of Apollo Bassitas* I. *The Architecture* Princeton, New Jersey, The American School of Classical Studies at Athens.

Cooper, Frederick A. (1996b) *The Temple of Apollo Bassitas* III. *The Architecture,* Princeton.

Crook, J. Mordaunt (1972) *The Greek Revival. Neo-Classical Attitudes in British Architecture 1760-1870.* London, John Murray.

De Keersmaecker, Roger O. (2001) *Travellers' Graffiti from Egypt and the Sudan. I. The Kiosk of Qertassi.* Berchem (Antwerp), Graffito Graffiti.

Dyson, Stephen L. (2006) *In Pursuit of Ancient Pasts. A History of Classical Archaeology in the Nineteenth and Twentieth Centuries.* New Haven and London, Yale University Press.

Eliot, C. W. J. (1968) 'Gennadeion Notes, III: Athens in the time of Lord Byron.' *Hesperia* 37 1968: pp. 134–58.

Finati, Giovanni (1830) *Narrative of the life and adventures of Giovanni Finati, native of Ferrara; who, under the assumed name of Mahomet, made the campaigns against the Wahabees for the recovery of Mecca and Medina; and since acted as interpreter to European travellers in some of the parts least visited of Asia and Africa. Translated from the Italian, as dictated by himself, and edited by William John Bankes, Esq.* London, John Murray.

Fisher, D. R. ed. (2009) *The History of Parliament: the House of Commons 1820–1832*, available online http://www.historyofparliamentonline.org/volume/1820–1832/member/legh-thomas-1793–1857

Heeren, A. H. L. (1832) *Historical Researches into the Politics, Intercourse, and Trade of the Carthaginians, Ethiopians, and Egyptians.* Translated from the German. Oxford, D.A. Talboys. Vol. I.

Henniker, Frederick (1823) *Notes During a Visit to Egypt, Nubia, the Oasis, Mount Sinai, and Jerusalem.* London, John Murray.

Irby, Charles and James Mangles (1823) *Travels in Egypt and Nubia, Syria and Asia Minor.* London, T. White.

Jenkins, Ian (1992) *Archaeologists and Aesthetes in the Sculpture Galleries of the British Museum 1800-1939.* London, British Museum Press.

Jenkins, Ian (2006) *Greek Architecture and its Sculpture*, Cambridge, Mass., Harvard University Press.

Jones, Sir William (1793) 'On the Borderers, mountaineers, and Islanders of Asia.' (Eighth Anniversary Discourse, delivered 24 February 1791). *Asiatic Researches* 3: p. 1–20. Calcutta; reprinted London 1796 and 1799.

Jungfleisch, Marcel (1946) 'Hasan Suliman, Kashif of Nubia.' *Sudan Notes and Records* 27: pp. 239–40.

Legh, Thomas (1816) *Narrative of a Journey in Egypt and the Country beyond the Cataracts.* First edition. London, John Murray.

Legh, Thomas (1817) *Narrative of a Journey in Egypt and the Country beyond the Cataracts.* Second edition. London, John Murray.

Light, Henry (1818) *Travels in Egypt, Nubia, Holy Land, Mount Libanon, and Cyprus in the year 1814.* London, Rodwell and Martin.

MacMichael, W. (1819) *Journey from Moscow to Constantinople, in the years 1817, 1818.* London, John Murray.

Madigan, Brian, and Frederick Cooper (1992) *The Temple of Apollo Bassitas 2 The Sculpture.* Princeton, Princeton University Press.

Markham, Clements R. (1881) *The Fifty years' work of the Royal Geographical Society*, London: John Murray.

Morkot, R. G. (2013a) 'George Hoskins, *Travels in Ethiopia* and the History of Meroe' in: *Souvenirs and New Ideas: Travel and Collecting in Egypt and the Near East*, edited by Diane Fortenberry, Oxbow Books and ASTENE: pp. 98–118.

Morkot, R. G. (2013b) 'Barry, Baillie, Godfrey and Wyse', *Bulletin of the Association for the Study of Travel in Egypt and the Near East*, no.55: pp. 12–13.

Morkot, R. G. (2013c) 'The "Irish lad" James Curtin, "servant" to the Belzonis', *Bulletin of the Association for the Study of Travel in Egypt and the Near East*, no.56: pp. 16–19.

Oliver, Andrew (2014) *American Travelers on the Nile. Early U.S. Visitors to Egypt, 1774--1839.* Cairo; New York, American University in Cairo Press.

Ouvaroff, M. [Count Sergey Semionovich Uvarov] (1817) *Essay on the Mysteries of Eleusis*, translated from the French by J. D. Price, with observations by J. Christie. London, Rodwell and Martin.

Russell, Michael (1833) *Nubia and Abyssinia: comprehending their civil history, antiquities, arts, religion, literature, and natural history*, 2nd ed. Edinburgh, Oliver and Boyd and Simpkin and Marshall, London.

Schmidt, Heike C. (2011) *Westcar on the Nile. A journey through Egypt in the 1820s*, Wiesbaden, Reichert Verlag.

Strong, E. (1903) 'Three sculptured stelai in the possession of Lord Newton at Lyme Park', *Journal of Hellenic Studies* 23: pp. 356–59.

Tinterow, Gary and Philip Conisbee eds (1999) *Portraits by Ingres. Image of an Epoch.* New York, The Metropolitan Museum of Art.

Vivian, Cassandra (2012) *Americans in Egypt 1770-1915. Explorers, Consuls,Travelers, Soldiers, Missionaries, Writers and Scientists.* Jefferson, North Carolina, McFarland.

Waddington, George and Barnard Hanbury (1822) *Journal of a Visit to Some Parts of Ethiopia.* London, John Murray.

Watkin, David (1999) 'The Travellers' Club and the Grand Tour: Correcting Raphael…', *The British Art Journal* 1.1: pp. 56–62.

13

'A Political Education':
Lady Augusta Gregory in Egypt

Cathy McGlynn

This paper focuses on the travels of Lady Augusta Gregory (née Persse, 1852–1932), an Irish dramatist and folklorist. An involvement with cultural nationalism and the Irish Literary Revival at the turn of the 20th century makes her one of the most significant women in Irish history. Born into an Anglo-Irish landowning family in Roxborough, County Galway, her upbringing was typically privileged. Her élite position in the landowning community was further reinforced through her marriage to Sir William Gregory, a landowner who had inherited Coole Park, a large country estate in County Galway. Sir William had recently retired from his exalted position as Governor of Ceylon, and he was knighted in 1875. As a young man, he travelled to Egypt in the winter of 1855–56 and shortly afterwards published an

account of his travels with the title *Egypt in 1855 and 1856 and Tunis in 1857 and 1858.* Sir William returned to Egypt with his new wife in the winter of 1881–82 and it was here, among key figures from the British administration in Egypt, that Lady Gregory first encountered nationalist politics, which shaped the complex trajectory of her own political outlook on nationalism in Ireland.

Several sources provide an account of Lady Gregory's time in Egypt. The most notable and valuable of these comes from the pen of Lady Gregory herself, in her autobiography *Seventy Years.*[1] Unpublished during her lifetime, the manuscript was discovered 40 years after her death, and offers a unique and intimate glimpse into her life before the

Fig 13.1 Lady Isabella Augusta Gregory in 1903, painted by J. B. Yeats.

First World War. An entire chapter is devoted to her time in Egypt, and this draws on extracts from the diary she kept while there. Likewise, her biographers have provided informative accounts of her Egyptian holiday;[2] while most, however, refer to her diary entries and autobiography, few make reference to her unpublished memoir, *An Emigrant's Notebook*[3] that Lady Gregory wrote at home in Ireland during the year following her travels. This memoir is significant in relation to this paper because, though it mostly focuses on childhood memories, the last section contains a beautiful and poetic evocation of Cairo – something that is entirely missing from her autobiography. Her romantic depiction of Cairo is followed by some observations on various aspects of Egyptian life, including the position of women, and musings on the importance of educating children. Both accounts of Lady Gregory's time in Egypt are woven together here to create a comprehensive picture of her sojourn in Egypt.

Lady Gregory's only son, Robert, was born in 1881, and when he was still an infant, Sir William decided they would spend a winter in Cairo. Leaving their baby boy behind with her sister, Lady Gregory sailed for Egypt with a broken heart. Sir William and Lady Gregory arrived on 18 November to stay at Shepheard's hotel.[4]

The chapter dealing with Egypt in Gregory's autobiography is entitled 'Education in Politics: Egypt' and this is indicative of its content; she focuses entirely on the Arabi Revolt, the Nationalist uprising that was taking place in Egypt at the time. The chapter is almost entirely lacking in any descriptions of Cairo or any other part of Egypt – and she does not mention any tourist attractions. Instead, it reads like a 'who's who' of British colonial figures and travellers in Egypt at the time. It offers a fascinating insight into the complex politics behind the revolution, including Arabi Bey himself, and provides a counter-narrative to the official story appearing contemporaneously in the British press.

The Arabi uprising was a nationalist revolt against the administration of the Khedive. The revolt was led by Arabi Bey, a colonel in the Egyptian army, in response to, not just the Khedive administration, but also 'French and English influence in the financing and governing of the country'.[5] Of the revolt, Gregory writes, 'It was in Egypt, where we spent the winter of 1881, that I first felt the real excitement of politics, for we tumbled into a revolution.'[6] When the Gregorys arrived in Egypt, Arabi had achieved moderate success, and 'in December the Khedive made Arabi Under-Secretary of War'.[7] Both Lady Gregory and her husband became interested in Arabi – she states that William 'was taken to see him and liked him. Arabi did not deny that much good had been done by foreign officials, but he thought it unfair that his countrymen were kept out of any important office'.[8] Here, Arabi is characterized as a fair-minded, unaggressive man who is campaigning against clear injustice.

So impressed was Sir William by Arabi that he 'wrote some letters to *The Times* to make his views known in England'.[9] In doing so, Sir William placed himself and his wife at the centre of the debate that was raging in British circles about the

Fig 13.2 Watercolour of the Colossi of Memnon viewed from the Ramesseum, probably painted by Lady Gregory during Sir William's and her stay at Luxor, 12-28 January 1882.

potential threat posed by Arabi. The Gregorys, from the start, were keen to defend him, and were influenced greatly by the views of the famed poet Wilfrid Scawen Blunt. Lady Gregory writes:

> It was one day at lunch at the Fitzgeralds,[10] we had met Wilfrid and Lady Anne Blunt,[11] the beginning to me of a long friendship... he and Lady Anne were now living in the garden they had bought in the Heliopolis desert, near Cairo, and they were convinced that Arabi's revolt was right, that it would lead to the Turks, as well as the Christians being turned out from the control of Egypt. And beyond that they had the vision of an Arab Caliphate, an independent Arab race.

Wilfrid Blunt was an anti-imperialist, and though he was most famous for his poetry, he published political pamphlets and essays, most notably, in 1907, *Atrocities of Justice under the English Rule in Egypt* and *Secret History of the English Occupation of Egypt*. In the latter, he frequently refers to the Gregorys, and the friendship between the Gregorys and the Blunts would have significant influence on the perception of Arabi in Britain. It is worth noting that like Lady Gregory, he was born into a privileged land-owning family, and early in his career, was supportive of colonialism. Fascinated with Arab culture, he and his wife

Anne 'travelled across the Arabian desert riding camels and sleeping in tents, enjoying the rigour of sparse food, privation and danger. They had observed the oppressiveness of Turkish imperialism and learnt Arabic'.[12] Blunt frequently dressed in traditional Bedouin attire, and devoted himself to the nationalist cause in Egypt.

Two months after the Gregory's arrival in Cairo, the British and French governments sent their 'Joint Note' to the Egyptian government. This, Lady Gregory writes, 'promised support of the Khedive and threatened armed intervention in case of disturbance. It made the National Party very angry. Arabi said to Mr. Blunt: "It is the language of menace, a menace to our liberties", and so indeed it was.'[13] Again, Lady Gregory offers a unique insight into Arabi's experience. The Egyptian government was being destabilized by the National Party and the threat of disorder loomed large. Battle lines were drawn between Blunt, the avid supporter of the Nationalist cause, and Mr Colvin (the British Controller of Finance in Egypt) who hoped for the annexation of Egypt to Britain.[14] Indeed, the Gregorys found themselves siding with the Blunts against the majority of Europeans in Egypt. At this point in her narrative, Lady Gregory goes on to list what she terms 'the gossip and rumours of the following days',[15] and she lists her encounters with many significant figures from both the British administration in Egypt and the Egyptian government, most of whom opposed Arabi's revolt:

> We dined with Sir E. Malet.[16] He is very anxious. The Chamber of Notables refuses to yield on the Budget question, he says, at Arabi's instigation. We went on with him to the opera. The Khedive was in his box looking dreary enough. He said to Sir Edward when he went to sit with him, 'Well, they can't do more than take my head...' On another day, W.S.B. came in Bedouin costume... He says that the Chamber is right in holding out, that if England intervenes there will be a bloody war, but that liberty has never been gained without blood. In the middle of this, Mr. Villiers Stuart[17] came in and began to talk of mummies and the covering of the Sacred Ark.[18]

> 3rd [February] We went with Lord Houghton[19] and Mrs Fitzgerald to see the Blunts at Heliopolis. They received us in Bedouin costumes at the door of their tent. Two or three Arab Sheiks to luncheon – first sweets, nougat etc. then incense burned and coffee; then a bowl of boiled lamb and one of rice.[20]

> 8th We lunched with Princess Said, in Turkish fashion, Princesses Monssor and Nazli there; some dancing girls, very young and pretty. Kiamil Pasha came in and announced that ten thousand Turks were on their way here, and there was consternation. We came back and found there was no truth in it... we dined with Count Sala. Sir E. Malet is more tolerant towards the new ministry... he has spoken to Arabi about the abolition of the Slave Trade (I asked him to do this).[21]

> 11th We dined at the Van der Nests' and heard the account of Arabi's reception at the Feast of the Sacred Carpet in the morning. The people rushed to him, kissed his hands, his feet, calling 'Long Life to him who has given us a Constitution!'[22]

12th We met the Duc d'Aumale at the La Salas and a Count – knowing the country well, who spoke of this wonderful National movement, he says it will go beyond the soldiers. Princess Nazli had heard the same account of Arabi's ovation. We dined with Sir E. Malet, Lord Houghton, Fitzgeralds, Sir F. Goldsmid there, we quarrelled over Arabi as usual, W and I against the rest.[23]

17th I met Arabi in the hall. I thanked him for the photograph he had sent me with the words written 'Arabi the Egyptian; I present my picture to Lady Gregory as a souvenir to preserve friendship'. He has the Slave Trade suppression 'next to his heart' and will carry it out.

25th W.S. Blunt in the afternoon. He says Arabi and the others are so exasperated by the false reports of their motives in the English papers that they have now a very bitter feeling towards England, and it may lead them to some rash act.[24]

This final entry is significant in terms of the efforts of the Gregorys and the Blunts to sway public opinion in Britain against the demonization of Arabi and the dominant view of Arabi's revolt as a threat to the stability of the Empire. The Blunts returned home to England, the Gregorys returned to London soon after, and Lady Gregory describes a series of dinners, parties and meetings with officials, and even with Gladstone and the Queen, against the backdrop of growing turbulence in Egypt. Sir William pleaded Arabi's case in a letter to Gladstone, to which Gladstone replied, '[Arabi] seems to me to represent at this time military violence and nothing else.' Interestingly, Gladstone's postscript reads, 'Will you be so kind as to breakfast here on Thursday at 10? Or on another Thursday? I will not come down upon you with Arabi!'[25] This is indicative of the exalted social position enjoyed by the Gregorys in London. They had influence and Lady Gregory herself used it.

The political crisis in Egypt deepened and eventually resulted in the British bombardment of Alexandria in July 1882. Lady Gregory wrote in her diary, 'Garden Party at Marlborough House. The Queen very grey, the Princess not so pretty as usual, in blue and white. The news of the massacre and burning of Alexandria cast rather a gloom over the party.'[26] Following this, she had a meeting with Thomas Chenery, the editor of *The Times*, and admonished him for publishing false reports on the Arabi affair, given his sympathy with 'the National Movement in Egypt'.[27] This sympathy worked in Lady Gregory's favour. Arabi was eventually arrested after the British entered Cairo on 14 September 1882.

Public opinion in Britain determined Arabi's fate; many were demanding his execution. At this point, Lady Gregory and Wilfrid Blunt campaigned vigorously in London for a fair trial for Arabi. Joseph Lennon explains that '[a]fter the physical battle had ended in Egypt, another continued in the press and political literature of Britain, both sides needing to publicly justify their arguments. The image of Arabi was the prize fought over.'[28] Control of this image was crucial if Arabi was going to be treated fairly and, encouraged by Blunt, Lady Gregory eventually persuaded William to allow her to send an article to Chenery for publication in *The Times*.

The article, 'Arabi and his Household', published on 23 October 1882 (her first published work) records details of Lady Gregory's and Anne Blunt's visit to Arabi's wife, mother and children in his home, and the images and descriptions of Arabi and his family counter the dominant views of Arabi at the time. Lady Gregory admitted this herself: 'I wrote down these recollections of Arabi and his family, which I knew must make him appear less of an ogre than he was generally supposed to be.' She described him as follows:

> In appearance, Arabi is a tall strongly-built man; his face is grave, almost stern, but his smile is very pleasant... I believe him to be exceedingly gentle and humane... I have an entire belief in his truthfulness; partly from his manner, partly because from everyone, without exception, who had known him long or watched his career... I heard on this point the same report – 'He is incapable of speaking untruth'; partly because it was many months ago – it was in November – that my husband first saw and spoke with him, and to every word he said then he has adhered ever since.

This image of Arabi directly subverted the conventional British view of Arabi as a threatening aggressive native needing containment. Words like 'pleasant', 'gentle' and 'humane', deliberately evoke 'a more human image of Arabi' and in doing so 'dismisses outright the 'ready belief' of the press and public that he is a violent monster.[29] Lady Gregory's description of her visit to his house emphasizes modesty and poverty to counter rumours of his 'avarice': the house is 'large and dilapidated looking', and 'the sole furniture consisted of small hard divans covered with brown linen and a tiny table'. On his family life, Gregory observed:

> His wife greeted us warmly... she has a pleasant, intelligent expression; but, having 5 children living out of 14 that have been born to her, looked rather overcome with the cares of maternity, her beauty dimmed since the time when the tall, grave soldier she had seen passing under the window every day, looked up at last, and saw and loved her. She wore a long dress of green silk. 'My husband hates this long train', she told us afterwards; 'he would like to take a knife and cut it off, but I say I must have a fashionable dress to wear when I visit the Khedive's wife and other ladies'. I think there are English husbands who, in this grievance at least, will sympathise with Arabi.

Here, Lady Gregory familiarized Arabi's home life. A snapshot of normal domesticity and typical conversations that might occur between a husband and his wife demanded both empathy and sympathy from the very 'English husbands' whose colonial outlook Gregory was attempting to influence. Indeed, 'the very process of representing the Orient'[30] is the subject of her essay. She goes on to describe Arabi's mother who was proud of, and worried about, the son she loved so much. They sat down to eat together and it is an idyllic domestic setting. She then described her final meeting with Arabi: 'Worried and troubled by false accusations made against him in English newspapers, he was still confident that someday his name would be cleared. "They must know some day that it is the good of the people that we seek". A little time before their work was judged, that was all he asked.' Arabi's motivations are presented by Lady Gregory as just and understandable.

Gregory reports in her diary that the letter was a huge success in Britain: 'Gladstone had said it was "very touching". And Greenwood, writing in his *St. James' Gazette*, had said it "made every woman in England Arabi's friend".'[31] At a reception in Downing Street, Gladstone asked Lady Gregory 'How are we to get peace and quiet in Egypt again?' to which she replied, 'Do what you like so that you don't touch my friend Arabi.'[32] Her letter, together with the efforts of her husband and Blunt (the latter of whom wrote numerous letters to *The Times* in support of Arabi and Egyptian Nationalism), did much to change British opinion of Arabi. He got his fair trial and his death sentence was commuted to banishment for life; Sir William ensured that he would be banished to Ceylon.

Lady Gregory concluded her chapter on Egypt with the following reflection:

> [T]hat was the end of my essay in politics, for though Ireland is always with me, and I first feared and then became reconciled to, and now hope to see even a greater independence than Home Rule, my saying has been long 'I am not fighting for it, but preparing for it'. And that has been my purpose in establishing a National Theatre, and for the revival of the language, and in making better known the heroic tales of Ireland... I am glad to have been in that fight for freedom, and glad my husband took freedom's side... And I like to remember also that I was of some service later on in making easier the circumstances of Arabi and his friends.[33]

In this final assessment of her political adventure, Lady Gregory wove together her early encounter, and sympathy with nationalism in Egypt, with her deep involvement in cultural nationalism in Ireland following the death of her husband in 1892. Born into a privileged landowning family, she had been attuned to an imperialist outlook from an early age, but this viewpoint would gradually change over time, and her experience in Egypt directly influenced the trajectory of her cultural and political activism. It is worth noting that her experience was in parallel with that of Wilfrid Scawen Blunt;[34] as Gattar notes, 'The path that Blunt travelled from unionist, to reforming liberal, to out-and-out nationalist would ultimately be her own, and the pivot of that swing was for her, as it had been for him, a perception of the failure of the British Crown, to honour its duties in Ireland, as in Egypt and elsewhere.'[35] Gregory gradually warmed to the idea of Irish independence and her founding of the Irish National Theatre, with W. B. Yeats, and the plays she wrote, supported that cause and played a significant part in paving the way for freedom.

Based on her autobiography alone, it is easy to interpret Gregory's experience in Egypt as an entirely political adventure, devoid of the usual pleasures of tourism. In *An Emigrant's Notebook*, however, a different experience of Egypt is evoked. Much of the notebook is a nostalgic yearning for pre-Land War stability in Ireland, and, more specifically, at her estate in Roxborough. However, as Gattar notes, the notebook (written in 1882), 'is equally important as a travel narrative'.[36] Indeed the section on Egypt in *An Emigrant's Notebook* omits any references whatsoever to Arabi, and in direct contrast to her diary and autobiography, the names of people she met in Egypt are also missing. The prose is more creative and imaginative, inviting the reader into a sensory experience of Cairo:

> Straight as the stork flies to the minarets of Cairo, the wonderful this loveable city... Rise in thy wondrous beauty – what remains of thy old glory is enough fortune! Come down by the markee to the narrow shaded stalls of the bazaar it is the hot hour of the day, all is drowsy and quiet. Turn with me then into the covered court wherein Abdullah sells his wares it will show you what carpets can be. Here are some of silk with a sheen upon them.[37]

Unlike her autobiography, the prose here is meandering, unstructured and Gregory often digresses from the topic at hand. At the start, her passion for Cairo is evoked in: 'Oh! I should like to live at Cairo 9 months of the year... The feast of colour always in the eyes the pleasure of doing nothing and never feeling that it is a crime'. She moves on to consider various aspects of Egyptian culture including the 'virtues of the Mohammedan' who has 'an unquestioning faith envied sometimes by us useless enquiring Western Christians'. He also has 'perfect resignation' and 'temperance patience obedience'. However, she warns that once one leaves 'mohammedan country for a christian one... what will strike you first will be the infinite difference of the position of the woman of the house in any rank of life'. The Western woman has a 'happier life, the greater possibility of bringing up her children well in the true family life – a lot that may well be envied by the veiled Eastern, at best but a slave liable to be dismissed by one word from her husband's lips and dismissal to poverty'. There is a significant and interesting contrast to be observed here between Gregory's view on Eastern women in general, and her depiction of Arabi's wife in 'Arabi and his Household'. The former is markedly different to the Western woman, yet the latter, in order to fulfil Gregory's political purposes, has much in common with the Western woman. Gregory is also critical of harem life, and in particular pities those women 'with intellect and education enough to know how much better life might be and yet with neither energy nor opportunity to make a change'.

Though *An Emigrant's Notebook* lacks the factual, detached political tone of Gregory's autobiography, it nevertheless briefly addresses politics in Egypt. The political climate is directly opposed to the passion Gregory initially expresses for Cairo. She writes:

> From the silent Cairene mosques and the shaded Cairene bazaars who would wish to plunge into the troubled changeful sea of Cairene politics: the selfish interests, the overbearing pride, the slanderous tongues, the interwoven intrigues, the bitter illwill, the unjust suspicions. Who will look ten years forward and prophesy that man's work will have stood the fire... Which of the actors will still be on the stage?

The amiable indolent minister full of good intentions but with no intention of ever carrying them out – the haughty high minded European official who will be Caesar or nobody, who will do his work well and thoroughly but must do it in his own way. The ambitious intriguer-in-exile yet feared. The beloved of the people, the just of the true... What will be the end? Can there be any peace before the day comes when the lion shall lie down with the lamb? I give no names you see, you may fit each to its epithet as you please.

Here, Gregory is unreserved in her judgement of various figures on the Cairene political scene, and refuses to name them, inviting the reader to engage in guesswork. Again there is a marked contrast between her autobiography and *An Emigrant's Notebook*. In her autobiography, a whole host of key political figures are named, but not judged.

The *Notebook* concludes with a brief consideration of a trip down the Nile on a Thomas Cook steamer. She does not give much attention to tourist attractions, with the exception of Cleopatra, of whom she opines, 'There does not seem to be much beauty about her my friend and yet we are told by history that her admirers were numerous but manner does a great deal – I think the attraction must have been in her nice manners (Oh thou great Anthony!).' In the final section, Gregory retells a story of romance told to her by a steward on the steamer, and so concludes her meandering meditation on her holiday in Egypt.

The three sources offering insight into Lady Gregory's experience of Egypt – her autobiography, 'Arabi and his Household', and *An Emigrant's Notebook* – offer together a composite portrait of a complex experience, one which would partly determine and shape Lady Gregory's political outlook and literary and cultural activity for years to come.

Endnotes

1   Gregory, A. (1976) *Seventy Years: 1852-1922*. New York, Macmillan.
2   Most notable of these sources is Colin Smythe's excellent account of the Gregorys' time in Egypt in *Literary Interrelations: Ireland, Egypt and the Far East.* (1987) Smythe is the copyright holder for much of Gregory's work and was the first to publish her autobiography. See also Hill, J. (2005) *Lady Gregory: An Irish Life.* Sutton Publishing, and Coxhead, E. (1961) *Lady Gregory: A Literary Portrait.* New York, Harcourt Brace.
3   For a sustained analysis of *An Emigrant's Notebook*, see Sinead Garrigan Mattar, 'Wage for Each People her Hand has Destroyed': Lady Gregory's Colonial Nationalism. *Irish University Review*, Vol. 34, No. 1, Special Issue: Lady Gregory (Spring–Summer 2004): pp. 49–66.
4   Hill, J. (2005) *Lady Gregory: An Irish Life.* Sutton Publishing: p. 38.
5   Garrigan Mattar, 'Wage for Each people her Hand has Destroyed': p. 55.
6   Gregory, *Seventy Years*: p.34.
7   *Ibid.*
8   Gregory, *Seventy Years*: p. 35.
9   *Ibid.*

10 Sir Gerald Fitzgerald, Director-General of Public Accounts in Egypt.
11 Lady Anne Blunt was the granddaughter of Lord Byron and the daughter of Ada Lovelace.
12 Hill, *Lady Gregory*: p. 41.
13 Gregory, *Seventy Years*: p. 36.
14 Hill, *Lady Gregory*: p. 43.
15 Gregory, *Seventy Years*: p. 35.
16 Sir Edward Malet was Agent and Consul-General in Egypt at the time.
17 Henry Windsor Villiers Stuart was an MP whose task was to report on post-revolt conditions in Egypt. He published *Egypt after the War* in 1883.
18 Gregory, *Seventy Years*: p. 36.
19 Described by Hill (*Lady Gregory*: p. 40) as 'the worldly, erudite and witty former politican... known among his male contemporaries for his collection of pornography'.
20 Gregory, *Seventy Years*: p. 37.
21 *Ibid.*
22 Gregory, *Seventy Years*: pp. 37–38.
23 Gregory, *Seventy Years*: p. 38.
24 *Ibid.*
25 Gregory, *Seventy Years*: p. 43.
26 Gregory, *Seventy Years*: p. 44.
27 *Ibid.*
28 Lennon, J. (2004) *Irish Orientalism: A Literary and Intellectual History*. New York, Syracuse University Press: p. 229.
29 Lennon, *Irish Orientalism*: p. 230.
30 Lennon, *Irish Orientalism*: p. 228.
31 Gregory, *Seventy Years*: p. 46.
32 Gregory, *Seventy Years*: p. 47.
33 Gregory, *Seventy Years*: p. 54.
34 With whom she would have an affair in the months following Arabi's banishment.
35 Mattar, 'Wage for Each People her Hand has Destroyed': p. 56.
36 *Ibid.*
37 *An Emigrant's Notebook*. MS 624: Box 46, Folder 8. Gregory Family Papers. Stuart A. Rose Manuscript, Archives and Rare Book Library. Robert W. Woodruff Library. Emory University.

14

Wilde about Egypt: Sir William Wilde in Egypt

Emmet Jackson

William Robert Wills Wilde was born in 1815, in the county of Roscommon, Ireland. As the plaque that now adorns his former residence at No. 1 Merrion Square, Dublin, states, he was to become a 'polymath, an aural and ophthalmic surgeon, archaeologist, ethnologist, antiquarian, biographer, statistician, naturalist, topographer, historian, and folklorist'. He had an incredible career in multiple fields, and in 1864, he was both knighted and had a degree of doctor of medicine conferred on him by the Board of Trinity College Dublin. His knighthood was primarily received for his work in relation to the 1841 and 1851 Irish censuses. As Malcom & Jones state, these 'were not merely detailed statistical surveys of contemporary public health, but massive and exhaustively researched histories of Irish epidemiology'[1] and his contribution to the 1851 census is 'arguably the finest of his polymathic achievements'.[2]

He was highly respected, and as the newspapers reported the day after his knighthood, no one 'more acceptable to all classes in Ireland, could not possibly have been made, for no member of the medical profession has been more prominently before the public for the last twenty-five years, in all useful and patriotic labours, than Dr. (now Sir William) Wilde'.[3] He was also other surgeon oculist to Her Majesty in Ireland, founder of the pioneering St Mark's Hospital and Dispensary for Diseases of the Eye and Ear in 1844,[4] an Honorary member of the Antiquarian Society of Berlin, Member of the Royal Society at Upsala, and was awarded the Order of the Polar Star by Carl XV of Sweden, and the Cunningham gold medal, the Royal Irish Academy's highest award.[5]

However, for all of his achievements William is often overlooked, outshone by the celebrated genius of his son Oscar Wilde. Tragically, William's life and fame were also marred by a libel case, one that would foreshadow his son's experience and subsequent, similar public demise. As 2015 saw the bicentennial of his birth, there has been renewed celebration of his genius with two separate symposiums being held in Dublin and his home county of Roscommon, plus new publications that focus on his medical career. However, there is little that touches on his travel to Egypt. This paper endeavours to capture some of the highlights of Wilde's Egyptian travels.

At the age of 22, on 16 March 11837, Wilde became a licentiate of the Royal College of Surgeons.[6] Sir Henry Marsh and Dr James Graves, his tutors, appointed Wilde as a medical attendant to a patient who was going on a cruise to Palestine, and in September 1837 he sailed on the yacht the *Crusader* with his patient, Mr Robert Meiklam of Glasgow. Stopping at the Canaries, Tenerife, the Rock of Gibraltar and Malta, they reached Alexandria on 13 January 1838. The voyage was as much for Wilde to restore his health as it was for his newly-found patient, as he had suffered ill health caused by asthma during and after his final exams. After some severe seasickness, the trip suited him and one of Wilde's biographers quips that 'Wilde performed prodigies on the tour; and if his

Fig 14.1 Sir William Robert Wills Wilde by Thomas Herbert Maguire. National Gallery of Ireland. NGI.10684

patient... attempted one-tenth of the exertions of his physician, it is little wonder that he expired apparently not long after their return'.[7]

Wilde wrote an account of his travel on his return with a typically lengthy Victorian title: *Narrative of a voyage to Madeira, Teneriffe and along the shores of the Mediterranean, including a visit to Algiers, Egypt, Palestine, Tyre, Rhodes, Telmessus, Cyprus and Greece. With observations on the present state and prospects of Egypt and Palestine, and on the climate, natural history, antiquities, etc, of the countries visited.*[8] The narrative, first published in 1840, was a huge success and an instant bestseller, becoming known as Wilde's Voyage.[9] It was a widely celebrated text for which Alexander von Humboldt forwarded Wilde an autograph letter of thanks from the then King of Prussia.[10]

The volume went into a second edition in 1844 with much revision and additions. Wilde indicates that, prior to his trip, he read many texts relating to Egypt and Egyptology, such as those written by Herodotus, Strabo, Pococke, Lane, Wilkinson, Lepsius and Waghorn. In his second edition, he removed many of his original notes as a result of reading Lane's *The manners & customs of the modern Egyptians* due to the 'accuracy' of his [Lane's] accounts. In other parts of the second edition, the text is augmented – parts of the text that appear as footnotes or appendices in the first edition now form part of the main text. Wilde also adds to his reading for the second edition, referring to other Egyptology sources, such as those of Sir John Gardner Wilkinson, Vivant Denon and McCullagh.[11]

Wilde's narrative is varied and very detailed, representing a 'contribution to the burgeoning genre of medical geography and travel writing'[12] which catered for the mass of wealthy Victorians seeking convalescent refuge from northern climes. Indeed, in the preface to his travel narrative he informs the reader that he 'undertook to collect information relative to the climate of the places we should visit, and also to keep a register of their temperature'.[13] But his narrative focuses on more than the weather: he moves from one observation to another, often without warning, devoting large passages to a multitude of subject matters in great detail, including local dress and customs, history, geography, sociology, zoology, economics, phrenology and medicine, to name a few. He includes appendices to expand upon his observations that range over topics as varied as the mode of suckling in cataceans to the linen of Ancient Egypt. It was this breath of demonstrated knowledge that gave Wilde a platform for lecturing, on his return, at the many respected institutions in Dublin, including Trinity College, Dublin, the Royal Dublin Society, the Royal College of Physicians and the Royal Irish Academy, all of which brought him notice as a gifted savant.

Wilde's travels only took him as far as Cairo, before he and his companion returned to Alexandria where, on the morning of 7 February, they set sail for Rhodes. Even though his stay was short, Egypt influenced Wilde greatly. In 1839, a year after his return, he decided to specialize in eye and ear diseases. It is interesting that Wilde makes so many entries about the 'eye' in Egypt; it suggests that his experience there may have influenced his choice of career.

Within minutes of landing in Alexandria, Wilde is struck by the filth and squalor in which people live and work:

> I was not many minutes in Alexandria until I was forcibly struck with the number of blind people I met at every turn; it is really incredible; the greater number had but one eye, and many others were groping their way through the streets in perfect darkness.' He continues, 'Squinting is a very common affection among the people of Alexandria, the greater number of the lower orders are what would be termed blear-eyed; and wherever we went we discovered lamentable traces of the ravages of ophthalmia.[14]

Later, he devotes pages to the description of the eye of the Egyptian, leading on from a somewhat lengthy and suggestive description of the female form. He describes them as 'bewitching and invariably black eyes rendered more sparling by the dark line of kohl... surrounding them... The eye of the Arab girl, and more particularly the Egyptian is so peculiar, and so often caused me to stop and admire its beauties; that I may be excused dwelling on it a few moments'.[15]

He continues to describe girls' eyes for a page, and concludes the passage by saying that 'there is a swimming loveliness in those brilliants set in jet that I cannot but admire. Unless when negro blood mingles with that of the Arab, the traveller can still recognise "A Helen's beauty in a brow of Egypt".'

The passage continues, but he concentrates less on matters of aesthetics when he discusses male eyes: 'Nearly all the young men you meet are blind of an eye, generally the right one, and have lost the index finger on the right hand; this act of mutilation is done by themselves to avoid the conscription... and what with the effects of ophthalmia and the terrors of the conscription, there will soon appear a cyclopean population.'[16]

His medical background also comes to the fore when visiting medical establishments and places for the incarceration of those with mental illness. He writes: 'Today I went to inspect two of the most revolting and disgusting sights at Cairo – the slave market, and the mad house.' On arrival at the latter, the institution called Morostàn [sic], their group were directed towards purchasing bread for the inmates. They were led into a large oblong room where 'a yell arose of the most unearthly kind my ears ever assailed by – so startling, that some of our party involuntary drew back with horror. Our sights – our smells – our hearing were overwhelmed with a combination of disgusting realities, such as I believe no other place allotted to mankind can exhibit.'

He continues with a harrowing description of the inmates, a group he describes as 'ravenous animals in a menagerie' – ending in a feeding frenzy. Wilde writes, 'Each in turn snatched his morsel, and devoured it with a growl I can only liken to a tiger's.' Wilde goes on to say that he 'will not disgust [his] readers with a recital of the sickening scene he witnessed in the female department'.[17] Instead, he quotes from Byron's poem 'The Lament of Tasso'.

After the visit, his medical concerns come to the fore and he laments that there is no treatment or cure available for the debilitating illness he witnesses. He scorns those who have visited these establishments but have not expressed their disgust, and he concludes that both Europeans and the medical men of Cairo should inquire into and reform this disgrace upon humanity. Things didn't change until the late 1880s, with reports from Nightingale, Flaubert and English psychiatrists visiting similar institutions in the 40s and 50s describing similar scenes.

While Wilde describes the Slave Market as revolting, his actual description of the slave market lacks any clear disapproval. He remarks that the slaves from Nubia and Dongola 'appear perfectly unconscious of their state, and, as far as appearance went, were very happy'.[18] He continues to say that 'apart from the miseries of separation from friends and country, it is an undoubted change to many for the better.... True it is that the master can kill his slave; but few are so foolish as to incur such a personal loss'. Wilde does make a distinction between the Nubian and Abyssinian slaves and says that of the latter, 'Our sympathies would be more excited' due to their 'interesting appearance and somewhat greater advances in civilisation'.[19] This is in stark contract to an earlier Irish traveller, Dr. R. R. Madden, who had stronger opinions on the matter[20] and went on to author a damming publication on slavery in the Ottoman Empire stating: 'On the subject of the slave trade carried on by the authorities – and it must be added, with the connivance of the present ruler of Egypt – the information that is given is full and authentic; and... can leave no possible doubt that the traffic is a source of revenue to the Pacha; and that he shelters the continuance of it under flimsy pretext.'[20]

A few days later, Wilde left his group to visit tourist attractions and with a letter of introduction to the Chief medical attendant, Dr Pruner, departed for the military hospital and medical college at Abouzabel (founded by Clot Bey). He is generous with his praise of the institution stating 'that a cleaner, better regulated, and better conducted medical establishment I never visited'.

There were several hundred patients out of the 1,200 with eye disease whom Wilde was especially anxious to see. However, he found cases of ophthalmia to be scarce, informing the reader that the disease was at its worst in autumn, when up to 700 cases were in the hospital at once. Wilde wrote a short treatise on the cause and treatment of this malady. He also toured the medical hospital, which he praised for its system of training and reflected that it should be imitated in Great Britain.

Coming from a medical school in Dublin, Wilde makes a point of mentioning the dissecting room whose establishment, he explains, was a major issue for a Muslim country – it was Mohammed Ali who enforced the practice of anatomy. The priesthood was against it, but Wilde recounts that 'it was the Pasha's royal wish and pleasure that they should legalise the act, and that, if they did not speedily do so, it was more than probable they themselves should form material for the first experiment in this branch of the practical sciences'.[21] In fact, it was Antoine Barthelemy Clot, later known as Clot Bey, who was appointed head of the army medical corps and who had convinced the Pasha to allow the study of anatomy.[22]

Not only did his experience of blindness, and obsession with 'eyes' in Egypt, go on to influence his career; the sales of his book which brought him £250[23] enabled him to study eye and ear surgery in London, Vienna, and Berlin. On his return from these studies abroad he set up a practice in Westland Row (around the corner from Merrion Square, where he would end up living), opened a dispensary for poor patients and engaged in numerous occupations.

Wilde was a gifted historian and produced celebrated texts on archaeology and folklore after his travels. His magnum opus was his volumes of the *Descriptive Catalogue of the Antiquities in the Museum of the Royal Irish Academy* (1857–62) that enumerated and illustrated the academy's large collections of historical artefacts.[24] It is not surprising then that he showed an early interest in antiquity while in Egypt. During his short stay in Alexandria, he explored as many sites as he could and his first visit was to Cleopatra's needle and Pompey's pillar. These were the first ancient monuments he saw and he was truly captivated by them: 'As these were the first objects of Egyptian grandeur and antiquity we had seen, we were greatly struck with them... how very difficult it is to convey by words, a description of objects such as these; or, without an appearance of affectations, to embody in language the feelings that their recollections will arouse.' He despairs at the graffiti on the monuments asking 'Young gentlemen of the royal navy, let me ask in sober earnestness, in what consist the honour and glory of having your names emblazoned upon every post and pillar'.[25]

He describes the monuments in detail; their appearance, position and history. He explains that the removal of one or other of these monuments to England has long been voiced and reflects a typical colonialist mind-set by commenting that 'the delay [in removing them] has never been satisfactorily accounted for; for they are ours by right of conquest and presentation'.[26] This was a subject matter that Wilde cared about greatly. He penned his thoughts on the matter in the *Dublin University Magazine* in 1839, and included the article as an appendix to the second edition of 'narrative of a voyage'. In it, he proposed to have the obelisk transported to England, where, along with some 'sphinxes and other memorial of [the] Egyptian conquest erected as the Nelson testimonial in Trafalgar-square'.[27]

In Cairo, he visited Absour, Dashur, Saqqara and Giza, exploring in a very claustrophobic manner the interiors of the stepped pyramid and the larger pyramids at Giza, and making astute observations on their construction and age. At Absour, he commented that the ground was strewn for miles with the sacking of the tombs consisting of quantities of linen, broken mummy cases, pottery and remains of human bones. Wilde was keen to stay to examine the material but was pushed on by their guide so they could reach the tomb in Saqqara that would be their shelter for the night. Discovering an abandoned mummy and case that was opened by a French traveller the day before, Wilde collected the remains which he describes as the 'most interesting objects I could have discovered'. Finding the mummy had disfigured arms, Wilde launched into an examination of the body, an early paleopathology study, and drew comparisons with Wilkinson's work on dwarf figures at Beni Hassan.

Later, at the Ibis catacombs at Saqqara, he informs us that 'he succeeded in removing six of these, and had them eventually conveyed to England'.[28] In his appendix on ancient Egyptian linen, he also refers to mummy linen that he brought back, so he did transport some artefacts home but it is not currently known where these objects ended up. He describes his descent into the mummy pits of the sacred animals in an excited fashion, conjuring up images of a Victorian treasure hunter. Having arrived at the catacombs, he was embarrassed to realize that he had forgotten 'the lights', but was determined to explore them saying, 'I resolved to feel my way into it [catacombs], and bring away some of the urns containing the embalmed ibises.'[29] Following a gruelling descent, during which he exclaims that 'I do not think in all my travels I ever felt the same strong sensation of being in an enchanted place... and lonely vaults of this immense mausoleum', he at last came to a spot where they could stand and Wilde informs us that 'thousands upon thousands of the urns have been removed and broken... yet thousands remain', before removing his own six urns. Wilde was keen to expand on his description of the Ibis, but stated that 'so very much has been written upon the sacred attributes and natural history of the Sacred Ibis, that I have little to add'. But Wilde in his typical search for knowledge informs that reader that he did 'in the museum of the school of medicine at Cairo... compare both black and the white Ibis with the bones of those found in the mummy-pits of Sackara [sic], and can add my testimony as to their identity'.[30]

After his visit to the catacombs, Wilde made his way to Giza, and climbed both pyramids. On scaling the pyramid of Khafre, Wilde forgets his earlier grievances with graffiti and writes, 'I saw two or three names scratched upon the central slab, to which of course I added my own.'[31]

Wilde's interest in the ancient lands mixed with his interest in Irish Mythology. Leaving Egypt and arriving at Tyre, he writes, 'As an Irishman I felt no small degree of interest on first touching the motherland, whose colony we claim to be.' One of his biographers finds this ironic, given that 'this young man who called himself so frequently an Englishman turned in Tyre, to the romantic origin of those paddies with large upper lips, cawbeens, shillelaghs, pigs with "Yer honour" ever on their lips, who graced the pages of Punch for the delectation of the English middle-class...'.[32] This description is arguably unfair, conflating Wilde's view, his 'Irishness', with a stage Irish persona. In fact, Wilde was touching on a deeper belief that he held, and which was common at the time, that Ireland had been colonized by people who had their origin in the Middle East. As Joseph Lennon observes, 'Long before it

Fig 14.2 'View of the Pyramid of Chephrenes [...] taken from the platform on the top of the great pyramid of Cheops'

was treated as Celtic, Irish culture was linked to the Orient. Ireland's ancient history and culture supposedly stemmed from Asian and Middle Eastern, or West Asian, cultures.'[33] Wilde expands on his ideas in the appendix to his wife's publication[34] entitled *On the Ancient Races of Ireland*.

His interest in the opposite sex is observed in the many biographical notes on Wilde. It is common, therefore, as de Vere writes, 'to all who write on him to repeat that he had a bastard in every cottage'.[35] Before his marriage, to Jane Francesca Elgee in 1851, Sir William had fathered three illegitimate children – one of whom, Henry, became a doctor and worked as his assistant. His two illegitimate daughters, Mary and Emily, lived with a cousin of his and he visited them regularly. Tragically, both died twhen their crinoline dresses caught fire at a ball.[36] The most famous of Wilde's affairs was with one of his patients, Mary Travers. Travers, self-published and disseminated a pamphlet, entitled 'Florence Boyle Price: A Warning' (1863), in which she describes a fictitious character modelled on Wilde, a 'Dr. Quilp', who rapes the fictional Florence Price. Lady Wilde, after several letters asking her to stop her campaign, sent a letter to Dr Travers, her father, saying, 'You may not be aware of the disreputable conduct of your daughter at Bray, where she consorts with all the low newspaper boys in the place, employing them to disseminate offensive placards, in which my name is given, and also tracts, in which she makes it appear that she has had an intrigue with Sir William Wilde.'[37] This letter was the catalyst of a libel case against the Wildes and became the talk of Dublin.

William and his wife had three children: William, Oscar and Isola, who died of a fever at the age of nine.[38] Lady Wilde was a nationalist and feminist and adopted the pseudonym 'Speranza' under which she wrote subversive, patriotic verse. She was the fiery poet of the *Nation* newspaper, and it was widely known that she had penned an unsigned editorial for the paper in 1848 which led the government to suppress the newspaper for sedition. Her fame as 'the heroine of [the] "Young Ireland" movement continued long after she abandoned militant nationalism'.[39]

The house on No 1 Merrion Square into which they moved in 1855 was one of the oldest and at the time on the most fashionable side of Merrion Square. When the square was built, it was largely inhabited by aristocrats attracted by the nearby presence of Leinster House, the home of the Duke of Leinster. After the Act of Union in 1800, the aristocrats living in the square were slowly replaced by the legal and medical professions and, by the time the Wildes moved, in several eminent medical, artistic and legal families were living in Merrion Square.[40]

From this house, Speranza ran her weekly salons, the most famous in Dublin, where the élite of Dublin gathered to argue over the pressing issues of the day.[41] Oscar considered that 'the best of his education in boyhood was obtained from [the] association with his father and mother and their remarkable friends'.[42] Yeats later to remarked that '[w]hen one listens to her [Lady Wilde] and remembers that Sir William Wilde was in his day a famous raconteur, one finds it no way wonderful that Oscar Wilde should be the most finished talker of our time'.[43]

Their social circle included some major literary luminaries of the day, and one of these was Bram Stoker, author of *Dracula*. He grew up among the Dublin élite, where he was a friend of the Wildes and was a regular visitor to Speranza's salons. Stoker had a specific relationship with Egyptology and published *The Jewel of Seven Stars* in 1903, his contribution to the Egyptian Gothic genre. Stoker's academic interest in ancient Egypt was evident in his library, which included a number of influential works by Petrie and Budge.[44] Notwithstanding the influence that Petrie and Budge, and specifically the discovery of Hatshepsut tomb, KV20, in 1902, had on Stoker, it is not too implausible to suggest that Stoker's interest was fired by Wilde's anecdotes and access to his house during his days in Dublin.

Wilde's house, like that of Abel Trelawney, in the novel, was reportedly filled with ancient Irish and Egyptian artefacts which influenced the bourgeoning writer. Some authors refer to the mummy that formed part of Wilde's collection.[45] However, it is not known for certain that Wilde had a mummy. When Wilde investigateds the deformed mummy parts at Saqqara, as previously described, he says that he 'carried them away with me'[46], but it is most likely that he did so to study them in situ and he does not state that he brought them back to Dublin.

William Wilde's amazing career has, to an extent, been overshadowed by the literary fame of his son. However, the notoriety that arose from his own illicit relationships and the scandal of the libel case against him left him tarnished. While his reputation somewhat recovered from the libel case, the death of his two illegitimate daughters and that of his daughter with Lady Wilde also took their toll, and he died on 19 April 1876 in his 62nd year. He was given a large, public funeral, and was buried at Mount Jerome Cemetery in Dublin on 22 April.[47] His *Narrative of a Voyage...* remains a fascinating read, not just for its observations on Egypt but also for all the places that he visited.

Endnotes

1   Malcom E., & Jones, G (eds) (1999) *Medicine, Disease and the State of Ireland 1650-1940.* Cork University Press. p. 5.

2   For more on Wilde's contribution to Famine Studies see Geary, L. (2015) 'William Wilde (1815–76) as Historian – A Bicentenary Appraisal'. *History Ireland*, Vol. 23, No. 5: pp. 28–33.

3   'Sir William Wilde'. *Freeman's Journal*, 29 January 1864. British Library Newspapers.

4   Ryder, S., 'Son and Parents: Speranza and William Wilde' in: Raby, P., K. Powell (Eds.). (2013) *Oscar Wilde in Context.* Cambridge, Cambridge University Press: p. 8.

5   Anon, (1876). Sir William Robert Willis Wilde M.D., F.R.C.S.I. *The British Medical Journal*, Vol. 1, No. 800 (Apr. 29, 1876): p. 553.

6   De Vere White, T. (1967). *The Parents of Oscar Wilde: Sir William and Lady Wilde.* London, Hodder and Stoughton: p. 37.

7   De Vere White, *The Parents of Oscar Wilde*, p. 38.

8   Wilde, W. (1844) *Narrative of a voyage to Madeira, Teneriffe and along the shores of the Mediterranean, including a visit to Algiers, Egypt, Palestine, Tyre, Rhodes, Telmessus, Cyprus*

and Greece. With observations on the present state and prospects of Egypt and Palestine, and on the climate, natural history and antiquities of the countries visited. Second Edition. Dublin. William Curry, Jun. and Company. Subsequent reference to this text will be denoted by the abbreviated version of the title, *Narrative of a Voyage*.

9   McGeachie, J. (2016) 'Wilde's Worlds: Sir William Wilde in Victorian Ireland', *Irish Journal of Medical Science*, 185: pp. 303–07.

10 'Sir William Wilde'. *Freeman's Journal*, 29 January 1864. British Library Newspapers.

11 MacCullagh, J. (1837) 'On the Chronology of Egypt'. *Proceedings of the Royal Irish Academy*, Vol. 1.: pp. 66–68.

12 McGeachie, J. (2016) 'Wilde's Worlds: Sir William Wilde in Victorian Ireland': p. 304.

13 Wilde, W. (1844) *Narrative of a Voyage*: p. v.

14 Wilde, W. (1844) *Narrative of a Voyage*: p. 174.

15 Wilde, W. (1844) *Narrative of a Voyage*: pp. 202–03.

16 Wilde, W. (1844) *Narrative of a Voyage*: p. 204.

17 Wilde, W. (1844) *Narrative of a Voyage*: p. 219.

18 Wilde, W. (1844) *Narrative of a Voyage*: p. 221.

19 Wilde, W. (1844) *Narrative of a Voyage*: p. 222.

20 Madden, R. R. (1833) *Travels in Turkey, Egypt, Nubia and Palestine in 1824, 1825, 1826 & 1827*. Vols. 1 & 2. London, Whittaker, Treacher, and Co.

21 Madden, R. R. (1841) *Egypt and Mohammed Ali: illustrative of the condition of his slaves and subjects, &c., &c.* London, Hamilton, Adams: p. vi.

22 Wilde, W. *Narrative of a Voyage*: p. 238.

23 Fahmy, K. (2012) 'The Sheikh and the Corpse' (Lecture delivered in the Oriental Hall, AUC on Monday, 5 November 2012). Al-Ahram, Issue No.1123, 22 November 2012.

24 Froggatt, P. (1977) 'Sir William Wilde, 1815–1876: A Centenary Appreciation Wilde's Place in Medicine.' *Proceedings of the Royal Irish Academy*. Section C: Archaeology, Celtic Studies, History, Linguistics, Literature, Vol. 77 (1977), pp. 261–78. p. 263.

25 See Wilde, W. R. (1857) *A Descriptive Catalogue of The Antiquities of Stone, Earthen, and Vegetable materials in The Museum of The Royal Irish Academy*, Vol. 1. Dublin, Hodges, Smith & Co.; Wilde, W. R. (1861) *A Descriptive Catalogue of The Antiquities of Animal Materials and Bronze in the Museum of The Royal Irish Academy*, Vol. 2. Dublin, Hodges, Smith & Co., and Wilde, W. R. (1862) *A descriptive catalogue of the antiquities of gold in the Museum of the Royal Irish Academy*. Dublin, London, Hodges, Smith and Co., Williams & Norgate.

26 Wilde, W. *Narrative of a Voyage*: p. 182.

27 Wilde, W. *Narrative of a Voyage*: p. 178.

28 Wilde, W. (1839) Proposal relative to the Nelson Testimonial. *The Dublin Magazine. A Literary and Political Journal.* Vol XIII. January to June, 1839. Dublin, William Curry, Jun. and Company, pp. 628–33.

29 For more on Animal Mummies see McKnight, L. M. & S. Atherton-Woolham (eds.) (2015) *Gifts for the Gods: Ancient Egyptian Animal Mummies and the British*. Liverpool, Liverpool University Press.

30 Wilde, W. *Narrative of a Voyage*: p. 267.

31 Wilde, W.. *Narrative of a Voyage*: p. 268.

32 Wilde, W. *Narrative of a Voyage*: p. 273.

33 De Vere White, *The Parents of Oscar Wilde*: p. 56.

34 Lennon, J. (2004) *Irish Orientalism: A Literary and Intellectual History*. New York, Syracuse University Press: p. xv.

35 Wilde, S., (1887) *Ancient Legends, Mystic Charms, and Superstitions of Ireland*. Boston, Ticknor and Co.

36 De Vere White, *The Parents of Oscar Wilde*: p. 37.

37 McMahon, T. (2003) 'The Tragic Deaths in 1871 in County Monaghan of Emily and Mary Wilde-Half-Sisters of Oscar Wilde'. *Clogher Record*, Vol. 18, No. 1 (2003): pp. 129–45.

38 'Extraordinary Action for libel against Sir William & Lady Wilde', *Liverpool Mercury*, 14 December 1864. British Library Newspapers.

39 Lyons J. B. *Wilde, Sir William Robert Wills*. Dictionary of Irish Biography Online © 2015 Cambridge University Press and Royal Irish Academy.

40 Ryder, S. 'Son and Parents: Speranza and William Wilde': p. 8.

41 For more on the history of Merrion Square, see. McEntegart, R. 'William Wilde and 1 Merrion Square'. *Ir J Med Sci* (2016) 185: pp. 285–89.

42 *Ibid.*: p. 288.

43 Coakley, D. (1994) *Oscar Wilde, The Importance of being Irish*. Town House: p. 38.

44 Ryder, S, 'Son and Parents: Speranza and William Wilde': p. 9.

45 Luckhurst, R. (2012) *The Mummy's Curse: The True History of a Dark Fantasy*. Oxford and New York, Oxford University Press: p. 173.

46 See *The Jewel of Seven Stars*, edited with an introduction and notes by Hebblethwaite, K. (2008), p. xix. and Luckhurst, R. (2012) *The Mummy's Curse*: p. 173.

47 Wilde, W. *Narrative of a Voyage*: p. 255.

48 Anon, (1876). Sir William Robert Willis Wilde M.D., F.R.C.S.I. *The British Medical Journal*, Vol. 1, No. 800 (Apr. 29, 1876): p. 553.

A French Traveller in the Levant: The Marquis Charles-Jean-Melchior de Vogüé (1829–1916), with reference to William Henry Waddington (1826–94)

Sheila McGuirk

The Marquis Charles-Jean-Melchior de Vogüé (Fig.15.1) was a diplomat and scholar, but also a traveller. As a traveller, he is best known for his discovery in 1861 of the ruined or, as they are often called, 'dead' Byzantine cities of northern Syria. Prominent among these was Qalb Lozeh with its large and beautiful stone church, thought to have set the pattern for the architecture of the region, including the Martyrium of Saint Simeon Stylites a little to the north.[1]

Others of the 'cities of the dead' that de Vogüé explored between 1860 and 1862 were Serjilla, Al-Bara, Deir Sobat, Ruweiha, Jerada and Dana, all in a group a little south of Qalb Lozeh. There are several hundred sites in this so-called dead cities area of northern Syria. On seeing the towns de Vogüé said: 'I would almost be tempted not to call them ruins, these towns are so intact; in some almost all the original

Fig 15.1 Marquis Charles-Jean Melchior de Vogüé. Private collection.

elements are still there, overturned perhaps, but never dispersed. The sight of them transports the traveller back to a lost civilization whose every secret is revealed.'[2]

English traders who settled in Aleppo in the 18th century probably knew of the sites, and by the time Karl Baedeker published his guide to Palestine and Syria in

1875, these places were on the tourist map. But there had been no systematic study before de Vogüé and his books on Syria and Jerusalem were listed in Baedeker's bibliography under Architecture and Art History.

Some of the ghost towns may be much as they were when the Marquis de Vogüé brought them to Western attention more than a century ago. In 2011, many were grouped into archaeological parks as a UNESCO World Heritage site. But the area is located between Antioch and Aleppo near the Turkish–Syrian border, so the physical remains are now being used by refugees from the Syrian civil war, and have been adapted accordingly. In some places, the old towns had already been overtaken by more recent construction and, as usual, *spolia* from the Byzantine ruins were used in the new houses. Much of the ransacking of the old structures occurred between de Vogüé's visit in 1861 (his second to the region) and that of a Princeton archaeological expedition some 50 years later. It is fortunate, therefore, that de Vogüé's detailed descriptions survive.

Charles-Jean-Melchior de Vogüé was born in Paris in 1829 into a minor aristocratic family from the Vivarais region of the Ardèche, near Aubenas. He was the eldest son of Léonce, Marquis de Vogüé (1805–77) and was proud to trace his family tree as far back as the 12th century and the time of the Crusaders, whom he admired immensely. He recounted this history in the book *Une Famille Vivaroise: histoires d'autrefois racontées à ses enfants*, which he wrote for his children, two girls from his first marriage in 1855 to his first cousin Adélaïde Marguerite de Vogüé and two sons from his second marriage in 1866. The family château still stands in the village of Vogüé and is open to the public, though Charles-Jean never actually lived there himself.

The family had a history of both military and literary achievement. On his seventh birthday, Charles-Jean allegedly received a Latin Grammar to encourage his growth in the humanities and a small cavalry sabre with the injunction 'Do not draw me without reason and do not sheathe me without honour'. He could have gone to the army officers' training school of St Cyr, but he chose the École Polytechnique, one of the most selective and prestigious of the French Grandes Écoles for studying science and engineering. Unfortunately, the revolution of 1848 caused him to miss the written entrance exam for the École Polytechnique and he failed the oral. This meant a complete change of plan, though apparently he never regretted giving up the study of mathematics in which he had been immersed up to then.

At this point, the young de Vogüé was talent-spotted by Alexis de Toqueville, then French Minister of Foreign Affairs and a friend of Léonce de Vogüé. In 1849, he was appointed attaché at the French Embassy in St Petersburg, and he set off in early 1850. This overland journey across the snowy wastes of Poland was as hazardous as any he subsequently undertook in the deserts of the Near East. In Russia, de Vogüé practised drawing and water-colouring, at both of which he was very talented, as the illustrations in his publications show.

In 1851, after two years in St Petersburg, de Vogüé left the diplomatic service. His departure was possibly hastened because his father was politically on the wrong side. The fractious nature of French politics in the 19th century, due to the tussle between Bourbon royalists, Bonapartists, and left or centrist republicans, made this a particularly complicated period to be in public life. In December that year, Louis Napoleon Bonaparte declared himself French President for Life and subsequently Emperor Napoleon III in 1852.

The young de Vogüé turned his hand to travel and archaeology in the Near East. De Vogüé was 24 when he first travelled through the Ottoman Empire. It was the beginning of a long life of scholarship in which he was a distinguished and prolific writer on many subjects. A list of de Vogüé's publications compiled in 1909 runs to 14 pages, and still doesn't include everything he published.

De Vogüé left from Marseilles in May 1853 for his first oriental voyage with two companions, Roger Anisson du Perron, a friend from his student days, and Alexandre de Boisgelin, both like him 'enthusiasts, interested in art, history, local colour, somewhat romantic and sincere believers', as he later recounted. He was away for a year, visiting first the classical sites of Greece. Then he and his companions sailed to Constantinople, Smyrna, Rhodes and Beirut. Arriving in Beirut, de Vogüé was immediately struck by the change in the landscape. He described 'groves of mulberry and pomegranate trees; sugar cane plantations; date palms; hedges of prickly pear cactus; and in the distance, beyond the great mountains which are white with snow in winter, the desert.' On leaving Beirut for Baalbek, de Vogüé complained that the arrangements made for them by their Ethiopian guide were extensive but not unusual: they had four donkey boys, 12 horses for the travellers and their baggage, tents, beds, tables, chairs, kitchen equipment and a cook. 'A large number of English including white-haired ladies, cross these regions every year and set the tone of these travels, which have become routine promenades, free from fatigue and danger,' he wrote rather disparagingly.

The trio became enamoured of desert travel with the Bedu and disliked towns and city dwellers. On arriving at Beirut he wrote, 'Here there are no more thieving Greeks; no more degenerate Turks. We were among the Arabs, whom it pleased our imaginations to embellish with exaggerated colours.'[3] Between Damascus and Palmyra they travelled like the Bedu, under the protection of a local sheikh, but were nevertheless required to pay tribute to others on the way. Everywhere he went de Vogüé took measurements with a mathematician's precision, copied inscriptions and made plans and drawings of the ruins, despite the impatience of his guides. Later, he tried to match the places they passed through on the Phoenician coast to the towns named by Strabo, Pliny, Polybius and other earlier visitors.

They arrived at Jerusalem in November. By December, the trio were at Alexandria, which was already a modern city on European lines. Cairo was more oriental, like Damascus, and wonderfully picturesque. The friends then sailed up the Nile as far as the second cataract, which took them 32 days. In Thebes, de Vogüé could barely tear himself away, he found the colours of the ruins and the hills in all lights to be magical for an artist.

In Cairo, he spent time with Mariette and he usually stayed with the French consul in towns such as Beirut and Jerusalem or called on them when passing through, as in Sidon. Meanwhile, de Vogüé had become friends with a M. de Guiraud with whom he had been crossing paths since Athens and who joined the three men up the Nile. At the end of the Nile trip, Guiraud and de Vogüé decided not to return from Cairo to France with the others but to go again to Jerusalem. Of the parting from his original companions, he wrote:

> For a year we travelled together, exposed to the same trials, sleeping in the same tent, tossed by the same wave, our tastes and emotions in total harmony, sharing the same joys and anxieties. Now for the first time in a year I was alone on the shore. It was true that the separation was not to be long, but on the banks of the Nile feelings and impressions were so much more intense. Once home would we find again the daily intimacy of travel, free from any other preoccupation? I felt strongly in bidding farewell to my friends that I was saying goodbye to all we had enjoyed together. Whatever should happen to me in future, a chapter of my life, one of the best, had just ended on the quayside in Bulaq.'[4]

As a passionate Roman Catholic, de Vogüé was overcome with emotion to be spending Easter 1854 in the Holy City. It was this second visit to Jerusalem that convinced him to spend the next six years back in France studying the churches of the Near East. He set about collecting documents to supplement his own careful on-site studies of the urban landscape. For his work and his travels de Vogüé eventually mastered Greek, Latin, Phoenician, Syriac and Hebrew. The book he finally produced six years later from all this research was called *Les Églises de la Terre Sainte*.

In the introduction to that book, he summarized his nine-day journey from Cairo across Sinai to Jerusalem in April 1854, with just one Bedouin guide from El-Arish, one camel boy and five camels, all obtained with the help of Linant de Bellefonds. In addition to de Vogüé and his friend de Guiraud, there was their dragoman Guiseppe, but he quickly became too ill to be of any help. To accomplish this journey at record speed, they ditched all superfluous baggage; 'all those comforts which the growing number of European tourists has brought to travelling in the Orient,' as he put it.

Les Églises de la Terre Sainte, which de Vogüé illustrated himself, was the first systematic account of churches from the Constantinian age to the Crusader period. It also included a description and analysis of their important art work. He discussed the influence of the work of Middle Eastern artisans employed by the barbarian kings of Europe. He pointed out that after the fall of Jerusalem its architectural style was continued in Cyprus and Rhodes. Even if his theories about the origins and cross fertilization of Byzantine and Romanesque styles are controversial, his research remains important for the many monuments he recorded that were later destroyed or irrevocably changed. He included in this book a study of mediaeval pilgrim and

Crusader guidebooks. De Vogüé categorized and summarized these guides in an appendix, and printed one complete Latin text dating from 1130 and a French text dating from 1187. He felt that this guide from 1187 could still be used to navigate Jerusalem, so little had the City changed since the Crusades.

In December 1861, shortly after the publication of *Les Églises de la Terre Sainte*, de Vogüé and the architect Edmond-Clément-Marie-Louise Duthoit (1837–89) travelled to Syria in the wake of the French armies which had gone to protect Syrian Christians following the Turkish and Druze massacres. The epigrapher William Henry Waddington (1826–94), who was already in Syria, had invited de Vogüé to join him. Waddington was an Anglo-Frenchman, educated at Rugby and Trinity College, Cambridge. He had previously published a report on Greek and Latin inscriptions in Asia Minor and Greece, including the Peloponnese. He and de Vogüé had become acquainted through the French Numismatic Society and used to see each other regularly in the Bibliothèque Nationale. De Vogüé was glad of the chance to travel again as he had just lost his young wife after only five years of marriage. The three scholars first conducted a survey of antiquities in Cyprus sending back inscriptions and statues to the Louvre. In Syria they travelled under English consular protection since France was unpopular after its recent military intervention.

Waddington left the Near East in spring 1862, but de Vogüé remained with Duthoit, researching in central Syria and the Hawrān. The results were published in 1864 as *Inscriptions araméennes et nabatéennes du Haouran*. But it was while travelling further north that de Vogüé made the detailed exploration of the deserted Byzantine villages for which he is most famous. The account of the ruins was published in fascicules over a period of 12 years as *Syrie central: Architecture civile et religieuse du Ier au VIIe siècle* (1865–77). The geographical concept of 'Central Syria', which we would today think of as just Syria, was one that he used primarily to designate the Limestone Massif where the dead cities lie; his Greater Syria encompassed areas of Byzantine and proto-Byzantine architecture north into Anatolia and south into Lebanon.

Of Duthoit, de Vogüé wrote, 'He is a well-trained and able architect, whose companionship added to the pleasure of the journey as much as his collaboration enhanced the results.'[5] Duthoit was also a brilliant draftsman and contributed detailed drawings to the joint work. The exactitude of their observations, particularly if the plates were coloured in, produced a record superior to any that could have been made via photography at the time, which was beginning to be used by other travellers and scholars.

Returning to Jerusalem gave de Vogüé the opportunity to work again in the Holy Land. The result of this trip was his 1864 study of the Temple of Jerusalem, published as *Le Temple de Jérusalem* (1864). And it seems de Vogüé *did* take photographs, because 50 years later the Sheikh who as a young man had conducted them around the Haram al-Sherif and Mosque of Omar remembered de Vogüé and said, 'There were three of you: one who wrote, one who drew and one who took photographs.' And it seems these were respectively Waddington, Duthoit and de Vogüé.[6]

Charles-Jean had earlier helped the career of the young orientalist Louis-Constantine-Henri-Francois Xavier De Clercq. Charles-Jean suggested to Emmanuel-Guillaume Rey, an historian of Crusader castles, that he take De Clercq as his assistant on an expedition to Syria and Asia Minor that was being commissioned by the French Ministry of Public Instruction. De Clercq travelled with Rey from August to December 1859. He was already an accomplished photographer using the calotype technique of waxed paper negatives. This technique had been popularized by Gustave le Gray, who himself subsequently travelled in Egypt and Syria in the 1860s. Photography was beginning to be used extensively by serious travellers and it is not surprising that de Vogüé's party would have had some such equipment, as well as more traditional scholarly tools.

Waddington recorded his experiences and discoveries in two *Mémoires*, and in his *Mélanges de numismatique et de philologie (Numismatic and Philological Miscellanies, 1862)*, a compendium of all his published articles up to that date. He published *Inscriptions Greques et Latines de la Syrie* in 1870. Georges Perrot, who in 1909 produced the encomium on Waddington for the Académie des Inscriptions, wrote that Waddington and de Vogüé had greatly helped him when he was also planning to travel in Palestine and Egypt in January 1862. 'De Vogué and Waddington', wrote Perrot, 'knew all about the countries we planned to visit: the ways, the means of transport, the best, or at any rate the least bad lodgings. They mapped out our route and individual stages. They helped us organize our caravans, obtaining for us tents, horses, both saddle horses and baggage animals, and the services of a dragoman who had the reputation of being one of the most intelligent and honest of that profession.'

Waddington and de Vogüé were relaxed travelling companions, the former also being a devout Christian, though in the Reformed tradition. De Vogüé commented later that Waddington had tremendous endurance. However long the stage, by sun or rain, he never seemed tired. If the wind tore out their tent pegs and they had to take refuge in some local habitation, de Vogüé would lie awake all night, tormented by bed bugs or mosquitoes. But Waddington would sleep through it all, awaking as refreshed as if he had spent the night in his own bed in Paris.

Waddington never bothered with the services of those facilitators whom ordinary tourists entrusted with the organization, direction and furnishing of their caravans. He just had two Albanian guards who served him devotedly and with whom he could converse with the smattering of Turkish he had acquired originally in Asia Minor eight years earlier.

In 1869, de Vogüé paid another visit to Palestine, partly in connection with the opening of the Suez Canal and partly to check for publication the report of an exploration of the Dead Sea carried out by his predecessor at the Académie des Inscriptions et Belles-Lettres, the duc de Luynes; the results were finally published in 1875. At the same time, Captain Warren's researches for the Palestine Exploration Fund at the Temple of Jerusalem vindicated de Vogüé's earlier theories about the site, and de Vogüé was delighted to visit Warren's subterranean excavations with him.

After the collapse of the Second Empire in 1870, de Vogüé was able to return to public life and a diplomatic career. By now an authority on the Holy Land and the Levant, in 1871, de Vogüé was appointed Ambassador of France in Constantinople by the new French President, Adolphe Thiers. He took along as his attaché his nephew, Eugène-Melchior de Vogüé, which resulted in the younger man also becoming an orientalist and traveller in the Holy Land through his next posting as Secretary at the French Embassy in Cairo.[7] De Vogüé had already assessed the weakness of the Ottoman Porte and the intrigues of the Europeans when he was first in Constantinople in 1853. Now, he was responsible for dealing with it first hand.

In the meantime, de Vogüé's friend Waddington had become a full-time, elected politician.[8] Waddington first served as the Minister of Public Instruction (essentially Minister of Education) for a month in 1873 and later for a little over a year between March 1876[9] and May 1877. This was the ministry under whose auspices he himself had gone to the Levant in 1861. After his stint as Minister of Education, Waddington was French Foreign Minister from 1877 to February 1879 and then Prime Minister till December 1879. He was Prime Minister at the height of the delicate negotiations over the Egyptian debt that ultimately resulted in the deposition and exile of the Khedive Ismail Pasha.

In 1875, while his political allies were still in power, de Vogüé was appointed French Ambassador to Vienna, and he held the post during the 1878 Congress of Berlin, which gave Cyprus to Britain and unofficially Tunisia to France and at which his former travelling companion, William Waddington, was the leader of the French delegation during his period as French Minister of Foreign Affairs.[10]

The changes in the French government at the end of 1879 turned against de Vogüé and his patrons and forced his final retirement from national political life, though he served for 30 years as a local councillor for the commune of Léré in the Cher region of France. Throughout his ambassadorial postings, de Vogüé continued to write and publish. He had inherited the title of Marquis on the death of his father in 1877. Now, de Vogüé devoted himself to archival research and to writing histories of his clan and of the château of Vogüé.

The family papers, including many boxes relating to Charles-Jean, were deposited in the French National Archives in 1994. The material has been used by Charles-Jean's biographers but must be a treasure trove for a scholar making a more detailed study as it was in letters home to his parents that de Vogüé described his travels. He tended to write publicly about his travels only as a preamble to scholarly descriptions of architecture and archaeology. Among the most useful secondary sources is the 'Notice sur la vie et les travaux de M. le Marquis de Vogüé' by René Cagnat in: *Comptes rendus des séances de l'Académie des Inscriptions et Belles-Lettres, 62e année*, N. 6, 1918: pp. 442–73.

The second major biographical source is the book by de Vogüé's son Louis, published in 1948. Like his father's own family history this was called *Une Famille Vivaroise*, qualified as the sequel to that work and sub-titled 'From the Vivarais to the Berry'. It covered the lives of Louis' grandfather Léonce and his father Charles-Jean using original letters, in addition to his father's published works.

Of de Vogüé's own extensive writings several have been re-published in facsimile editions or can be read via Gallica, the Bibliotheque Nationale de France's digital archive. These books bear witness to the thoroughness of his research, the brilliance of his drawings and his earnest, occasionally purple, writing style when narrating his travels. An 1864 copy of *Le Temple de Jérusalem* was advertised for sale in 2015 at £3,800 (originals of his illustrated works are very rare).

De Vogüé had been a member of the French Asiatic Society since 1856 and of the Society of Antiquaries since 1860. In 1868, he was nominated a member of the Académie des Inscriptions et Belles-Lettres, three years after Waddington achieved the same distinction. He assisted in the compilation of the *Corpus Inscriptionum Semiticarum*, published by the Académie des Inscriptions, a work supervised by Ernst Renan from 1881 until his death in 1892, and subsequently by de Vogüé himself. At one time, de Vogüé was considered as important a pioneering scholar as Austen Henry Layard, Heinrich Schliemann or Arthur Evans because he provided the foundations and inspiration for later scholars in his field.

From 1891, he was President of the Society of the History of France. In 1901, in the same year that Edmond Rostand was elected to seat 31, de Vogüé was elected to the Académie Française in seat 18, joining in that distinguished company among others, Anatole France and Pierre Loti. The most famous previous occupant of seat 18 was Alexis de Toqueville, who held it from 1841 to 1860 and had been a patron to Charles-Jean when the young man was starting his diplomatic career.[11] One of the 40 other members when de Vogüé attained his seat was his other political patron, Adolphe Thiers.[12]

In old age, de Vogüé was showered with awards and accolades. The Festschrift in honour of his 80th birthday was introduced by Gaston Maspero and included contributions from scholars in England, America and Germany, as well as in France and in Switzerland from Édouard Naville.

Charle-Jean's final trip to Jerusalem was made over two weeks in February and March 1911 when he was aged 82. He still hoped to correct errors and omissions from his earlier work. In 1912, after the trip, he published a small and nostalgic book, *Jérusalem hier et aujourd'hui*, revisiting his 50 years of experiences in the Levant. As his biographer paraphrased:

> The Jerusalem of 1911 was one where you arrived and left by train from a non-descript train station, rather than on foot or horseback. The Garden of Gethsemane, which fifty years earlier had retained the aspect which it had the eve of the first Holy Thursday when the bare earth bore the prostrate body of the Saviour and soaked up his tears, was now surrounded by walls, adorned with flowers, clipped box hedges and raked paths. All those who have travelled in a country still primitive, full of

poetry and great memories and who return there some years later will recognise the disillusion which de Vogüé experienced when faced with these distressing but inevitable improvements of civilisation.

As for William Waddington, he spent the last ten years of his life as French Ambassador to the Court of St James, in London, and was simultaneously the elected senator for the department of l'Aisne. He died at the age of 67 in 1894, and is buried in Père Lachaise cemetery. Charles-Jean de Vogüé died in 1916 aged 87, and is buried in Boulleret, near Bourges.

This brief account of a member of the French petty aristocracy and one Anglo-Frenchman who briefly ruled France barely scratches the surface of the importance of these travellers and their work. Their public careers rose and fell depending on which faction was in power in 19th century France. But like Renaissance men, and men of the Enlightenment, they combined a life in public service with one of travel, scholarship and research. Through birth and connections, they could become distinguished members of the French establishment. Through their energy and diligence, they joined that coterie of enthusiasts who have preserved for us something of the past wonders of the Levant.

Acknowledgments

Thank you to Arnaud Crevolin of the Chateau de Vogüé, Ardèche, who was helpful with sources and who obtained permission from the family for use of the photograph of the sketch of the Marquis J-C M de Vogüé, taken by Russell McGuirk at the chateau in July 2015. I am grateful to the current Marquis de Vogüé for this permission.

Endnotes

1   In 1878, together with the photographer Albert Poche (1842–1929), of Aleppo, de Vogüé published a monograph on this church – Saint Simeon Stylite.

2   *Je serais presque tenté de refuser le nom de ruines à une série de villes presque intactes ou, du moins, dont tous les éléments se retrouvent, renversés quelquefois, jamais dispersés, dont la vue transporte le voyageur au milieu d'une civilisation perdue et lui en révèle, pour ainsi dire, tous les secrets ; en parcourant ces rues désertes, ces cours abandonnées, ces portiques où la vigne s'enroule autour des colonnes mutilées, on ressent une impression analogue à celle que Ton éprouve à Pompéi, moins complète, car le climat de la Syrie n'a pas défendu ses trésors comme les cendres du Vésuve, mais plus nouvelle, car la civilisation que l'on contemple est moins connue que celle du siècle d'Auguste.*
    Introduction to the three-volume book de Vogüé subsequently published on the architecture and archaeological ruins of central Syria, *Syrie Central: Architecture civile et religieuse du Ier au VIIe siècle (1865–1877).*

3   Quotations from *Fragments d'un journal de voyager en Orient (1855)*, translated from the French. See bibliography.

4   *Les Églises de la Terre Sainte* – Introduction.

5   *Syrie Centrale* – Avertissement.

6 *Jerusalem, hier et aujourd'hui.*
7 Eugène-Melchior published his *Syrie, Palestine, Mont Athos* in 1876 as well as *Boulacq et Saqquarah* in 1879, followed by *Chez les Pharaons* in the same year. However, following a posting to St Petersburg, where in 1878 he married the daughter of General Annenkoff, aide-de-camp to the Tzar, Eugène-Melchior eventually became a Russian rather than Middle East specialist.
8 Waddington was elected to the Chamber of Deputies in February 1871.
9 Waddington was elected to the Senate in January 1876.
10 Waddington was always considered a better scholar than politician by his more ambitious rivals, but his diplomatic successes have been recognized by subsequent historians.
11 De Vogüé was himself succeeded in Chari 18 by two famous military leaders: Maréchal Ferdinand Foch, in the seat from 1918 to 1929, and Philippe Pétain, who held it from 1929 to 1952.
12 De Vogüé's nephew, Eugène Melchior, had been elected to the Academie earlier, based on his work on Russian literature and history. He occupied seat 39 from 1888 to 1910.

Bibliography

Cagnat René. *Notice sur la vie et les travaux de M. le Marquis de Vogüé*. In: Comptes rendus des séances de l'Académie des Inscriptions et Belles-Lettres, 62e année, N. 6, 1918: pp. 442–73.

Macadam, Henry I. (1991) *William Henry Waddington, Orientalist and Diplomat*. Arabic and Islamic Studies in Memory of Malcolm H. Kerr. Eds. Seikaly, Baalbaki, Dodd. American University of Beirut.

Perrot, Georges. *Notice sur la vie et les travaux de William-Henry Waddington*. Paris in: Comptes rendus des séances de l'Académiedes Inscriptions et Belles-Lettres, 53e année, N. 11, 1909:. pp. 876–938.

Vogüé, J-C Melchior (1858) *Fragments d'un Journal de Voyage en Orient*. E. Thunot et Cie. Kissinger Legacy Reprints.

Vogüé, J-C Melchior (1912) *Jerusalem Hier et Aujourd'hui*. Librairie Plon – Hachette Digital reprint from Bibliotheque Nationale de France copy.

Vogüé, J-C Melchior (1860) *Les Eglises de la Terre Sainte*. Paris. Victor Dedron.

Vogüé, J-C Melchior (1865–77) *Syrie central: Architecture civile et religieuse du Ier au VIIe siècle*, 3 vols. Paris. J. Baudrey

De Vogüé, Louis-Antoine Melchior (1948) *Une famille vivaroise suite. Du Vivarais au Berry*. Reims, Impr. du Nord-Est

16

In Constantinople During the Crimean War

Peta Rée

Accounts by two different travellers of their experiences in the same place at the same time may not be too uncommon; that the writers should be husband and wife is unusual. The accounts of Mr and Mrs Hornby of their time in Constantinople in 1855–56, during the Crimean War, are complementary, though differing for various reasons.

Mr Hornby was there to do an important job, and was very occupied by it and the people he was dealing with; Mrs Hornby had the leisure to observe her surroundings. His account is but a few chapters in his autobiography written many years later; hers is told in contemporary letters to her family and friends. He is blunt, irreverent and displays an easy-tempered humour; she is deeply sensitive to atmosphere and sympathetic to the people around her.

Edmund Grimani Hornby was born in 1825. His father came from Yorkshire, his mother from Venice. In 1841, he became private secretary to his uncle, the British Minister at Lisbon and, in 1848, was called to the Bar. In 1850, Hornby was visiting Weybridge in Surrey when he rescued a girl who had fallen out of her punt, dragging her to shore by her crinoline. 'She was a girl of pluck,' said he, and so he married her.

She was Emilia Bithnia, the beautiful and accomplished daughter of a 'cultured lady who ran a boarding-house in Weybridge and had a vaguely deceased Italian husband', Colonel Maceroni, who had been aide-de-camp to General Murat. (Fig.16.1)

In 1855, Edmund was asked by the Foreign Secretary to go to Constantinople to manage the loan of £5 million that the British had granted to the Turks to enable them to fight the war in the Crimea against Russia. Edmund's instructions were 'casually given' (his phrase) by the Chancellor of the Exchequer: 'All I had to do was to get the money from the Bank of England out to Turkey as it was required and by the cheapest means; to keep accurate accounts of its expenditure, and above all to see that it went to the troops and was not spent on palaces, harams and backshish… Thus fully accoutred, I sallied forth as a knight of finance.'

Emilia went with him. Eighteen months into the Crimean War, on 30 August 1855, at Marseilles, they boarded the *Simois*, a steamer crowded with French soldiers bound for the Crimea, their horses stalled on the deck, and below a hold full of packages addressed to Florence Nightingale at Scutari, and to the Army in the east.

Fig 16.1 Emelia Hornby with her dogs Fuad and Arslan from
Constantinople during the Crimean War, 1863.

A week later, Emilia was on deck to 'admire the white castles of the Dardanelles... we passed some great ships-of-war, French and English, every sail set to a fair wind, and crowded with troops'.

Constantinople was reached after a night of violent tempest:

> But as we approached the Golden Horn the clouds were breaking up... the wind gradually dropped... and the beautiful city... burst upon our charmed sight... There was Mount Olympus, its summit glittering with snow, there the shadowy islands of the Propontis, there the sparkling Bosphorus, gay with innumerable caiques, then the dark cypress groves and white hospital of Scutari, where the 'heroic Miss Nightingale lay sick', then beautiful Stamboul itself, with its crowning mosque of Santa Sophia and lofty minarets.

They landed at Pera,

> among most wretched, dilapidated wooden houses, on a filthy, broken, crowded pavement, amidst a motley of Greeks and Turks, soldiers and sailors, fruit-sellers and money-changers... We soon found a couple of porters, whose backs were bowed almost to a crescent by constantly carrying heavy loads; and after a rapid walk up the steep and narrow streets, after being jostled by strings of donkeys, after having narrowly escaped being trampled on by caparisoned horses, treading on dead rats, melon rinds, and cats, – confused, enchanted with the without, disgusted beyond measure at the within, – we arrived, tired and almost breathless, at Mysseri's Hotel. They have given me such a delightful room, with four large windows looking down the Golden Horn, and on the distant mountains.'

At meals:

> One can scarcely see to the end of the table. Almost all the guests are English and French officers, either in uniform, or in odd and semi-eastern costume – long beards and sunburnt faces. The din of so many voices is almost as confusing, I should think, as the roar of cannon at Sebastopol; but by degrees I began to pick up a few sentences here and there....
>
> 'Come and try a day or two over there,' says one handsome boy-officer to another, 'I can give you a plank and some capital straw in my tent, within a quarter of an hour from the Redan. You won't mind a shell now and then.'
>
> 'Beastly shell!' drawled a tremendously tall, affected Rifle; 'spoiled the best dinner we had for a long time, and killed that very amusing fellow Ross, who sat next to me. It was par-ti-cu-larly awkward; for the tent fell down upon us. And we were obliged to crawl out.'
>
> 'I felt quite out of sorts when it was all over – missed my arm so confoundedly, and got no dinner, for poor Smith had asked me to dine with him, and he was killed an hour before.'
>
> You may easily imagine how it startles one at first to hear all the horrible incidents of war spoken of after this fashion.... It seems indeed a strange war-gathering here. Everyone is anxious for news from Sebastopol; and even the sick and wounded are angry and impatient at being away from the scene of action, and from the tremendous attack which it is expected will soon take place. Numbers of English and French ships, crowded with troops, are constantly going up to Balaklava... What a relief it will be to one's mind when this dreadful place is taken!

A few days later, came the news of Sebastopol's fall to the French on 10 September:

> The Bosphorus on Monday morning presented a gay and beautiful spectacle. All the ships-of-war and crowds of merchant ships of all nations were decked with flags, and many large and splendid ones floated from the principal balconies. The roar of guns from the different vessels was tremendous, – enough to startle the echoes of Olympus, whose snows glittered brightly above the clouds of smoke... The firing began again at eight in the evening; and as far as noise and the rattle of windows went, gave us a good idea of a bombardment. All the ships... were illuminated, as far as the eye could reach. Some of the French men-of-war burned coloured lights... Pera and Stamboul glittered with lamps; palaces and minarets illuminated... like pale clusters of stars shining here and there in the deep grey light and over the shifting ripples of the sea.

Sadly, the fall of Sebastopol did not mean the end of the war, which was to drag on for another six months.

Emilia Hornby commented, 'Edmund has been very much engaged.' When he introduced himself to his French colleague in the negotiations, the 64-year-old M. de Cadrossi, surprised at Edmund's youthful appearance (he was just 30), asked how long he had been engaged in the Department of Finance. 'On my assuring him that I had never seen the inside of it and that I knew nothing of finance, but had journeyed expressly to Constantinople to give him the pleasure of teaching me, he laughed heartily and declared nothing could please him more. We became excellent friends....'

The first interview with the British Ambassador, Lord Stratford de Redcliffe, went less well, though Edmund describes it as 'a decidedly funny one' and wrote:

> He received me in his grey dressing gown in his study... looking anything but pleased and without offering to shake hands. I had hardly finished my bow before he let fly at the Government for not appointing the man he had nominated – a Greek and competent financier and one who had his confidence. Having abused the Foreign Office to his heart's content, he wound up... by wishing them joy of their nominee – meaning me – to whom, of course, he could not be expected to render any assistance, and therefore I was at liberty to manage the loan as I thought fit, as that could alone have been the intention of the Government in sending me out. I was thunderstruck.... However, his venerable appearance [he was nearly 70 at this time], as well as his evident conviction that he had been ill-used by the Foreign Office, made me keep a civil tongue in my head and I let him finish without saying a word; but as he was walking to his dressing room with an evident intention of disappearing, I ventured on a placid "Good Morning my Lord", adding that as it was his intention not to assist me it was my intention to telegraph to the Foreign Office begging to be relieved from my duties, as without his assistance, and perhaps in the face of his opposition, I simply could not and would not even attempt to perform them, and without adding a word left the room.
>
> On the stairs I met Lady Stratford... she put out her hand, saying, "Mr Hornby, I think, I am afraid my husband was not quite himself this morning as he was very much put out at Mr— not being appointed; but I hope you will not take to heart anything he may have said, as – with this terrible war going on – he is sadly harassed and overworked."

This was said, and clearly meant, so kindly, that Edmund could not vent his anger on her 'and then there was a worn, anxious look on her nice intelligent English face and in her eyes that plainly told that all the labour did not rest on the Ambassador's shoulders... I simply said that I was afraid my visit had been at an inopportune moment; but I suppose I looked as if that visit would be my last, as she added, "Don't say or do anything until you hear either from me or Lord Stratford."'

Edmund returned to Emilia, telling her 'to be prepared to leave by the next mail, and to calm my ruffled temper took her for a walk along the shore of the Bosphorus... The loveliness of the scene soon soothed me, and as for my wife, she was enchanted – to leave she declared to be simply impossible, and if I did she would remain and manage the loan herself.'

Back at the hotel, they found Lady Stratford had left a note inviting them to dinner, and begging Emilia to bring him nolens volens. They were received most kindly by both Lord and Lady Stratford.

After dinner Lord Stratford came up to Edmund and said, 'I am afraid – nay indeed I am certain – I was most unjustly rude to you this morning. Will you accept an old man's apology who has much to trouble him?'

Edmund stopped him at once and said, 'I have already forgotten everything except your and Lady Stratford's kind welcome to my wife and myself.' From that moment to the day of his death, Edmund and Lord Stratty as he used to call him, were the best of friends.

Emilia describes the Christmas party at the British Embassy. (Fig.16.2) She travelled from the hotel in a 'ridiculously painted and gilded sedan-chair'. Few people were about, and the houses were closely shut up: 'Every now and then a dark figure steals by, wrapped in a dark cloak, and you feel, what is so strange to the English, that murder lurks in every dark place. Edmund, with several officers, walked by my chair. The street dogs eyed us suspiciously from their lairs.' A guard of Turkish soldiers was drawn up in the narrow street leading to the palace, and various sightseers had gathered – 'Greeks, Turks and groups of mounted officers in full dress look so well by torchlight, – very different certainly to the black coats and carriages of a London dinner party.'

The Embassy was decorated with orange and lemon trees in both flower and fruit, with myrtle and scarlet cacti, and even holly, though sadly it had no berries. Lady Stratford entered with her daughters behind her, and at her side a modest nun-like figure in a black dress and a close cap. It was Florence Nightingale. Emilia felt quite dumb as she observed her 'wasted figure and the short brown hair combed over her forehead like a child's, cut so, when her life was despaired of from fever' a short time before.

Fig 16.2 Pera House, the British Embassy in Constantinople built in 1844 to the designs of Sir George Gilbert Scott.

> Miss Nightingale is by no means striking in appearance... she is very slight, rather above the middle height; her face is long and thin. But this may be from recent illness and great fatigue. She has a very prominent nose, slightly Roman; and small dark eyes, kind, yet penetrating; but her face does not give you at all the idea of great talent. She looks a quiet, persevering, orderly, ladylike woman ....
>
> After dinner there was great fun; for all the midshipmen of the different men-of-war lying here were invited; such fine, brave-looking little fellows!... They came marching in, looking so fresh and nice in their little, old-fashioned blue coatees with gilt buttons.

A little overawed at first, when Christmas games were started, in which almost everyone joined, 'the middies were wild with delight... their feeling of the excessive fun of playing with their Admiral, Sir Houston Stewart, was intense.' Florence Nightingale, too weak to join in, 'sat on a sofa, laughing until the tears came into her eyes. I said to her, "How delighted the mothers of these boys would be to see them now!" She replied, "Ah! The poor mothers!"'

Emilia thought, looking around, what a curious group it was playing children, even the children having acted their part in the fighting. The Admiral told Emilia that most of the boys had been under fire, and had behaved gallantly. Edmund had charge of them to their hotel, and 'we were a merry torchlight party scrambling through the quaint and narrow streets. It seemed so odd to see such little fellows going to an hotel alone in a country like this.'

'As to the Commission, nothing has been done as yet,' Emilia had written in November. At first the Turks had thought that Edmund and M. de Cadrossi 'were quiet, gentlemanly men, whom, no doubt it would be easy to manage... but after further negotiation, and when Edmund had sent in his plans of operation, they changed their opinion as to the firmness of the English and French Commissioners.' They were bent (three or four of them especially, who were furious at the idea of not being able to finger some thousands for their own private purse) on getting the whole of the loan into their own hands, though they knew full well that it was only the solemn agreement that England and France should direct the disbursement, that it was lent. Edmund had asked that no more instalments should be sent out, and was nervous about how much the Commissariat was already sitting on.

Eventually, things began to move. Cadrossi did the office work and accounts, while Edmund went about 'to different parts of the country where the Turkish troops were supposed to be, to vouch that the men were paid and not cheated'. He soon found that, whatever pay lists and commissariat lists said, it was necessary to count the soldiers and ask them if they had been paid, and what pay was in arrears. Clothing, provisions and ammunition also had to be checked. Several times, Edmund had to get Turkish officers suspended for activities of malversation and embezzlement. The officers, declared Edmund, were not to be trusted, 'either in the field or out of it'.

This stricture did not apply to the Uzbashis and Bimbashis, the non-commissioned officers – 'these were really splendid fellows, selected from the ranks for courage and knowledge of regimental duty – they led the troops under fire – and to these men is due the gallant front the rank and file so constantly showed when before an enemy.'

One social occasion was mentioned by both the Hornbys – the fancy-dress ball given by the Stratfords in February 1856, to which the Sultan Abdul Mejid was invited. (Fig.16.3) Emilia wrote:

> He walked quietly up the ballroom with Lord and Lady Stratford, their daughters, and a gorgeous array of Pashas in the rear... He was dressed in a plain dark-blue frock-coat, with cuffs and collar of crimson, studded with brilliants ... he stood looking about him with the undisguised pleasure and simplicity of a child... He looks languid and careworn, but, when spoken to, his fine dark eyes brighten up and he smiles the most frank and winning of smiles... I am quite charmed by the Sultan... so touchingly kind and simple and sorrowful.

Suddenly, a veiled Turkish lady appeared, hanging on the arm of General Mansfield. At first, she seemed somewhat timid, but soon she began to go boldly up to the English officers and stare in their faces. Then, bolder still, she began

Fig 16.3 Lord and Lady Stanhope welcome Sultan Abdul Mejid at the Embassy Ball February 1856. (© Pictorial Press Ltd / Alamy Stock Photo).

'intriguing' (Edmund's word) with the Sultan himself – 'Poor Abdul, I do not think he ever laughed so much in his life as during the quarter of an hour the lady poured into his ear a lot of witty nonsense.' In vain, the Grand Vizier tried to draw her away, but 'all he got for his pains was significant motions of the Sultan's hands suggestive that his interference was not welcome, and from the lady a torrent of Turkish eloquence such perhaps as never flowed from a harem favourite's lips.' The Vizier sought Lord Stratford's help, finally Lady Stratford succeeded in diverting the Sultan's attention. 'The lady then "intrigued"; with all the Ministers in turn, giving it to them hot and strong.'

Emilia says the lady was making such remarks as "Ah! You see we are coming out now. No more cages for us. We are going to see the world and judge for ourselves, and love whom we like."

At length, the fair one was unmasked – and revealed as Percy Smythe, one of the English Diplomatic Secretaries, a thorough Turkish, Arabic and Persian scholar. It seems an amazingly 'politically incorrect' prank, but was apparently accepted without offence, probably because the Sultan had been so delighted by it.

So much for parties; but a bloody and horrible war still raged on. As part of Edmund's job, he had to go up to the Crimea – 'I only got up... for a day or two but what I saw there sickened my stomach for months.' With the signing of a peace treaty the war ended in March 1856.

By this time, the Hornbys had removed from the environs of Constantinople to a house (or kiosk, as Emilia calls it) in a village called Orta-Kioy, from which Edmund rode nine miles each day into the city. Emilia was always relieved to see him back, for the Pashas were very angry that they were being prevented from getting their hands on the Loan.

On 18 March 1856, Emilia's neighbour brought news of the peace; 'The Emperor of Russia is at peace with the Emperor of Turkey... The village watchmen went through the streets, striking their staves on the ground... and chanting the news of Peace. They ended by asking a few piastres from each house, as a subscription towards lighting up the Greek churches. In the evening, all the ships were illuminated and lamps were hung out at the gates of the palaces by the edge of the Bosphorus.'

Emilia and her friend Mrs Brett went up to Balaklava towards the end of April, to see the grand encampment at Sebastopol before it broke up. 'We have pressing and hospitable invitations from all our Crimean acquaintance, to spare tents, clean straw, ruined out-houses, and capital horses and mules.'

After a miserably rough voyage up the Black Sea, it was extremely depressing to arrive at Balaklava to find the harbour so crowded with shipping that they had to anchor outside. Fortunately, the Commandant at Balaklava, Colonel Hardinge, invited them to stay at his Headquarters. (Fig.16.4)

At the crowded harbour of Balaklava, they saw

Fig 16.4 House of the Governor of Balaclava, used as a Headquarters by Colonel Hardinge, and where the Hornbys stayed.

the vast preparations for the return home of a great army! Some of the countless ships were taking in crowds of hurrying soldiers; others, loads of shot and shell... commissariat stores of all kinds, Russian cannons, vast quantities of iron, soldiers' clothing and accoutrements. The railway cars were busily at work, transporting huge bales and packages... After hearing all the horrors of this place when our army landed – men and horses sticking in mud and mire, – it seems now, with its railway and fine roads, a marvellous picture of skill and industry. People in England can hardly form an idea of what our officers and men have accomplished; of the gigantic difficulties overcome at a fearful cost.

Colonel Hardinge's headquarters, which had been the house of the Governor of Balaklava, was a low-roofed, white building with a large central room, off which others led. Emilia, Mrs Brett and their two maids were lodged in the former chamber of the Governor's wife.

Colonel Hardinge had given strict orders that nothing should be disturbed, and even himself watered a large and beautifully trained hay-plant in the window, which had evidently been a great favourite with the owner. In another recess of the window lay a touching evidence of hasty flight; it was a little doll's cap, with the gay ribbons not yet quite sewn on, and a small toy of seed-beads, of many colours, containing tiny rings and necklaces, – threaded perhaps with childish delight just as our great ships of war were coming up.

It was a shock, when Emilia opened the wardrobe, to see the Governor's uniform hanging there. 'There were two rents on the breast of the coat; I suppose the poor man had cut off his Orders in the hurry of flight.' The two ladies were glad to remind each other that the Governor and his family were alive and well.

On that first day, they walked up to the heights of Balaklava, by the old Genoese castle. 'On one side is a solitary and magnificent view of the sea and cliffs; but pass a sharp and lofty turning, and the crowded port beneath, and all the active military movements, are instantly before your eyes.'

> We then walked among the scattered wooden huts a little lower down... beautifully neat and clean, with broad and well-swept roads between. Many of the occupants evidently took great pleasure in the names so carefully painted on some of them, – perhaps the same as those in which their wives and children lived in England. 'Albert Terrace', 'Prospect Cottage', amused us so much, and especially one tiny wooden hut, dignified with the appellation of 'Marine Villa'. Many of these had pretty little flower-borders, about two feet wide, with not a weed to be seen, and carefully watered. Higher up, we came to Miss Nightingale's hospital huts, built of the same long planks, and adorned with the same neatly-bordering flowers.

The next day they set out further afield, Mrs Brett riding, and Emilia and the rest of the party in an ambulance, drawn by four mules. 'We came to the different town-like encampments of our army, scattered over the vast steppes and plains... Every moment something ingenious met the eye... nicely contrived and sheltered little gardens, – tub sentry boxes, prettily roofed with turf, a fir-tree planted on each side by way of ornament, – neat little fowls' houses, and flourishing-looking cocks and hens sunning themselves at the doors, – a cosy turf dog-kennel ...'

The white tents of the French army, which could be seen in the distance, with a glimpse of the sea before them, formed a beautiful picture.

> A more touching one was the wayside cemetery of the 33rd Regiment. The graves were very thick, and rows of white stones, inscribed with many a gallant name stood out in sad array against the clear blue sky. Soldiers were busy laying turf around them, planting arbor vitae and juniper trees, and placing shot and shell at the head and foot of each. The little paths were also bordered with fresh green turf; and it seems to have been a labour of love to leave these graves as fair as possible.

Further on was the ravine called the Valley of the Shadow of Death (the scene of the ill-fated charge of the Light Brigade). They were not the only visitors:

> We met a large party of Russians officers, driving handsome droshkys, with four horses abreast. They bowed to us with the greatest politeness, and each party regarded the other with interest....
>
> We stopped at the foot of the ravine, and collected as relics a few pieces of the vast quantities of shot and shell scattered about. The ground was torn up in every direction, the banks of the little mountain stream broken down here and there, and its clear waters bubbling over more shot and fragments of shell than pebbles.

Emilia, Mrs Brett and the rest of their party toiled up the height of the Malakoff,

> looking frowning and formidable still, though conquered... it seemed almost startling not to hear the cries and din of war... torn and empty cartridge boxes lay thick on the ground – shot and shell, as hail after a storm, – here a torn shoulder-knot, there a broken scabbard. It was sunset when we gained the tower of the Malakoff; and oh what a magnificent spectacle it was... the distant range of mountains, the ruined city and the sunken ships, – the Mamelon, the Redan, the Garden Battery, – all the grand plan of attack and defence, bathed in the purple and violet light of the sun's parting rays!

At the Redan, they saw

> the sun sink beneath the waves, bathing the whole scene and every object, from the broken cannon to the little purple iris flowers springing up on the trampled earth in the same unclouded blaze of golden light. Then in the profound silence, when the grey twilight came falling sadly over all, it seemed to us that the splendour that had entranced us was like the glory our brave men had gained, and the darkness, like the pain and sorrow for their loss.

They passed through the

> vast camp in profound darkness, excepting the light afforded by the large, bright stars – encampment after encampment each marked out by its numerous twinkling lights stretching far and wide over the hills and plains and valleys... Everything was profoundly tranquil, only now and then we passed a soldier wrapped in his long cloak... It was bitterly cold and we were glad to hear the challenge of a sentinel, on arriving at last at Balaklava....
> Is it not well to have a few days in one's life like this?

Bibliography

Lady Hornby (1863) *Constantinople during the Crimean War*. London, Richard Bentley.
Sir Edmund Hornby (1928) *An Autobiography*. London, Constable.

Joun Encounter: Alexander William Kinglake meets Lady Hester Stanhope

Paul Starkey

This chapter will consider the circumstances that brought together two of the most notable English Middle Eastern travellers of the first half of the nineteenth century: Alexander William Kinglake (1809–91), whose work entitled *Eothen; or, Traces of travel brought home from the East* – a travelogue of a young Englishman's journey through Syria, Palestine and Egypt in the mid-1830s – was first published in 1844 and has since become a classic of Middle Eastern travel writing;[1] and the eccentric adventurer and traveller Lady Hester Stanhope (1776–1839) who, in 1831, had settled in the Lebanese mountain village of Joun,[2] in the Chouf region near Sidon, from where for a time she wielded considerable authority over the surrounding area, and where she later died.

Both A. W. Kinglake and Lady Hester Stanhope (who in some respects form a study in contrasts) will already be well known to many readers – the adventures of Lady Hester in particular having attracted the attention of a considerable number of writers and biographers, including, most recently, full-length accounts of her life by Lorna Gibb[3] and Kirsten Ellis.[4] The extent of her reputation as a great British eccentric may best be gauged by the fact that she merits a place (along with Sir Richard Burton and Kinglake himself, among others) in the 'Great British Nutters' blogspot, on which she is introduced with the words: 'Lady Hester Stanhope: Kooky Desert Queen… They don't come madder than Lady Hester Stanhope. They don't come much braver either.'[5]

Being mainly concerned here with the latter period of her life, we need devote no more than a few lines to Lady Hester's early years. Born in 1776 to Lady Hester Pitt and Charles Stanhope, she was the granddaughter of Pitt the Elder and niece of William Pitt the Younger, who served two spells as Prime Minister between 1783 and 1806, and for whom she acted as a hostess and performed other duties – by virtue of which she was awarded an annual pension of several hundred pounds, which she enjoyed to the end of her days. Her early life was perhaps more noteworthy for a series of largely unsatisfactory love affairs, and it was probably as a result of a romantic disappointment that Lady Hester (who had already travelled abroad) took the decision in 1810 to leave England for good and embark on a long sea voyage, taking with her an entourage that included not only Michael Bruce, who became her lover, but also her private physician, Dr Charles Meryon, who later served as her first biographer. Things, however, did not go according to plan. After visiting Athens, where the poet Lord Byron is said to have dived into the sea to greet her, the party travelled to Constantinople, intending to proceed to Cairo, but before reaching Cairo they encountered a storm and were shipwrecked on Rhodes.

It is arguably at this point that the unbalanced, delusional streak in Lady Hester's personality first became apparent. As her party had lost all their clothes, they had to borrow Turkish costumes. Lady Hester refused to wear a veil, preferring to dress as a Turkish male, in robe, turban and slippers – an outfit that became more elaborate, and more varied, as she embarked on an extensive tour of the Middle East, visiting Damascus and Jerusalem, as well as Palmyra, where she was famously crowned 'Queen of the Desert'.[6] It is the last quarter or so of her life that most concerns us here, when, tired of wandering the Middle East, she decided to settle in the south of Lebanon; first, in the disused Mar Elias monastery in the village of 'Abra, near Sidon; then in another monastery, Dayr Mashmushah,[7] before eventually settling – again, in a former monastery – at Joun, a village about eight miles from Sidon, where she lived from 1831 until her death in 1839, and where she was visited by the considerably younger Alexander William Kinglake. Her residence, known locally as Dār al-Sitt,[8] was at the top of a hill, 'whence comers and goers might be seen on every side', as she reported to Dr Meryon – and may still be seen today, in a rather miserable condition, surrounded by its venerable olive trees, and marked (unusually) by a sign from the country's main motorway.[9]

Preceded by her formidable reputation, Lady Hester exercised an extraordinary authority over the surrounding area from her various residences, to such an extent that the Egyptian Ibrāhīm Pasha thought it advisable to seek her neutrality before invading Syria in 1832.[10] Like other travellers to the region both before and after her, she could not avoid becoming caught up in local sectarian disputes, so that, although at first she had been regarded favourably by the emir Bashīr Shihāb II (1767–1850),[11] the support that she provided for some hundreds of Druze refugees eventually turned his favour to hostility. Her real downfall seems to have been caused not so much by the local ethnic environment but her own inability to handle money. A famously hospitable character, she lived constantly beyond her means, and eventually found herself unable to pay her debts, dying in Joun in lonely penury, with her life apparently in pieces.

Even in death, she continued to cause controversy and confusion. In August 1988, as the Lebanese civil war entered its final phases, the British FCO received news that 'the earthly remains of Lady Hester Stanhope had been found in the hills around Sidon', and a series of frantic negotiations ensued, involving, inter alia, a missing skull and a grey cardboard box containing her remains, which was stored in the Ambassador's office, before they were re-interred in the garden of the British Ambassador's summer residence overlooking Beirut on 2 February 1989. Only on 23 June 2004, 165 years after her death, were her ashes thought to have been finally scattered across her garden in Joun – until, that is, one of her biographers visited the area some years later, only to be shown a container holding Lady Hester's remains, which had been duly gathered up from the garden by the local priest to be preserved for posterity.[12]

By contrast with that of Lady Hester Stanhope, the life of Alexander William Kinglake seems a rather conventional one – certainly less complicated and eccentric than Lady Hester's, though it was not without its excitements. He was born in the West Country in 1809 to a family of apparently Scottish descent, and educated at Eton and Trinity College, Cambridge. Called to the Bar in 1837, he built up a successful legal practice, but abandoned the law in 1856 to devote himself to public life and to writing about history, in which he had long had an interest. As a member of the Whig Party, he unsuccessfully contested one of the two Bridgwater (Somerset) Commons seats in 1852; standing again, he was elected in the 1857 general election and re-elected at the next two general elections. But on 26 February 1869, the Bridgwater result for the general election held the previous year was declared void on petition; no by-election was held, and following a Royal Commission finding of extensive corruption, the borough was disenfranchised, thus bringing Kinglake's political career to an end.

Both Lady Hester Stanhope and Alexander Kinglake left substantial bodies of writing of historical as well as literary importance. Three volumes of Lady Hester's memoirs, entitled *Memoirs of the Lady Hester Stanhope as related by herself in Conversations with her Physician*,[13] were published by Dr Meryon in 1845, and these were followed in 1846 by three further volumes, entitled *Travels of Lady Hester Stanhope*.[14] The interest of these memoirs goes well beyond that of 'ordinary' travellers in or to the Middle East, and the various ways of regarding her life are well illustrated by the different approaches of her two most recent biographers: to quote a review of Kirsten Ellis's book by Lesley McDowell:

> In Gibb's account, Lady Hester came across as hedonistic, often foolish, occasionally delusional and very capable of bad judgment. In Ellis's account, however, we have a very different Hester Stanhope: a woman who has inherited the mantle of her Prime Minister forebears, showing due leadership, courage under fire, and a mission to count in the imperial power games being played in the East... To read Gibb is to picture a dynamic, unstable, privileged aristocrat having adventures in the desert; to read Ellis is to encounter a strong-willed, passionate, politically astute individual trying to make the world a better place. The truth probably lies somewhere between the two.[15]

For his part, Alexander Kinglake's magnum opus was undoubtedly the massive, nine-volume *The Invasion of the Crimea*, published between 1863 and 1887.[16] The work reflects the author's interest in military history, as well as in travel, which had already led him to visit Algeria in 1845 to witness the French campaign, and to follow the British army to the Crimea in 1854. By contrast with this massive work, his only other literary production of major significance, *Eothen* (the work which concerns us here), is a rather slight work, of a couple of hundred or so modestly-sized pages; first published in London in 1844 (having previously been rejected by John Murray on account of its 'wicked spirit of jesting at everything'), it enjoyed an immediate success, and has subsequently been reprinted on numerous occasions.[17] The work that, on the evidence of the author's original preface, had been abandoned on two previous attempts at writing it, describes a Near Eastern journey undertaken a decade or so earlier, in 1834–35, before the author had settled on his legal career (a sort of 'gap year', if we may use modern terminology) and leads us from the frontier of the Ottoman Empire at Semlin[18] near Belgrade, through Constantinople and Smyrna [İzmir], to Cyprus, then on to modern-day Lebanon, Palestine and Jordan, then across the desert to Cairo, where the author visits the Sphinx and the Pyramids, before setting out again homewards by way of Damascus and Baalbec.

Described by Edward Said as an 'undeservedly famous and popular work... a pathetic catalogue of pompous ethnocentrisms and tiringly nondescript accounts of the Englishman's East',[19] it has to be admitted that *Eothen* (the title means 'from the early dawn' or 'from the East' in Greek) is not exactly an obvious candidate for the status of a 'classic' of travel writing. We start in Semlin, though without any idea of how the author got there; and are rudely dumped at the end of the book somewhere in the Taurus mountains, 'joyfully winding our way through the first of his rugged defiles'.[20] At times, Kinglake's route is obscure, and it is frequently unclear with whom the author is travelling at any particular stage. In many respects, the author seems lamentably ill-prepared for his journey: he knows 'hardly one word of Arabic', for example; he arrives at Cairo knowing no one in the place, and with no letters of introduction;[21] he heads off into the desert on the way from Cairo to Suez with the thought that 'although I might miss the line leading most directly to Suez, I could not well fail to find my way sooner or later to the Red Sea. The worst of it was that I had no provision of food or water with me and already I was beginning to feel thirst.'[22] In light of these passages (among others), Edward Said's observation that 'the form of such works as Kinglake's *Eothen* (1844)... is rigidly chronological and dutifully linear, as if what the [author was] describing was a shopping trip to an Oriental bazaar rather than an adventure'[23] seems curiously misplaced. It is indeed true that the book often seems less a travel account than a series of personal *vignettes* – in many of which, so it has been suggested, the main focus of the author is less on his surroundings than on his own reactions to them.

Arguably, the most interesting of Kinglake's descriptions are those of the plague – a hazard that he encountered at several points in his journey, though with most immediacy in Cairo, where he was 'awakened in the night by the wail of death in the next house, and another time by a like howl from the house opposite; and there were two or three minutes, I recollect, during which the howl seemed to be actually *running* along the street'.[24] Throughout it all, he remains cool and superior, at one point summarizing his situation by stating simply, and with what appears to be an almost inhuman lack of emotion: 'It so happened that most of the people with whom

I had anything to do during my stay in Cairo were seized with plague; and all these died.'[25] Indeed, all in all, Kinglake seems never to feel happier than when he is alone, for it is not so much the sights, the culture, or the people he encounters as his own experiences that provide him with his biggest thrills. Riding from Cairo to Suez, he records that:

> It was not without a sensation of awe that I swept with my sight the vacant round of the horizon, and remembered that I was all alone and unprovisioned in the midst of the arid waste; but this very awe gave tone and zest to the exultation with which I felt myself launched. Hitherto in all my wanderings I had been under the care of other people – sailors, Tatars, guides and dragomen had watched over my welfare, but now, at last, I was here in this African desert, and I *myself, and no other, had charge of my life*: I like the office well: I had the greater part of the day before me, a very fair dromedary, a fur pelisse, and a brace of pistols, but no bread, and worst of all, no water; for that I must ride – and ride I did.[26]

As a guidebook, the work would surely rate very poorly on any Google or Amazon scale: in Cairo, Kinglake opines, for example, that 'there is not much in the way of public buildings to admire at Cairo, but I saw one handsome mosque…';[27] while the principal outcome of his visit to the Sphinx is a series of reflections on the passage of time, concluding with the words: 'And we, we shall die, and Islam will wither away; and the Englishman, straining far over to hold his loved India, will plant a firm foot on the banks of the Nile and sit in the seats of the Faithful, and still that sleepless rock will lie watching and watching the works of the new busy race, with those same sad earnest eyes, and the same tranquil mien everlasting. You dare not mock at the Sphynx.'[28]

That said, it is fair to say that in his preface to the first edition, Kinglake had already covered himself against such charges: 'It is right to forewarn people', he observes,

> … that the book is quite superficial in its character. I have endeavoured to discard from it all valuable matter derived from the works of others, and it appears to me that my efforts in this direction have been attended with great success. I believe I may truly acknowledge that from all details of geographical discovery, or antiquarian research – from all display of 'sound learning and religious knowledge' – from all historical and scientific illustrations – from all useful statistics – from all political disquisitions – and from all good moral reflections, the volume is thoroughly free'.[29]

Amid this general attitude of studied detachment and superiority (not without a hint of anti-Semitism at times, one might add), Kinglake's account of his meeting with Lady Hester Stanhope in some respects seems out of place. Indeed, the author himself acknowledges in his preface that his approach to the writing of the chapter in question (which takes up roughly a tenth of the total work, in terms of the number of pages) has been somewhat different to the rest of the work, and declares that:

> My scheme of refusing to dwell upon matters which failed to interest my own feelings has been departed from in one instance – namely, in my detail of the late Lady Hester Stanhope's conversation on supernatural topics. The truth is, that I have been much questioned on this subject, and I thought that my best plan would be to write down at once all that I could ever have to say concerning the personage whose career has excited so much curiosity amongst Englishwomen. The result is, that my account of the lady goes to a length which is not justified either by the importance of the subject, or by the extent to which it interested the narrator.[30]

Having thus noted Kinglake's 'disclaimer', let us turn to his account of the meeting itself. Arriving in Beirut, Kinglake found that '[I]n all society the standing topic of interest was an Englishwoman (Lady Hester Stanhope) who lived in an old convent in the Lebanon range, at a distance of about a day's journey from the town [Beirut]. The lady's habit of refusing to see Europeans added the charm of mystery to a character which, even without that aid, was sufficiently distinguished to command attention.'[31]

Kinglake, in fact, was well placed to overcome Lady Hester's inhibitions about meeting Europeans, since his mother had been a childhood friend of hers, and indeed he makes reference to this in the letter he wrote to her requesting an interview.[32] He recalls that the name of Lady Hester, the 'Queen of the Desert',

> ... was made almost as familiar to me in my childhood as the name of Robinson Crusoe... The subject, however, died away, and from the ending of my childhood up to the period of my arrival in the Levant, I had seldom if ever heard a mentioning of [Lady Hester Stanhope]; but now wherever I went I was met by the name so familiar in sound, and yet so full of mystery... I heard it too connected with fresh wonders; for it was said that the woman was now acknowledged as an inspired being by the people of the mountains, and it was even hinted with horror that she claimed to be *more than a prophet*.'[33]

Lady Hester's reply arrived in due course, to the effect that 'it will be a great satisfaction to have an opportunity of enquiring after your mother'; and after negotiating his arrangements for the trek up to Joun, the author – having first 'enjoyed a dinner of an oriental kind' – was admitted to the presence of the Lady Prophetess for an interview that lasted until well after midnight, before being renewed and extended the following evening. The conversation during these several hours ranged widely, sustained by a regular supply of coffee and tchibouks, which are replenished from time to time by black slave girls. In the course of the conversation, Lady Hester related a number of incidents from her own life, and did outrageous impressions of Lord Byron and the Frenchman Lamartine; she also opined on the current political situation, describing Ibrahim Pasha, who had led the Egyptian invasion of Syria in 1831–32, as a 'bold, bad man'.[34] 'In truth', Kinglake noted, 'this half-ruined convent, guarded by the proud heart of an English gentlewoman, was the only spot throughout all Syria and Palestine in which the will of Mehemet Ali and his fierce lieutenant [Ibrahim] was not the law.'[35]

Race also formed a topic of conversation: Kinglake records that Lady Hester Stanhope 'set great value upon the ancient French, not Norman, blood', and rather cryptically adds that she had a 'vast idea of the Cornish miners on account of their race'.[36] Most of all, however, it was on the subject of religion, magic and the like on which the conversation turned:

> For hours and hours this wondrous white woman poured forth her speech, for the most part concerning sacred and profane mysteries; but every now and then she would stay her lofty flight, and swoop down upon the world again; whenever this happened, I was interested in her conversation... And when she engaged in this more worldly chat, then she was no longer the prophetess, but the sort of woman that you sometimes see, I am told, in London drawing rooms – cool, decisive in manner, unsparing of enemies full of audacious fun... .

(Note here not only the implication that most of Lady Hester's conversation was of little or no interest to Kinglake in itself – an implication confirmed explicitly in the preface to the work – but also the elliptical, enigmatic phrase, 'I am told', distancing the narrator from the phenomenon that he purports to describe.)

What, then, does Kinglake's account tell us about the two protagonists of this meeting? About Lady Hester Stanhope, it would be possible to argue that it tells us little or nothing that we did not know already. As previously noted, there is a wide range of different views concerning Lady Hester, most obviously encapsulated, perhaps, in the review by Leslie McDowell already quoted of her two most recent biographers.[37]

Given the choice, I think there can be little doubt that Kinglake would have inclined to Gibb's view (as summed up by McDowell) rather than Ellis's; and indeed, although one at times needs to read between the lines of Kinglake's narrative, his description of the meeting would make a contrary view difficult to sustain. What is also clear, however, is that Alexander Kinglake emerges from the account as a master of irony and sarcasm: clearly, he thought Lady Hester a pretentious poser, but he skilfully succeeds in conveying this to the reader without explicitly saying so. Kinglake's skill in this respect arguably augurs well for the successful legal career on which he subsequently embarked. But as not infrequently with this sort of retrospective literary interpretation, questions remain: for example, why exactly did Kinglake choose to devote around a tenth of his memoir to a woman he apparently thought did not deserve it? Are the remarks in his preface merely a literary conceit? Or did he perhaps simply think that talking extensively about Lady Hester Stanhope would help to sell his book?

Whatever the answers to these questions, it should be self-evident that *Eothen* does not deserve to be dismissed in the contemptuous terms employed by Edward Said in *Orientalism*. In the preface to a modern reprint of the work, Jonathan Raban suggested that 'Eothen needs to be read with more subtlety than most readers have brought to it in the past. It is a very *slippery* book'.[38] That is not the most obvious adjective, perhaps, to apply to a work that has become a classic of its genre; not a word, indeed, much used by literary critics at all, but it is certainly one that ought to give us pause for thought. It is indeed high time for a critical re-evaluation of this slim, but fascinating, volume.

Endnotes

1   Kinglake, A. W. (1844) *Eothen; or, Traces of travel brought home from the East*. London, John Ollivier. The work has been reprinted several times; references in the current essay are to the edition first published in the Everyman's Library series, London, J.M. Dent & Sons Ltd; New York, E.P Dutton & Co. Inc., 1908, and reprints.

2   Otherwise spelled Joon or Dhoun. The village is not to be confused with the better known Jounieh (also formerly occasionally spelled Jouni), a coastal town to the north of Beirut, which came to prominence as a Maronite stronghold during the Lebanese civil war of 1975–1990.

3   Gibb, Lorna (2005) *Lady Hester: Queen of the East*. London: Faber.

4   Ellis, Kirsten (2008) *Star of the Morning: The Extraordinary Life of Lady Hester Stanhope*. London, HarperPress.

5   http://greatbritishnutters.blogspot.co.uk/2008/07/lady-hester-stanhope-kooky-desert-queen.html (accessed 26 November 2016).

6   For further details of Lady Hester's early life, see, inter alia, the two biographies referred to above in notes 3 and 4. Earlier biographies were written by Virginia Childs, Joan Haslip, and others, and there have also been numerous articles devoted to her life. For a short biography, see https://en.wikisource.org/wiki/1911_Encyclop%C3%A6dia_Britannica/Stanhope,_Lady_Hester_Lucy

7   Also (among various other spellings) spelled Deir Mashmousheh.

8   'The Lady's House'.

9   Personal observations from a visit to the site in 2009.

10 For Ibrāhīm Pasha's Egyptian expedition, see Khaled Fahmy, 'The era of Muhammad 'Ali Pasha' in M. W. Daly (ed.), *The Cambridge History of Egypt*, vol. 2: *Modern Egypt from 1517 to the End of the Twentieth Century*: pp. 165 ff.

11 For whom, see William Harris, *Lebanon: A History 600–2011*, New York, Oxford University Press: pp. 124 ff.

12 On this, see http://www.kirstenellis.net/musings/the-curious-case-of-hesters-remains/ (last accessed 2 December 2016).

13 *Memoirs of the Lady Hester Stanhope, as related by herself in conversations with her physician [i.e. Charles Lewis Meryon, 1783-1877]: comprising her opinions and anecdotes of some of the most remarkable persons of her time.* London, Henry Colburn, 1845.

14 *Travels of Lady Hester Stanhope: forming the completion of her memoirs, narrated by her physician [C.L. Meryon].* London, 1846.

15 http://www.scotsman.com/lifestyle/book-review-the-extraordinary-life-of-lady-hester-stanhope-1-1086915.

16 Kinglake, A. W (1863–87) *The Invasion of the Crimea: its origin, and an account of its progress down to the death of Lord Raglan*, 9v., Edinburgh, W. Blackwood, and reprints.

17 For publication details, see above, note 1.

18 Modern Zemun, now integrated into urban Belgrade.

19 Said, Edward (1978) *Orientalism*, London & Henley, Routledge and Kegan Paul: p. 193.

20 *Eothen*: p. 238.

21 *Ibid.*: p. 160.

22 *Ibid.*: p. 184.

23 Said, *Orientalism*: p. 193.

24 *Eothen*: pp. 155 ff.

25 *Ibid.*: p. 172.

26 *Ibid.*: pp. 184–85.

27 *Ibid.*: p. 165.

28 *Ibid.*: p. 182.

29 From Kinglake's original preface to *Eothen* (not included in the Everyman edition used for the preparation of this chapter).

30 *Ibid.*

31 *Eothen*: p. 62.

32 *Ibid.*: pp. 62–63.

33 *Ibid.*: p. 63.

34 *Ibid.*: p. 74.

35 *Ibid.*: p. 75.

36 *Ibid.*: p. 77.

37 See quotation above on p.275.

38 As quoted by Allan Massie in http://staging.spectator.co.uk/2008/10/a-very-slippery-book/

18

'A Mani Splendoured Thing' – or Fermor's Folly

John Chapman

We are on a boat in the Bay of Limeni, on the west coast of the Mani peninsula in southern Greece sometime in midsummer in the early 1950s.

> A derelict, shadowless little port and a group of empty houses bereft of life appeared at the bottom of steep olive covered rocks. The engine fell silent, and, as we drew alongside, the roar of millions of cicadas burst on the ear. It came from the shore in rhythmic, grating, metallic waves like the engines of an immense factory in a frenzy – the electric rattle of innumerable high-powered dynamos whirling in aimless unison. There was not a breath of wind and on the quay when we left the caique's cool awning the sun came stampeding down to attack. We plunged for shelter into a slovenly kapheneion awhirl with flies. Lulled by their buzz and by the ear splitting clatter outside we lay on the sticky benches for an hour or two, till the sun should decline a little and declare a truce'. (Fermor, 1958: p. 41.)

This passage is typical of the honed lyricism of Patrick (Paddy) Leigh Fermor's classic travel book of 1958, *Mani* – subtitled, 'Travels in the Southern Peloponnese'. I don't use the word classic lightly, since critics, pundits and observers queue up to praise it as a great work of literature. There are some, such as Robert Eisner, who challenge this view, but even he admits that he feels guilty about his cavils, writing, 'In criticizing him I may be revealing more about my deficiencies as a reader than his as a writer.' (Eisner, 1993: p. 236.) Though there are other dissenting views. The novelist Jane Stevenson gives these bitter words to her fictional narrator in the short story 'The Island of the Day Before Yesterday': 'Daddy... did know T. E. Lawrence, and go around with Peter Fleming and Paddy Leigh Fermor, which is to say he was genuinely part of that strange and very British little clique of men of action with a tiny gift for prose about whom the world has heard so unnecessarily much.' (Stevenson, 1999: p. 3.) And one wonders if Paul Theroux had Paddy in mind when he wrote that when he first assayed travel writing himself in 1973 with *The Great Railway Bazaar*, he thought, 'The travel book was a bore. A bore wrote it and bores read it.' (Theroux, 2011: p. 323.)

Travel accounts of Greece are not in short supply. There are literally thousands. Indeed, Shirley Weber's 1953 catalogue of travellers' accounts held in the Gennadion Library in Athens was thought important enough to have had a 2002 reprint. Major studies of Anglo-Saxon writing on Greece have followed: Terence Spencer's 1954 study of literary philhellenism from Shakespeare to Byron; Robert Eisner's witty 1993 overview; David Roessel's 2002 exhaustive and exhaustively scholarly *In Byron's Shadow*; Edmund Keeley's 1999 study of the writings of the 1930s; and David Wills' 2007 analysis of the hundred or so post war Greek travel books published in the UK. (Spencer, 1954; Eisner, 1993; Roessel, 2002; Keeley, 1999 and Wills, 2007.)

This paper concentrates on one place, Mani, that is often on the edge of the Greek world, and on one book.

In the 19th century, Mani was visited with regularity. In fact, western travellers positively wanted to go there, if only to gawp at the strange breed of mountaineers, who were fiercely independent, given to piracy and over fond of fighting one another and building defensive tower houses. (Fig.18.1) By the beginning of the 20th century, Mani was a backwater, visited merely by scholars of the British School at Athens, who described the churches and the dialect, but rarely the people or the landscape. Mani then goes off radar for half a century. Compare in the on-line *Times* the scores of references to Mani in the 19th century with the few in the 20th and 21st centuries, which are mostly after 1958, and only with regards to *Mani* by Patrick Leigh Fermor.

Fig 18.1 The village of Vathia – Deep Mani. Although spending only a few nights on the roof of a locals' tower house, Paddy stretched the passage in his book Mani over three chapters. The village is now deserted and mostly in ruins. (Illustrations in this chapter © John Chapman.)

What makes Paddy's *Mani* a classic? Well the prose is lapidary and Paddy's erudition is remarkable. Paddy claimed that his ideals in prose are clarity, brevity and euphony. His close friend and fellow hero of the Cretan resistance Xan Fielding commented wryly that Paddy's forte was euphony. But there are other factors at work – the book is, as Robert Eisner points out, like the author's mind – a miscellany. Paddy often described the book as a clothes horse on which he could hang any number of things about Greece, therefore the narrative is broken off for musings and diversions that are engrossing if you know a modicum about the huge arc of Hellenic history, but frankly baffling if you don't. An early review of *Mani* pointed out that '... for his readers, it is amusing in small doses; but Mr. Leigh-Fermor's doses often last for several pages and his book, good as it is, would have been still better... if he had curbed his exuberances and stuck to his main subject.' (Collier, 1959: p. 251.)

Then there is the imprecision of the narrative. In his 2008 BBC TV documentary on Fermor, Benedict Allen questioned whether Paddy had made anything up and was surprised to find that his memory was remarkably acute. However, there is a deliberate vagueness about Paddy's narrative journey through Mani. We are never given any clues as to exactly when the trip took place, it is clearly midsummer from the reference to cicadas, but what year was it? In her biography (Cooper, 2012: p. 261), Artemis Cooper dates it to 1951 but the only way I could guess is from a photograph from the hardback version and from my being a personal friend of the little boy who is in the picture.

Fermor and his travelling companion, Joan, rather typically enter Mani by climbing over an 8,000-ft mountain. Paddy also wanted somewhere remote (and found it in Mani), though he could easily have driven in as Robert Liddell did in his relatively contemporaneous *The Morea* (Liddell, 1958). By the 1950s, travellers had to go off piste to avoid the clichés of tourism. In 1869, the 4th Earl of Carnarvon published an abridged version of his father's journals of a Greek journey in 1839, and wrote in his introduction that he was excising most of his father's descriptions of Athens because most readers would be far too familiar with the Acropolis and other famous sites. The 3rd Earl's account of Mani, however, was given prominence. (Carnarvon, 1869.)

It is a cliché-cum-truism that travel writers often reveal more about themselves than the places they visit. And for 1930s' travellers to Greece, famously Lawrence Durrell and Henry Miller, this was part of the quest – to find oneself through some spiritual interaction with Greece. Some even add Paddy's name to the list of these seekers after themselves, but it's really not true.

In the latest American edition of *Mani*, Michael Gorra wrote in his introduction:

> Where those digressions almost never take us is into Leigh Fermor himself. His eyes look out, not in. We know him by the pace of his sentences, his fondness for lists, his expertly mixed cocktails of metaphor. We know him by his passions, his taste in books and buildings. We know him by his friends. Yet there is little here about his private life – just the Christian name of his travelling companion, and eventual wife, Joan Eyres Monsell. (Fermor, 1958. Introduction Gorra, 2006: p. x.)

Which leads us to the two other charms of the book: John Craxton's original dust-jacket design for the original hardback edition (another Englishman who settled in Greece) and the hardback edition itself contain the black-and-white photographs by Joan Eyres Monsell, who married Paddy in the 1960s. Oddly, the cover has been changed on occasion for the paperback versions, but Joan's photographs have never made the leap to the paperback. The book, by the way, seems never to have been out of print in the 50 years since its publication.

Mary Beard wrote of this:

> Leigh Fermor was accompanied on many of his journeys after the war by his partner, and later wife, Joan; but she very rarely gets a look in, and when she does it's usually in a decidedly passive role... This absence is exacerbated in the recent reprints, which have retained John Craxton's characteristic cover designs, but omitted the arresting black and white photographs taken by Joan that were included in the first editions.' (Beard 2014: p. 239.)

In the 1950s, the roads into Mani were few, travel was either by boat or by donkey track, the trip to Athens was at least a day. Paddy delighted in the lack of electricity so that Mani was preternaturally devoid of the jabbering backdrop of radio which filled its social spaces. But how does this select snapshot of a golden age really match up to the realities of post-war Mani? And more importantly, given media comments that many tourists visiting Mani are seen clutching a copy, how does it match 60 years on with a Mani where four-wheel drives criss-cross the mountains and mobile phones trill in the olive groves?

With regards the ease of travelling there: the journey that Fermor took through Mani, which provides the clothes horse, is so interrupted by asides that his trip seems to take place in a Shangri-La dream sequence. There are hints of a world outside, but generally the world of Byzantium and the Ottoman era take precedence. Greece had only recently emerged from a bitter civil war that was particularly divisive and nasty in Mani. A political discussion in the village of Lagia is reported, but curiously, Fermor refuses to pass comment. A pelvis, possibly human, is seen in the crossing of the Taygetus mountains. But from *Mani*, you would get little idea of the turmoil of contemporary Greek politics, or the viciousness of the recent war. It is a narrative with no context. For this, one has to read Kevin Andrew's 1959 *The Flight of Ikaros* which draws a much darker picture of Mani in 1949: 'The place was empty but for a few boys who lounged around the wine shop door. They had pimpled necks and wore heterogeneous pieces of military clothing... later a few small children played about on the cobblestones with the bodies of some live rock-pigeons, pulling their beaks open till they broke, or squeezing the downy heads between their fingers – soft little hands lingering absently over the extinction of life.' (Andrews, 1959/1984: p. 101.)

It reminds me of Sam Peckinpah's movie *The Wild Bunch*, where small children torture scorpions before the adult world explodes into slow motion bloodletting. And the bloodletting in Mani *was* prodigious. Fermor would have been vividly aware of this, but some inner politeness restrains him from passing comment on the dark side of recent Greek history.

My second point is, how do we continue to create narratives of place in a modern world where Athens is only three hours' drive away, everyone has a mobile phone and every savvy café owner has wireless broadband?

There is still travel writing on Greece, much of which has little literary merit but which hopes to inject a modicum of humour into the interface between the British and the Hellenic mentalities.

In some way, all explore a particularly intimate ethnographical theatre. This is perhaps the only valid expression of travel writing about Greece, or almost anywhere else, these days. Unless of course you can carry a fridge around Ireland, or beat every member of the Moldavian football team at tennis. Benedict Allen is quick to revere his heroes, Paddy, Eric Newby and Laurie Lee but they all knew a soft voyage when they saw one, and when to give up. He seems hell bent on killing himself in search of going somewhere no white Anglo-Saxon, middle-class man has ever been before. Allen calls himself an explorer, while Paddy hated the term 'travel writing', but it seems to me that both are playing semantic tricks to hoodwink themselves and their audience that there is a huge gap between them and the tourist.

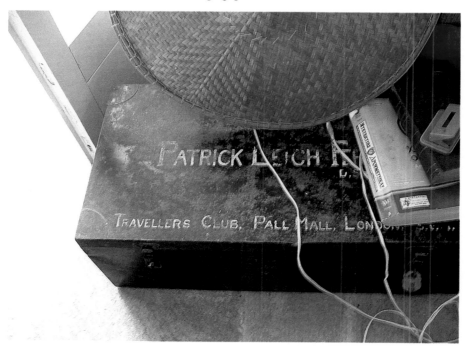

Fig 18.2 Although Paddy disliked the term 'travel writer' his trunk clearly announced his membership of The Travellers Club.

Anthropological studies, even of the very driest kind, are yet another way of providing prospective visitors with a way in. In the 1960s, a number of American anthropologists studied the Mani. One, Peter S. Allen, studied the village of Skoutari, which he disguised as Aspida (the Greek word for 'shield'). (Allen, 1976.) Much has changed since he was there in the early 1970s, when there were no cars, merely a few motor-cycles, electricity had only arrived in 1968 and there was only one, communal telephone, and most of the economy was based on self-sufficiency and communal barter. In a later article, Allen returned to Skoutari, and was generally disappointed with the changes. (Allen, 1998.) 'Never Go Back' is perhaps a discerning visitor's mantra, but the speed of change, even in Mani, can happen with brutal speed.

One of Joan's 1950s photographs is of a threshing floor in Mani – an *aloni*. Today these, and there are many of them, are uniformly abandoned to weeds. I was told the other day of how in the 1970s the colonels pushed roads into the deepest part of Mani. The Maniates, at the time were mostly right-wing monarchists with a tiny leavening of communists, so the colonels curried favour. The first year after the roads appeared so, at harvest time, did a man in a truck towing a milling machine. He did the job in a fraction of the time and without using donkey power. The next year, the local stores stocked bags of flour. The locals stopped growing subsistence grain crops, donkey numbers declined and wild bird populations plummeted due to a lack of food.

Paddy knew his Greece and his Greeks, but he presents us with a Land of Cockaigne. But if we are going on a two-week holiday, do we really want to be faced by the visceral reality of quotidien Maniat life? Or would we prefer a *Shirley Valentine*-like experience with a better vocabulary?

Although the first package tour to Greece is claimed to have taken place in 1834, it is only in the last 30 years that Greece has become infested by tourism. Mani survives, just, although Paddy seemed to want it both ways – to write about it, yet deplore the toll it takes on its specialness. Paddy's own house was built with extreme discretion into the bay of Kalamitsi. In the intervening 40 years it has been surrounded by hotels, villas and infill. In his preface to the 1991 photo album *Vanishing Greece*, he wrote from the self-same house at Kalamitsi, stating that Mani was 'a land as pocked with pumice, and choked with prickly pear; a land of lizards and tortoises and scarce water and circular threshing floors and dirges, too strange and solemn and beautiful a place to be ruined.' And then adds, 'The least said the better lest bulldozers and mixers move in and finish the job.' (Perry, 1991.)

As Mary Beard wrote in 2005: 'What he failed to predict was that he might become an object of tourism himself. The *Lonely Planet* guide directs its readers to the village in the Mani where, it emphasises, Leigh Fermor (now ninety) still lives for part of the year – and to the taverna run by his former housekeeper.'

I know, for, to my consternation, I got myself invited to tea with Paddy, and history is rich in such pilgrimages to the feet of the master. Bruce Chatwin foisted himself upon Paddy (as, one could add, he did many people), and a whole horde of poets, novelists and writers have supped at Paddy's table. (Fig.18.3) He was, I have to point out, rarely resentful of these intrusions, and in the case of Chatwin, he laid his ashes to rest in the hills above his house. He was a man who enjoyed any chance to chat and imbibe.

Authentic Greece is as impossible to pinpoint as is authentic England. It is forever changing, evolving and it depends very much on who is looking and at what. A book written 60 years ago by a man who only, perforce, in his nineties, learnt to use a typewriter is hardly going to reflect modern realities.

How can we create new narratives of our own? Hollywood is quite capable of recreating good stories many times, with varying success. *King Kong* for example, springs to mind. But a classic travel narrative is another matter. Especially one so covered with fairy dust as Paddy's *Mani*. Others have written accounts, such as Greenhalgh & Eliopoulos' 1985 *Deep Into Mani*, but, if anything, they revealed even less about the contemporary state of Mani than Paddy did 30 years earlier. (Greenhalgh, 1985.) Others have tried to pinpoint the landscape in privately published volumes and walking guides. But what we want from travel books is, I would argue, escapism. And walking guides are directional rather than inspirational. Although novelists such as Don DeLillo and the British crime writer Paul Johnston have tapped into the dark side of Mani, both deliberately describing a midwinter dystopic Mani (DeLillo, 1999; Johnston, 2003).

Do we want our dreams of a land where we spend a few weeks of relaxation to resonate with the chaotic, cacophonous reality of modern Greece?

But I fear we can never sweep away a classic account, nor really should we. Too many of us have bought into the dream.

When Benedict Allen proposed in his TV documentary programme that he was going to follow in Paddy's footsteps to check that Paddy told the truth in his books (many travel writers, Bruce Chatwin *primus inter pares*, don't), the columnist on *The Independent*, Deborah Orr, and her friends, who had briefly met the great man, and therefore naturally felt they owned a bit of him, were seething with indignation. (Orr, 1988.)

Fig 18.3 Paddy Leigh Fermor in his house, May 2005. At the age of 90, he was ever talkative and fond of drinking tea and ouzo.

As late as 1997, Lord Renton of Mount Harry was reported in the House of Lords (Hansard, Lords 1997) as saying 'I remember visiting the Mani... about whom Paddy Leigh-Fermor wrote in a brilliant book. How could that part of Greece, which still appears totally medieval, be at the same economic level as Frankfurt, Bonn or Brussels?' Indeed, but why would anyone ever want it to be the same?

Bibliography

Allen, P. (1976) *Aspida: A Depopulated Maniat Community* in *Regional Variation in Modern Greece and Cyprus: Towards a Perspective on the Ethnography of Greece*, Ernestine Friedl and Muriel Dimen, eds. Annals of the New York Academy of Sciences (268): pp. 168–98.

Allen, P. (1998) *Returning to the Field: A Sabbatical in Greece*. FAS/Rhode Island College 18 (October): pp. 22–30.

Andrews, K (1959/1984) *The Flight of Ikaros: Travels in Greece During a Civil War*. London, Weidenfeld & Nicolson.

Beard, M. (2014). 'Don't forget your pith helmet' in *Confronting the Classics: Traditions, Adventures and innovations*. London, Profile Books.

Carnarvon, Henry John George Herbert Earl of (1800–49) (1869) *Reminiscences of Athens and the Morea*. London, John Murray.

Collier L. Review: 'Mani: Travels in the Southern Peloponnese; The Private Sea', *The Geographical Journal*, Vol.125, No 2, June 1959: pp. 251–52.

Cooper, A. (2012) *Patrick Leigh Fermor: An Adventure*. London, John Murray.

DeLillo, D. (1999) *The Names*. London, Picador.

Eisner, R. (1993) *Travelers to an Antique Land: The History and Literature of Travel to Greece*. Ann Arbor, University of Michigan Press.

Fermor, P. (1958) *Mani: Travels in the Southern Peloponnese*. London. John Murray.

Fermor, P. (2006) *Mani: Travels in the Southern Peloponnese*. New York Review of Books.

Greenhalgh, P. (1985) *Deep into Mani: Journey to the Southern Tip of Greece. London*. Faber & Faber.

Hansard, Lords. 14 July 1997, Vol. 581: pp. 824–63.

Johnston, P. (2003) *The Last Red Death*. London, Hodder & Stoughton.

Keeley, E. (1999) *Inventing Paradise: The Greek Journey. 1937-47*. Evanston Illinois, Northwestern University Press.

Liddell, R. (1958) *The Morea*. London. Jonathan Cape.

Orr, D. (2008) 'Last Night's TV: The Travellers' Century', *The Independent*, 7 August 2008.

Perry, C. (1991) *Vanishing Greece*. London, Conrad Octopus.

Roessel, D. (2002) *In Byron's Shadow: Modern Greece in the English & American Imagination*. Oxford, Oxford University Press.

Spencer, T. (1954) *Fair Greece, Sad Relic: Literary Philhellenism from Shakespeare to Byron*. London, Weidenfeld & Nicolson.

Stevenson, J. (1999) *Several Deceptions*. London, Jonathan Cape.

Theroux, P. (2011) *Fresh-air Fiend: Travel Writings, 1985-2000*. London, Penguin.

Wills, D. (2007) *The Mirror of Antiquity: 20th Century British Travellers in Greece*. Newcastle, Cambridge Scholars Publishing.

Index